W9-AWF-250

The Complete
ITALIAN VEGETARIAN
Cookbook

The Complete ITALIAN VEGETARIAN Cookbook

350 Essential Recipes for Inspired Everyday Eating

JACK BISHOP

PHOTOGRAPHY BY
ANN STRATTON

A Chapters Book
HOUGHTON MIFFLIN COMPANY
BOSTON NEW YORK
1997

Library of Congress Cataloging-in-Publication Data

Bishop, Jack

The complete Italian vegetarian cookbook: 350 essential recipes for inspired everyday eating/by Jack Bishop; photography by Ann Stratton.

p. cm.

Includes index.

ISBN 1-57630-044-7

1. Vegetarian cookery. 2. Cookery, Italian. I. Title.

TX837.B527 1997

641.5'636'0945—dc21 97-16879

Printed in the United States of America

RMT 10 9 8 7 6 5 4 3 2 1

Designed by Susan McClellan

Front Cover: Polenta with Garlicky Greens (page 192) by Ann Stratton

Food Stylist: Rori Spinelli

Prop Stylist: Betty Alfenito

To my parents

Contents

Acknowledgments

Many people helped make the writing of this book possible.

As always, I first shared my ideas with Angela Miller, my agent and friend. I want to thank her for her wise counsel and constant good humor.

My editor, Rux Martin, challenged me with her careful readings, insightful comments and ability to focus on the details while keeping the big picture in her head. Her warmth and intelligence made editing this book a pleasure.

I appreciate the efforts of Barry Estabrook, editor-in-chief of Chapters, on my behalf. Also at Chapters, I would like to thank Jessica Sherman for corrections to the manuscript, Susan McClellan for her functional, attractive design, Susan Derecskey for her diligent copyediting, Rose Grant for her thorough indexing and Susan Dickinson for her careful proofreading.

Thank you to photographer Ann Stratton and stylist Rori Spinelli for capturing my food so beautifully.

My colleagues at *Cook's Illustrated* and *Natural Health* have been a valuable source of support and advice over the years. Anne Alexander, Pam Anderson, Mark Bittman, Stephanie Lyness, Eva Katz, Chris Kimball, Adam Ried and John Willoughby have all encouraged my writing about Italian food, even when it bordered on obsession.

Thank you to my wife, Lauren Chattman, for sharing my passion for all things Italian, and to our daughter, Rose, for having the good sense to like Daddy's cooking.

Yvette Willock joined Rose and me at many enjoyable lunches, always offering her honest assessment of my day's work.

Andrea Ackerman, Alexandra Fischman and Harry Fischman have been our good neighbors and friends, helping us settle into our new home and life in Sag Harbor.

The presence of Beth Bloomberg, Dana Bishop, Doug Bishop, Patty Bishop, Patrick Bishop, Barri Chattman, Stacey Chattman, Kurt Kruger and Sophia Okorn makes any meal a special occasion.

My grandfather, James Bishop, has set an example for the entire family and shown us the rewards of hard work.

My grandmother, Katherine Pizzarello, is always with me in the kitchen, even when I'm not talking to her on the phone. Thank you for introducing me to so much great Italian cooking at an early age.

My in-laws, Marty and Marilyn Chattman, have turned over their kitchen to my mad antics on many occasions and always appreciated the results.

Finally, thank you to my parents, who gave me the skills and the room to make my own way.

INTRODUCTION

WHEN I LIVED IN FLORENCE in the early 1980s, I took some classes at the home of a well-known local cook. Besides the food and camaraderie, I remember his words of advice to the young students. They went something like this: "Good cooking is about turning a few humble ingredients into nourishing and enticing meals. Nothing more, and nothing fancy." As his ideal, my teacher would point to his mother, who could transform something as basic as ripe summer tomatoes, arugula from her garden, fine olive oil and linguine into a remarkably delicious and simple pasta dish.

Such seasonal food from the garden or local produce market is the essence of Italian home cooking. Pasta and pizza may be Italy's most eye-catching exports, but it is the country's varied and sensible use of vegetables that provides the best inspiration for American cooks. While traveling throughout Italy, I ate many vegetarian meals almost unconsciously, whether a pizza topped with sliced baby artichokes and crisp bread crumbs or a simple dish of orecchiette (ear-shaped pasta) tossed with ricotta, garden-fresh peas and Parmesan. Although vegetarianism as a movement does not have a strong history in Italy, few cuisines put a greater emphasis on vegetables.

Especially in poorer rural areas, many Italians have traditionally eaten meatless meals several times a week. They do so not to follow a strict dietary regimen but, rather, to make good use of the ingredients at hand. Asparagus spears coated with a little olive oil, sprinkled with salt and roasted to intensify their flavor; thick slices of country bread grilled over an open fire, rubbed with garlic, drizzled with recently pressed olive oil and topped with diced tomatoes and shredded basil from the garden; or a fragrant stew with fennel and peas—Italians enjoy dishes like these because of what they *do* contain, not what they don't.

When I lived in Florence, I made a daily pilgrimage to the giant central market, where I practiced my language skills with the vendors while buying eggplants or artichokes. Along the way, I picked up tips for preparing and cooking vegetables like fava beans that I had never seen at home. Soon I was sautéing swiss chard and garlic and using the mixture as a topping for soft, creamy polenta. I made my own black olive paste and layered it into crusty rolls with slices of creamy fresh mozzarella. Pasta, always an important part of my diet, took on new life when combined with the incomparable market produce—with tomatoes and rosemary, or perhaps zucchini, lemon and mint.

THIS BOOK TAKES THE SIMPLE ITALIAN WAY with vegetables as its starting point. Most of the following recipes are my renditions of classic dishes I have tasted in various parts of Italy. Some are family favorites adapted from my Italian grandmother's recipes. While the fresh, uncomplicated flavors and improvisational spirit of my recipes remain true to their traditional origins, I have simplified many dishes and adapted them to the realities of shopping and cooking in the United States. The result is everyday eating for people who want meatless meals occasionally or exclusively.

In my travels, I have frequently seen the same dish made in different ways. Unlike French cooks, who can turn to several encyclopedic reference books, Italian home cooks generally rely on their own personal experience, preparing food the way they always have or the way their mother, neighbor, grandmother or friend does. I have offered my own version, often incorporating elements from various methods to arrive at something that offers a combination of the best results with a minimum of effort.

In so doing, I have not been a slave to tradition. For example, conventional recipes call for stirring polenta constantly for 40 minutes. If you turn down the heat to low and cover the pot, a quick stir every 10 minutes or so is enough to keep the polenta from sticking. Similarly, frequent rather than constant stirring gives the traditional creamy texture to risotto.

Each chapter begins with an overview of a particular group of dishes or a technique, followed by recipes that illustrate some of the myriad possibilities. Once you master a basic technique, you can make variations easily, both those included in this book and those inspired by your own trips to the market.

Throughout, I have attempted to keep fat in check. I use butter and cheese when needed, but I like the fresh flavor of vegetables. For the most part, that means just enough olive oil to coat the pan or to sauce some linguine. While I have been following the path of healthier eating for many years, I have recently noticed that the rest of my family is slowly but surely joining me. My Italian grandmother rarely prepares the elaborate Sunday feast with four kinds of meat that I remember from my childhood. At 86, she would rather have a simple supper of pasta sauced with cauliflower and onions or a soup made with pasta, beans and tomatoes. I couldn't agree more.

The traditional Italian multicourse meal structure—antipasto, *primo* (a first course that can be soup, pasta or risotto) and *secondo* (meat, poultry or fish) accompanied by a vegetable side dish—is impractical for most American cooks who have a limited amount of time to spend in the kitchen. However, dinner is more enjoyable when there are at least two components—a colorful salad after a bowl of risotto or a quickly cooked vegetable with pizza.

BECAUSE MANY PEOPLE TELL ME they have trouble composing a complete meal when meat is not on the plate, I've added specific suggestions for accompaniments at the end of each recipe. Most are simple pairings for quick weeknight dinners—a mushroom and spinach frittata with pan-roasted leeks or wilted escarole with garlic and lemon after a dinner of polenta and portobello mushrooms. A few of the suggestions offer more elaborate possibilities for when company comes—for example, an artichoke and sun-dried tomato tart with a bowl of chickpea and fennel soup to start, followed by a salad of radicchio, arugula and endive.

In addition to the serving suggestions at the end of each recipe, I have listed some of my favorite menus on pages 13 to 16. Some of these are quite simple, consisting of a main course and a salad or vegetable, while others are celebratory, starting with an antipasto and ending with dessert. Feel free to put your personal stamp on these menus or yield completely to your own impulses, keeping in mind that a meal should contain a mix of colors, textures and flavors that will complement each other.

The recipes themselves are easy enough. Use high-quality ingredients and trust your own judgment, and the results are certain to be satisfying.

Sag Harbor, 1997

Suggested Menus

Weeknight Meal in a Flash, Southern Italian Style

Spaghetti with Tomatoes, Olives and Capers (*page 75*)

Tender Green Salad with Pine Nuts and Yellow Raisins (*page 375*)

Simple Autumn Supper

Polenta with Portobello Mushrooms (*page 190*)

Wilted Escarole with Garlic and Lemon (*page 343*)

Harvest Party

Potato Fritters with Parmesan (*page 41*)

Mushroom Crespelle (*page 277*)

Mixed Greens with Tomatoes, Yellow Pepper and Fennel (*page 377*)

Baked Peaches Stuffed with Almond Macaroons (*page 496*)

Weeknight Dinner for Winter

Onion and Mushroom Frittata (*page 247*)

Wilted Spinach with Garlic (*page 360*)

Sunday Supper with Children

Baked Ziti with Tomatoes, Basil and Mozzarella (*page 113*)

Focaccia with Sage (*page 452*)

Tender Greens and Vegetables with Blood Orange Vinaigrette (*page 376*)

Dinner in the Kitchen with Friends

Pesto Pizza (*page 432*)

Risotto Cakes Stuffed with Mozzarella (*page 172*)

Swiss Chard with Raisins and Almonds (*page 340*)

Red Leaf Lettuce, Arugula and Fennel Salad (*page 374*)

Pink Grapefruit Sorbet (*page 511*)

Casual Weekend Lunch

Mozzarella Spiedini with Lemon-Caper Sauce (*page 475*)

Roasted Peppers Marinated in Garlic Oil (*page 25*)

Special Winter Meal

Crostini with Oven-Roasted Mushrooms (*page 37*)

Squash Ravioli with Sage and Parmesan (*page 126*)

Wilted Spinach Salad with Polenta Croutons (*page 379*)

Blood Orange Sorbet (*page 512*)

Cornmeal Biscotti with Dried Cherries (*page 501*)

Holiday Cocktail Party

Marinated Black Olives with Rosemary and Lemon Zest (*page 20*)

Marinated Sun-Dried Tomatoes with Thyme and Garlic (*page 22*)

Crostini with Arugula and Ricotta Puree (*page 30*)

Spiced Baked Chickpeas (*page 39*)

Rosemary Nuts (*page 40*)

Frittata with Potatoes, Onions and Thyme (*page 256*)

Porcini Mushroom Tart (*page 408*)

Dinner by the Fire

Swiss Chard and Parmesan Tart (*page 410*)

Polenta with Mascarpone, Rosemary and Walnuts (*page 186*)

Tender Greens and Vegetables with Blood Orange Vinaigrette (*page 376*)

Classic Almond Biscotti (*page 498*)

Simple Spring Supper

Lemon Risotto (*page 162*)

Roasted Asparagus with Olive Oil (*page 330*)

Spring Meal for Company

Roasted Yellow Pepper Soup (*page 53*)

Artichoke and Sun-Dried Tomato Tart (*page 406*)

Fennel and Orange Salad (*page 389*)

Macerated Strawberries with Balsamic Vinegar (*page 492*)

Do-Ahead Spring Meal

Lasagne with Asparagus, Fresh Herbs and Parmesan (*page 118*)

Red Leaf Lettuce, Arugula and Fennel Salad (*page 374*)

Oranges Poached in Syrup (*page 494*)

Pine Nut Macaroons (*page 502*)

Light Summer Dinner for Guests

Potato Gnocchi with Pesto (*page 223*)

Arugula, Tomato and Black Olive Salad (*page 372*)

Watermelon-Campari Granita (*page 520*)

Do-Ahead Room-Temperature Meal for Summer

Zucchini Frittata with Parmesan (*page 259*)

Roasted Potato Salad with Herbs and Red Wine Vinegar (*page 391*)

Tomato Salad with Black Olives, Capers and Herbs (*page 394*)

Steamed Green Beans with Tarragon (*page 347*)

Caffè Latte Granita (*page 516*)

Summer Meal by the Grill

Bruschetta with Tomatoes and Basil (*page 476*)

Grilled Portobello Mushrooms, Red Onions and Bell Peppers (*page 320*)

Summer Rice Salad with Tomatoes, Cucumber and Yellow Pepper (*page 175*)

Peaches with Ricotta-Walnut Filling (*page 497*)

Lunch for the Beach

Grilled Eggplant and Red Pepper Sandwiches with Olivada (*page 471*)

Marinated Tomato and Red Onion Salad (*page 395*)

Summer Picnic

Ricotta Torta with Herbs (*page 417*)

Bread Salad with Roasted Peppers and Black Olives (*page 400*)

Marinated Yellow Beans and Summer Tomato Salad (*page 383*)

Antipasto

THE WORD ANTIPASTO TRANSLATES as "before the meal." A good antipasto should stimulate the appetite yet be light enough not to overwhelm or satiate. For that reason, antipasti (antipasto in the plural) are often quite pungent, with salty, spicy and/or acidic ingredients, like olives, lemon juice and hot red pepper flakes. All of these elements quell hunger pangs without filling the stomach and go well with a glass of wine or a cocktail.

Many antipasti are vegetable-based, highlighting what is freshest at local markets or in backyard gardens. For example, *Pinzimonio* (page 28), a selection of raw vegetables dipped in the finest olive oil, can be varied to suit the season. For a spring dinner, serve fava beans, carrots and radishes. In summer, a combination of bell peppers, zucchini, cucumber and cherry tomatoes signals the height of the harvest.

Other antipasti can act as "pantry" items, gaining flavor as they marinate for days or weeks in the refrigerator. They are ideal for impromptu entertaining. Adding rosemary and lemon zest to black olives, for instance, recovers some of their sun-drenched taste. Likewise, sun-dried tomatoes can be reconstituted in hot water, then drained and seasoned with olive oil, thyme and garlic to re-create summer in the dead of winter. Nuts may be mixed with brown sugar and rosemary, and chickpeas can be spiced with cumin and baked until crunchy.

High-quality cheeses also have a place at the start of a meal. Small balls of fresh mozzarella, called bocconcini ("little mouthfuls"), may be marinated in good olive oil with hot red pepper flakes and fresh thyme.

Slices of toasted bread slathered with various toppings, known as crostini, are especially convenient. Cut from a thin loaf of Italian bread, a baguette or a loaf of country bread, they are meant to be eaten out of hand with drinks. The toppings must be light—creamy arugula and ricotta puree, melted Gorgonzola cheese or pureed black olives. A couple of toasts are sufficient before a meal. Eat six, and you won't want dinner!

For a cocktail party, you'll want to select several antipasti to be served together. Before a meal, one—or at most two—should suffice.

Cold Antipasto

Hot Antipasto

Marinated Black Olives with Rosemary and Lemon Zest

MAKES ABOUT 1½ CUPS

I ALWAYS HAVE A JAR of these olives on hand in my refrigerator. Other herbs, such as thyme or oregano, are nice, but I particularly like the combination of woodsy rosemary with the lemon and garlic. *See the photograph on page 199.*

- **1 large lemon**
- **8 ounces black olives, such as gaeta, niçoise or kalamata**
- **1 teaspoon chopped fresh rosemary leaves**
- **2 large garlic cloves, thinly sliced**
- **½ cup extra-virgin olive oil**
- **Freshly ground black pepper**

1. Use a vegetable peeler to remove the yellow skin from the lemon, leaving behind the bitter white pith. Cut the lemon zest into very thin ½-inch-long strips.

2. Combine the olives, lemon zest, rosemary and garlic in a large jar with a lid. Add the oil and a few grindings of black pepper. Cover the jar and turn several times to distribute the oil over the olives.

3. Marinate the olives in the refrigerator for at least 1 day, turning the jar occasionally to redistribute its contents. *(The olives can be kept in the refrigerator for several weeks and will improve with time.)* Bring the olives to room temperature before serving.

SERVING SUGGESTIONS

Whenever guests are expected, I take some of these olives out of the refrigerator. Even if I serve nothing else, I like to have something a little salty with cocktails to stimulate appetites. Of course, adding a vegetable antipasto or some cheese and bread is a good way to provide a more substantial start to a meal.

Marinated Green Olives with Pickled Red Onions

MAKES ABOUT 2 CUPS

ONIONS CAN BE PICKLED QUICKLY by boiling thin slices until tender, draining them and covering with red wine vinegar. After an hour, the onions will emerge from the pickling liquid a beautiful pinkish purple color. The pickled onions are tossed with green olives, olive oil and a fresh herb (here, oregano) and then marinated overnight to allow the flavors to blend. Feel free to use parsley, mint, marjoram or thyme instead of the oregano.

- **1 medium red onion, thinly sliced**
- **1 bay leaf**
- **¼ cup red wine vinegar**
- **10 ounces large green olives, drained**
- **¼ cup extra-virgin olive oil**
- **1 tablespoon minced fresh oregano leaves**
- **Salt and freshly ground black pepper**

1. Bring 1 quart water to a boil in a medium saucepan. Add the onion and bay leaf and simmer for 1 minute. Drain and place the onion slices in a small bowl along with the bay leaf. Add the vinegar and enough cold water (about ¾ cup) to completely cover the onion slices. Let stand for 1 hour.

2. Toss the olives, oil and oregano in a large jar with a lid. Drain the onions and discard the bay leaf. Add the onions to the jar along with salt and pepper to taste. Cover the jar and turn several times to distribute the oil evenly.

3. Marinate the olives and onions in the refrigerator for at least 1 day, turning the jar occasionally to redistribute its contents. *(The olives and onions can be refrigerated for up to 1 week.)*

4. Bring the olives and onions to room temperature. Pile the onions into the bottom of a small serving bowl. Place the olives on top and serve immediately.

SERVING SUGGESTIONS

These marinated olives can be served with aperitifs while you wait for dinner. Or include them in a large party spread with breads, crackers, cheeses and other antipasti.

Marinated Sun-Dried Tomatoes with Thyme and Garlic

MAKES ABOUT 1 CUP

I SOMETIMES RECONSTITUTE dried tomatoes, add my own seasonings and olive oil and serve them as part of an antipasto. This way, I can choose the flavors I like—thyme and garlic—and have control over the amount and quality of the oil that goes into the dish. Also, I find that many brands of sun-dried tomatoes packed in oil are mushy. When I reconstitute dried tomatoes myself, I use hot (not boiling) water and make sure to drain the tomatoes before they become too soft.

2 ounces sun-dried tomatoes, not packed in oil (about 1 cup) or 1 recipe Oven-Dried Tomatoes (page 525)
1 teaspoon minced fresh thyme leaves
1 medium garlic clove, minced
2 tablespoons extra-virgin olive oil
Salt

1. If using sun-dried tomatoes, place them in a small bowl and add hot tap water to cover. Soak until the tomatoes are pliable but not mushy, about 20 minutes. Drain the tomatoes and blot them completely dry with paper towels. (Oven-Dried Tomatoes do not need to be soaked.)

2. Combine the tomatoes, thyme, garlic and oil in a small bowl. Add salt to taste and adjust the other seasonings. Cover and marinate at room temperature for 1 hour. *(The tomatoes can be placed in an airtight container, just barely covered with oil, and refrigerated for several weeks. Bring to room temperature before using.)*

SERVING SUGGESTIONS

The flavor of these tomatoes is intense, so I generally just put out a few. They are especially nice with goat cheese and crackers. Leftovers can be covered with olive oil and used as needed to perk up sandwiches or a winter tomato sauce. Sliver a couple of these tomatoes and add them to any sauce based on canned tomatoes for a stronger tomato flavor.

Marinated Bocconcini with Cherry Tomatoes and Hot Red Pepper

MAKES ABOUT 5 CUPS

BOCCONCINI ARE TINY BALLS of fresh mozzarella cheese packed in water. They are sold in many supermarkets. The name translates as "little mouthfuls," so make sure to buy balls of mozzarella that are small enough to be skewered on toothpicks as part of an antipasto spread. You could also cut a large piece of fresh mozzarella into small chunks. The cheese can be marinated in a mixture of seasoned olive oil for several hours or several days. In either case, add the tomatoes just before serving. A mixture of tiny red and yellow cherry tomatoes is especially attractive. *See the photograph on page 199.*

1 pound bocconcini (tiny mozzarella balls)
½ teaspoon dried hot red pepper flakes, or to taste
Salt
Several sprigs fresh thyme
⅓ cup extra-virgin olive oil
1 pint small cherry tomatoes, either red or yellow, stemmed

1. Drain the bocconcini and pat dry on paper towels. Place them in a large bowl, sprinkle with the hot red pepper and salt to taste. Add the thyme sprigs.

2. Drizzle the oil over the bocconcini and seasonings. Toss gently to coat the cheese with the oil. Cover the bowl and place it in the refrigerator for several hours. Gently toss the bocconcini once or twice. *(If desired, the bocconcini can marinate for several days in the refrigerator. Make sure to turn the bocconcini once or twice a day to promote even flavoring.)*

3. Remove the bocconcini mixture from the refrigerator and bring it to room temperature. Add the tomatoes and toss gently. Add more oil if necessary to moisten the ingredients. Serve immediately with toothpicks.

SERVING SUGGESTIONS

This spicy marinated dish makes a great addition to a summer antipasto spread. It goes with marinated olives or either of the roasted pepper recipes that follow.

Roasted Yellow Peppers with Capers, Parsley and Balsamic Vinegar

SERVES 6

YELLOW BELL PEPPERS are roasted and marinated in their own juices and a little balsamic vinegar to intensify their sweetness. Capers add a salty, piquant note, while a last-minute drizzle of extra-virgin olive oil provides silkiness. *See the photograph on page 199.*

- **4 large yellow bell peppers (about 1¾ pounds)**
- **1 tablespoon aged balsamic vinegar**
- **1 teaspoon drained capers, rinsed**
- **15 fresh parsley leaves**
- **1 tablespoon extra-virgin olive oil**

1. Roast and peel the peppers as directed on page 526, working over a bowl to catch their juices. Core and seed the peppers and cut them into 1-inch-wide strips.

2. Add the vinegar to the pepper juices. Add the pepper strips and toss gently. Cover and marinate at room temperature for at least 30 minutes or up to 2 hours.

3. Transfer the peppers from the marinating liquid to a large platter. Sprinkle the capers and parsley leaves over the peppers. Drizzle with the oil and serve immediately.

SERVING SUGGESTIONS

This dish is a wonderful addition to almost any antipasto spread. You may want to have some bread close at hand. Diners can spoon some of the peppers onto bread or enjoy them as is with a plate, knife and fork.

Roasted Peppers Marinated in Garlic Oil

SERVES 8 TO 10

DIFFERENT-COLORED PEPPERS are roasted and then lightly drizzled with homemade garlic oil. Arrange the peppers on a platter and garnish with basil leaves.

- 1½ tablespoons extra-virgin olive oil
- 1 medium garlic clove, lightly smashed
- 2 medium red bell peppers (about ¾ pound)
- 2 medium yellow bell peppers (about ¾ pound)
- 2 medium orange bell peppers (about ¾ pound)
- 6-8 large fresh basil leaves

1. Place the oil and garlic in a small skillet set over medium-low heat. Cook, turning the garlic occasionally, until it is golden brown, about 10 minutes. Remove and discard the garlic. Cool the oil to room temperature.

2. Roast and peel the peppers as directed on page 526. Core and seed the peppers and cut them into ¾-inch-wide strips.

3. Arrange the peppers on a large platter, alternating red, yellow and orange strips. Drizzle the garlic oil over the peppers and marinate at room temperature for at least 1 hour. *(The peppers can be covered and kept at room temperature for up to 4 hours.)*

4. Garnish the peppers with the basil leaves and serve immediately.

SERVING SUGGESTIONS

This dish is the perfect addition to a summer buffet or meal. Serve with toasted slices of bread and let guests make their own crostini. Or offer the peppers as is with plates, forks and knives.

Caponata

MAKES ABOUT 6 CUPS

MANY AMERICANS think of caponata as an eggplant relish. While eggplant is an important ingredient, this Sicilian dish is more complex than that. Sautéed onions and red bell peppers contribute sweetness, while cooked celery adds a fresh, crisp note. The salty olives and capers are balanced by red wine vinegar and a little sugar.

- ¾ cup extra-virgin olive oil
- 2 medium onions, halved and cut into very thin strips
- 1 medium red bell pepper, halved crosswise, cored, seeded and cut into very thin strips
- Salt
- 2 cups canned crushed tomatoes
- 1 teaspoon minced fresh oregano leaves
- 3 large celery ribs with leaves, stalks cut into ½-inch dice, leaves minced
- 1 large eggplant (about 1 pound), ends trimmed and cut into ½-inch dice
- 3 ounces large green olives (about ½ cup), rinsed, pitted and chopped
- 2 tablespoons drained capers, rinsed (chopped if large)
- ⅓ cup red wine vinegar
- 1 tablespoon sugar

1. Heat ¼ cup of the oil in a large sauté pan. Add the onions and sauté over medium heat until translucent, about 6 minutes. Add the bell pepper and a pinch of salt and cover the pan. Cook, stirring occasionally, until the pepper starts to soften, about 6 minutes.

2. Add the tomatoes and oregano and simmer, uncovered, until the mixture thickens somewhat, about 5 minutes. Remove from the heat and set aside.

3. Heat another ¼ cup oil in a large skillet. Add the celery ribs and leaves and sauté over medium heat until the celery starts to soften, about 6 minutes. Use a slotted spoon to transfer the celery to the pan with the tomato mixture.

4. Add the remaining ¼ cup oil to the oil already in the skillet. Add the eggplant and cook, stirring often, until it softens and shrinks considerably, about 6 minutes. Lower the heat if the eggplant starts to burn, but do not add more oil. Scrape the eggplant into the pan with the other ingredients.

5. Place the sauté pan over medium-low heat. Cover and simmer, stirring occasionally, until the flavors blend and the vegetables are tender but still distinct, about 20 minutes.

6. Uncover the pan and stir in the olives, capers, vinegar and sugar. Simmer for 1 to 2 minutes to blend the flavors. Adjust the seasonings. Cool the caponata to room temperature before serving. *(The caponata can be refrigerated in an airtight container for 4 days. Bring it to room temperature before serving.)*

SERVING SUGGESTIONS

Serve caponata as a dip with pita crisps—crackers made from pita breads that have been cut into triangles and either baked or fried. If served with another antipasto or two, the caponata should satisfy a party of fifteen or so. Good choices to round out the antipasto table would be Marinated Bocconcini with Cherry Tomatoes and Hot Red Pepper (page 23) and Spiced Baked Chickpeas (page 39). Leftover caponata can be served as an accompaniment to most frittatas or used as a room-temperature pasta sauce.

Raw Vegetables with Olive Oil Dipping Sauce

THIS IS ONE OF ITALY'S SIMPLEST and most delicious antipasto dishes. It is called *Pinzimonio,* which loosely translates as "pinch and marry." Seasonal vegetables are trimmed and arranged on a large platter. Guests gather around the table, and the host pours extra-virgin olive oil into bowls set before each person. The guests add coarse salt and pepper to suit their taste and "pinch" off small pieces of vegetables and "marry" them with the seasoned oil by dipping.

This antipasto can be prepared for two people or twelve, depending on how many vegetables and bowls you have on hand. I find that a selection of four vegetables is about right. See the recipe below for some suggestions, but feel free to add anything you like. Of course, there is no point in using anything but the finest oil.

Extra-virgin olive oil
Kosher salt or coarse sea salt
Coarsely ground black pepper

Selection of several young vegetables, including:
- **Carrots, peeled, quartered lengthwise and cut into short lengths**
- **Celery ribs, cut into short lengths**
- **Cherry tomatoes, stemmed**
- **Cucumber, peeled, quartered lengthwise, seeded and cut into short lengths**
- **Fava beans in pods (each person can shell them at the table)**
- **Fennel bulb, cut into thin strips**
- **Red, yellow or orange bell peppers, cut into thick wedges**
- **Radishes, halved**

1. For each person, pour a little oil in 1 small ramekin. Place salt and pepper (or a pepper mill) on the table.

2. Arrange the vegetables on a large platter. Give guests small plates and allow them to season their ramekins of oil with salt and pepper as desired. Dip vegetables, one at a time, into the seasoned oil.

Herbed Cheese Spread

MAKES ABOUT ⅔ CUP

IN ITALY, this simple snack might be made with a fresh ricotta cheese. If you have access to creamy homestyle ricotta, by all means use it. However, fresh goat cheese makes an excellent substitute. As for herbs, choose whatever looks freshest in your garden or refrigerator. I especially like tarragon or thyme.

- **2 teaspoons whole fresh herb leaves**
- **1 small garlic clove**
- **4 ounces fresh goat cheese or ⅔ cup homestyle ricotta cheese**
- **2 teaspoons extra-virgin olive oil**

1. Place the herbs and garlic in the work bowl of a food processor. Process, scraping down the sides of the bowl once, until roughly chopped. Add the cheese and oil and process, scraping down the sides of the bowl once again, until smooth and creamy.

2. Scrape the cheese spread into a small ramekin or dish. Serve immediately or cover and refrigerate for later use. (The garlic flavor will become more intense with time, so serve the cheese spread within a few hours.)

SERVING SUGGESTIONS

Put this cheese spread out as a snack for a small group, adding crackers, pita bread triangles or thin slices of good Italian or peasant bread. A bowl of olives and/or some raw vegetables (carrots are nice) would make a suitable antipasto for four. This recipe can be doubled or tripled as needed.

Crostini with Arugula and Ricotta Puree

SERVES 6 TO 8

A CREAMY ARUGULA AND RICOTTA PUREE is slathered over small pieces of toasted bread for a quick antipasto. Parsley is added to smooth the flavor of the arugula. The puree can be made a day in advance and then spread over the toasts at the last minute.

- 2 tablespoons walnut pieces
- 1½ cups packed arugula leaves, washed, excess water shaken off
- 1½ cups packed fresh parsley leaves
- 2 tablespoons extra-virgin olive oil
- ½ cup ricotta cheese, homestyle or supermarket
- Salt
- 1 narrow loaf Italian bread, cut into 24 slices, each ½ inch thick
- 4 sun-dried tomatoes packed in oil, drained and cut into very thin slivers

1. Place the walnuts in a small skillet set over medium heat. Toast, shaking the pan often to turn the nuts, until they are fragrant. Transfer to a plate. Let cool.

2. Place the walnuts, arugula and parsley in the work bowl of a food processor or blender. Pulse, scraping down the sides as needed, until the ingredients are finely chopped. With the motor running, slowly pour the oil through the feed tube and process until smooth. Add the ricotta and process until it is incorporated into the puree.

3. Scrape the puree into a small bowl. Add salt to taste. *(Refrigerate the puree for at least 2 hours or up to 2 days to allow the flavors to develop.)*

4. Preheat the oven to 400 degrees F. Place the bread slices on a baking sheet. Bake, turning the slices once, until they are lightly browned and crisp, 8 to 10 minutes.

5. Place the toasted bread slices on a large platter. Spoon 1 generous teaspoon of the arugula puree over each slice. Garnish each with a sliver of sun-dried tomato and serve immediately.

SERVING SUGGESTIONS

These crostini make an excellent beginning to a spring or summer meal. Follow with Onion and Mushroom Frittata (page 247) or a simple pasta dish such as Linguine with Grilled Plum Tomato Sauce (page 106). Extra arugula-ricotta puree can be used as a pasta sauce or stirred into steamed white rice.

Crostini with Ricotta and Herbs

SERVES 6 TO 8

SUPERMARKET RICOTTA CHEESE tends to be a bit watery and curdish compared with the homestyle versions sold in Italian markets and gourmet stores. For this recipe, it's important that the cheese be firm and dry. If you cannot find homestyle ricotta, you can remove some of the liquid from supermarket ricotta as directed in the recipe. You may use all basil in this recipe, but the contrast of basil and mint is more interesting.

1 cup ricotta cheese, preferably homestyle
1 tablespoon minced fresh basil leaves
1 tablespoon minced fresh mint leaves
Salt and freshly ground black pepper
1 narrow loaf Italian bread, cut into 24 slices, each ½ inch thick

1. If using supermarket ricotta, line a small colander or mesh sieve with several layers of paper towels. Spread the cheese over the towels and let drain until thickened and creamy, about 1 hour. Remove the cheese from the colander and discard the paper towels; they should be quite moist. (Homestyle ricotta does not need to be drained.)

2. Combine the ricotta, herbs and salt and pepper to taste in a medium bowl. Set aside. *(The cheese mixture can be refrigerated for several hours.)*

3. Preheat the oven to 400 degrees F. Place the bread slices on a baking sheet. Bake, turning the slices once, until they are lightly browned and crisp, 8 to 10 minutes.

4. Place the toasted bread slices on a large platter. Spread a scant 2 teaspoons of the cheese mixture over each slice. Serve immediately.

SERVING SUGGESTIONS

These crostini give a light start to a spring or summer meal. Do not follow with dishes that contain large amounts of cheese. Good choices include Summer Spaghetti with Raw Arugula and Tomatoes (page 85), Fusilli with Summer Tomatoes and Olivada (page 107) and Polenta with Garlicky Greens (page 192).

Crostini with Pesto and Ricotta

SERVES 6 TO 8

PESTO IS A BIT TOO STRONG to spread alone on crostini. Some creamy ricotta cheese tames the rough edges.

¼ cup ricotta cheese, preferably homestyle
½ cup Pesto, My Way (page 531)
Salt and freshly ground black pepper
1 narrow loaf Italian bread, cut into 24 slices, each ½ inch thick

1. If using supermarket ricotta, line a small colander or mesh sieve with several layers of paper towels. Spread the cheese over the towels and let drain until thickened and creamy, about 1 hour. Remove the cheese from the colander and discard the paper towels; they should be quite moist. (Homestyle ricotta does not need to be drained.)

2. Combine the ricotta, pesto and salt and pepper in a small bowl. Mix well and adjust the seasonings, adding more salt or pepper if needed.

3. Preheat the oven to 400 degrees F. Place the bread slices on a baking sheet. Bake, turning the slices once, until they are lightly browned and crisp, 8 to 10 minutes.

4. Place the toasted bread slices on a large platter. Spread 1 generous teaspoon of the pesto mixture over each slice. Serve immediately.

SERVING SUGGESTIONS

These toasts make a fine beginning to a summer meal. Follow with a vibrant main course, such as Fettuccine with Zucchini, Lemon and Mint (page 112), Red Pepper Frittata with Mint (page 250) or Zucchini Frittata with Parmesan (page 259).

Crostini with Black Olive Spread and Capers

SERVES 6 TO 8

OLIVADA, A PUNGENT BLACK OLIVE PUREE, is spread over toasts for a simple antipasto. The puree is intensely flavored, so use a light hand.

1 narrow loaf Italian bread, cut into 24 slices, each ½ inch thick
6 tablespoons Olivada (page 553)
24 small drained capers, rinsed

1. Preheat the oven to 400 degrees F. Place the bread slices on a baking sheet. Bake, turning the slices once, until they are lightly browned and crisp, 8 to 10 minutes.

2. Place the toasted bread slices on a large platter. Spread ¾ teaspoon of the Olivada over each slice. Garnish each with a caper and serve immediately.

SERVING SUGGESTIONS

These robust toasts should be followed with foods that can stand up to olives. Good choices include Summer Spaghetti with Raw Arugula and Tomatoes (page 85), Linguine with Grilled Plum Tomato Sauce (page 106) and Artichoke and Sun-Dried Tomato Tart (page 406).

Crostini with Sun-Dried Tomato and Black Olive Puree

SERVES 6 TO 8

SUN-DRIED TOMATOES AND BLACK OLIVES make a rich, potent topping for crostini. This recipe calls for store-bought sun-dried tomatoes. However, you may use Marinated Sun-Dried Tomatoes with Thyme and Garlic (page 22). If you do, omit the garlic and thyme in the recipe.

- 15 sun-dried tomatoes packed in oil, drained (about ⅔ cup)
- 8 large black olives, pitted
- 1 medium garlic clove
- 2 tablespoons whole fresh parsley leaves
- 1 teaspoon whole fresh thyme leaves
- 2 tablespoons extra-virgin olive oil
- Salt
- 1 narrow loaf Italian bread, cut into 24 slices, each ½ inch thick

1. Place the sun-dried tomatoes, olives, garlic, parsley and thyme in the work bowl of a food processor. Pulse, scraping down the sides of the bowl as needed, until the ingredients are coarsely chopped. Pulse in the oil, 1 tablespoon at a time, to form a smooth but still slightly coarse paste.

2. Scrape the puree into a small bowl. Add salt to taste. If the olives are salty, you may need very little salt. *(The puree can be refrigerated in an airtight container for 1 day. To prolong storage, pour a thin film of oil over the puree.)*

3. Preheat the oven to 400 degrees F. Place the bread slices on a baking sheet. Bake, turning the slices once, until they are lightly browned and crisp, 8 to 10 minutes.

4. Place the toasted bread slices on a large platter. Spread 1 generous teaspoon of the puree over each slice. Serve immediately.

SERVING SUGGESTIONS

Serve these boldly flavored crostini at the start of a meal with equally assertive tastes. Extra sun-dried tomato-olive puree can be used as a pasta sauce. Toss dripping-wet spaghetti or linguine with some of the puree for a great late-night snack or simple meal.

Crostini with Roasted Eggplant, Tomato and Herbs

SERVES 6 TO 8

ROASTING EGGPLANT instead of sautéing it gives it a smoky flavor and also cooks this spongelike vegetable without adding any oil. Peel and chop the eggplant and combine it with fresh tomato and herbs to make a summery spread for toasts. Unlike Caponata (page 26), this spread is fairly lean; the focus is squarely on the eggplant itself.

2 medium eggplants (about 1 pound)
1 large tomato (about 8 ounces), peeled, cored, seeded and finely chopped
1½ tablespoons minced fresh parsley leaves
1½ tablespoons minced fresh basil leaves
2 tablespoons extra-virgin olive oil
Salt and freshly ground black pepper
1 narrow loaf Italian bread, cut into 24 slices, each ½ inch thick

1. Preheat the oven to 400 degrees F. Place the eggplants on a small baking sheet and roast until they have collapsed and are very soft, about 45 minutes. (Leave the oven on if serving the crostini right away.) Cool slightly.

2. Remove the ends and skins from the eggplants. Halve lengthwise and remove as many of the seeds as possible using a fork. Finely chop the flesh and place it in a large bowl.

3. Add the tomato, parsley and basil to the eggplant. Mix well and stir in the oil. Add salt and pepper to taste. *(The eggplant mixture can be refrigerated overnight in an airtight container. Bring to room temperature before using.)*

4. If necessary, preheat the oven to 400 degrees F. Place the bread slices on a baking sheet. Bake, turning the slices once, until they are lightly browned and crisp, 8 to 10 minutes.

5. Place the toasted bread slices on a large platter. Spread 2 teaspoons of the eggplant mixture over each slice. Serve immediately.

SERVING SUGGESTIONS

These crostini make a good start to a summer meal. Follow with Fettuccine with Zucchini, Lemon and Mint (page 112) or Zucchini Frittata with Parmesan (page 259).

Gorgonzola Crostini

SERVES 6 TO 8

UNLIKE MOST CROSTINI RECIPES, which call for spreading ingredients over toasted bread, this one bakes the bread and topping together. The topping is a mixture of mild Gorgonzola cheese, toasted pine nuts and basil. If you can only find aged, crumbly Gorgonzola, you are better off buying a non-Italian creamy blue cheese like Saga Blue.

2 tablespoons pine nuts
5 ounces mild Gorgonzola *(dolcelatte)* cheese (about ¾ cup), left at room temperature until soft
2 tablespoons minced fresh basil leaves
Freshly ground black pepper
16 ½-inch-thick slices country white bread, each about 3 inches across

1. Preheat the oven to 375 degrees F.

2. Place the pine nuts in a small skillet over medium heat. Toast, shaking the pan occasionally to turn the nuts, until golden. Transfer to a plate. Cool the nuts and chop them into a fine powder.

3. Combine the nuts, Gorgonzola, basil and pepper to taste in a small bowl, using a fork to work the mixture into a smooth paste. *(The paste may be refrigerated for up to 2 hours.)*

4. Place the bread slices on a medium baking sheet. Spread about 1 tablespoon of the cheese mixture over the top of each slice. Bake just until the edges of the toasts become golden, about 8 minutes. Remove the toasts from the oven and allow them to cool for several minutes. Serve warm.

SERVING SUGGESTIONS
Serve these toasts with drinks before a robust dish like Spaghetti with Spicy Spinach and Toasted Bread Crumbs (page 104) or Polenta with Garlicky Greens (page 192).

Crostini with Oven-Roasted Mushrooms

SERVES 4

ROASTING MUSHROOMS IN THE OVEN concentrates their flavor. Brown cremini mushrooms, which resemble regular button mushrooms but have a superior taste and texture, are my first choice for this recipe, but anything other than plain white button mushrooms would be fine. Creminis are sold loose in most supermarkets. The three-inch toasts for this recipe can be made by cutting larger slices in half. *See the photograph on page 199.*

¾ pound cremini or wild mushrooms
¼ cup extra-virgin olive oil
Salt and freshly ground black pepper
Several sprigs fresh thyme
8 ½-inch-thick slices country white bread, each about 3 inches across

1. Preheat the oven to 400 degrees F. Trim a thin slice from the stem end of each mushroom. Wipe the caps clean with a towel. Halve the smaller ones and quarter the larger ones. Place the mushrooms in a roasting pan large enough to hold them in a single layer. Drizzle the oil over them and toss gently to coat evenly. Season with salt and pepper to taste. Scatter the thyme sprigs around the mushrooms.

2. Roast, turning the mushrooms once or twice, until golden brown and a bit crusty, about 20 minutes. During the last 10 minutes of the cooking time, place the bread slices on a baking sheet. Bake on another shelf of the oven, turning the slices once, until lightly browned and crisp, 8 to 10 minutes.

3. When the mushrooms are done, taste them and adjust the seasonings. Place the toasted bread slices on a large platter. Spoon some of the mushrooms over each slice. Serve immediately.

SERVING SUGGESTIONS

These crostini are a good starter for what I call a "serious" fall dinner that might also include Risotto with Butternut Squash and Sage (page 149) or Squash Ravioli with Sage and Parmesan (page 126). The crostini are substantial enough to make a light lunch for two or three, especially if served with a mixed green salad.

Crostini with Pureed Fava Beans

SERVES 4

THIS RECIPE IS A LABOR-INTENSIVE but lovely way to start a spring meal. Fava beans require a two-step shelling and skinning process before they can be boiled, pureed, enriched with a little olive oil and spread on toasts. First, the beans must be removed from their pods, much as you shell garden peas. Unlike peas, though, the beans are covered with a thick skin that must be loosened by blanching and then peeled away with your fingers. The time to do this is when there are several hands working in the kitchen; the delicate flavor of the beans makes it well worth the effort.

2 pounds fresh fava beans in pods
Salt
1 tablespoon extra-virgin olive oil
Freshly ground black pepper
12 ½-inch-thick slices bread, each about 3 inches across

1. Bring 2 quarts water to a boil in a medium saucepan. Shell the fava beans. There should be about 2 cups shelled beans. Add the beans to the boiling water and simmer for 2 minutes. Use a slotted spoon to transfer the favas to a large bowl. (Turn off the heat but keep the pan on the stove.) Cover the beans with cold water and drain again. Use your fingers to scrape away part of the outer light green skin on each fava. Squeeze the skin to pop out the dark green bean.

2. Bring the water in the pan back to a boil. Add the peeled beans and 1 teaspoon salt. Cook until the beans are quite tender, about 4 minutes. Drain the beans and place them in a small bowl. Mash the beans with a potato masher and then beat in the oil with a fork. Season with salt and pepper to taste. Keep warm.

3. Preheat the oven to 400 degrees F. Place the bread slices on a baking sheet. Bake, turning the slices once, until they are lightly browned and crisp, 8 to 10 minutes.

4. Place the toasted bread slices on a large platter. Spread a little of the fava bean puree over each slice and serve immediately.

SERVING SUGGESTIONS

To continue the spring theme, follow with a light risotto or pasta dish, such as Risotto with Asparagus, Ricotta and Mint (page 156) or Spaghetti with Asparagus, Tomatoes and Lemon (page 88). You might conclude the meal with Roasted Beet Salad with Watercress, Walnuts and Fresh Pecorino (page 384).

Spiced Baked Chickpeas

MAKES ABOUT 2½ CUPS

THIS SIMPLE FINGER FOOD is the perfect accompaniment to cocktails before a meal. The chickpeas, cooked until tender but still firm, are seasoned with a little olive oil, cumin and salt and baked until crisp. The effect depends on the contrast between the crunchy exterior and tender center of the beans. Avoid canned beans: They are too mushy for this dish.

1 cup dried chickpeas, soaked overnight in cold water to cover (for quick-soak instructions, see page 293)
1 bay leaf
Salt
2 tablespoons extra-virgin olive oil
½ teaspoon ground cumin

1. Bring 2 quarts water to a boil in a medium saucepan. Drain the chickpeas and add them to the boiling water along with the bay leaf. Simmer for 25 minutes, then add 2 teaspoons salt to keep the skins from blistering. Continue cooking until the chickpeas are mostly cooked but still a bit firm, 5 to 20 minutes more.

2. Drain the chickpeas and gently toss them in a medium bowl with the oil and cumin. Add salt to taste. Pick out and discard any papery skins that have fallen off the chickpeas. Spread the chickpeas out in a single layer on a large baking sheet. *(The chickpeas may be loosely covered with plastic wrap and set aside at room temperature for several hours.)*

3. Preheat the oven to 400 degrees F. Bake the chickpeas, turning them once or twice, until they are a bit crunchy on the outside but still tender on the inside, about 10 minutes.

4. Remove the chickpeas from the oven and cool slightly. Transfer to a serving bowl and serve warm.

SERVING SUGGESTIONS

These chickpeas made a good snack anytime. As an antipasto, they work with lusty southern Italian dishes like Rigatoni with Stewed Eggplant Sauce (page 91) or Artichoke Pizza with Garlicky Bread Crumbs (page 426).

Rosemary Nuts

Makes about 4 cups

Rosemary, melted butter, a little brown sugar and salt lend a wonderful aroma and flavor to toasted mixed nuts. Any unsalted nuts may be used in this recipe.

- **4 ounces walnut halves (about 1 cup)**
- **4 ounces pecan halves (about 1 cup)**
- **4 ounces whole almonds with skins (about 1 cup)**
- **2 ounces pine nuts (about ⅓ cup)**
- **1 tablespoon unsalted butter, melted**
- **1 tablespoon minced fresh rosemary leaves**
- **2 teaspoons dark brown sugar**
- **1 teaspoon salt**

1. Preheat the oven to 350 degrees F. Spread the nuts on a baking sheet large enough to hold them in a single layer. Toast until fragrant, about 10 minutes. Be careful not to burn them.

2. Meanwhile, combine the butter, rosemary, brown sugar and salt in a large bowl.

3. Add the hot nuts to the bowl with the butter and flavorings. Toss gently to coat evenly. Transfer the nuts to a serving bowl and cool slightly. They are best served warm. *(The nuts can be placed in an airtight container and stored at room temperature for 2 days. Reheat just before serving.)*

Serving Suggestions

These nuts are a light accompaniment to cocktails. I particularly like them with Campari drinks. The brown sugar and rosemary work well with the bitter citrus flavor in the liquor.

Potato Fritters with Parmesan

SERVES 6

THESE POTATO FRITTERS ARE ADDICTIVE. That's why I like to serve just a few with drinks. Otherwise, guests would make a meal of the cheese-and-herb-flavored morsels. It's important that the potatoes be free of lumps. A ricer does the best job of transforming potatoes into a fluffy, snowy mound. A food mill is also fine. Do not use a food processor, which will make the potatoes gluey. You may mash them by hand (the fritters will not be quite as light), as long as all the lumps are broken up. Yukon Gold potatoes make especially ethereal fritters.

1 pound Yukon Gold or baking potatoes, scrubbed
Salt
½ cup freshly grated Parmigiano-Reggiano cheese
1 teaspoon minced fresh thyme or sage leaves
Pinch of freshly grated nutmeg
Freshly ground black pepper
2 large egg yolks
At least ½ cup olive oil
Lemon wedges, for serving

1. Bring several quarts water to a boil in a medium saucepan. Add the potatoes and salt to taste and simmer until the potatoes can be pierced with a skewer, about 30 minutes. They should be tender but not falling apart. Drain and set aside to cool for several minutes. Peel the potatoes and pass them through a ricer or the fine disk of a food mill into a large bowl.

2. Beat the cheese, thyme or sage, nutmeg and salt and pepper to taste into the potatoes. Stir in the egg yolks. Shape the potato mixture into patties that measure about 2 inches across and ½ inch thick. There should be about 15 patties.

3. Heat ½ cup oil in a medium skillet. When it is quite hot, place as many patties into the pan as can fit comfortably in a single layer. Fry, turning once, until crisp and golden brown on both sides, about 6 minutes. Transfer the fritters to a platter lined with paper towels. Fry the remaining fritters, adding more oil if needed. Serve immediately with the lemon wedges.

SERVING SUGGESTIONS

These fritters are a good choice when you want something with a little heft while waiting for dinner. They can also be served with Marinated Black Olives with Rosemary and Lemon Zest (page 20).

SOUPS

ITALIAN COOKS PREPARE ALL KINDS of vegetarian soups, from light summer broths made with fresh tomatoes to hearty winter classics loaded with vegetables, potatoes, beans and pasta. Most are easy to prepare and allow for a fair amount of improvisation.

The main area of concern for vegetarians is the stock. Like cooks in other affluent areas of the world, Italians generally use chicken stock as the liquid base for their vegetable, bean and pasta soups. But there is also an established tradition, especially in poor rural areas, of using water.

A more complex but hardly more difficult vegetable stock is my preference for most of the recipes in this chapter. Like chicken stock, a good vegetable stock adds body and richness that plain water cannot. Sautéing carrots, onions, leeks and celery in a little oil before adding the liquid and other ingredients to the pot is vastly preferable to tossing everything in all at once, for sautéing brings out the natural sweetness and full flavor of the vegetables.

Homemade stock is often the difference between good soup and great soup, so it's worth taking the time to make it and keeping some on hand in the freezer. While a few canned chicken stocks are marginally acceptable, canned vegetable stocks are uniformly wretched. The light, fresh flavor of good homemade stock is totally absent in canned versions, replaced by added sweeteners, chemicals and too much salt. Vegetable bouillon cubes are a fine shortcut in rice dishes, where they blend in with the other ingredients and add flavor without being too noticeable. In soups, however, their less-than-fresh taste is too prominent.

If homemade stock is not an option, water is the best alternative, especially in soups with lots of flavorful ingredients like beans and tomatoes. Soups made with water may not taste as rich as those made with stock, but they are more than acceptable.

ONE WAY TO BOOST THE FLAVOR OF A SOUP, especially one in which water instead of stock is used, is to toss in a rind of Parmigiano-Reggiano. I keep old rinds in the freezer and drop one into the kettle for any soup that will be served with cheese. The rind softens and adds a nutty, buttery flavor. When the soup is done, simply fish out and discard the rind before serving.

Another fast source of potent flavor is the liquid used to rehydrate dried porcini mushrooms; this liquid can be saved and added to the stock.

When pureeing soups, I find that the blender is the best tool for the job. Food processors usually leak when quantities of liquid are added, and food mills are messy to use and require more effort. To puree, simply pour the contents of the saucepan in batches into the container of the blender and whir until smooth. I prefer soup when it has cooled a bit from the boil, but if you like your soup warmer, pour it back into the saucepan and reheat it for several minutes, or until piping hot.

Unless otherwise noted, the soups in this chapter are designed to be served as a main course for dinner. Smaller portions may be offered as a first course or with a sandwich or piece of pizza or focaccia for lunch.

Soup

Creamy Carrot Soup

SERVES 4 TO 6

THIS SOUP IS BURSTING WITH CARROT FLAVOR. Although the texture is smooth as can be, there is no cream. The carrots themselves are the thickener.

8 medium carrots (about 1½ pounds)
2 tablespoons unsalted butter
3 medium shallots, minced
2¼ cups Vegetable Stock (page 529) or water, plus more as needed to thin the soup
1 teaspoon salt
Freshly ground white pepper
Pinch of freshly grated nutmeg
1 cup whole milk
1 tablespoon minced fresh parsley leaves or chives

1. Peel and halve the carrots lengthwise. Cut them crosswise into ¼-inch-thick half circles. There should be about 4 cups. Set aside.

2. Heat the butter in a medium pot or soup kettle. Add the shallots and sauté over medium heat until golden, about 6 minutes. Add the carrots and cook, stirring often, for about 2 minutes.

3. Add the stock or water, salt, white pepper to taste and nutmeg and bring to a boil. Lower the heat, cover and simmer until the carrots are tender, about 20 minutes.

4. Transfer the carrot mixture to a blender or food processor. Add the milk and puree, working in batches. Add hot stock, water or milk if necessary to thin the soup. Adjust the seasonings. *(The soup can be refrigerated for 2 days and reheated just before serving.)* If necessary, return the soup to the pot and reheat.

5. Ladle the soup into warm bowls and garnish with the parsley or chives. Serve immediately.

SERVING SUGGESTIONS

This soup is a good first course before egg dishes, such as Onion and Mushroom Frittata (page 247) or Parmesan Soufflé (page 266), and a leafy green salad.

Chard and Spinach Soup with Lemon-Parsley Pesto

SERVES 6

RED-VEINED SWISS CHARD AND LEAFY GREEN SPINACH make an attractive combination in this soup, which is brightened by adding a lemon-parsley pesto just before serving. Any mix of tender greens or just one kind can be used, including swiss chard (either red- or white-veined), spinach, beet greens or escarole. Just make sure that the total amount equals two pounds before stemming and cleaning.

1 pound red-veined swiss chard
1 pound flat-leaf spinach
6 tablespoons extra-virgin olive oil
1 medium onion, minced
4 medium garlic cloves, minced
Salt and freshly ground black pepper
6 cups Vegetable Stock (page 529) or water
¾ cup packed fresh parsley leaves
1 teaspoon grated lemon zest

1. Remove and discard the stems from the swiss chard and spinach. Wash the leaves in successive bowls of cold water until grit no longer appears in the bottom of the bowl. Shake the leaves to remove excess water but do not dry them. Coarsely chop the leaves and set aside.

2. Heat 3 tablespoons of the oil in a large soup kettle or stockpot. Add the onion and sauté over medium heat until translucent, about 5 minutes. Add the garlic and cook until golden, about 2 minutes more.

3. Add the damp swiss chard and spinach and stir to coat with the oil. Cover the pot and cook, stirring occasionally, until the greens are wilted, about 5 minutes. Season generously with salt and pepper to taste.

4. Add the stock or water and bring to a boil. Lower the heat and simmer to blend the flavors, about 10 minutes.

5. While the soup is simmering, place the parsley and lemon zest in the work bowl of a food processor or a blender. Process until finely minced. With the motor running, slowly pour the remaining 3 tablespoons oil through the feed tube and process until the pesto is smooth. Scrape the pesto into a small bowl and season with salt and pepper to taste.

6. Adjust the seasonings in the soup. Ladle the soup into warm bowls. Swirl some of the lemon-parsley pesto into each bowl and serve immediately.

SERVING SUGGESTIONS

The lemon-parsley pesto makes this soup a perfect winter pick-me-up. Accompany it with a bread dish to make a complete meal. Good choices include a bruschetta, light sandwich or light pizza, especially Bruschetta with Grilled Portobello Mushrooms (page 482), Garlic and Rosemary Pizza (page 425) and Mozzarella and Arugula Panini with Roasted Red Pepper Spread (page 470).

Pureed Cauliflower Soup with Pesto

SERVES 4 TO 6

A SILKY SMOOTH CAULIFLOWER SOUP is the perfect foil for pesto. This soup is especially good in fall.

- 1 large cauliflower head (about 2½ pounds)
- 2 tablespoons extra-virgin olive oil
- 1 medium onion, minced
- 2 tablespoons dry white wine
- 3 cups Vegetable Stock (page 529) or water, plus more as needed to thin the soup
- 1 teaspoon salt
- Freshly ground white pepper
- ¼ cup Pesto, My Way (page 531)

1. Discard the leaves and stems from the cauliflower. Cut the florets into bite-size pieces. There should be about 6 cups.

2. Heat the oil in a medium pot or soup kettle. Add the onion and sauté over medium heat until golden, about 6 minutes. Add the wine and cook until the alcohol aroma fades, about 1 minute.

3. Add the cauliflower and stir well to coat it with the oil and onions. Add the stock or water, salt and white pepper to taste and bring to a boil. Lower the heat, cover and simmer until the cauliflower is tender, about 12 minutes.

4. Transfer the cauliflower mixture to a blender and puree, working in batches. Add hot stock or water if necessary to thin the soup. Adjust the seasonings. *(The soup can be refrigerated for 3 days and reheated just before serving.)*

5. Ladle the soup into warm bowls. Swirl 2 teaspoons pesto into each bowl and serve immediately.

SERVING SUGGESTIONS

This soup makes a full meal when accompanied by a focaccia or pizza. Good choices include Focaccia with Black Olives and Thyme (page 447) or Focaccia with Sun-Dried Tomatoes and Garlic (page 454).

Kale and Red Potato Soup with Garlic-Rubbed Croutons

SERVES 6

ONE LARGE BUNCH OF KALE should be enough for this recipe. Trim and discard the tough stems just below the base of the leaves. Tear off and discard the veins of the leaves. Wash thoroughly to remove all traces of sand and dirt. Drain and chop the leaves and measure out six cups. Some markets sell prewashed kale with the stems already removed in plastic packages. Look for this item near the packaged spinach.

- **2 pounds red new potatoes, scrubbed but not peeled**
- **6 cups Vegetable Stock (page 529) or water**
- **6 cups loosely packed chopped kale leaves**
- **Salt and freshly ground black pepper**
- **12 ¾-inch-thick slices Italian bread**
- **1 large garlic clove**
- **3 tablespoons extra-virgin olive oil**

1. Cut the potatoes into ½-inch cubes and place them in a large soup kettle or stockpot. Add the stock or water and bring to a boil. Lower the heat and simmer for 10 minutes.

2. Stir in the kale and season generously with salt and pepper to taste. Continue simmering until the potatoes are cooked through and the kale is tender, about 10 minutes.

3. While the soup is simmering, preheat the broiler. Rub both sides of the bread slices with the garlic clove. Generously brush both sides of the bread with 2 tablespoons of the oil. Place the bread on a baking sheet and slide the sheet under the broiler. Toast, turning once, until both sides are golden brown.

4. Remove 2 cups of soup from the pot and puree it in a food processor or blender. Return the pureed soup to the pot and adjust the seasonings.

5. Ladle the soup into warm bowls. Float 2 garlic toasts in each bowl and drizzle the remaining 1 tablespoon oil over the soup. Serve immediately.

SERVING SUGGESTIONS

This soup is quite substantial and should be followed by a crisp, lightly acidic salad, such as Tender Greens and Vegetables with Blood Orange Vinaigrette (page 376) or Fennel and Orange Salad (page 389).

Porcini Mushroom and Barley Soup

SERVES 6

DRIED PORCINI MUSHROOMS are especially well suited to making soup. While they are soaking, prepare the soup base by sautéing carrots, celery, onion and fresh mushrooms. Then add the dried mushrooms and their richly flavored soaking liquid to the aromatic vegetables. A handful of barley cooked in the soup gives it plenty of heft. Rice can be substituted for the barley if desired.

- **2 ounces dried porcini mushrooms**
- **¼ cup extra-virgin olive oil**
- **2 medium carrots, peeled and diced**
- **2 celery ribs, diced**
- **1 medium onion, chopped**
- **1 pound white button mushrooms, wiped clean, stems trimmed, thinly sliced**
- **Salt and freshly ground black pepper**
- **½ cup pearl barley**
- **¼ cup minced fresh parsley leaves**

1. Place the porcini mushrooms in a medium bowl and cover with 3½ cups hot water. Soak until softened, about 20 minutes. Carefully lift the mushrooms from the liquid and pick through them to remove any foreign debris. Wash the mushrooms if they feel gritty. Strain the soaking liquid through a sieve lined with a paper towel. Set aside the mushrooms and the strained soaking liquid separately.

2. While the porcini mushrooms are soaking, heat the oil in a large soup kettle or stockpot. Add the carrots, celery and onion and sauté over medium heat until softened slightly, about 8 minutes.

3. Add the button mushrooms and raise the heat to medium-high. Cook, stirring often, until they give off their liquid, about 6 minutes. Season generously with salt and pepper.

4. Add the porcini mushrooms, their soaking liquid and 4 cups cold water and bring to a boil. Lower the heat and simmer for 5 minutes to combine the flavors. Stir in the barley and simmer, stirring occasionally, until the barley is tender, about 45 minutes. *(The soup can be refrigerated for 3 days and reheated just before serving.)*

5. Stir in the parsley and adjust the seasonings. Ladle the soup into warm bowls and serve immediately.

SERVING SUGGESTIONS

A leafy salad, such as Arugula, Pine Nut and Parmesan Salad (page 370) or Tender Greens and Vegetables with Blood Orange Vinaigrette (page 376), would round out this wintry meal.

Rice and Pea Soup

SERVES 4 TO 6

THIS SOUP HAILS FROM VENICE, where it is called *risi e bisi*. It is very thick—some Venetian restaurants actually serve it with a fork. I prefer a medium thickness, somewhere between a creamy risotto and regular soup. If you like, you can adjust the thickness of the soup by adding more water when the rice is tender or allowing excess stock to simmer off. Like risotto, this soup is better when made with stock or a vegetable bouillon cube rather than plain water.

- **2 tablespoons unsalted butter**
- **1 tablespoon extra-virgin olive oil**
- **1 medium onion, minced**
- **6 cups Vegetable Stock (page 529) or 1 vegetable bouillon cube dissolved in 6 cups boiling water**
- **1½ cups Arborio rice**
- **2 pounds fresh peas, shelled (about 2½ cups), or a 10-ounce package frozen peas, thawed**
- **3 tablespoons minced fresh parsley leaves**
- **Salt**
- **Freshly grated Parmigiano-Reggiano cheese**

1. Heat the butter and oil in a large soup kettle or stockpot. Add the onion and sauté over medium heat until golden, about 6 minutes. Add the stock or bouillon and bring to a boil.

2. Stir in the rice and lower the heat to medium-low. Cover and simmer, stirring occasionally, until the rice is almost tender, about 15 minutes.

3. Stir in the peas. Cook, uncovered, until the rice and peas are tender, 5 to 7 minutes for fresh peas or 3 to 4 minutes for frozen. Stir in the parsley and salt to taste.

4. Ladle the soup into warm bowls. Serve immediately with grated cheese passed separately at the table.

SERVING SUGGESTIONS

This dish can be served as a first course, as it traditionally is in Italy. Instead of following it with meat or fish, try Roman-Style Stuffed Artichokes with Garlic and Mint (page 304) or Zucchini Stuffed with Ricotta and Herbs (page 308). While you should be able to get six first-course portions from this recipe, it can also be served as a main course for four, followed by Fava Bean and Asparagus Salad with Basil Toasts (page 382) or a salad of bitter greens.

Roasted Yellow Pepper Soup

SERVES 6 TO 8

I FIRST TASTED THIS SOUP AT CIBRÈO, my favorite restaurant in Florence, and was determined to make it myself. The roasted yellow peppers give the soup a rich texture and an intense, sweet flavor. The drizzle of oil and the croutons are a must. This soup makes a great first course.

6 medium yellow bell peppers (about 2 pounds), roasted and peeled (see page 526)
3 tablespoons extra-virgin olive oil, plus more for drizzling over the soup
1 medium carrot, peeled and diced small
1 celery rib, diced small
1 medium onion, minced
Salt
1¼ pounds baking potatoes, peeled and diced
6 cups Vegetable Stock (page 529) or water
6 ¾-inch-thick slices Italian bread

1. Core and seed the roasted peppers and cut them into ½-inch-wide strips.

2. Heat 2 tablespoons of the oil in a large soup kettle or stockpot. Add the carrot, celery and onion and sauté over medium heat until the vegetables are tender, about 10 minutes. Add the pepper strips and a pinch of salt. Cook, stirring often, for 2 minutes.

3. Add the potatoes and stock or water and bring to a boil. Lower the heat, cover and simmer until the potatoes begin to fall apart, about 20 minutes. Transfer the soup to a blender and puree, working in batches. *(The soup can be refrigerated for 2 days and reheated just before serving.)* Return to the pot and keep warm.

4. Preheat the broiler. Generously brush both sides of the bread with the remaining 1 tablespoon oil. Place the bread on a baking sheet and slide the sheet under the broiler. Toast, turning once, until both sides are golden brown. Cut the toasts into small croutons.

5. Adjust the seasonings in the soup. Ladle into warm bowls. Float several croutons in each bowl and then drizzle with a little oil. Serve immediately.

SERVING SUGGESTIONS

Follow the soup with Orecchiette with Fava Beans, Plum Tomatoes and Ricotta Salata (page 94) or any pizza with tomatoes.

Potato, Spinach and Bread Soup

SERVES 4

DESPITE THE HUMBLE ORIGINS OF THIS SOUP, it is by no means hardship eating. Made with newly dug potatoes, fresh spinach and good country bread, it is marvelous. The drizzle of olive oil is imperative and should be the finest.

4 cups packed spinach leaves
1½ pounds Yukon Gold potatoes, peeled and cut into ½-inch dice
4½ cups Vegetable Stock (page 529) or water
Salt and freshly ground black pepper
2 cups cubed (½ inch) stale country white bread
2 tablespoons extra-virgin olive oil, or to taste

1. Remove and discard the stems from the spinach. Wash the leaves in successive bowls of cold water until grit no longer appears in the bottom of the bowl. Dry the leaves and cut them into ¾-inch-wide strips.

2. Place the potatoes and stock or water in a medium pot or soup kettle. Bring to a boil and cook briskly for 15 minutes. Add the spinach and salt and pepper to taste and cover the pot. Continue cooking until the potatoes are falling apart and the spinach is tender, about 10 minutes.

3. Remove from the heat, stir in the bread cubes and cover the pot. Let stand for 5 minutes, or until the bread is very soft. Adjust the seasonings and add hot water to thin the texture if desired. (This soup is designed to be quite thick but can be thinned to any consistency.)

4. Ladle the soup into warm bowls. Drizzle ½ tablespoon oil (or more to taste) over each bowl and serve immediately.

SERVING SUGGESTIONS

This stick-to-your-ribs soup is designed to be a meal-in-one. Add a light salad, such as Radicchio, Arugula and Endive Salad with Balsamic Vinaigrette (page 373) or Arugula Salad with Sliced Radishes and Carrots (page 371), to round out the meal.

Chilled Potato and Zucchini Soup with Fresh Tomato Garnish

SERVES 4

THIS SOUP IS DESIGNED FOR THE SUMMER COOK who wants to do as much of the work as possible during the cool morning hours. The potatoes are simmered until they fall apart, providing an almost creamy base for the bits of zucchini. The soup is thoroughly chilled and then flavored with mint or basil and garnished with diced tomato.

- 3 tablespoons extra-virgin olive oil
- 1 medium onion, minced
- 3 medium garlic cloves, minced
- 4 medium new potatoes, peeled and diced (about 2 cups)
- 3½ cups Vegetable Stock (page 529) or water
- Salt and freshly ground black pepper
- 4 small zucchini (about 1 pound), scrubbed, ends trimmed and cut into ½-inch dice
- 1 tablespoon minced fresh mint or basil leaves
- 1 large, ripe tomato, cored and diced very small

1. Heat the oil in a medium pot or soup kettle. Add the onion and sauté over medium heat until translucent, about 4 minutes. Add the garlic and continue cooking until golden, about 2 minutes.

2. Add the potatoes, 1½ cups of the stock or water and salt and pepper to taste. Bring to a boil. Lower the heat, cover and simmer until the potatoes are tender and starting to fall apart, about 25 minutes.

3. Add the zucchini and the remaining 2 cups stock or water to the pot. Simmer, uncovered, until the zucchini is tender, about 20 minutes. Cool slightly, then pour into an airtight container. Chill for at least 4 hours or up to 2 days.

4. When ready to serve, stir in the mint or basil and adjust the seasonings. Ladle the soup into individual bowls and garnish each serving with some of the diced tomato. Serve immediately.

SERVING SUGGESTIONS

As a first course, follow with Spinach Crespelle (page 279), Three-Cheese Pizza (page 439) or Artichoke and Sun-Dried Tomato Tart (page 406). As a light main course, serve with a salad, such as Arugula, Pine Nut and Parmesan Salad (page 370), or Bruschetta with Fresh Herbs (page 477).

Butternut Squash Soup with Parmesan and Sage

Serves 6

This pureed soup is garnished with whole sage leaves and dusted with Parmesan cheese. Despite its rich texture, the soup contains no cream, just a dash of milk.

- **1 medium butternut squash (about 2½ pounds)**
- **2 tablespoons unsalted butter**
- **1 medium onion, chopped**
- **2½ cups Vegetable Stock (page 529) or water**
- **1 teaspoon salt**
- **Freshly ground white pepper**
- **½–¾ cup whole milk**
- **12 whole fresh sage leaves**
- **6 tablespoons freshly grated Parmigiano-Reggiano cheese**

1. Halve the squash and scoop out and discard the seeds and stringy pulp. Use a large knife to cut away and discard the tough skin. Cut the flesh into ½-inch chunks. There should be about 6 cups. Set aside.

2. Heat the butter in a medium pot or soup kettle. Add the onion and sauté over medium heat until golden, about 6 minutes. Add the squash and cook, stirring often, for 2 minutes more.

3. Add the stock or water, salt and white pepper to taste. Bring to a boil. Lower the heat, cover and simmer until the squash is tender, about 15 minutes.

4. Transfer the squash mixture to a blender. Add ½ cup milk and puree, working in batches. Add more milk if necessary to thin the soup. Adjust the seasonings. *(The soup can be refrigerated for 3 days and reheated just before serving.)* If necessary, transfer the soup to the pot and reheat.

5. Ladle the soup into warm bowls and garnish each bowl with 2 whole sage leaves. Sprinkle 1 tablespoon cheese over each bowl and serve immediately.

Serving Suggestions

This soup makes an excellent start to an autumnal or winter meal. Follow with Penne with Portobello Mushroom Ragù (page 99), Mushroom Tortellini with Brown Butter and Pine Nuts (page 128) or Risotto with Savoy Cabbage (page 140) and then a leafy green salad.

Tomato and Bread Soup

SERVES 4

PAPPA AL POMODORO REPRESENTS TUSCAN COOKING AT ITS SIMPLEST. This thick soup is nothing more than garden-ripe tomatoes, stale bread, olive oil, garlic and basil. Thrifty Italian cooks have traditionally added bread to soups to give them bulk. The bread softens and swells into a comforting consistency. Be sure to choose a high-quality stale loaf—nothing sliced, please.

¼ cup extra-virgin olive oil
2 medium garlic cloves, minced
4 large, ripe tomatoes (about 2 pounds), cored, peeled, seeded and diced
8 large fresh basil leaves, cut into thin strips
Salt and freshly ground black pepper
4 cups Vegetable Stock (page 529), Light Tomato Stock (page 530) or water
5 cups cubed (½ inch) stale country white bread (about ½ pound)

1. Heat the oil in a medium pot or soup kettle. Add the garlic and sauté over medium heat until golden, about 2 minutes. Add the tomatoes and basil and cook just until the tomatoes soften, about 10 minutes.

2. Season the tomatoes with salt and pepper to taste. Add the stock or water and bring to a boil. Lower the heat and simmer just until the flavors are combined, about 5 minutes.

3. Stir in the bread and simmer until it swells, about 2 minutes. Cover the pot and remove from the heat. Let stand until the bread softens and breaks down, about 30 minutes. Adjust the seasonings.

4. Ladle the soup into warm bowls and serve immediately.

SERVING SUGGESTIONS

For a summer meal, follow with a green vegetable or salad. Good choices include Steamed Green Beans with Tarragon (page 347), Grilled Vegetables with Thyme and Garlic (page 365) and Arugula, Pine Nut and Parmesan Salad (page 370).

Summer Tomato, Caramelized Leek and Bread Soup

SERVES 4

STALE BREAD GETS RECYCLED IN MANY WAYS by thrifty Italian cooks. In this recipe, it plumps up leek and tomato soup. Fairly stale bread, at least two or three days old, is best, since it will absorb more liquid. If you need to, dry out cubed bread in a warm oven until stale. Although fresh summer tomatoes are best in this recipe, it can also be prepared with seeded and chopped canned tomatoes.

- **3 medium leeks (about 1½ pounds)**
- **¼ cup extra-virgin olive oil, plus more for drizzling over the soup**
- **3 large, ripe tomatoes (about 1½ pounds), cored, peeled, seeded and chopped**
- **Salt and freshly ground black pepper**
- **3½ cups Vegetable Stock (page 529), Light Tomato Stock (page 530) or water**
- **2½ cups cubed (½ inch) stale country white bread**
- **8 large fresh basil leaves, cut into thin strips**
- **Freshly grated Parmigiano-Reggiano cheese**

1. Trim and discard the dark green tops and tough outer leaves from the leeks. Remove the roots along with a very thin slice of the nearby white part. Halve the leeks lengthwise and wash them under cold running water. Gently spread apart but do not separate the inner layers to remove all traces of soil. If the leeks are particularly sandy, soak them in several changes of clean water. Slice the cleaned leeks crosswise into thin strips.

2. Heat the oil in a medium pot or soup kettle. Add the leeks and sauté over medium heat just until they become golden brown, 12 to 15 minutes.

3. Add the tomatoes and salt and pepper to taste. Cook, stirring often, until the tomatoes soften, about 10 minutes. Add the stock or water and simmer for 10 minutes to blend the flavors.

4. Add the bread to the pot and stir well. Cover the pot and remove from the heat. Let stand until the bread softens and starts to fall apart, about 40 minutes. Stir well and adjust the seasonings.

5. Ladle the soup into warm bowls. Garnish each bowl with basil strips, sprinkle with cheese to taste and drizzle with oil to taste. Serve immediately.

Serving Suggestions

This soup makes a meal-in-a-bowl that is suitable for a September night when tomatoes are still in high season and you want something substantial for dinner. Wilted Spinach with Garlic (page 360) or Swiss Chard with Raisins and Almonds (page 340) would be good vegetable side dishes. A leafy salad is an equally fine way to round out the meal.

Classic Minestrone with Pesto

SERVES 6

EVERY FAMILY IN ITALY MAKES ITS OWN VARIATION of this classic vegetable soup. One may insist on using spinach, while another may argue for leeks and swiss chard. The combination that follows, which is made in the Genoa area, is my favorite. The vegetables are to some extent interchangeable (use swiss chard instead of spinach, or extra onions and no leeks). The taste of slow-simmered vegetables and cannellini beans contrasts with the bright flavors of basil and garlic in the pesto. If you have a rind of Parmigiano-Reggiano in the freezer, this is a good place to use it. *See the photograph on page 203.*

- 4 cups tightly packed spinach leaves
- ¼ cup extra-virgin olive oil
- 2 medium leeks, trimmed, washed thoroughly and white and light green parts thinly sliced
- 2 medium carrots, peeled and chopped
- 1 medium onion, chopped
- 1 celery rib, chopped
- 7 cups Vegetable Stock (page 529) or water
- 1 medium baking potato (about 8 ounces), peeled and cut into ½-inch dice
- 1 medium zucchini (about 6 ounces), scrubbed, ends trimmed and cut into ½-inch dice
- 1 28-ounce can whole tomatoes, drained and chopped
- 1½ cups Basic Cannellini Beans (page 286)
- Salt
- ¼ cup Pesto, My Way (page 531)
- Freshly grated Parmigiano-Reggiano cheese

1. Remove and discard the stems from the spinach. Wash the leaves in successive bowls of cold water until grit no longer appears in the bottom of the bowl. Shake the leaves to remove excess water but do not dry them. Chop and set aside.

2. Heat the oil in a large soup kettle or stockpot. Add the leeks, carrots, onion and celery and sauté over medium heat until softened, about 10 minutes.

3. Add the stock or water, potato, zucchini, spinach and tomatoes. Bring to a boil, reduce the heat and simmer gently for 1 hour. Stir in the beans and salt to taste. Simmer just until the flavors have blended, about 10 minutes. *(The soup can be refrigerated for 2 days and reheated just before serving.)*

4. Remove the pot from the heat and stir in the pesto. Adjust the seasonings.

5. Ladle the soup into warm bowls and serve immediately with grated cheese passed separately at the table.

Serving Suggestions

With cannellini beans and so many vegetables, this soup is a meal in itself. Add bread for a hearty winter supper.

Leftover Vegetable Soup with Rice

SERVES 2 TO 3

THE ADDITION OF ARBORIO RICE transforms leftover minestrone. This is the perfect recipe when you have leftover soup on hand but don't want to eat the same thing two days in a row. Long-grain rice may be used, but it lacks the pleasantly chewy, firm texture of Arborio.

2 cups leftover Classic Minestrone with Pesto (page 60)
⅓ cup Arborio rice
Salt and freshly ground black pepper
Freshly grated Parmigiano-Reggiano cheese

1. Place the leftover minestrone in a large saucepan. Add 2½ cups cold water and bring to a boil.

2. Stir in the rice and bring the soup back to a boil. Lower the heat and simmer until the rice is tender, about 15 minutes. Add salt and pepper to taste.

3. Ladle the soup into warm bowls. Serve immediately with grated cheese passed separately at the table.

SERVING SUGGESTIONS
Make this recipe for lunch or a quick dinner. Add some bread to sop up the extra soup.

Pasta and White Bean Soup with Garlic and Rosemary

SERVES 6

THIS CLASSIC PASTA AND BEAN SOUP, called *pasta e fagioli*, is found all over Italy. In this version, the pasta is cooked in an aromatic tomato broth flavored with garlic and rosemary. You may substitute two 19-ounce cans of cannellini beans, drained and rinsed, for home-cooked cannellini beans.

- **¼ cup extra-virgin olive oil, plus more for drizzling over the soup**
- **4 large garlic cloves, minced**
- **2 teaspoons minced fresh rosemary leaves**
- **1½ cups drained canned whole tomatoes, chopped**
- **Salt and ground black pepper**
- **7 cups Vegetable Stock (page 529) or water**
- **6 ounces small pasta, such as small elbows or tiny shells**
- **4 cups Basic Cannellini Beans (page 286)**

1. Heat the oil in a large soup kettle or stockpot. Add the garlic and rosemary and sauté over medium heat for about 2 minutes.

2. Add the tomatoes and a generous amount of salt and pepper. Simmer for 3 to 4 minutes, or until the tomatoes soften.

3. Add the stock or water and bring to a boil. Lower the heat and simmer for 5 minutes. Add the pasta to the simmering broth and cook until almost tender, 7 to 10 minutes, depending on the shape.

4. Add the cooked beans and simmer for 2 to 3 minutes to blend the flavors and finish cooking the pasta. Adjust the seasonings.

5. Ladle the soup into warm bowls and drizzle with oil to taste. Serve immediately.

SERVING SUGGESTIONS

This soup can be served as a main course. Add a leafy salad, such as Arugula Salad with Sliced Radishes and Carrots (page 371) or Spinach Salad with Orange Juice Vinaigrette and Toasted Walnuts (page 380), and some good crusty bread.

Chickpea Soup with Fennel and Orange Zest

SERVES 6

ANISE-FLAVORED FENNEL strips are paired with chickpeas in a light broth sparked by orange zest, tomatoes, onions and garlic. Make this soup with dried chickpeas that you soak and cook yourself or use two 19-ounce cans of chickpeas, drained and rinsed. For an even heartier soup, add one cup orecchiette or small shells along with the chickpeas and simmer until tender.

- **1 medium fennel bulb (about 1 pound)**
- **¼ cup extra-virgin olive oil**
- **2 medium onions, chopped**
- **4 medium garlic cloves, minced**
- **1 teaspoon grated orange zest**
- **1 cup drained canned whole tomatoes, chopped**
- **Salt and freshly ground black pepper**
- **6 cups Vegetable Stock (page 529)**
- **4 cups Basic Chickpeas (page 293)**

1. Trim the stems and fronds from the fennel. Discard the stems. Mince and reserve 1 tablespoon of the fronds. Trim a thin slice from the base of the bulb and remove any tough or blemished outer layers. Cut the bulb in half through the base and use a small, sharp knife to remove the triangular piece of the core from each half. With the flat side of the fennel bulb down and your knife parallel to the work surface, slice each fennel half crosswise to yield several ½-inch-thick slices. Cut the slices lengthwise to yield long strips about ⅛ inch thick. Set aside.

2. Heat the oil in a large soup kettle or stockpot. Add the onions and sauté over medium heat until translucent, about 5 minutes. Stir in the garlic and orange zest and cook for 2 minutes more. Stir in the tomatoes and cook for 2 minutes more.

3. Add the fennel strips and cook, stirring occasionally, until they begin to soften, about 7 minutes. Season generously with salt and pepper to taste.

4. Pour the stock into the pot and bring to a boil. Lower the heat and simmer, stirring occasionally, until the fennel is quite tender, about 15 minutes.

5. Add the chickpeas and simmer for about 5 minutes to blend the flavors. Adjust the seasonings.

6. Ladle the soup into warm bowls and garnish with the minced fennel fronds. Serve immediately.

SERVING SUGGESTIONS

Since the flavors in this soup are bold, I like to serve it with an equally assertive dish, like Mozzarella Panini with Black Olive Paste (page 465).

Kale and White Bean Soup

SERVES 4 TO 6

HEARTY, BITTER GREENS MAKE A GOOD FOIL for the soft, creamy beans in this soup, which is especially easy to prepare, since it does not require any stock. The water from cooking the greens as well as the bean-cooking liquid are used instead. Other greens, such as swiss chard, turnip greens or mustard greens, may be substituted for the kale. You may need to reduce the cooking time for tender greens like chard, but not for the others.

¾ pound kale
Salt
¼ cup extra-virgin olive oil
4 medium garlic cloves, minced
1 teaspoon minced fresh sage leaves
4½ cups Basic Cannellini Beans (page 286), with about 1 cup cooking liquid reserved
Freshly ground black pepper
Freshly grated Parmigiano-Reggiano cheese

1. Trim and discard the tough kale stems just below the base of the leaves. Tear off the tender, dark green leafy portion on either side of the center veins. Discard the veins. (There should be about 6 cups firmly packed leaves.) Wash the leaves in successive bowls of cold water until grit no longer appears in the bottom of the bowl. Shake the leaves to remove excess water but do not dry them. Coarsely chop the leaves.

2. Bring 1 quart water to a boil in a large soup kettle or stockpot. Add the kale and 1 teaspoon salt and simmer until tender, about 15 minutes. Drain, reserving the cooking liquid in a measuring cup. There should be about 2 cups.

3. Heat the oil in the empty stockpot. Add the garlic and sauté over medium heat until golden, about 2 minutes. Stir in the sage and cook for 20 seconds to release its flavor. Add the kale and cook, stirring often, until well coated with oil, about 1 minute.

4. Add the beans. Add enough bean-cooking liquid to the measuring cup with the kale-cooking liquid to make 2½ cups. Add to the pot along with salt and pepper to taste. Simmer just until the flavors have blended, about 5 minutes.

5. Transfer 2 cups of the soup to a food processor or blender and puree until smooth. Stir the pureed soup back into the pot. If desired, the soup may be thinned with the remaining bean-cooking liquid. Adjust the seasonings.

6. Ladle the soup into warm bowls and serve immediately with grated cheese passed separately at the table.

SERVING SUGGESTIONS

The soup makes a meal if served with bread. For lunch, add a basic focaccia, such as Focaccia with Sage (page 452), or just a loaf of crusty bread. For a more substantial meal, add Pesto Pizza (page 432) or Bruschetta with Grilled Portobello Mushrooms (page 482).

Lentil and Tomato Soup with Escarole

SERVES 6

UNLIKE MOST HEARTY SOUPS, this one is quick, with lentils, which, unlike other legumes, do not need to be soaked, as well as tomatoes, escarole and basil. Spinach or swiss chard may be substituted for the escarole. If you have a rind of Parmesan in the freezer, add it with the water. It contributes a mellow richness to soups, especially to those made without stock. Remove the rind just before adding the escarole.

- 2 tablespoons extra-virgin olive oil
- 1 medium onion, minced
- 1 medium carrot, peeled and chopped
- 1 celery rib with leaves, chopped
- 3 medium garlic cloves, minced
- 1 28-ounce can whole tomatoes drained and chopped, juice reserved
- 1½ cups brown lentils (about 10 ounces)
- 1 medium head escarole (about ¾ pound), washed, tough ends removed and leaves thinly sliced crosswise
- 2 tablespoons minced fresh basil leaves
- Salt and freshly ground black pepper
- Freshly grated Parmigiano-Reggiano cheese

1. Heat the oil in a large soup kettle or stockpot. Add the onion, carrot and celery and sauté over medium heat until the vegetables begin to soften, 8 to 10 minutes. Stir in the garlic and cook for 1 to 2 minutes more.

2. Add the tomatoes and simmer just until they soften, about 5 minutes. Measure the reserved tomato juice and add enough water to make 8 cups. Add the liquid to the soup and bring to a boil.

3. Add the lentils, lower the heat to medium-low and simmer until they are tender, 35 to 45 minutes. Stir in the escarole, basil and salt and pepper to taste and cook just until the escarole is tender, about 5 minutes. Adjust the seasonings. *(The soup can be refrigerated for 2 days and reheated just before serving.)*

4. Ladle the soup into warm bowls and sprinkle with grated cheese to taste. Serve immediately.

SERVING SUGGESTIONS

This soup is substantial enough for a main course. Serve it with crusty bread.

PASTA

PASTA IS A WORKHORSE in both American and Italian kitchens. One Italian cookbook in my collection contains literally one thousand recipes using both dried and fresh pasta. Pasta can be a simple 20-minute meal or a three-hour project. In this chapter, I have focused mainly on simple sauces for dried pasta. I have also added a few recipes for baked pasta, using dried noodles. The final portion of the chapter deals with fresh pasta and its main uses, namely lasagne, ravioli and tortellini. Of course, if you prefer, you can also pair the sauces in the first part of this chapter with fresh pasta for a different effect.

My emphasis on dried pasta should not be construed as some sort of compromise. Fresh pasta is wonderful, but it is not superior to dried. Day in and day out, Italians use dried pasta with most sauces. Fresh pasta is made at home (or in a local shop that prepares sheets daily), mainly for filled pastas like ravioli and for lasagne. There are exceptions—fresh fettuccine is great with a cream sauce—but dried pasta is the first choice for most dishes because it is more resilient than fresh. The tenderness of fresh pasta as well as its eggy flavor make it less versatile.

If you decide to buy fresh, go to an Italian market or a gourmet store that makes pasta every day. So-called fresh pasta that sits for weeks on the shelves of supermarket refrigerated cases is expensive, tasteless and mushy. Or make your own: The recipes for plain and spinach pasta in this chapter are remarkably easy. To do this, you will want to invest in a manual hand-cranked pasta machine that clamps onto a counter or worktable. Electric pasta machines that knead and extrude the dough are very expensive and do not produce good pasta. Another approach, favored by generations of Italian grandmothers, is to use a rolling pin, but even very experienced cooks have trouble rolling sheets of dough thin enough. A manual pasta machine from Italy costs about $40 and is the best choice. (For mail-order sources, see page 554).

Most manual machines can be fitted with attachments to produce ravioli and other filled pastas, but you are better off making these delicate shapes by hand with long, wide sheets of pasta. Most models also come with two cutting blades. The wider cutters for fettuccine are better than the thin cutters, which often do a poor job of separating individual strands of pasta.

AS FOR DRIED PASTA, my favorite is DeCecco, an Italian brand that my family has used for as long as I can remember. From blind taste tests, however, I know that most cooks, including Italians, cannot tell the difference between Italian brands and American brands. Almost all pasta tastes good. The biggest difference is the array of shapes that Italian manufacturers offer. For this reason alone, you may prefer Italian.

More important than the brand of pasta is how you cook it. If you can boil water, you can cook pasta. But there are some tricks. The number-one complaint I hear is that the pasta sometimes sticks together. If this happens, you probably aren't using enough water. Pasta needs room to swell and rehydrate. Use at least four quarts of water per pound of pasta. Although many Americans add oil to the cooking water to prevent sticking, this is not necessary if you use enough water. Oil tends to make pasta slick and prevents the sauce from adhering properly.

Many cooks mistakenly skimp on the salt in the cooking water. No matter how salty the sauce, pasta cooked without salt will be bland. My advice: Go lightly on salt in the sauce and use a freer hand in the water. Most of the salt, after all, will go down the drain with the water, but the flavor that remains is essential. I use one tablespoon of salt for four quarts of water. Some Italian cooks use more, even two or three tablespoons. Experiment and find out how much tastes right to you, but remember, ¼ teaspoon cannot possibly flavor a whole pot of pasta.

I've heard some funny "tips" for telling when pasta is done, such as throwing it against the refrigerator door to see if it will stick. The only way to know when pasta is ready is to taste it. After the pasta has boiled for five minutes (or in the case of fresh pasta, three minutes), fish out a strand. Keep tasting until the pasta is al dente, just a little resistant in the center. In southern Italy, many people serve pasta that is so al dente the pieces stick to your back molars. In general, I prefer it to be slightly more cooked than that, as it usually is in northern regions. It should still have some bite but should not be chewy.

I HAVE LEFT COOKING TIMES OUT of my pasta recipes. This does not mean you should follow the times listed on the box. On the contrary, package instructions are widely inaccurate, and cooking times will also vary from stove to stove. There is no substitute for tasting. Fresh fettuccine and filled pastas can become al dente in as little as three or four minutes, and very small or thin dried pasta shapes, such as orzo and spaghettini, may not take much longer. Thick rigatoni or farfalle, with its thick center, may require 12 minutes. Watch the pot, not the clock.

My last bit of advice concerns draining. Like many people, I have bad memories of old-style Italian-American restaurants that served spaghetti in a pool of water with some thick red sauce on top. The reaction of many cooks has been to shake the pasta in the colander until it is bone-dry. They are overcompensating. Retaining some of the water helps spread the sauce over the noodles. This is especially important for oil-based sauces that contain large chunks of vegetables but no tomatoes or cream. Many recipes even call for reserving a little cooking water to mix into the pasta along with the sauce.

Whatever you do, never rinse drained pasta under running water. Rinsing cools the pasta down, makes it taste watery and removes the starchy coating that helps bind the sauce to the noodles.

The sauces in this chapter are divided into two categories: those that rely on shelf-stable items and can be made year-round and those that use fresh vegetables. Some of my favorites fall into the first group because they require little or no planning, so long as you have a pantry stocked with canned tomatoes, dried porcini mushrooms, olives and capers, and lemons and fresh herbs in the refrigerator.

Vegetable sauces should change with the seasons; select a recipe based on what looks good at your local market. Springtime favorites include fava beans, asparagus and artichokes. Summer is the time for vine-ripened tomatoes, eggplant and zucchini. Broccoli, cauliflower, mushrooms and squash are particularly good in fall and winter.

Pasta with Sauces Made from the Pantry

Pasta with Vegetable Sauces

Baked Pasta

Lasagne, Ravioli and Tortellini

Spaghetti with Tomatoes, Olives and Capers

SERVES 4

THIS RECIPE IS MY FAVORITE version of the famed *spaghetti alla puttanesca,* or "whore's pasta." The spicy, strong flavors in the sauce have made it a classic. We often have it when there's nothing for dinner in the refrigerator.

- **3 tablespoons extra-virgin olive oil**
- **3 medium garlic cloves, minced**
- **½ teaspoon dried hot red pepper flakes or to taste**
- **1 28-ounce can whole tomatoes, drained and chopped**
- **15 large black and/or green olives, pitted and chopped (about ½ cup)**
- **1 tablespoon drained capers, rinsed**
- **Salt**
- **1 pound spaghetti**

1. Bring 4 quarts water to a boil in a large pot for cooking the pasta.

2. Heat the oil in a large skillet. Add the garlic and hot red pepper flakes and sauté over medium heat until the garlic is golden, about 2 minutes.

3. Add the tomatoes, olives and capers. Simmer, stirring occasionally, until the tomatoes soften and the sauce thickens, about 15 minutes. Taste and add salt if needed.

4. When the water comes to a boil, add salt to taste and the spaghetti. Cook until al dente and then drain.

5. Toss the spaghetti with the tomato sauce and mix well. Divide among individual bowls and serve immediately.

SERVING SUGGESTIONS

More often than not, I prepare this dish as a late-night snack or for a quick meal on the run. I might add some bread or a leafy green salad, but anything more seems out of place with the improvised spirit of this dish.

Fusilli with Tomato and Porcini Sauce

SERVES 4

THIS TOMATO SAUCE derives its richness from dried porcini mushrooms and the liquid used to rehydrate them. The aromatic vegetables—onion, celery and carrot—add another layer of flavor.

- 1 ounce dried porcini mushrooms
- 1 28-ounce can whole tomatoes, drained
- 3 tablespoons extra-virgin olive oil
- 1 medium onion, minced
- 1 celery rib, minced
- 1 small carrot, peeled and minced
- Salt
- 1 pound fusilli
- Freshly grated Parmigiano-Reggiano cheese

1. Bring 4 quarts water to a boil in a large pot for cooking the pasta.

2. Place the porcini mushrooms in a small bowl and cover with 1 cup hot water. Soak until softened, about 20 minutes. Carefully lift the mushrooms from the liquid and pick through them to remove any foreign debris. Wash them if they feel gritty. Chop them. Strain the soaking liquid through a sieve lined with a paper towel. Set aside the mushrooms and the strained soaking liquid separately.

3. Working over the sink, open each tomato and push the seeds and liquid out with your fingers. Chop the tomato meat and set aside.

4. Heat the oil in a large sauté pan. Add the onion, celery and carrot and cook, stirring often, over medium heat until the vegetables soften, about 10 minutes. Add the chopped mushrooms and salt to taste and cook for 1 to 2 minutes more to release their flavor.

5. Add the tomatoes and mushroom soaking liquid. Bring to a boil, lower the heat and simmer until the sauce thickens, about 15 minutes. Adjust the seasonings.

6. When the water comes to a boil, add salt to taste and the fusilli. Cook until al dente and then drain.

7. Toss the fusilli with the tomato-porcini sauce and mix well. Divide among individual bowls and serve immediately with grated cheese passed separately at the table.

SERVING SUGGESTIONS

Follow this dish with some sharp greens. Radicchio, Arugula and Endive Salad with Balsamic Vinaigrette (page 373) is a good choice, as is Wilted Spinach with Garlic (page 360).

Fusilli with Spicy Tomato Sauce and Ricotta Salata

SERVES 4

THIS PASTA DISH IS REMARKABLY SIMPLE and yet seems a bit exotic. The sweet tomatoes, pungent garlic and hot red pepper flakes are balanced by the salty, creamy cheese. Ricotta salata, which is a lightly pressed salted form of ricotta, softens when combined with the hot sauce and pasta but does not melt.

2 tablespoons extra-virgin olive oil
3 medium garlic cloves, minced
1 teaspoon dried hot red pepper flakes, or to taste
1 28-ounce can whole tomatoes, drained and coarsely chopped
Salt
1 pound fusilli
6 ounces ricotta salata cheese, shredded in a food processor or on the large holes of a box grater (about 1½ cups)

1. Bring 4 quarts water to a boil in a large pot for cooking the pasta.

2. Heat the oil in a large skillet. Add the garlic and hot red pepper flakes and sauté over medium heat until the garlic is golden, about 2 minutes.

3. Add the tomatoes and simmer, occasionally using a wooden spoon to break apart the tomatoes, until the sauce thickens, about 10 minutes. Adjust the seasonings.

4. When the water comes to a boil, add salt to taste and the fusilli. Cook until al dente and then drain.

5. Toss the fusilli with the tomato sauce and ricotta salata. Mix until the cheese softens slightly, about 30 seconds. Divide among individual bowls and serve immediately.

SERVING SUGGESTIONS

This spicy, somewhat salty pasta should be followed by a green salad, perhaps one that has a little sweetness and acidity. Good choices include Tender Greens and Vegetables with Blood Orange Vinaigrette (page 376), Tender Green Salad with Pine Nuts and Yellow Raisins (page 375) and Spinach Salad with Orange Juice Vinaigrette and Toasted Walnuts (page 380).

Penne with Tomatoes, Rosemary and Balsamic Vinegar

SERVES 4

ROSEMARY ADDS A RESINOUS FLAVOR to a basic tomato sauce. A little balsamic vinegar is stirred in at the end of the cooking time to maximize the sauce's sweet-and-sour punch.

- **3 tablespoons extra-virgin olive oil**
- **1 medium onion, minced**
- **1 teaspoon minced fresh rosemary leaves**
- **1 28-ounce can whole tomatoes, drained and chopped**
- **Salt and freshly ground black pepper**
- **1 pound penne or ziti**
- **2 teaspoons aged balsamic vinegar**
- **Freshly grated Parmigiano-Reggiano cheese**

1. Bring 4 quarts water to a boil in a large pot for cooking the pasta.

2. Heat the oil in a large skillet. Add the onion and sauté over medium heat until translucent, about 5 minutes. Stir in the rosemary and cook for 30 seconds to release its flavor.

3. Add the tomatoes and salt and pepper to taste. Simmer until the sauce thickens, about 10 minutes. Adjust the seasonings.

4. When the water comes to a boil, add salt to taste and the penne or ziti. Cook until al dente and then drain.

5. Stir the vinegar into the tomato sauce and toss with the penne or ziti, mixing well. Divide among individual bowls and serve immediately with grated cheese passed separately at the table.

SERVING SUGGESTIONS

This quick pasta recipe should be followed by a salad of bitter greens. Since a vinegary dressing may seem out of place after the balsamic vinegar in the pasta sauce, Arugula Salad with Sliced Radishes and Carrots (page 371), which is dressed with olive oil only, is the perfect choice.

Penne with Oven-Dried Tomatoes, Olives and Herbs

SERVES 4

OVEN-DRIED TOMATOES GIVE A JOLT to this southern Italian pasta sauce sparked by olives, capers, hot red pepper flakes, garlic and herbs. Other herbs may be used in place of the oregano and mint, including basil, parsley, cilantro or thyme.

- **1½ cups Oven-Dried Tomatoes (page 525)**
- **10 large black olives, pitted and chopped**
- **2 teaspoons drained small capers, rinsed**
- **1 medium garlic clove, minced**
- **½ teaspoon dried hot red pepper flakes, or to taste**
- **1 tablespoon minced fresh oregano leaves**
- **1 tablespoon minced fresh mint leaves**
- **⅓ cup extra-virgin olive oil**
- **Salt**
- **1 pound penne**

1. Bring 4 quarts water to a boil in a large pot for cooking the pasta.

2. Slice the tomatoes lengthwise into long, thin strips. Place them in a bowl large enough to hold the penne when cooked. Add the olives, capers, garlic, hot red pepper flakes, oregano and mint and toss gently. Drizzle the oil over the tomato mixture and sprinkle with salt to taste. Toss gently and set aside.

3. When the water comes to a boil, add salt to taste and the penne. Cook until al dente and then drain.

4. Transfer the penne with a little water still dripping from the noodles to the bowl with the tomato mixture. Toss gently to combine the ingredients. Divide among individual bowls and serve immediately.

SERVING SUGGESTIONS

This full-flavored pasta dish should be served with plenty of bread and followed with a salad, preferably one with a citrus dressing that will stand up to the sauce. Good choices include Spinach Salad with Orange Juice Vinaigrette and Toasted Walnuts (page 380), Fennel and Orange Salad (page 389) and Tender Greens and Vegetables with Blood Orange Vinaigrette (page 376).

Penne with Ricotta, Parmesan and Mint

SERVES 4

NOTHING SAYS SPRING QUITE like this simple pasta dish. I sampled something akin to it many years ago on my first visit to Florence. The fresh mint releases its fragrance when tossed with the hot pasta and perfumes the whole kitchen: Get the bowls to the table as quickly as possible so that everyone can enjoy the aroma. This dish calls out for the creamy, fresh-tasting ricotta—either whole milk or part skim—sold in many Italian and gourmet-food stores. Bland supermarket ricotta is just not the same.

¾ cup ricotta cheese, preferably homestyle
¼ cup freshly grated Parmigiano-Reggiano cheese
2 tablespoons unsalted butter, diced
2 tablespoons minced fresh mint leaves
Salt and freshly ground black pepper
1 pound penne

1. Bring 4 quarts water to a boil in a large pot for cooking the pasta.

2. Place the ricotta, Parmigiano-Reggiano, butter, mint, ½ teaspoon salt and pepper to taste in a bowl large enough to hold the penne when cooked. Stir well to combine.

3. When the water comes to a boil, add salt to taste and the penne. When the penne is nearly finished cooking, remove ¼ cup hot water from the pot and stir it into the bowl with the cheese mixture. Adjust the seasonings.

4. Continue cooking the penne until al dente and then drain.

5. Toss the penne with the cheese sauce and mix well. Divide the pasta among individual bowls and serve immediately.

SERVING SUGGESTIONS

This is a perfect light lunch. Followed by an orange eaten out of hand, it satisfies for the rest of the day. For dinner, conclude the meal with Fennel and Orange Salad (page 389) or Tender Greens and Vegetables with Blood Orange Vinaigrette (page 376).

Linguine with Crushed Green and Black Olives

SERVES 4

IF YOU HAVE A SELECTION OF GOOD OLIVES and some fine extra-virgin olive oil on hand, you have the makings for this sauce. A combination of olives is best; I often buy the mixed marinated olives at my local Italian market. Parsley or basil is essential here, while thyme or oregano makes a nice addition if you have some on hand or in the garden. Add hot red pepper flakes if you want a spicy sauce.

8 ounces mixed green and black olives (2-3 dozen, depending on size)
1 medium garlic clove, minced
2 tablespoons minced fresh parsley or basil leaves
1 teaspoon minced fresh thyme or oregano leaves (optional)
6 tablespoons extra-virgin olive oil
Salt
½ teaspoon dried hot red pepper flakes (optional)
1 pound linguine

1. Bring 4 quarts water to a boil in a large pot for cooking the pasta.

2. Use the side of a large chef's knife to crush each olive and loosen the pit. Pull out and discard the pit and then throw the 2 or 3 pieces of the olive into a bowl large enough to hold the linguine when cooked. Repeat with the remaining olives. Add the garlic, parsley or basil, thyme or oregano (if using), oil, salt to taste and the hot red pepper flakes (if using).

3. When the water comes to a boil, add salt to taste and the linguine. Cook until al dente and then drain, leaving a little cooking liquid dripping from the noodles.

4. Toss the linguine with the olive sauce. Divide among individual bowls and serve immediately.

SERVING SUGGESTIONS
Round out the meal with a leafy green salad. Tender Green Salad with Pine Nuts and Yellow Raisins (page 375) is an especially good choice.

Linguine with Garlic, Olive Oil and Lemon

SERVES 4

THIS RECIPE IS THE ITALIAN ANSWER TO THE QUESTION "What's for dinner?" when few ingredients are on hand. Anyone who does even a little cooking is bound to have some garlic, olive oil and pasta in the kitchen. I like to perk up this classic, called *aglio e olio*, or garlic and oil, with a little lemon juice and hot red pepper flakes, though neither is strictly traditional. Note that the sauce can be prepared in the time it takes to bring the water to a boil and cook the pasta.

6 tablespoons extra-virgin olive oil
8 medium garlic cloves, minced
1 tablespoon lemon juice
Salt
½ teaspoon dried hot red pepper flakes, or to taste
1 pound linguine

1. Bring 4 quarts water to a boil in a large pot for cooking the pasta.

2. Heat the oil in a large skillet. Add the garlic and sauté over medium-low heat until golden but not browned, about 4 minutes. The garlic will become bitter if browned but should be a deep golden color.

3. Stir in the lemon juice, 1 teaspoon salt and hot red pepper flakes. Cook for 30 seconds more to blend the flavors. Remove from the heat.

4. When the water comes to a boil, add salt to taste and the linguine. Cook until al dente and then drain.

5. Add the linguine to the skillet with the oil and garlic and mix well. Divide among individual bowls and serve immediately.

SERVING SUGGESTIONS

As late-night fare or dinner when the cupboard is bare, this dish is designed to stand alone. Of course, a green vegetable or leafy salad could be added for a more substantial meal, but neither is required.

Fettuccine with Mascarpone, Toasted Walnuts and Basil

SERVES 4

RICH MASCARPONE, A KIND OF ITALIAN CREAM CHEESE, makes an excellent sauce for fresh or dried fettuccine. Make sure that the pasta is still dripping with water in order to thin the cheese to sauce consistency. Reserve a little extra cooking water as well, in case the pasta needs more moistening. Do not use American cream cheese as a substitute. Homestyle ricotta would be a better, if imperfect, choice.

½ cup chopped walnuts
3 tablespoons unsalted butter
2 tablespoons chopped fresh basil or parsley leaves
½ cup mascarpone cheese
Salt and freshly ground black pepper
1 pound fettuccine

1. Bring 4 quarts water to a boil in a large pot for cooking the pasta.

2. Place the walnuts in a medium skillet over medium heat. Toast, shaking the pan occasionally to turn the nuts, until fragrant, about 5 minutes. Transfer to a plate.

3. Melt the butter in the skillet. Add the nuts and basil or parsley and cook just until heated through. Place the mascarpone in a bowl large enough to hold the fettuccine when cooked. Stir in the walnut mixture and add salt and pepper to taste.

4. When the water comes to a boil, add salt to taste and the fettuccine. Cook until al dente and then drain, reserving ¼ cup of the cooking liquid.

5. Toss the fettuccine, still dripping with cooking water, with the walnut sauce and mix well. Add as much reserved cooking liquid as needed to thin the sauce. Divide among individual bowls and serve immediately.

SERVING SUGGESTIONS

This dish is rich and should be followed by a light salad of bitter greens, such as Radicchio, Arugula and Endive Salad with Balsamic Vinaigrette (page 373), Arugula Salad with Sliced Radishes and Carrots (page 371) or Red Leaf Lettuce, Arugula and Fennel Salad (page 374).

Summer Spaghetti with Raw Arugula and Tomatoes

SERVES 4

A FRESH TOMATO SAUCE WITH OLIVE OIL AND GARLIC is tossed with spaghetti and arugula cut into ribbons for a quick summer dish. The tomatoes are just warmed in the hot oil and should not be cooked so long that they lose their shape. *See the photograph on page 194.*

4 cups stemmed arugula leaves
3 tablespoons extra-virgin olive oil
2 medium garlic cloves, minced
3 medium, ripe tomatoes (about 1¼ pounds), cored and cut into ½-inch cubes
Salt
1 pound spaghetti

1. Bring 4 quarts water to a boil in a large pot for cooking the pasta.

2. Wash and dry the arugula. Slice the leaves crosswise into thin strips and set them aside in a bowl large enough to hold the spaghetti when cooked.

3. Heat the oil in a large skillet. Add the garlic and sauté over medium heat until golden, about 2 minutes. Add the tomatoes and salt to taste and cook, stirring occasionally, just until the tomatoes are heated through, about 2 minutes.

4. When the water comes to a boil, add salt to taste and the spaghetti. Cook until al dente and then drain.

5. Toss the pasta and the tomato sauce with the arugula, mixing until the arugula wilts. Divide among individual bowls and serve immediately.

SERVING SUGGESTIONS

The aggressive flavors in this summer dish make it right with any number of dishes. Start with Raw Vegetables with Olive Oil Dipping Sauce (page 28) or perhaps Crostini with Black Olive Spread and Capers (page 33). Finish off with Marinated Zucchini Salad with Lemon and Thyme (page 396) or Raw Zucchini Salad with Lemon and Basil (page 397).

Fettuccine with Braised Artichoke Sauce

SERVES 4

THIS SAUCE OF SLOW-COOKED ARTICHOKES AND TOMATOES is substantial and satisfying. The artichokes will need at least 40 minutes to soften properly; the flavor achieved is worth the wait.

1 lemon, halved
4 medium artichokes (about 2 pounds)
¼ cup extra-virgin olive oil
1 medium onion, minced
3 medium garlic cloves, minced
1 28-ounce can whole tomatoes, drained and chopped, juice reserved
2 teaspoons minced fresh oregano leaves
Salt and freshly ground black pepper
1 pound fettuccine
Freshly grated Parmigiano-Reggiano cheese

1. Squeeze the lemon halves into a large bowl of cold water and add the lemon to the bowl. Working with 1 artichoke at a time, bend back and snap off the tough outer leaves. Remove several layers until you reach the leaves that are mostly pale green or yellow except for the tips. With a sharp knife, slice off the dark green pointed tip of the artichoke. Trim the end of the stem and use a vegetable peeler to peel the outer layer. Use the peeler to remove any dark green leaf bases that may surround the top of the stem. Quarter the artichoke lengthwise, leaving a part of the stem attached to each piece. Slide a small, sharp knife under the fuzzy choke and cut toward the leaf tips to remove it. Slice the cleaned quarters into ¼-inch-thick wedges and drop them into the bowl of cold lemon water. Repeat with the remaining artichokes. Set aside.

2. Heat the oil in a large sauté pan. Add the onion and sauté over medium heat until translucent, about 5 minutes. Drain the artichokes and add them to the pan. Add the garlic. Cook for 1 to 2 minutes, stirring, until the garlic is golden and the artichokes are well coated with oil.

3. Add 1 cup water, cover and simmer until most of the liquid has evaporated, about 10 minutes. Add the tomatoes and their juice, the oregano and salt and

pepper to taste. Cover and simmer, stirring occasionally, until the artichokes are tender, 30 to 40 minutes. Adjust the seasonings.

4. When the sauce is nearly done, bring 4 quarts water to a boil in a large pot.

5. When the water comes to a boil, add salt to taste and the fettuccine. Cook until al dente and then drain.

6. Toss the fettuccine with the artichoke sauce and mix well. Divide among individual bowls and serve immediately with grated cheese passed separately at the table.

Serving Suggestions

Follow this dish with a light salad. Good choices include Red Leaf Lettuce, Arugula and Fennel Salad (page 374) and Fava Bean and Asparagus Salad with Basil Toasts (page 382).

Spaghetti with Asparagus, Tomatoes and Lemon

SERVES 4

A SQUIRT OF LEMON JUICE enlivens a simple plum tomato sauce that does not overwhelm steamed asparagus.

- **1 pound medium asparagus**
- **Salt**
- **3 tablespoons extra-virgin olive oil**
- **3 medium garlic cloves, minced**
- **7 medium plum tomatoes (about 1½ pounds), cored, seeded and diced**
- **1 tablespoon lemon juice**
- **1 pound spaghetti**
- **Freshly grated Parmigiano-Reggiano cheese**

1. Bring 4 quarts water to a boil in a large pot for cooking the asparagus and the pasta.

2. Snap off the tough ends of the asparagus spears. Cut the spears lengthwise in half (quarter thicker spears) and slice them on the bias into 1-inch pieces. When the water comes to a boil, add the asparagus and salt to taste and cook until almost tender, about 1½ minutes. Use a slotted spoon to transfer the asparagus to a medium bowl. (Leave the pot on the heat.)

3. Heat the oil in a large skillet. Add the garlic and sauté over medium heat until golden, about 2 minutes. Add the tomatoes and cook until they soften slightly, about 3 minutes. Add the asparagus and lemon juice and cook just until the asparagus is heated through, 1 to 2 minutes. Adjust the seasonings.

4. When the water comes back to a boil, add salt to taste and the spaghetti. Cook until al dente and then drain.

5. Toss the spaghetti with the tomato-asparagus sauce and mix well. Divide among individual bowls and serve immediately with grated cheese passed separately at the table.

SERVING SUGGESTIONS

Bruschetta with Fresh Herbs (page 477) makes a good accompaniment. I like to conclude the meal with Arugula Salad with Sliced Radishes and Carrots (page 371) because it does not contain any acid that might conflict with the lemon juice in the pasta sauce.

Whole Wheat Spaghetti with Spicy Broccoli and Pecorino

Serves 4

This southern Italian sauce is easy to prepare, since the broccoli cooks right along with the pasta. The full-flavored sauce has enough bite to stand up to whole wheat pasta. Of course, regular spaghetti may be used.

2 pounds broccoli
¼ cup extra-virgin olive oil
4 medium garlic cloves, minced
½ teaspoon dried hot red pepper flakes, or to taste
Salt
1 pound whole wheat or regular spaghetti
Freshly grated Pecorino Romano or Parmigiano-Reggiano cheese

1. Bring 4 quarts water to a boil in a large pot for cooking the pasta.

2. Remove and discard the stalks from the broccoli. Cut the florets into bite-size pieces. There should be about 5 cups. Set aside.

3. Heat the oil in a skillet large enough to hold the spaghetti when cooked and the broccoli. Add the garlic and hot red pepper flakes and sauté over medium heat until the garlic is golden, about 2 minutes. Turn off the heat and stir in 1 teaspoon salt.

4. When the water comes to a boil, add salt to taste and the spaghetti. When the spaghetti is almost al dente, add the broccoli. Continue cooking until the pasta is al dente and the broccoli is tender, about 2 minutes. Drain, reserving ½ cup of the cooking liquid.

5. Add the spaghetti and broccoli to the skillet. Toss over high heat, adding most, if not all, of the reserved cooking liquid to moisten the dish. Divide among individual bowls and serve immediately with grated cheese passed separately at the table.

Serving Suggestions

Follow this assertive dish with a salad, preferably one with a citrus vinaigrette. Good choices include Tender Green Salad with Pine Nuts and Yellow Raisins (page 375), Spinach Salad with Orange Juice Vinaigrette and Toasted Walnuts (page 380) and Tender Greens and Vegetables with Blood Orange Vinaigrette (page 376).

Penne with Cauliflower, Onions and Saffron

SERVES 4

IN THIS EASY DISH, CAULIFLOWER IS SAUTÉED WITH ONIONS AND SAFFRON, which gives a bright yellow color and a subtle, haunting flavor.

- **1 small cauliflower head (about 1¾ pounds)**
- **¼ cup extra-virgin olive oil**
- **2 medium onions, halved and sliced crosswise into thin strips**
- **¼ teaspoon saffron threads**
- **Salt**
- **1 pound penne or orecchiette**
- **2 tablespoons minced fresh parsley leaves**

1. Bring 4 quarts water to a boil in a large pot for cooking the pasta.

2. Trim and discard the leaves and stems from the cauliflower. Cut the florets into bite-size pieces. There should be about 5 cups. Set aside.

3. Heat the oil in a large sauté pan. Add the onions and sauté over medium heat until light gold in color, about 6 minutes. Add the cauliflower and cook, stirring often, until the florets are pale gold, about 10 minutes.

4. While the onions and cauliflower are cooking, place the saffron in a small bowl. Add ¾ cup boiling water and let stand for 2 minutes. Add the saffron mixture and salt to taste to the pan. Reduce the heat to medium-low, cover and cook, stirring occasionally, until the cauliflower is tender and bright yellow in color, about 10 minutes.

5. When the water comes to a boil, add salt to taste and the penne or orecchiette. Cook until al dente and then drain.

6. Toss the penne or orecchiette with the cauliflower sauce and parsley and mix well. Divide among individual bowls and serve immediately.

SERVING SUGGESTIONS

Serve with a green leafy salad with a citrus dressing, such as Spinach Salad with Orange Juice Vinaigrette and Toasted Walnuts (page 380) or Tender Green Salad with Pine Nuts and Yellow Raisins (page 375).

Rigatoni with Stewed Eggplant Sauce

SERVES 4

USE CANNED TOMATOES PACKED IN JUICE for this hearty eggplant sauce with onion, olives and red bell pepper. The juice becomes the cooking medium for the vegetables and reduces to a sauce.

- 3 tablespoons extra-virgin olive oil
- 1 medium onion, minced
- 3 medium garlic cloves, minced
- 2 cups drained canned whole tomatoes, coarsely chopped, juice reserved
- 1 large eggplant (about 1 pound), ends trimmed and cut into ½-inch dice
- 1 large red bell pepper, cored, seeded and cut into ½-inch dice
- 12 large black olives (about 3 ounces), pitted and chopped
- Salt and freshly ground black pepper
- 1 pound rigatoni
- Freshly grated Pecorino Romano or Parmigiano-Reggiano cheese

1. Bring 4 quarts water to a boil in a large pot for cooking the pasta.

2. Heat the oil in a Dutch oven. Add the onion and sauté over medium heat until translucent, about 5 minutes. Stir in the garlic and cook until it is golden, about 1 minute.

3. Add the tomatoes and 1 cup of the juice. Add the eggplant, bell pepper, olives and salt and pepper to taste. Cover and simmer, stirring occasionally, until the eggplant is almost tender, about 20 minutes. Uncover and simmer until the sauce thickens a bit and the vegetables are quite tender, about 5 minutes. Adjust the seasonings.

4. When the water comes to a boil, add salt to taste and the rigatoni. Cook until al dente and then drain.

5. Toss the rigatoni with the eggplant sauce and mix well. Divide among individual bowls and serve immediately with grated cheese passed separately at the table.

SERVING SUGGESTIONS

Accompany this dish with bread and follow it with a simple salad, such as Radicchio, Arugula and Endive Salad with Balsamic Vinaigrette (page 373) or Tender Green Salad with Pine Nuts and Yellow Raisins (page 375).

Ziti with Roasted Eggplant, Fresh Tomato Sauce and Ricotta

SERVES 4

ROASTING CUBES OF EGGPLANT in the oven requires much less oil than sautéing and has the same effect: it concentrates the flavor and turns them golden brown. The eggplant is then added to a fresh tomato sauce with fresh basil. A small amount of ricotta cheese provides a good counterpoint.

- 2 small eggplants (about ¾ pound)
- ¼ cup extra-virgin olive oil
- 2 medium garlic cloves, lightly smashed
- 3 medium, ripe tomatoes (about 1¼ pounds), cored, peeled, seeded and diced small
- Salt and freshly ground black pepper
- 10 large fresh basil leaves, cut into thin strips
- ½ cup ricotta cheese, homestyle or supermarket
- 1 pound ziti or penne

1. Preheat the oven to 400 degrees F. Trim and discard the ends from the eggplants. Peel and cut the eggplants into ½-inch cubes. Place on a baking sheet, drizzle 2 tablespoons of the oil over and toss gently. Spread the cubes on the baking sheet in a single layer. Bake, turning twice, until the eggplant is golden brown, about 20 minutes.

2. While the eggplant is cooking, bring 4 quarts water to a boil in a large pot for cooking the pasta.

3. Heat the remaining 2 tablespoons oil in a medium saucepan. Add the garlic and sauté over medium heat until it is golden, about 3 minutes. Remove and discard the garlic.

4. Add the tomatoes and salt and pepper to taste. Simmer, stirring occasionally, until the tomatoes soften and form a sauce, 5 to 10 minutes, depending on their initial firmness. Stir in the roasted eggplant and basil. Cook for 1 to 2 minutes more to heat through. Adjust the seasonings.

5. Place the ricotta in a bowl large enough to hold the ziti or penne when cooked.

6. When the water comes to a boil, add salt to taste and the ziti or penne. Cook until al dente and then drain, reserving ¼ cup of the cooking liquid. Stir the cooking liquid into the ricotta to thin it.

7. Add the ziti or penne and tomato-eggplant sauce to the ricotta and mix well. Divide among individual bowls and serve immediately.

SERVING SUGGESTIONS

To balance the rich taste of cheese in this recipe, follow it with a salad of bitter greens, such as Red Leaf Lettuce, Arugula and Fennel Salad (page 374).

Orecchiette with Fava Beans, Plum Tomatoes and Ricotta Salata

SERVES 4

EAR-SHAPED ORECCHIETTE trap small bits of this spring pasta sauce, which features fava beans and ricotta salata cheese. Like feta cheese, ricotta salata can be crumbled finely by hand. Its flavor, however, is much milder and less salty than that of feta. *See the photograph on page 200.*

- 1½ pounds fresh fava beans in pods
- ¼ cup extra-virgin olive oil
- 3 medium shallots, minced
- 5 medium plum tomatoes (about 1 pound), cored and cut into ½-inch cubes
- Salt and freshly ground black pepper
- 2 tablespoons minced fresh chives or scallions
- 1 pound orecchiette or small shells
- 2 ounces ricotta salata cheese, finely crumbled

1. Bring 4 quarts water to a boil in a large pot for cooking the fava beans and the pasta.

2. Shell the fava beans. There should be about 1½ cups shelled beans. Add the beans to the boiling water and simmer for 2 minutes. Use a slotted spoon to transfer the favas to a large bowl. (Leave the pot on the heat.) Cover the beans with cold water and drain. Use your fingers to scrape away part of the outer light green skin on each fava. Squeeze the skin to pop out the dark green bean. Set aside.

3. Heat the oil in a large skillet. Add the shallots and sauté over medium heat until translucent, about 3 minutes. Stir in the tomatoes and salt and pepper to taste and simmer until the tomatoes soften slightly but do not lose their shape, about 4 minutes.

4. Stir in the fava beans and chives or scallions. Cook until the beans are completely tender, 2 to 3 minutes. Adjust the seasonings.

5. Add salt to taste to the large pot of water and the orecchiette or small shells. Cook until al dente and then drain.

6. Toss the orecchiette or small shells with the tomato-fava sauce and mix well. Divide among individual bowls, sprinkle the crumbled cheese over each bowl and serve immediately.

Serving Suggestions

This dish is ideal for early spring when favas first arrive in the stores. Serve it with bread and follow with a leafy salad, such as Tender Green Salad with Pine Nuts and Yellow Raisins (page 375) or Fennel and Orange Salad (page 389).

Farfalle with Sautéed Fennel and Fresh Tomatoes

SERVES 4

THE FENNEL MUST BE DICED SMALL for this recipe and then cooked in garlicky oil until tender. Do not let it burn or brown; it's sweet enough, so there's no need to caramelize it. When cooking farfalle, be prepared to boil this butterfly-shaped pasta a bit longer than usual. It takes quite a while for the double-thick portions near the center to cook through.

2 small fennel bulbs (about 1¾ pounds)
¼ cup extra-virgin olive oil
3 medium garlic cloves, minced
2 small, ripe tomatoes (about ½ pound), cored and cut into ½-inch cubes
Salt
1 pound farfalle
Freshly grated Parmigiano-Reggiano cheese

1. Bring 4 quarts water to a boil in a large pot for cooking the pasta.

2. Trim the stems and fronds from the fennel. Discard the stems. Mince 1 tablespoon of the fronds and set aside. Trim a thin slice from the base of the bulb and remove any tough or blemished outer layers. Cut the bulb in half through the base and use a small, sharp knife to remove the core. Lay the halves flat side down on a cutting board and chop into ¼-inch dice. Set aside.

3. Heat the oil in a large skillet. Add the garlic and sauté over medium heat until golden, 1 to 2 minutes. Add the diced fennel and cook, stirring occasionally, until quite tender, 15 to 20 minutes. Lower the heat if the fennel starts to brown.

4. Stir in the tomatoes and salt to taste. Cook just until the tomatoes soften and are heated through, about 3 minutes. Stir in the minced fennel fronds and adjust the seasonings.

5. When the water comes to a boil, add salt to taste and the farfalle. Cook until al dente and then drain.

6. Toss the pasta with the fennel-tomato sauce and mix well. Divide among individual bowls and serve immediately with grated cheese passed separately at the table.

Serving Suggestions

Serve as the centerpiece for an easy-to-prepare late-summer meal, with Bruschetta with Fresh Herbs (page 477) and a leafy green salad.

Linguine with Leeks and Tomatoes

SERVES 4

LEEKS TRANSFORM A PLAIN TOMATO SAUCE into something extraordinary. Sautéing leeks until they start to brown brings out their sweetness.

- **4 medium leeks (about 2 pounds)**
- **¼ cup extra-virgin olive oil**
- **1 28-ounce can whole tomatoes, drained and chopped, juice reserved**
- **1 teaspoon minced fresh thyme leaves**
- **Salt and freshly ground black pepper**
- **1 pound linguine**
- **Freshly grated Parmigiano-Reggiano cheese**

1. Bring 4 quarts water to a boil in a large pot for cooking the pasta.

2. Trim and discard the dark green tops and tough outer leaves from the leeks. Remove the roots along with a very thin slice of the nearby white part. Halve the leeks lengthwise and wash them under cold running water. Gently spread apart but do not separate the inner layers to remove all traces of soil. If the leeks are particularly sandy, soak them in several changes of clean water. Slice the cleaned leeks crosswise into thin pieces.

3. Heat the oil in a large skillet. Add the leeks and sauté over medium heat just until they start to brown, 10 to 12 minutes. Do not let the leeks burn, or they will become bitter.

4. Add the tomatoes and ½ cup of the reserved juice. Use the back of a wooden spoon to break apart the tomatoes. Add the thyme and salt and pepper to taste. Simmer until the sauce thickens, about 10 minutes. Adjust the seasonings.

5. When the water comes to a boil, add salt to taste and the linguine. Cook until al dente and then drain.

6. Toss the linguine with the tomato-leek sauce and mix well. Divide among individual bowls and serve immediately with grated cheese passed separately at the table.

SERVING SUGGESTIONS

The caramelized leeks make this tomato sauce especially sweet, so follow with a salad with a lemony dressing, such as Wilted Spinach Salad with Polenta Croutons (page 379) or Fava Bean and Asparagus Salad with Basil Toasts (page 382).

Penne with Portobello Mushroom Ragù

SERVES 4

RED WINE AND MEATY PORTOBELLO MUSHROOMS give this sauce the flavor of a slow-cooked ragù. I add rosemary, but oregano or thyme would also work.

- **2 medium portobello mushrooms (about 8 ounces)**
- **3 tablespoons extra-virgin olive oil**
- **1 medium onion, minced**
- **1 teaspoon minced fresh rosemary leaves**
- **Salt and freshly ground black pepper**
- **½ cup dry red wine, such as Chianti**
- **1½ cups drained canned whole tomatoes, chopped**
- **1 pound penne**
- **Freshly grated Parmigiano-Reggiano cheese**

1. Bring 4 quarts water to a boil in a large pot for cooking the pasta.

2. Remove and discard the mushroom stems. Wipe the caps clean. Cut the mushrooms in half; slice each half crosswise into ¼-inch-thick strips. Set aside.

3. Heat the oil in a large skillet. Add the onion and sauté over medium heat until translucent, about 5 minutes. Add the mushrooms and cook, stirring occasionally, until they are quite tender and have begun to give off some liquid. Stir in the rosemary and salt and pepper to taste and cook for 30 seconds more.

4. Add the wine and simmer until it reduces by half, about 3 minutes. Add the tomatoes and simmer until the sauce thickens considerably, 10 to 15 minutes. Adjust the seasonings.

5. When the water comes to a boil, add salt to taste and the penne. Cook until al dente and then drain.

6. Toss the penne with the mushroom sauce and mix well. Divide among individual bowls and serve immediately with grated cheese passed separately at the table.

SERVING SUGGESTIONS

Serve this dish with bread and some of the same red wine used for the sauce. Follow with a green salad, such as Red Leaf Lettuce, Arugula and Fennel Salad (page 374) or Tender Greens and Vegetables with Blood Orange Vinaigrette (page 376).

Orecchiette with Two Mushrooms and Rosemary

Serves 4

Button mushrooms get a boost from a handful of dried porcini mushrooms. In this recipe, the drained pasta is added to the pan with the sauce so that it can absorb some of the porcini liquid. Thyme or oregano can be used in place of the rosemary.

1 ounce dried porcini mushrooms
2 tablespoons unsalted butter
1 tablespoon extra-virgin olive oil
1 medium onion, minced
2 medium garlic cloves, minced
1 teaspoon minced fresh rosemary leaves
1 pound white button mushrooms, wiped clean, stems trimmed, thinly sliced
Salt and freshly ground black pepper
1 pound orecchiette or small shells
⅓ cup freshly grated Parmigiano-Reggiano cheese
2 tablespoons minced fresh parsley leaves

1. Bring 4 quarts water to a boil in a large pot for cooking the pasta.

2. Place the porcini mushrooms in a small bowl and cover with 1 cup hot water. Soak until softened, about 20 minutes. Carefully lift the mushrooms from the liquid and pick through them to remove any foreign debris. Wash the mushrooms if they feel gritty. Chop them. Strain the soaking liquid through a sieve lined with a paper towel. Set aside the mushrooms and strained soaking liquid separately.

3. Heat the butter and oil in a large sauté pan. Add the onion and sauté over medium heat until translucent, about 5 minutes. Add the garlic and rosemary and cook until the garlic is golden, about 1 minute.

4. Add the button mushrooms and sauté until golden brown and the liquid they give off has evaporated, about 8 minutes. Season with salt and pepper to taste. Add the chopped porcini and cook for 1 to 2 minutes more to release their flavor. Add the soaking liquid and bring to a boil. Cover and remove from the heat.

5. When the water comes to a boil, add salt to taste and the orecchiette or small shells. Cook until al dente and then drain.

6. Add the orecchiette or small shells, cheese and parsley to the pan with the mushroom sauce. Toss over medium-low heat just until the cheese melts and the pasta absorbs the liquid in the pan. Divide among individual bowls and serve immediately.

Serving Suggestions

Follow this dish with something leafy, green and distinctive. Good choices include Wilted Spinach with Garlic (page 360), Radicchio, Arugula and Endive Salad with Balsamic Vinaigrette (page 373) and Spinach Salad with Orange Juice Vinaigrette and Toasted Walnuts (page 380).

Orecchiette with Peas, Ricotta and Parmesan

SERVES 4

RICOTTA CHEESE FORMS A CREAMY SAUCE FOR PASTA. Orecchiette are small bowl-shaped pasta shells—the name actually means "little ears"—that do a good job of trapping the peas. Small shells or fusilli will work as well. If shelling fresh peas, buy a little over a pound to yield 1½ cups.

- 1½ cups shelled fresh or frozen peas
- 2 tablespoons extra-virgin olive oil
- 1 medium onion, minced
- 1 cup ricotta cheese, preferably homestyle
- ⅓ cup freshly grated Parmigiano-Reggiano cheese
- Salt and freshly ground black pepper
- 1 pound orecchiette or small shells

1. Bring 4 quarts water to a boil in a large pot for cooking the pasta. Bring several cups water to a boil in a small pot for cooking the peas.

2. Add the peas to the small pot of boiling water and cook until tender, about 4 minutes for fresh and about 1 minute for frozen. Drain and set aside.

3. Heat the oil in a small skillet. Add the onion and sauté until lightly browned, about 7 minutes. Stir in the peas and cook for 30 seconds.

4. Scrape the onion and peas into a bowl large enough to hold the orecchiette or small shells when cooked. Stir in the ricotta and Parmigiano-Reggiano cheeses and salt and pepper to taste.

5. When the water comes to a boil, add salt to taste and the orecchiette or small shells. Cook until al dente and then drain, reserving ½ cup of the cooking liquid.

6. Toss the pasta with the cheese sauce, adding as much cooking water as needed to thin the sauce. Divide among individual bowls and serve immediately.

SERVING SUGGESTIONS

This pasta should be followed with a sharp salad, like Marinated Tomato and Red Onion Salad (page 395) or Marinated Yellow Beans and Summer Tomato Salad (page 383). If tomatoes are not in season, try Wilted Spinach Salad with Polenta Croutons (page 379) or Fennel and Orange Salad (page 389).

Spaghetti with Roasted Red Peppers and Basil

SERVES 4

SILKEN ROASTED RED BELL PEPPERS make a rich sauce for pasta. You can use an assortment of colored peppers (yellow and orange peppers are good) or stick with red peppers. Make sure to reserve the juices given off by the peppers to help moisten the pasta.

- **6 large red bell peppers (about 2½ pounds), roasted and peeled (see page 526)**
- **¼ cup extra-virgin olive oil**
- **3 tablespoons minced fresh basil leaves**
- **Salt and freshly ground black pepper**
- **1 pound spaghetti**
- **Freshly grated Parmigiano-Reggiano cheese**

1. Bring 4 quarts water to a boil in a large pot for cooking the pasta.

2. Core and seed the roasted peppers and cut them into very thin strips. Place the pepper strips and their juice in a bowl large enough to hold the spaghetti when cooked. Add the oil, basil and salt and pepper to taste. Toss gently. *(The peppers can be covered and set aside for several hours.)*

3. When the water comes to a boil, add salt to taste and the spaghetti. Cook until al dente and then drain.

4. Toss the spaghetti with the roasted-pepper sauce and mix well. Divide among individual bowls and serve immediately with grated cheese passed separately at the table.

SERVING SUGGESTIONS

This dish is sweet and needs a leafy green salad with a bite. Follow with Arugula Salad with Sliced Radishes and Carrots (page 371) or Radicchio, Arugula and Endive Salad with Balsamic Vinaigrette (page 373).

Spaghetti with Spicy Spinach and Toasted Bread Crumbs

SERVES 4

IN SOUTHERN REGIONS OF ITALY, bread crumbs are often used in place of grated cheese over simple pasta dishes. Homemade crumbs, made by grinding fresh or stale bread in a food processor, are best. However, commercial plain bread crumbs will be fine, especially when toasted.

- **⅓ cup plain bread crumbs**
- **¼ cup extra-virgin olive oil**
- **½ teaspoon dried hot red pepper flakes**
- **Salt**
- **1½ pounds spinach, preferably flat-leaf**
- **1 pound spaghetti**

1. Bring 6 quarts water to a boil in a large pot for cooking the pasta.

2. Set a small skillet over medium heat. Add the bread crumbs and toast, shaking the pan occasionally, until golden brown. Do not let them burn. Set aside in a small bowl.

3. Combine the oil, hot red pepper flakes and ¾ teaspoon salt in another small bowl. Set aside.

4. Remove and discard the stems from the spinach. Wash the leaves in successive bowls of cold water until grit no longer appears in the bottom of the bowl. Shake the leaves to remove excess water but do not dry them.

5. When the water comes to a boil, add salt to taste and the spaghetti. Cook almost al dente. Add the spinach, stir well to submerge the leaves in the water and continue cooking for 1½ minutes, or until the pasta is done.

6. Drain the pasta and spinach and toss with the oil mixture, mixing well. Divide among individual bowls, sprinkle with the toasted bread crumbs and serve immediately.

SERVING SUGGESTIONS

Follow with Marinated Yellow Beans and Summer Tomato Salad (page 383), Tomato Salad with Black Olives, Capers and Herbs (page 394) or Fennel and Orange Salad (page 389).

Spaghetti with Barely Cooked Summer Tomato Sauce

SERVES 4

WHEN TOMATOES ARE AT THEIR FINEST, consider making this sauce, which cooks in less time than it takes to boil pasta. The tomatoes are cooked just long enough to heat them through. If possible, use a combination of yellow and red tomatoes. Choose the finest fruity olive oil. This also goes well with fresh pasta.

- **Salt**
- **1 pound spaghetti**
- **6 tablespoons extra-virgin olive oil**
- **4 medium garlic cloves, minced**
- **4 large, ripe tomatoes (about 2 pounds), cored and cut into ½-inch cubes**
- **20 large fresh basil leaves, cut into thin strips**
- **Freshly ground black pepper**

1. Bring 4 quarts water to a boil in a large pot for cooking the pasta.

2. When the water comes to a boil, add salt to taste and the spaghetti. As soon as the spaghetti is in the pot, heat the oil in a large skillet. Add the garlic and cook for about 20 seconds to release its flavor. Add the tomatoes and basil and cook just until the tomatoes are warmed through and slightly softened, about 2 minutes. Season with salt and pepper to taste. Remove from the heat. Cover and keep warm.

3. When the spaghetti is al dente, drain and toss it with the tomato sauce. Divide among individual bowls and serve immediately.

SERVING SUGGESTIONS

This dish should be served with plenty of bread to sop up the extra sauce that collects at the bottom of the bowl. Follow with a green salad, such as Arugula, Pine Nut and Parmesan Salad (page 370) or Red Leaf Lettuce, Arugula and Fennel Salad (page 374).

Linguine with Grilled Plum Tomato Sauce

SERVES 4 TO 6

LIGHTLY CHARRED PLUM TOMATOES tossed with olive oil and fresh herbs make a fast sauce for pasta. The smoky flavor is a sure sign of summer.

10 medium plum tomatoes (about 2 pounds), halved lengthwise
4 tablespoons extra-virgin olive oil
3 tablespoons minced fresh basil leaves
1 tablespoon minced fresh mint leaves
Salt and freshly ground black pepper
1 pound linguine

1. Light the grill or make a charcoal fire. Bring 4 quarts water to a boil in a large pot for cooking the pasta.

2. Lay the tomatoes on a large baking sheet and brush them with 1 tablespoon of the oil.

3. When the grill is medium-hot, place the tomatoes over the fire. Grill, turning once, until the flesh is streaked with dark grill marks and the skins are quite blistered, about 8 minutes.

4. Transfer the tomatoes to a cutting board and cool them slightly. Peel and discard the charred tomato skins. Chop the tomatoes and place them in a medium bowl. Drizzle the remaining 3 tablespoons oil over the tomatoes. Sprinkle with the basil, mint and salt and pepper to taste. Stir gently and adjust the seasonings. *(The sauce can be covered and kept at room temperature for several hours.)*

5. When the water comes to a boil, add salt to taste and the linguine. Cook until al dente and then drain.

6. Toss with the tomato sauce and mix well. Divide among individual bowls and serve immediately.

SERVING SUGGESTIONS

This dish works well as a first course for six people or as a main course for four. For a simple main course, pair it with salad and bread, such as Bruschetta with Fresh Herbs (page 477). When serving as a first course, follow with something else from the grill, perhaps Grilled Portobello Mushrooms, Red Onions and Bell Peppers (page 320).

Fusilli with Summer Tomatoes and Olivada

SERVES 4

A FEW TABLESPOONS OF OLIVADA, a pungent black olive paste, jazzes up a simple raw tomato sauce. If you don't feel like making Olivada especially for this dish, pit and finely chop a handful of large black olives and a small garlic clove and add the mixture to the tomatoes along with two tablespoons extra-virgin olive oil and one tablespoon lemon juice. The effect is slightly different but the flavors are similar. Many gourmet stores sell a similar olive paste in jars, which can be used here as well.

- **4 medium, ripe tomatoes (about 1½ pounds), cored and cut into ½-inch cubes**
- **⅓ cup Olivada (page 533)**
- **1 teaspoon minced fresh thyme leaves**
- **Salt**
- **1 pound fusilli**

1. Bring 4 quarts water to a boil in a large pot for cooking the pasta.

2. Place the tomatoes in a bowl large enough to hold the fusilli when cooked. Stir in the Olivada and thyme. Taste and add salt sparingly.

3. When the water comes to a boil, add salt to taste and the fusilli. Cook until al dente and then drain.

4. Add the linguine to the bowl with the tomatoes and mix well. Divide among individual bowls and serve immediately.

SERVING SUGGESTIONS

This pasta needs to be followed by a simple but bracing salad, such as Radicchio, Arugula and Endive Salad with Balsamic Vinaigrette (page 373) or Red Leaf Lettuce, Arugula and Fennel Salad (page 374).

Fusilli with Spinach and Ricotta Puree

SERVES 4

RAW SPINACH MAKES AN EXCELLENT BASE for a pestolike sauce. The ricotta cheese is a mellow partner to the spinach and also helps reduce the oil content in the puree to just two tablespoons. Substitute walnuts for pine nuts if you like.

- **2 tablespoons pine nuts**
- **8 ounces flat-leaf spinach**
- **1 medium garlic clove**
- **2 tablespoons extra-virgin olive oil**
- **½ cup ricotta cheese, homestyle or supermarket**
- **¼ cup freshly grated Parmigiano-Reggiano cheese**
- **Salt**
- **1 pound fusilli**

1. Bring 4 quarts water to a boil in a large pot for cooking the pasta.

2. Place the pine nuts in a medium skillet over medium heat. Toast, shaking the pan occasionally to turn the nuts, until golden, about 5 minutes. Transfer to a plate.

3. Remove and discard the stems from the spinach. You should have about 3 cups tightly packed leaves. Wash the leaves in successive bowls of cold water until grit no longer appears in the bottom of the bowl. Shake the leaves to remove excess water but do not dry them.

4. Place the spinach, pine nuts and garlic in the work bowl of a food processor. Process, scraping the sides of the bowl once, until the ingredients are finely chopped. With the motor running, slowly pour the oil through the feed tube and process until smooth. Add the ricotta cheese and process until well combined.

5. Scrape the spinach puree into a bowl large enough to hold the fusilli when cooked. Stir in the Parmigiano-Reggiano and salt to taste.

6. When the water comes to a boil, add salt to taste and the fusilli. Cook until al dente and then drain, reserving ½ cup of the cooking water.

7. Stir ¼ cup of the reserved water into the bowl with the spinach puree to thin it. Toss the pasta with the sauce, adding more of the cooking liquid if needed and mixing well. Divide among individual bowls and serve immediately.

SERVING SUGGESTIONS

Follow this dish with an assertive salad without leafy greens, such as Fennel and Orange Salad (page 389). In the summer, serve Marinated Tomato and Red Onion Salad (page 395) or Tomato Salad with Black Olives, Capers and Herbs (page 394) after the pasta.

Fusilli with Grilled Vegetables

SERVES 4

THIS LATE-SUMMER PASTA features thin strips of grilled fennel, red onion and red bell pepper along with a handful of shredded basil leaves. Grilling brings out the sweetness of the vegetables and gives this dish a caramelized flavor. Since the vegetables may be prepared several hours in advance, the dish is a good choice for entertaining.

- 2 small fennel bulbs (about 1½ pounds)
- 1 large red onion (about ½ pound), cut crosswise into ½-inch-thick slices
- 1 medium red bell pepper (about 6 ounces), cored, seeded and cut into 2-inch-wide pieces
- 5 tablespoons extra-virgin olive oil
- Salt and freshly ground black pepper
- ¼ cup shredded fresh basil leaves
- 1 pound fusilli

1. Light the grill or make a charcoal fire. Bring 4 quarts water to a boil in a large pot for cooking the pasta.

2. Remove and discard the stems and fronds from the fennel. Remove any tough or blemished outer layers. Slice the bulb vertically through the base into ½-inch-thick fan-shaped wedges.

3. Place the fennel, onion and bell pepper on a large baking sheet and brush with 3 tablespoons of the oil. Season generously with salt and pepper to taste.

4. When the grill is ready, place the vegetables over the medium-hot fire. Grill the vegetables, turning once, until they are streaked with dark grill marks, about 10 minutes for the peppers and onions and 15 minutes for the fennel.

5. Briefly cool the grilled vegetables and cut them into thin strips. Place the vegetables in a bowl large enough to hold the fusilli when cooked. Add the remaining 2 tablespoons oil along with the basil. Adjust the seasonings. *(The vegetables can be covered and kept at room temperature for several hours.)*

6. When the water comes to a boil, add salt to taste and the fusilli. Cook until al dente and then drain.

7. Toss the fusilli with the vegetables. Divide among individual bowls and serve immediately.

SERVING SUGGESTIONS

Because it has so many vegetables, this dish is almost a complete meal. A simple leafy green salad may be added if desired. Grilled bread, such as Bruschetta with Fresh Herbs (page 477), is also a good accompaniment.

Fettuccine with Zucchini, Lemon and Mint

SERVES 4

FOR THIS DISH, zucchini is cut into very thin matchstick-size strips that cook quickly and absorb the flavors in the sauce.

- 4 medium zucchini (about 1½ pounds), scrubbed
- ⅓ cup extra-virgin olive oil
- 3 medium garlic cloves, minced
- ½ teaspoon grated zest and 2 tablespoons juice from 1 medium lemon
- 12 large fresh mint leaves, shredded
- Salt and freshly ground black pepper
- 1 pound fettuccine
- Freshly grated Parmigiano-Reggiano cheese

1. Bring 4 quarts water to a boil in a large pot for cooking the pasta.

2. Trim the ends from the zucchini and cut them slightly on the bias into ¼-inch-thick rounds. Cut the rounds into thin strips the size of matchsticks.

3. Heat the oil in a large skillet. Add the garlic and sauté over medium heat until golden, about 2 minutes. Add the lemon zest and zucchini and cook over medium-high heat, stirring often, until the zucchini is tender and starting to brown, about 8 minutes.

4. Stir in the lemon juice, mint and salt and pepper to taste. Cook, stirring often, until the flavors are combined, about 1 minute. Adjust the seasonings.

5. When the water comes to a boil, add salt to taste and the fettuccine. Cook until al dente and then drain.

6. Toss the fettuccine with the zucchini sauce and mix well. Divide among individual bowls and serve immediately with grated cheese passed separately at the table.

SERVING SUGGESTIONS

Pair this dish with a few perfectly ripe sliced tomatoes and a good loaf of bread. If you want something slightly more elaborate, make Marinated Tomato and Red Onion Salad (page 395) or Tomato Salad with Black Olives, Capers and Herbs (page 394).

Baked Ziti with Tomatoes, Basil and Mozzarella

SERVES 4 TO 6

THIS HOMEY BAKED PASTA DISH combines ziti, tomato sauce, plenty of creamy mozzarella and a little grated Parmigiano-Reggiano. Use fresh mozzarella if you can—it adds extra moisture and richness. Shrink-wrapped cheese will work but is a distant second choice.

1 tablespoon extra-virgin olive oil
3 cups Quick Tomato Sauce made with basil (page 522)
8 ounces fresh mozzarella cheese packed in water, drained
Salt
1 pound ziti
¼ cup freshly grated Parmigiano-Reggiano cheese

1. Bring 4 quarts water to a boil in a large pot for cooking the pasta. Preheat the oven to 400 degrees F. Brush a 13-by-9-inch ceramic or glass baking dish with the oil and set aside.

2. Prepare the tomato sauce and place in a bowl large enough to hold the ziti when cooked. Shred the mozzarella and set aside.

3. When the water comes to a boil, add salt to taste and the ziti. Cook until it is 1 to 2 minutes shy of al dente and then drain.

4. Stir the ziti into the bowl with the tomato sauce. Toss to coat well.

5. Pour half of the mixture into the baking dish. Sprinkle with half the mozzarella and half the Parmigiano-Reggiano. Top with the remaining ziti and tomato sauce and sprinkle with the remaining mozzarella and then the remaining Parmigiano-Reggiano.

6. Bake until the cheese turns golden brown in spots, about 20 minutes. Serve immediately.

SERVING SUGGESTIONS

This old-style comfort dish is perfect for a Sunday family dinner. Kids love baked pasta, especially when made with tomato sauce and cheese. Add a loaf of bread, a tossed green salad and plenty of red wine (for the grown-ups).

Baked Ziti with Spinach and Gorgonzola

SERVES 4

BAKING ZITI IN A CREAMY BÉCHAMEL SAUCE flavored with Gorgonzola cheese and spinach allows the sauce to penetrate the noodles. Stir the noodles twice while they are in the oven so that they absorb the sauce evenly.

- 2½ tablespoons unsalted butter
- 2 cups Classic Béchamel (page 527) or Low-Fat Béchamel (page 528), hot
- 4 ounces Gorgonzola cheese, crumbled (about ⅔ cup)
- 1 pound flat-leaf spinach
- 1 medium onion, minced
- Salt
- Pinch of freshly grated nutmeg
- 1 pound ziti
- ¼ cup freshly grated Parmigiano-Reggiano cheese

1. Bring 4 quarts water to a boil in a large pot for cooking the pasta. Preheat the oven to 375 degrees F. Use ½ tablespoon of the butter to grease a 13-by-9-inch ceramic or glass baking dish and set aside.

2. Pour the hot béchamel into a bowl large enough to hold the ziti when cooked. Add the Gorgonzola and stir on and off for several minutes until the cheese has melted. Set aside.

3. Remove and discard the stems from the spinach. Wash the leaves in successive bowls of cold water until grit no longer appears in the bottom of the bowl. Shake the leaves to remove excess water but do not dry them. Set aside.

4. Heat the remaining 2 tablespoons butter in a deep pot. Add the onion and sauté over medium heat until translucent, about 5 minutes. Add the spinach and stir to coat the leaves evenly with the butter. Sprinkle with salt to taste. Cover and cook, stirring occasionally, until the spinach has wilted, about 5 minutes.

5. Stir the spinach mixture, including any liquid in the pot, into the bowl with the béchamel. Add the nutmeg and adjust the seasonings. Set aside.

6. When the water comes to a boil, add salt to taste and the ziti. Cook until it is 1 to 2 minutes shy of al dente and then drain.

7. Stir the ziti into the bowl with the sauce. Toss to coat well. Pour the mixture into the baking dish. Sprinkle the Parmigiano-Reggiano over the pasta.

8. Bake, stirring twice, until the pasta has absorbed most of the sauce in the baking dish and is just beginning to turn golden brown in spots, about 25 minutes. Serve immediately.

Serving Suggestions

Follow this rich pasta with a crisp salad of contrasting colors and textures, like Radicchio, Arugula and Endive Salad with Balsamic Vinaigrette (page 373), Red Leaf Lettuce, Arugula and Fennel Salad (page 374) or Tender Greens and Vegetables with Blood Orange Vinaigrette (page 376).

Baked Shells with Fontina and Parmesan Bread Crumbs

SERVES 4 TO 6

IN THIS ITALIAN VERSION OF MACARONI AND CHEESE, small shells soak up a thick sauce made with cream, butter and fontina cheese. Parmesan-flavored bread crumbs add a crunchy topping. Use only fontina from Valle d'Aosta in the foothills of the Alps. Fontina cheese from other places lacks the creamy, buttery texture and nutty flavor of the real article. *See the photograph on page 196.*

5½ tablespoons unsalted butter
1 cup heavy cream
8 ounces Italian fontina cheese
Salt
1 pound small shells
Pinch of freshly grated nutmeg
⅓ cup plain bread crumbs
¼ cup freshly grated Parmigiano-Reggiano cheese

1. Bring 4 quarts water to a boil in a large pot for cooking the pasta. Preheat the oven to 400 degrees F. Use ½ tablespoon of the butter to grease a 13-by-9-inch ceramic or glass baking dish and set aside.

2. Dice 4 tablespoons of the butter and place in a large bowl. Pour the cream into a small saucepan and heat. Cover, remove from the heat and keep the cream warm. Shred the fontina (you should have about 2 cups). Set aside.

3. When the water comes to a boil, add salt to taste and the shells. Cook until they are 1 to 2 minutes shy of al dente and then drain.

4. Stir the shells into the bowl with the butter. Toss to coat well. Stir in the warm cream and fontina and stir until the cheese starts to melt. Season with salt to taste and the nutmeg.

5. Pour the mixture into the baking dish. Combine the bread crumbs and Parmigiano-Reggiano and sprinkle over the pasta. Dice the remaining 1 tablespoon butter and dot the crumb topping with small pieces of butter.

6. Bake until the sauce is bubbling and the topping turns golden brown, about 20 minutes. Serve immediately.

SERVING SUGGESTIONS

Serve with a tossed green salad, such as Red Leaf Lettuce, Arugula and Fennel Salad (page 374) or Tender Greens and Vegetables with Blood Orange Vinaigrette (page 376).

Lasagne with Asparagus, Fresh Herbs and Parmesan

SERVES 6

WITHOUT TOMATO SAUCE OR MOZZARELLA, this dish is especially light and delicate. Dried lasagne noodles are simply too thick to work here; if you don't have the time to make or buy fresh, choose another recipe. It's also imperative to use thin asparagus, which will fit snugly between the layers of fresh pasta when halved lengthwise. Otherwise, you will need to quarter larger spears. All basil or all parsley may be substituted for the combination of herbs listed below.

- **2½ pounds thin asparagus**
- **Salt**
- **2 tablespoons unsalted butter**
- **2 tablespoons extra-virgin olive oil**
- **3 medium shallots, minced**
- **Freshly ground black pepper**
- **¼ cup minced fresh parsley leaves**
- **¼ cup shredded fresh basil leaves**
- **¼ cup shredded fresh mint leaves**
- **1 recipe Fresh Egg Pasta (page 130) or Fresh Spinach Pasta (page 132), rolled into thin sheets for lasagne, or 1 pound fresh store-bought noodles**
- **1¾ cups Classic Béchamel (page 527) or Low-Fat Béchamel (page 528)**
- **1¼ cups freshly grated Parmigiano-Reggiano cheese**

1. Bring 4 quarts water to a boil in a large pot for cooking the asparagus.

2. Snap off the tough ends of the asparagus spears. Cut the spears lengthwise in half (quarter thicker spears) and slice them on the bias into ½-inch pieces. When the water comes to a boil, add the asparagus and salt to taste and cook until crisp-tender, about 1 minute. Drain and set aside.

3. Heat the butter and oil in a large sauté pan. Add the shallots and sauté over medium heat until golden, about 5 minutes. Add the asparagus, 1 teaspoon salt and pepper to taste. Cook, stirring constantly, for about 1 minute. Stir in the herbs and set aside.

4. Bring 4 quarts water to a boil in a large pot for cooking the pasta. Add salt to taste and 3 or 4 sheets of pasta. Cook the pasta, stirring occasionally, for 2 minutes. Use a slotted spoon to transfer the noodles to a large bowl filled with cold water. Let the noodles cool for about 30 seconds and then transfer them to a clean kitchen towel to dry. Repeat, cooking 3 or 4 sheets of pasta at a time. *(The cooked pasta can be set aside for up to 1 hour.)*

5. Preheat the oven to 400 degrees F. Grease a 13-by-9-inch lasagne pan.

6. Smear 3 tablespoons of the béchamel across the bottom of the pan. Line the pan with a layer of pasta, cutting with scissors as necessary so the noodles touch but do not overlap. Spread 1 cup of the asparagus mixture over the noodles. Drizzle ¼ cup béchamel over the asparagus and sprinkle with 3 tablespoons cheese. Repeat the layering of pasta, asparagus, béchamel and cheese four more times. For the sixth and final layer, coat the noodles with the remaining 5 tablespoons béchamel and remaining 5 tablespoons cheese.

7. Bake the lasagne until the top turns golden brown in spots, about 20 minutes. Let stand for 5 minutes. Cut into squares and serve immediately.

Serving Suggestions

This lasagne celebrates spring. Start a multicourse meal with Chickpea Soup with Fennel and Orange Zest (page 64) or Roasted Yellow Pepper Soup (page 53). Conclude with a complex salad, such as Tender Greens and Vegetables with Blood Orange Vinaigrette (page 376) or Spinach Salad with Orange Juice Vinaigrette and Toasted Walnuts (page 380).

Lasagne with Broccoli and Carrots

SERVES 6

ALTERNATE LAYERS OF TWO COLORFUL VEGETABLES make this lasagne especially attractive. The vegetables are cooked separately in garlic-infused butter to bring out their natural sweetness. To speed the cooking of the vegetables, make sure they are cut into very small pieces. Although better with fresh pasta, the dish can be made with dried. Fresh sheets of pasta must be boiled in batches, but all 18 dried noodles can be cooked at one time, then drained in a colander and refreshed in cold water as directed in Step 4.

4 tablespoons (½ stick) unsalted butter
4 medium garlic cloves, lightly crushed
1 pound carrots, peeled and cut into ¼-inch dice
Salt
3 pounds broccoli (2 medium bunches)
1 recipe Fresh Egg Pasta (page 130), rolled into thin sheets for lasagne, or 1 pound fresh store-bought noodles or 18 dried noodles
2½ cups Classic Béchamel (page 527) or Low-Fat Béchamel (page 528)
1¾ cups freshly grated Parmigiano-Reggiano cheese

1. Melt 1½ tablespoons of the butter in a large skillet. Add 2 garlic cloves and sauté over medium heat until golden, about 5 minutes. Remove and discard the garlic and add the carrots and 2 tablespoons water. Cook the carrots, stirring occasionally, until tender but not mushy, 10 to 15 minutes. The carrots should start to shrink in size and become lightly colored. Set aside in a medium bowl and season with salt to taste.

2. Bring several quarts water to a boil in a large saucepan. Remove and discard the stalks from the broccoli. (You should have about 9 cups florets.) When the water comes to a boil, add the broccoli and salt to taste and cook for 2 minutes. Drain the broccoli, refresh it under cold running water and drain again. Chop the broccoli into ¼-inch dice.

3. Melt the remaining 2½ tablespoons butter in a clean skillet. Add the remaining 2 garlic cloves and sauté over medium heat until golden, about 5 minutes. Remove and discard the garlic and add the broccoli and 2 tablespoons water. Cook the broccoli, stirring occasionally, until tender but not mushy, about 6 minutes. Set aside in a separate medium bowl.

4. Bring 4 quarts water to a boil in a large pot for cooking the pasta. Add salt to taste and 3 or 4 sheets of pasta. Cook the pasta, stirring occasionally, for 2 minutes for fresh pasta or about 6 minutes for dried. Use a slotted spoon to transfer the noodles to a large bowl filled with cold water. Let the noodles cool for about 30 seconds and then transfer them to a clean kitchen towel to dry. Repeat, cooking 3 or 4 sheets of pasta at a time. *(The cooked pasta can be set aside for up to 1 hour.)*

5. Preheat the oven to 400 degrees F.

6. Grease a 13-by-9-inch lasagne pan. Set ½ cup béchamel aside. Stir ¾ cup béchamel into the bowl with the carrots, and 1¼ cups béchamel into the bowl with the broccoli. Mix well and adjust the seasonings.

7. Smear 3 tablespoons of the reserved béchamel across the bottom of the pan. Line the pan with a layer of pasta, cutting fresh pasta with scissors so the noodles touch but do not overlap. Spread one third of the broccoli mixture over the noodles, making sure the noodles are well coated with the béchamel from the mixture. Sprinkle with ¼ cup cheese and top with another layer of pasta. Repeat the process, using half of the carrot mixture and another ¼ cup cheese for a second layer. Make a third layer with broccoli, a fourth layer with carrots and a fifth layer with broccoli, sprinkling each layer with ¼ cup cheese. For the sixth layer, coat the noodles with the remaining reserved béchamel and sprinkle with the remaining ½ cup cheese.

8. Bake the lasagne until the top turns golden brown in spots and the sauce is bubbling, about 20 minutes. Let stand for 5 minutes. Cut the lasagne into squares and serve immediately.

Serving Suggestions

With pasta, cheese and two vegetables, this lasagne makes a special one-dish meal. Follow with a light salad of tender greens, perhaps Radicchio, Arugula and Endive Salad with Balsamic Vinaigrette (page 373) and serve with bread.

Lasagne with Porcini Mushrooms, Tomatoes and Parmesan

SERVES 6 TO 8

THIS HEARTY LASAGNE is made with a porcini and fresh mushroom sauce. The sauce is used to coat the layers of pasta along with béchamel and grated Parmesan. Fresh pasta is my first choice, but dried can also be used. See the dried-noodle cooking instructions on page 120.

- 2 ounces dried porcini mushrooms
- 2 tablespoons unsalted butter
- 2 tablespoons extra-virgin olive oil
- 1 medium onion, minced
- 2 pounds white button mushrooms, wiped clean, ends trimmed, thinly sliced
- Salt and freshly ground black pepper
- 2 cups canned crushed tomatoes
- 1 tablespoon minced fresh oregano leaves
- 1 recipe Fresh Egg Pasta (page 130), rolled into thin sheets for lasagne, or 1 pound fresh store-bought noodles or 18 dried noodles
- 1½ cups Classic Béchamel (page 527) or Low-Fat Béchamel (page 528)
- 1 cup freshly grated Parmigiano-Reggiano cheese

1. Place the porcini mushrooms in a small bowl and cover them with 2 cups hot water. Soak until softened, about 20 minutes. Carefully lift the mushrooms from the liquid and pick through them to remove any foreign debris. Wash the mushrooms if they feel gritty and chop them. Strain the soaking liquid through a sieve lined with a paper towel. Set aside the mushrooms and the strained soaking liquid separately.

2. Heat the butter and oil in a large sauté pan. Add the onion and sauté over medium heat until translucent, about 5 minutes. Add the button mushrooms and cook, stirring occasionally to bring up the cooked mushrooms from the bottom of the pan, until golden brown, about 9 minutes. Season with salt and pepper to taste.

3. Add the porcini mushrooms and cook for 1 minute. Add the soaking liquid, tomatoes and oregano and simmer, stirring occasionally, until the sauce thickens and most of the liquid has evaporated, about 20 minutes. Adjust the seasonings and set aside.

4. Bring 4 quarts water to a boil in a large pot for cooking the pasta. Add salt to taste and 3 or 4 sheets of pasta. Cook the pasta, stirring occasionally, for 2 minutes for fresh pasta or about 6 minutes for dried. Use a slotted spoon to transfer the noodles to a large bowl filled with cold water. Let the noodles cool for about 30 seconds and then transfer them to a clean kitchen towel to dry. Repeat, cooking 3 or 4 sheets of pasta at a time. *(The cooked pasta can be set aside for up to 1 hour.)*

5. Preheat the oven to 400 degrees F. Grease a 13-by-9-inch lasagne pan.

6. Smear ¼ cup of the béchamel across the bottom of the pan. Line the pan with a layer of pasta, cutting fresh pasta with scissors as necessary so the noodles touch but do not overlap. Spread 1 cup of the mushroom sauce over the noodles. Drizzle with 3 tablespoons béchamel and sprinkle with 2 tablespoons cheese. Repeat the layering of pasta, mushroom sauce, béchamel and cheese four more times. For the sixth and final layer, coat the pasta with the remaining 5 tablespoons béchamel and sprinkle with the remaining 6 tablespoons cheese.

7. Bake the lasagne until the top turns golden brown in spots and the sauce is bubbling, about 20 minutes. Let stand for 5 minutes. Cut the lasagne into squares and serve immediately.

SERVING SUGGESTIONS

This festive lasagne is a good choice for parties. It can be made in the morning (or afternoon), refrigerated until guests arrive and then baked. The dish is quite rich and needs only a leafy green salad and some bread to accompany it.

Spinach and Ricotta Ravioli with Garden Tomato Sauce

SERVES 6

THESE RAVIOLI ARE FILLED WITH A MIXTURE OF SPINACH AND RICOTTA and topped with a simple tomato sauce sweetened with onions and carrots. Other leafy vegetables, such as kale or swiss chard, may be substituted for the spinach in this recipe. Frozen spinach will work as well. Defrost ¾ cup frozen chopped spinach and squeeze out the excess moisture before adding it to the butter and onions.

- ¾ pound flat-leaf spinach
- 5 tablespoons unsalted butter
- 1 medium onion, minced
- Salt
- 1 cup ricotta cheese, preferably homestyle
- ¾ cup freshly grated Parmigiano-Reggiano cheese, plus more for the table
- 1 large egg yolk
- 1 pound Fresh Egg Pasta (page 130), rolled into thin sheets
- 1 medium carrot, peeled and minced
- 1 28-ounce can crushed tomatoes
- 2 tablespoons minced fresh basil or parsley leaves

1. Remove and discard the stems from the spinach. Wash the leaves in successive bowls of cold water until grit no longer appears in the bottom of the bowl. Shake the leaves to remove excess water but do not dry them. Place the damp leaves in a large saucepan. Cover and cook over medium heat, stirring occasionally, until the spinach wilts, about 5 minutes. Cool. Squeeze out all excess liquid from the leaves with your hands. Finely chop the spinach and set aside.

2. Heat 2 tablespoons of the butter in a small skillet. Add half of the onion and cook over medium heat until translucent, about 5 minutes. Stir in the chopped spinach and salt to taste. Cook for about 1 minute more.

3. Transfer the spinach mixture to a medium bowl. Stir in the ricotta, ¾ cup Parmigiano-Reggiano and the egg yolk. Set aside. *(The filling can be refrigerated overnight.)*

4. Use a pizza wheel or sharp knife to cut the pasta sheets into long rectangles that measure 4 inches across. Place small balls of the filling (each about 1 rounded teaspoon) in a line about 1 inch from the bottom of the pasta sheet. Leave about 1¼ inches between each ball of filling. Fold over the top of the pasta sheet, lining it up with the bottom edge. Seal the bottom and 2 open sides with your finger. Use a fluted pastry wheel to cut along the 2 sides and bottom of the sealed pasta sheet. Run the pastry wheel between the balls of filling to cut out individual ravioli. You should have about 60 ravioli. Place the ravioli in a single layer on a large baking sheet and put it in the refrigerator.

5. Melt the remaining 3 tablespoons butter in a medium skillet. Add the remaining onion and the carrot and cook over medium heat, stirring often, until the vegetables soften, about 5 minutes. Add the tomatoes and salt to taste. Bring the sauce to a boil, reduce the heat and simmer until it thickens, about 1 hour. Stir in the basil or parsley and adjust the seasonings. Cover and keep warm.

6. Bring 4 quarts water to a boil in a large pot for cooking the ravioli. Add salt to taste and add half the ravioli. Cook until the doubled edges are al dente, 4 to 5 minutes. Use a slotted spoon to transfer the ravioli to warm pasta bowls. Add the remaining ravioli to the boiling water while you spoon half of the tomato sauce over the cooked ravioli. By the time you get the first batch on the table, the second batch should be ready to be drained and sauced. Serve immediately with grated cheese passed separately at the table.

SERVING SUGGESTIONS

These ravioli should be served with bread (to sop up any extra sauce) and followed by a simple tossed green salad such as Radicchio, Arugula and Endive Salad with Balsamic Vinaigrette (page 373).

Squash Ravioli with Sage and Parmesan

SERVES 6

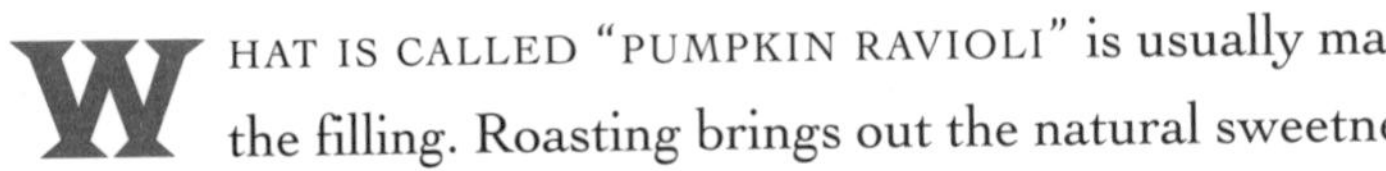

WHAT IS CALLED "PUMPKIN RAVIOLI" is usually made with butternut squash in the filling. Roasting brings out the natural sweetness of the squash.

- ½ large butternut squash (about 1½ pounds), stringy pulp and seeds discarded
- 1 large egg yolk
- 1½ cups freshly grated Parmigiano-Reggiano cheese, plus more for the table
- 2 tablespoons minced fresh sage leaves
- ⅛ teaspoon freshly grated nutmeg
- Salt
- 1 pound Fresh Egg Pasta (page 130), rolled into thin sheets
- 8 tablespoons (1 stick) unsalted butter

1. Preheat the oven to 400 degrees F. Place the squash cut side down on a small baking sheet. Bake until it is very tender, about 45 minutes. Cool and scoop out the flesh with a spoon. You should have about 1½ cups.

2. Mash the squash in a medium bowl. Stir in the egg yolk, 1 cup of the Parmigiano-Reggiano, 1 tablespoon of the sage, the nutmeg and ½ teaspoon salt. Set aside. *(The filling can be refrigerated overnight.)*

3. Use a pizza wheel or sharp knife to cut the pasta sheets into long rectangles that measure 4 inches across. Place small balls of the filling (each about 1 rounded teaspoon) in a line about 1 inch from the bottom of the pasta sheet. Leave about 1¼ inches between each ball of filling. Fold over the top of the pasta sheet, lining it up with the bottom edge. Seal the bottom and 2 open sides with your finger. Use a fluted pastry wheel to cut along the 2 sides and bottom of the sealed pasta sheet. Run the pastry wheel between the balls of filling to cut out individual ravioli. You should have about 60 ravioli. Place the ravioli in a single layer on a large baking sheet and put it in the refrigerator.

4. Bring 4 quarts water to a boil in a large pot for cooking the ravioli.

5. While the water is heating, melt the butter in a small skillet. Add the remaining 1 tablespoon sage and sauté for 1 to 2 minutes over medium heat to release its flavor. Do not let the butter brown or burn. Remove from the heat and keep warm.

6. Add salt to taste to the boiling water. Add half the ravioli and cook until the doubled edges are al dente, 4 to 5 minutes. Use a slotted spoon to transfer the ravioli to warm pasta bowls. Add the remaining ravioli to the boiling water while you spoon half of the butter sauce over the cooked ravioli. Sprinkle the ravioli with some of the remaining ½ cup cheese. By the time you get the first batch on the table, the second batch should be ready to be drained and sauced. Serve immediately with grated cheese passed separately at the table.

Serving Suggestions

This dish can be the centerpiece of a fall meal. Start with Porcini Mushroom Tart (page 408) and finish with Wilted Spinach Salad with Polenta Croutons (page 379).

Mushroom Tortellini with Brown Butter and Pine Nuts

SERVES 6

IF YOU HAVE NEVER MADE TORTELLINI BEFORE, don't imagine these are like the gummy, store-bought versions with bland fillings. The pasta dough is rolled thin, cut into small squares, dolloped with an intensely flavored filling and wrapped around the finger into small O-shaped rings. Preparing so many individual pastas takes time, but there is no substitute for doing this yourself.

- 1 ounce dried porcini mushrooms
- 2 tablespoons extra-virgin olive oil
- 2 medium garlic cloves, minced
- 10 ounces white button mushrooms, wiped clean, stems trimmed, minced
- ¼ cup minced fresh parsley leaves, plus more for garnish
- Salt and freshly ground black pepper
- 1 cup ricotta cheese, homestyle or supermarket
- ⅓ cup freshly grated Parmigiano-Reggiano cheese, plus more for the table
- 1 large egg yolk
- 1 pound Fresh Egg Pasta (page 130), rolled into thin sheets
- ½ cup pine nuts
- 8 tablespoons (1 stick) unsalted butter

1. Place the porcini mushrooms in a small bowl and cover them with 1 cup hot water. Soak until softened, about 20 minutes. Carefully lift the mushrooms from the liquid and pick through them to remove any foreign debris. Wash the mushrooms if they feel gritty. Mince them. Strain the soaking liquid through a sieve lined with a paper towel. Set aside the mushrooms and the strained soaking liquid separately.

2. Heat the oil in a medium skillet. Add the garlic and cook over medium heat until golden, about 2 minutes. Add the button mushrooms and cook, stirring often, until tender, about 5 minutes. Stir in the porcini, ¼ cup parsley and salt and pepper to taste. Cook until all the liquid in the pan evaporates, about 2 minutes.

3. Remove the pan from the heat and stir in the ricotta, ⅓ cup Parmigiano-Reggiano and the egg yolk. Set aside. *(The filling can be refrigerated overnight.)*

4. Use a pizza wheel or sharp knife to cut the pasta sheets into 2½-inch squares. Lift 1 square from the work surface (otherwise, it may stick when stuffed) and transfer it to a clean part of the counter. Place ½ teaspoon filling in the center of the square. Lift one corner of the pasta dough over the filling and bring it down so that it rests just below the opposite corner to make a triangle shape that completely encloses the filling. Seal the edge with your finger.

5. Lift the filled triangle from the counter and wrap the back of the triangle around the top of your index finger, point up. Squeeze the 2 bottom corners of the triangle together. Finally, pull back the top point of the triangle, gently folding it over the top of the ring of pasta. Slide the filled pasta off your finger and repeat with the remaining pieces of dough. You should have about 90 tortellini.

6. Bring 4 quarts water to a boil in a large pot for cooking the tortellini.

7. While the water is heating, place the pine nuts in a medium skillet over medium heat. Toast, shaking the pan occasionally to turn the nuts, until golden, about 5 minutes. Remove the nuts from the pan and add the butter. Cook over medium-low heat, swirling the pan occasionally, until the butter turns golden brown, about 5 minutes. Do not let the butter burn. Stir in the toasted nuts and ½ teaspoon salt. Cover and keep warm while you cook the pasta.

8. Add salt to taste and half the tortellini to the boiling water. Cook until the doubled edges are al dente, 4 to 5 minutes. Use a slotted spoon to transfer the tortellini to warm pasta bowls. Spoon half of the brown butter sauce over the cooked tortellini and garnish with parsley. Add the remaining tortellini to the boiling water. By the time you get the first batch on the table, the second batch should be ready to be drained and sauced. Serve immediately with grated cheese passed separately at the table.

SERVING SUGGESTIONS

Follow this rich dish with a simple vegetable course, such as Roasted Asparagus with Olive Oil (page 330) or Wilted Spinach with Garlic (page 360).

Fresh Egg Pasta

MAKES ABOUT 1 POUND

KNEADING THE DOUGH for homemade pasta in a food processor makes the job much easier, although a little hand kneading is still required (no more than a minute or two). Once the dough has been formed, a hand-cranked pasta machine is best for rolling out thin sheets. A rolling pin (preferably one that is as long as possible) may be used, but the resulting sheets will probably be on the thick side, posing a problem with filled pastas like ravioli that have doubled edges. The sheets of pasta can be boiled for lasagne, run through the cutters on the pasta machine for fettuccine or spaghetti or used for filled pastas like ravioli and tortellini.

2 cups unbleached all-purpose flour
3 large eggs, lightly beaten

1. Place the flour in the work bowl of a food processor and pulse several times. Add the eggs and process until the dough forms a rough ball, about 30 seconds. (If the dough refuses to come together, add water, ½ teaspoon at a time, and continue processing until a ball forms. If the dough sticks to the sides of the work bowl, add flour, 1 tablespoon at a time, and continue processing until a ball forms.)

2. Turn the dough out onto a dry work surface. Knead by hand until the dough is smooth, 1 to 2 minutes. Cover with plastic wrap and set aside for 15 to 30 minutes.

3. Cut about one quarter of the dough from the ball and flatten the piece into a disk. (Rewrap the remaining dough.) Run the dough through the widest setting on a manual pasta machine. Bring the ends of the dough toward the middle of the sheet of pasta and press them together. Run the dough, open side first, through the widest setting again. Fold, seal and roll again. Without folding, run the pasta through the widest setting 2 more times, or until the dough is smooth. If at any point the dough seems sticky, lightly dust it with flour.

4. Continue to run the dough through the pasta machine, narrowing the setting each time. When you reach the last setting, the outline of your hand should be visible through the pasta. Lay the sheet of pasta on a dry kitchen towel and cover with a second towel. Repeat with the rest of the dough. If using the pasta for lasagne, ravioli or tortellini, proceed with the recipe.

5. If making fettuccine, take the first sheet of pasta (it will have had a little time to dry out but should not be tough or brittle) and run it through the fettuccine cutters on the pasta machine. Carefully spread out the fettuccine on kitchen towels. Repeat with the remaining sheets, making sure they have dried for 15 to 20 minutes before cutting. Use the pasta within a few hours or place it in zipper-lock plastic bags and freeze for up to several months.

6. When you are ready to cook the pasta, bring 4 quarts water to a boil in a large pot. Add salt to taste and the fettuccine. Fresh pasta will be ready in about 3 minutes. Frozen pasta should not be defrosted before cooking. It will require 4 to 5 minutes cooking time.

Fresh Spinach Pasta

MAKES ABOUT 1 POUND

THIS RECIPE IS SIMILAR TO FRESH EGG PASTA but has different uses. While plain egg pasta is pliable and therefore suitable for ravioli or tortellini, spinach pasta is too tender to fold and shape. Rather, cut it into fettuccine and serve it with cream or tomato sauces. The sheets can also be used for lasagne. This is one dish where fresh spinach affords no advantages.

½ 10-ounce package frozen chopped spinach, thawed
3 large eggs, lightly beaten
2½ cups unbleached all-purpose flour

1. Bring 1 cup water to a boil in a small saucepan. Add the spinach and cook until tender, about 3 minutes. Drain and refresh the spinach under cold running water. Use your hands to squeeze as much moisture as you can from the spinach. It must be as dry as possible.

2. Place the spinach on a cutting board and finely chop it. Press your hands against the spinach and tilt the board over the sink to drain off the liquid. You should have about ⅓ cup finely chopped spinach that is totally dry. Beat the spinach and eggs lightly with a fork in a bowl. Set aside.

3. Place the flour in the work bowl of a food processor and pulse several times. Add the spinach and eggs and process until the dough forms a rough ball, about 30 seconds. (If the dough refuses to come together, add water, ½ teaspoon at a time, and continue processing until a ball forms. If the dough sticks to the sides of the work bowl, add flour, 1 tablespoon at a time, and continue processing until a ball forms.)

4. Turn the dough out onto a dry work surface. Knead by hand until the dough is smooth, 1 to 2 minutes. Cover with plastic wrap and set aside for 15 to 30 minutes.

5. Cut about one quarter of the dough from the ball and flatten the piece into a disk. (Rewrap the remaining dough.) Run the dough through the widest setting on a manual pasta machine. Bring the ends of the dough toward the middle of the sheet of pasta and press them together. Run the dough, open side first, through the widest setting again. Fold, seal and roll again. Without folding, run the pasta through the widest setting 2 more times, or until the dough is smooth. If at any point the dough seems sticky, lightly dust it with flour.

6. Continue to run the dough through the pasta machine, narrowing the setting each time. Lay the sheet of pasta on a dry kitchen towel and cover with a second towel. Repeat with the rest of the dough. If using the pasta for lasagne, proceed with the recipe.

7. If making fettuccine, take the first sheet of pasta (it will have had a little time to dry out but should not be tough or brittle) and run it through the fettuccine cutters on the pasta machine. Carefully spread out the fettuccine on kitchen towels. Repeat with the remaining sheets, making sure they have dried for 15 to 20 minutes before cutting. Use the pasta within a few hours or place it in zipper-lock plastic bags and freeze for up to several months.

8. When you are ready to cook the pasta, bring 4 quarts water to a boil in a large pot. Add salt to taste and the fettuccine. Fresh pasta will be ready in about 3 minutes. Frozen pasta should not be defrosted before cooking. It will require 4 to 5 minutes cooking time.

RICE

IN NORTHERN REGIONS OF ITALY ESPECIALLY, rice is an important carbohydrate, appearing in salads, side dishes and stuffings. For the vegetarian, the most adaptable and important rice dish is risotto.

Risotto is truly more than the sum of its parts. Something magical happens when rice is sautéed in oil and broth is gradually stirred in. The rice softens but does not become mushy; the sauce thickens and becomes creamy. This creamy texture is what makes risotto so satisfying and substantial and no doubt accounts for its popularity on both sides of the Atlantic.

I know many cooks avoid risotto, though I'm not sure why. Some may not realize that the dish transforms rice into an appealing main course, either with or without meat. Others may have been discouraged by instructions that the rice must be stirred constantly for half an hour or more. This is too bad, since this admonition is completely unfounded.

While frequent stirring is necessary to produce the characteristic creaminess of a good risotto, constant stirring is not. When I make risotto, I walk over to the pot every minute or two and stir the rice for about 10 seconds with a long wooden spoon or flat spatula (rice sticks to metal utensils, which should be avoided). The dish does require attention, but it is not an all-consuming culinary job. Between stirs, you can mince an herb, grate some cheese or even make a salad.

The choice of rice allows no such flexibility, however. You must use the Italian medium-grain rice Arborio, which is sold in most supermarkets. If you can find them, premium Italian rices such as Vialone Nano and Carnaroli make excellent risotto, but other medium-grain or long-grain rices are not suitable. These other types of rice have a different ratio of starches and will not yield slightly chewy grains swimming in a creamy sauce.

The other essential ingredient that merits some discussion is the stock. There is some leeway here. Purists insist that only meat or chicken stock is acceptable, but I find they can overwhelm the flavor of delicate vegetables. Vegetable stock is preferable.

Of course, many cooks don't want to be bothered making any stock. In Italy, most home cooks simply dissolve a bouillon cube in water when making risotto. Some of the vegetable cubes sold in natural-food stores are relatively good and free of weird chemicals. And there are times when plain water is just fine. For instance, a risotto made with tomatoes will get plenty of flavor from their juice and does not need stock or a bouillon cube. A risotto with delicate ingredients like asparagus, however, may seem bland if made with plain water. For each recipe, I have indicated whether stock, water or a bouillon cube is appropriate.

AS FOR THE ACTUAL TECHNIQUE, most risotto starts with the sautéing of onion and/or garlic in oil or butter. Slow-cooking vegetables like fennel are added at this point, while fast-cooking spinach, for example, is held back until the last moment. After the onion and other seasonings have softened, the rice is sautéed in the fat for a minute or so to bring out its flavor.

At this point, warm stock or other liquid is poured over the rice in small increments, about one-half cup at a time, just enough so that the liquid comes up to the top of the rice. Then it is stirred every minute or so, and more stock is added when the rice has absorbed the liquid in the pot. This goes on until the rice is al dente, usually about 25 minutes. Given the relatively long cooking time, it's essential to choose a heavy-bottomed pot to prevent scorching. I use a 4½-quart saucepan, but any medium casserole or sauté pan will work just fine.

When the rice is done, butter and cheese are beaten in. Even just a tablespoon of butter and one-quarter cup of grated Parmigiano-Reggiano transform risotto, adding flavor and richness. Beating also lightens the consistency of the sauce by whipping some air into it.

Like pasta, risotto can be served in small portions as a first course, as it traditionally is in Italy. Also like pasta, it makes an excellent main course if portions are more generous. Select a particular risotto recipe based on what vegetables look good at the market. For that reason, the recipes have been grouped according to season.

The chapter ends with a number of other rice dishes, including savory rice cakes, boiled rice dishes and a baked casserole with marinated artichokes. While it may be possible to make these recipes with other rices, the pleasantly chewy texture of Arborio rice is welcome.

Risotto for Fall and Winter

Risotto for Spring and Summer

Other Rice Dishes

Red Wine Risotto with Rosemary and Garlic

SERVES 4

RED WINE turns the risotto an attractive mauve color and adds good flavor as well. Chianti or another red wine that is fairly fruity works nicely. This risotto may seem plain, but the rosemary and garlic are pronounced.

- 6 cups Vegetable Stock (page 529) or 1 vegetable bouillon cube dissolved in 6 cups boiling water
- 3 tablespoons unsalted butter
- 1 tablespoon extra-virgin olive oil
- 2 teaspoons minced fresh rosemary leaves
- 4 medium garlic cloves, minced
- 1½ cups Arborio rice
- ½ cup dry red wine
- ½ cup freshly grated Parmigiano-Reggiano cheese, plus more for the table
- Salt and freshly ground black pepper

1. Bring the stock to a simmer in a medium saucepan. Keep it warm over low heat.

2. Heat 2 tablespoons of the butter and the oil in a heavy-bottomed medium pot. Add the rosemary and garlic and sauté over medium heat until the garlic is golden, about 2 minutes. Using a wooden spoon, stir in the rice and cook for 1 minute. Add the wine and cook just until the alcohol aroma fades, 1 to 2 minutes.

3. Add ½ cup of the warm stock and cook, stirring frequently, until the rice absorbs the liquid. Continue adding stock in ½-cup increments, stirring, until the rice is creamy and soft but still a bit al dente, about 25 minutes. (Add hot water if you run out of stock.)

4. Remove the pot from the heat and vigorously stir in the remaining 1 tablespoon butter and the ½ cup cheese. Add salt and pepper to taste. Divide the risotto among individual soup bowls. Serve immediately with more grated cheese passed separately at the table.

SERVING SUGGESTIONS

Since there are no vegetables in this dish, look for a salad that has some, such as Tender Greens and Vegetables with Blood Orange Vinaigrette (page 376), Roasted Beet Salad with Watercress, Walnuts and Fresh Pecorino (page 384) or Wilted Spinach Salad with Polenta Croutons (page 379).

Risotto with Savoy Cabbage

SERVES 4

SAVOY CABBAGE IS A BIG CABBAGE WITH SOFT, CRINKLY LEAVES. It is a favorite in northern Italy, where it is used in pasta sauces as well as rice dishes. Blanching the cabbage removes some of the sulfurous compounds that many people find objectionable. Sautéing it highlights its sweetness.

- **6 cups Vegetable Stock (page 529) or 1 vegetable bouillon cube dissolved in 6 cups boiling water**
- **½ medium savoy cabbage head (about 1 pound)**
- **3 tablespoons extra-virgin olive oil**
- **1 medium onion, minced**
- **2 medium garlic cloves, minced**
- **2 tablespoons unsalted butter**
- **1½ cups Arborio rice**
- **½ cup freshly grated Parmigiano-Reggiano cheese, plus more for the table**
- **Salt and freshly ground black pepper**

1. Bring the stock to a simmer in a medium saucepan. Keep it warm over low heat.

2. Bring several quarts water to a boil in a large saucepan for blanching the cabbage. Remove and discard any tough outer leaves from the cabbage half and cut the cabbage in half through the stem end. Remove and discard the core and stem. Slice the cabbage crosswise into very thin strips. You should have about 5 cups. Add the cabbage to the boiling water and cook until crisp-tender, about 5 minutes. Drain and set aside.

3. Heat the oil in a heavy-bottomed medium pot. Add the onion and sauté over medium heat until slightly softened, about 3 minutes. Add the garlic and cook for 30 seconds. Add 1 tablespoon of the butter and the cabbage and cook, stirring often, until the cabbage softens and starts to brown, about 15 minutes.

4. Using a wooden spoon, stir in the rice and cook for 1 minute. Add ½ cup of the warm stock and cook, stirring frequently, until the rice absorbs the liquid. Continue adding stock in ½-cup increments, stirring, until the rice is creamy and soft but still a bit al dente, about 25 minutes. (Add hot water if you run out of stock.)

5. Remove the pot from the heat and vigorously stir in the remaining 1 tablespoon butter and the ½ cup cheese. Add salt and pepper to taste. Divide the risotto among individual soup bowls. Serve immediately with more grated cheese passed separately at the table.

SERVING SUGGESTIONS

Because this dish is fairly monochromatic, follow it with something colorful, such as Tender Greens and Vegetables with Blood Orange Vinaigrette (page 376) or Roasted Beet Salad with Watercress, Walnuts and Fresh Pecorino (page 384).

Risotto with Fennel

SERVES 4

DICED FENNEL FLAVORS THIS SIMPLE RISOTTO. On its own, the fennel is pallid, echoing the creamy whiteness of the rice, but the minced fennel fronds and parsley add herbal notes and needed color.

- **6 cups Vegetable Stock (page 529) or 1 vegetable bouillon cube dissolved in 6 cups boiling water**
- **1 medium fennel bulb (about 1¼ pounds)**
- **2 tablespoons extra-virgin olive oil**
- **1 medium onion, minced**
- **1½ cups Arborio rice**
- **⅓ cup dry white wine**
- **½ cup freshly grated Parmigiano-Reggiano cheese, plus more for the table**
- **2 tablespoons minced fresh parsley leaves**
- **1 tablespoon unsalted butter**
- **Salt and freshly ground black pepper**

1. Bring the stock to a simmer in a medium saucepan. Keep it warm over low heat.

2. Trim the stems and fronds from the fennel. Discard the stems. Mince 2 tablespoons of the fronds and set aside. Trim a thin slice from the base of the bulb and remove any tough or blemished outer layers. Cut the bulb in half through the base and use a small, sharp knife to remove the core. Lay the halves flat side down on a cutting board and chop into ½-inch dice. Set aside.

3. Heat the oil in a heavy-bottomed medium pot. Add the onion and sauté over medium heat until softened, about 3 minutes. Add the diced fennel and cook, stirring occasionally, until the vegetables start to brown around the edges, about 6 minutes. Add ½ cup of the warm stock and cook until the fennel is fairly soft, about 3 minutes.

4. Using a wooden spoon, stir in the rice and cook for 1 minute. Add the wine and cook just until the alcohol aroma fades, 1 to 2 minutes. Add ½ cup of the warm stock and cook, stirring frequently, until the rice absorbs the liquid. Continue adding stock in ½-cup increments, stirring, until the rice is creamy and soft but still a bit al dente, about 25 minutes. (Add hot water if you run out of stock.)

5. Remove the pot from the heat and vigorously stir in the ½ cup cheese, parsley, minced fennel fronds and butter. Add salt and pepper to taste. Divide the risotto among individual soup bowls. Serve immediately with more grated cheese passed separately at the table.

SERVING SUGGESTIONS

The gentle, aniselike sweetness of this dish is best followed by a leafy salad with a lemony dressing. Tender Green Salad with Pine Nuts and Yellow Raisins (page 375) or Wilted Spinach Salad with Polenta Croutons (page 379) would be appropriate.

Risotto with Porcini Mushrooms

Serves 4

Dried porcini mushrooms are supplemented by white button mushrooms to keep the cost of this dish down as well as to provide a pleasant contrast in taste and texture. When rehydrated, the porcini are chewy and woodsy-tasting, while the button mushrooms are tender and mild. The soaking liquid from the mushrooms is so potent that water may be used in place of the customary vegetable stock with no sacrifice in flavor.

- 1 ounce dried porcini mushrooms
- 3 tablespoons unsalted butter
- 1 medium onion, minced
- 1 pound white button mushrooms, wiped clean, stems trimmed, thinly sliced
- Salt and freshly ground black pepper
- 2 teaspoons minced fresh oregano leaves
- 1½ cups Arborio rice
- ½ cup freshly grated Parmigiano-Reggiano cheese, plus more for the table

1. Warm 6 cups water in a medium saucepan. Place the porcini mushrooms in a medium bowl and cover with 2 cups of the warm water. Soak until softened, about 20 minutes. Carefully lift the mushrooms from the liquid and pick through them to remove any foreign debris. Wash the mushrooms if they feel gritty. Coarsely chop them and set aside. Strain the soaking liquid through a sieve lined with a paper towel. Return the soaking liquid to the saucepan with the remaining 4 cups water. Keep warm over low heat.

2. Heat 2 tablespoons of the butter in a heavy-bottomed medium pot. Add the onion and sauté over medium heat until translucent, about 5 minutes. Add the button mushrooms and cook until they turn golden brown, about 8 minutes. Season with salt and pepper to taste.

3. Add the porcini mushrooms and oregano and cook for 1 minute. Using a wooden spoon, stir in the rice and cook for 1 minute.

4. Add ½ cup of the warm soaking liquid and cook, stirring frequently, until the rice absorbs the liquid. Continue adding warm liquid in ½-cup increments, stirring, until the rice is creamy and soft but still a bit al dente, about 25 minutes. (Add hot water if you run out of the soaking-liquid mixture.)

5. Remove the pot from the heat and vigorously stir in the remaining 1 tablespoon butter and the ½ cup cheese. Add salt and pepper to taste. Divide the risotto among individual soup bowls. Serve immediately with more grated cheese passed separately at the table.

SERVING SUGGESTIONS

This risotto should be followed by something green and colorful like Wilted Spinach with Garlic (page 360). As a first course, try Radicchio, Arugula and Endive Salad with Balsamic Vinaigrette (page 373). Or start with Wilted Spinach Salad with Polenta Croutons (page 379) and follow with Asparagus with Lemon-Shallot Vinaigrette (page 331).

Risotto with Radicchio

SERVES 4

THIN STRIPS OF RADICCHIO lose their shape when cooked slowly with rice, forming a magenta sauce. The radicchio also loses much of its bitterness and takes on a slightly smoky flavor. For an even more intense color, the dish can be made with a young, fruity red wine rather than white wine.

- **6 cups Vegetable Stock (page 529) or 1 vegetable bouillon cube dissolved in 6 cups boiling water**
- **2 medium radicchio heads (about 1¼ pounds)**
- **2 tablespoons extra-virgin olive oil**
- **1 medium onion, minced**
- **1½ cups Arborio rice**
- **½ cup dry white wine**
- **2 tablespoons unsalted butter**
- **½ cup freshly grated Parmigiano-Reggiano cheese, plus more for the table**
- **Salt and freshly ground black pepper**

1. Bring the stock to a simmer in a medium saucepan. Keep it warm over low heat.

2. Discard any tough or dry outer leaves from the radicchio. Use a small, sharp knife to remove the cores. Slice the heads in half through the stem end. Lay the halves down on a work surface and slice crosswise into ¼-inch-wide strips. Set aside.

3. Heat the oil in a heavy-bottomed medium pot. Add the onion and sauté over medium heat until it turns a rich golden color but has not yet started to brown, about 6 minutes. Add the radicchio and cook, stirring often, until soft and wilted, about 4 minutes.

4. Using a wooden spoon, stir in the rice and cook for 1 minute. Add the wine and cook just until the alcohol aroma fades, 1 to 2 minutes. Add ½ cup of the warm stock and cook, stirring frequently, until the rice absorbs the liquid. Continue adding stock in ½-cup increments, stirring, until the rice is creamy and soft but still a bit al dente, about 25 minutes. (Add hot water if you run out of stock.)

5. Remove the pot from the heat and vigorously stir in the butter and the ½ cup cheese. Add salt and pepper to taste. Divide the risotto among individual soup bowls. Serve immediately with more grated cheese passed separately at the table.

Serving Suggestions

End the meal with a light salad, such as Tender Green Salad with Pine Nuts and Yellow Raisins (page 375), Tender Greens and Vegetables with Blood Orange Vinaigrette (page 376) or Spinach Salad with Orange Juice Vinaigrette and Toasted Walnuts (page 380), or a leafy green vegetable, such as Swiss Chard with Raisins and Almonds (page 340).

Risotto with Butternut Squash and Sage

SERVES 4

WITH MELTINGLY TENDER PIECES OF SAGE-FLAVORED SQUASH, this dish needs no embellishment, though you can garnish the risotto with fried sage leaves. To fry sage leaves, heat two tablespoons olive oil in a small nonstick skillet until quite hot. Add eight large whole sage leaves and sauté them, turning once, until crisp. Drain on paper towels. *See the photograph on page 206.*

- 6 cups Vegetable Stock (page 529) or 1 vegetable bouillon cube dissolved in 6 cups boiling water
- 1 tablespoon extra-virgin olive oil
- 3 tablespoons unsalted butter
- 1 medium onion, minced
- 6 large fresh sage leaves, minced, plus 8 leaves for frying (optional)
- ½ small butternut squash (about 1 pound), stringy pulp and seeds discarded, peeled and cut into ½-inch cubes
- ½ cup dry white wine
- 1½ cups Arborio rice
- ½ cup freshly grated Parmigiano-Reggiano cheese, plus more for the table
- Salt and freshly ground black pepper

1. Bring the stock to a simmer in a medium saucepan. Keep it warm over low heat.

2. Heat the oil and 2 tablespoons of the butter in a heavy-bottomed medium pot. Add the onion and sauté over medium heat until translucent, about 5 minutes. Stir in the minced sage and cook for 30 seconds to release the flavor. Stir in the squash and cook for 2 minutes, stirring often to coat the pieces.

3. Add the wine and 1 cup of the warm stock and bring to a boil. Reduce the heat to low, cover and simmer until the squash is very tender, about 25 minutes. (If the pot runs dry, add more warm stock as needed.) Uncover the pot and cook off any extra liquid.

4. Using a wooden spoon, stir in the rice and cook for 1 minute. Add ½ cup of the warm stock and cook, stirring frequently, until the rice absorbs the liquid. Continue adding stock in ½-cup increments, stirring, until the rice is creamy and soft but still a bit al dente, about 25 minutes. (Add hot water if you run out of stock.)

5. Remove the pot from the heat and vigorously stir in the remaining 1 tablespoon butter and the ½ cup cheese. Add salt and pepper to taste. Divide the risotto among individual soup bowls and garnish with the fried sage leaves, if using. Serve immediately with more grated cheese passed separately at the table.

SERVING SUGGESTIONS

This dish makes an impressive main course. Follow with a green salad, such as Red Leaf Lettuce, Arugula and Fennel Salad (page 374), Tender Green Salad with Pine Nuts and Yellow Raisins (page 375), Wilted Spinach Salad with Polenta Croutons (page 379) or Spinach Salad with Orange Juice Vinaigrette and Toasted Walnuts (page 380).

Saffron Risotto

SERVES 4

CLASSIC RISOTTO ALLA MILANESE is made with beef stock, but the meat stock can overwhelm the delicate saffron. Vegetable stock is a better choice. You can maximize the impact of the saffron by dissolving it in a little hot stock and adding it to the rice toward the end of the cooking time. This dish is plain—there are no vegetables other than shallots or onions—but satisfying.

6 cups Vegetable Stock (page 529) or 1 vegetable bouillon cube dissolved in 6 cups boiling water
¼ teaspoon saffron threads
1 tablespoon extra-virgin olive oil
4 tablespoons (½ stick) unsalted butter
3 medium shallots or 1 medium onion, minced
1½ cups Arborio rice
½ cup dry white wine
½ cup freshly grated Parmigiano-Reggiano cheese, plus more for the table
Salt

1. Bring the stock to a simmer in a medium saucepan. Keep it warm over low heat. Place the saffron threads in a small bowl. Add ¼ cup of the warm stock and set aside to infuse.

2. Heat the oil and 2 tablespoons of the butter in a heavy-bottomed medium pot. Add the shallots or onion and sauté over medium heat until softened, about 3 minutes. Using a wooden spoon, stir in the rice and cook for 1 minute. Add the wine and cook just until the alcohol aroma fades, 1 to 2 minutes. Add ½ cup of the warm stock and cook, stirring frequently, until the rice absorbs the liquid. Continue adding stock in ½-cup increments, stirring, for 20 minutes. Add the saffron-infused stock and continue cooking, stirring, until the rice is creamy and soft but still a bit al dente, about 5 minutes. (Add hot water if you run out of stock.)

3. Remove the pot from the heat and vigorously stir in the remaining 2 tablespoons butter and the ½ cup cheese. Add salt to taste. Divide the risotto

among individual soup bowls. Serve immediately with more grated cheese passed separately at the table.

Serving Suggestions

This dish should be followed by one or two vegetables. Roasted Asparagus with Olive Oil (page 330) and Oven-Roasted Portobello Mushrooms (page 353) make a good pairing. You might also try a substantial vegetable side dish, such as Roasted Fennel, Carrots and Red Onion (page 346), followed by a green salad, such as Tender Green Salad with Pine Nuts and Yellow Raisins (page 375). Or serve a leafy salad that also contains vegetables, such as Tender Greens and Vegetables with Blood Orange Vinaigrette (page 376).

Risotto with Artichokes and Mushrooms

SERVES 4

SMALL ARTICHOKES WILL YIELD THIN WEDGES that are just the right size for this risotto. Larger ones may be substituted, but the wedges should be cut in half crosswise so that they are not too big for the rice. Any kind of fresh mushroom, either domestic or wild, can be used.

- 6 cups Vegetable Stock (page 529) or 1 vegetable bouillon cube dissolved in 6 cups boiling water
- 1 lemon, halved
- 6 small artichokes (about 1 pound)
- 2 tablespoons extra-virgin olive oil
- 1 medium onion, minced
- ½ cup dry white wine
- ½ pound mushrooms, preferably cremini, wiped clean, stems trimmed, thinly sliced
- 1½ cups Arborio rice
- ⅓ cup freshly grated Parmigiano-Reggiano cheese, plus more for the table
- 2 tablespoons unsalted butter, diced
- 2 tablespoons minced fresh parsley leaves
- Salt and freshly ground black pepper

1. Bring the stock to a simmer in a medium saucepan. Keep it warm over low heat.

2. Squeeze the lemon halves into a large bowl of cold water and add the lemon to the bowl. Working with 1 artichoke at a time, bend back and snap off the tough outer leaves. Remove several layers until you reach the leaves that are mostly pale green or yellow except for the tips. With a sharp knife, slice off the dark green pointed tip of the artichoke. Trim the end of the stem and use a vegetable peeler to peel the outer layer. Use the peeler to remove any dark green leaf bases that may surround the top of the stem. Quarter the artichoke lengthwise, leaving a part of the stem attached to each piece. Slide a small, sharp knife under the fuzzy choke and cut toward the leaf tips to remove it. Slice the cleaned quarters into ⅛-inch-thick wedges and drop them into the bowl of cold lemon water. Repeat with the remaining artichokes. Set aside.

3. Heat the oil in a heavy-bottomed medium pot. Add the onion and sauté over medium heat until translucent, about 5 minutes. Drain the artichokes and add them to the pot, discarding the lemon halves. Cook, stirring often, for 2 minutes. Add the wine and cover the pot. Simmer, checking often, until the artichokes have absorbed almost all of the liquid in the pot, about 8 minutes.

4. Add the mushrooms. Cook, stirring often, until they are nicely browned, about 7 minutes. Using a wooden spoon, stir in the rice and cook for 1 minute.

5. Add ½ cup of the warm stock and cook, stirring frequently, until the rice absorbs the liquid. Continue adding stock in ½-cup increments, stirring, until the rice is creamy and soft but still a bit al dente, about 25 minutes. (Add hot water if you run out of stock.)

6. Remove the pot from the heat and vigorously stir in the ⅓ cup cheese, butter and parsley. Add salt and pepper to taste. Divide the risotto among individual soup bowls. Serve immediately with more grated cheese passed separately at the table.

Serving Suggestions

This risotto needs little more than a leafy salad to make a meal. Tender Green Salad with Pine Nuts and Yellow Raisins (page 375) would be a good choice.

Risotto with Artichokes and Tomatoes

SERVES 4

IN THIS RISOTTO, ARTICHOKES COOK IN A ROSY TOMATO BASE. Use plum tomatoes that are firm enough to skin with a vegetable peeler. Wedges of small artichokes are just right for this risotto. Larger ones may be substituted, with the wedges cut in half crosswise.

- **6 cups Vegetable Stock (page 529), Light Tomato Stock (page 530) or water**
- **1 lemon, halved**
- **6 small artichokes (about 1 pound)**
- **2 tablespoons extra-virgin olive oil**
- **1 medium onion, minced**
- **2 medium garlic cloves, minced**
- **4 medium plum tomatoes (about ¾ pound), peeled, cored, seeded and diced small**
- **Salt and freshly ground black pepper**
- **1½ cups Arborio rice**
- **½ cup freshly grated Parmigiano-Reggiano cheese, plus more for the table**
- **1 tablespoon unsalted butter**

1. Bring the stock or water to a simmer in a medium saucepan. Keep it warm over low heat.

2. Squeeze the lemon halves into a large bowl of cold water and add the lemon to the bowl. Working with 1 artichoke at a time, bend back and snap off the tough outer leaves. Remove several layers until you reach the leaves that are mostly pale green or yellow except for the tips. With a sharp knife, slice off the dark green pointed tip of the artichoke. Trim the end of the stem and use a vegetable peeler to peel the outer layer. Use the peeler to remove any dark green leaf bases that may surround the top of the stem. Quarter the artichoke lengthwise, leaving a part of the stem attached to each piece. Slide a small, sharp knife under the fuzzy choke and cut toward the leaf tips to remove it. Slice the cleaned quarters into ⅛-inch-thick wedges and drop them into the bowl of cold lemon water. Repeat with the remaining artichokes. Set aside.

3. Heat the oil in a heavy-bottomed medium pot. Add the onion and sauté over medium heat until translucent, about 5 minutes. Add the garlic and cook until lightly colored, about 1 minute. Add the tomatoes and salt and pepper to taste and cook until they soften a bit, about 3 minutes.

4. Drain the artichokes and add them to the pot, discarding the lemon halves. Add 1 cup of the warm stock or water and cover the pot. Simmer, stirring occasionally, until the artichokes have started to soften and have absorbed most of the liquid, 10 to 12 minutes.

5. Using a wooden spoon, stir in the rice and cook for 1 minute. Add ½ cup of the warm stock or water and cook, stirring frequently, until the rice absorbs the liquid. Continue adding stock or water in ½-cup increments, stirring, until the rice is creamy and soft but still a bit al dente, about 25 minutes. (If you are using stock and run out of it, add hot water.)

6. Remove the pot from the heat and vigorously stir in the ½ cup cheese and the butter. Adjust the seasonings. Divide the risotto among individual soup bowls. Serve immediately with more grated cheese passed separately at the table.

SERVING SUGGESTIONS

This dish can be the centerpiece for a spring meal. Add a simple leafy green salad to round out the meal or, if you want something more ambitious, follow with Fava Bean and Asparagus Salad with Basil Toasts (page 382).

Risotto with Asparagus, Ricotta and Mint

SERVES 4

A SWIRL OF RICOTTA CHEESE adds extra creaminess to this risotto. For more tang, substitute an equal amount of fresh goat cheese. Note that the asparagus is precooked and added to the rice as it finishes cooking. Don't overcook the asparagus pieces when you boil them. They will soften further when added to the risotto.

- **6 cups Vegetable Stock (page 529) or 1 vegetable bouillon cube dissolved in 6 cups boiling water**
- **¾ pound medium asparagus**
- **2 tablespoons extra-virgin olive oil**
- **2 medium shallots, minced**
- **1½ cups Arborio rice**
- **⅓ cup dry white wine**
- **¼ cup ricotta cheese, homestyle or supermarket**
- **¼ cup freshly grated Parmigiano-Reggiano cheese, plus more for the table**
- **1½ tablespoons minced fresh mint leaves**
- **Salt and freshly ground black pepper**

1. Bring the stock to a simmer in a medium saucepan. Keep it warm over low heat.

2. Bring several quarts water to a boil in a medium saucepan. Snap off the tough ends of the asparagus spears. Cut the spears in half lengthwise and then on the diagonal into 1½-inch pieces. Add the asparagus to the boiling water and cook until crisp-tender, about 2 minutes. Drain and set aside.

3. Heat the oil in a heavy-bottomed medium pot. Add the shallots and sauté over medium heat until softened, about 3 minutes. Using a wooden spoon, stir in the rice and cook for 1 minute. Add the wine and cook just until the alcohol aroma fades, 1 to 2 minutes.

4. Add ½ cup of the warm stock and cook, stirring frequently, until the rice absorbs the liquid. Continue adding more stock in ½-cup increments, stirring, until the rice is creamy and soft but still a bit al dente, about 25 minutes.

(Add hot water if you run out of stock.) Add the asparagus during the last 1 to 2 minutes of cooking and keep the pot over the heat until the asparagus pieces are heated through.

5. Remove the pot from the heat and vigorously stir in the ricotta, the ¼ cup Parmigiano-Reggiano and the mint. Add salt and pepper to taste. Divide the risotto among individual soup bowls. Serve immediately with more grated cheese passed separately at the table.

SERVING SUGGESTIONS

This creamy risotto is a good choice for a multicourse dinner. Start with Roasted Yellow Pepper Soup (page 53) and follow with Spinach Salad with Orange Juice Vinaigrette and Toasted Walnuts (page 380). It's also nice for a simpler meal, served with bread and a leafy salad.

Golden Risotto with Carrots and Peas

SERVES 4 TO 6

CARROTS GIVE THIS RISOTTO AN APPEALING YELLOW-ORANGE COLOR as well as sweetness. I first tasted this dish in a small trattoria in Rome. Although the chef there used a mixture of chicken stock and carrot juice, water can easily take the place of the chicken stock, for the carrot juice brings plenty of flavor and color to the dish. If you own a juice extractor, make your own carrot juice. Otherwise, pick up fresh juice at a natural-foods store or supermarket.

- 3 cups carrot juice
- 3 tablespoons extra-virgin olive oil
- 1 medium onion, chopped
- 2 medium garlic cloves, minced
- 2 cups Arborio rice
- ½ cup white wine
- 4 medium carrots, peeled and chopped
- 2 cups fresh peas or frozen, thawed
- 2 tablespoons minced fresh parsley leaves
- ½ cup freshly grated Parmigiano-Reggiano cheese, plus more for the table
- 1 tablespoon unsalted butter
- Salt and freshly ground black pepper

1. Combine the carrot juice and 3 cups water in a medium saucepan and bring the mixture to a simmer. Keep it warm over low heat.

2. Heat the oil in a heavy-bottomed medium pot. Add the onion and sauté over medium heat until translucent, about 5 minutes. Stir in the garlic and continue cooking for 1 minute more. Using a wooden spoon, stir in the rice and cook for 1 minute. Add the wine and simmer, stirring constantly, until the alcohol aroma fades, 1 to 2 minutes.

3. Add the carrots and ½ cup of the warm carrot-juice mixture. Stir frequently until the rice absorbs the liquid. Continue adding more carrot-juice mixture in ½-cup increments, stirring, until the rice is almost al dente, 20 to 25 minutes.

4. Stir in the peas and parsley. Continue cooking and stirring, adding more liquid as necessary, until the rice is creamy and soft but still a bit al dente. (Add hot water if you run out of the carrot-juice mixture.)

5. Remove the pot from the heat and vigorously stir in the ½ cup cheese and butter. Add salt and pepper to taste. Divide the risotto among individual soup bowls. Serve immediately with more grated cheese passed separately at the table.

Serving Suggestions

The carrots make this risotto fairly sweet. Therefore, this dish needs a strong partner, such as Wilted Spinach with Garlic (page 360) or Roasted Asparagus with Olive Oil (page 330).

Eggplant Risotto with Fresh Tomatoes and Basil

SERVES 4

THIS RISOTTO IS BEST MADE with small eggplants. The flesh is usually firm, and they contain few, if any, seeds. Ripe summer tomatoes give this dish a full flavor, but fresh plum tomatoes or even three cups of seeded and diced canned plum tomatoes may be used. The tomatoes will completely fall apart, turning the sauce an attractive orange-red color. Stock is not needed here.

- **3 tablespoons extra-virgin olive oil**
- **4 medium garlic cloves, minced**
- **3 large, ripe tomatoes (about 1½ pounds), peeled, cored, seeded and diced small**
- **Salt and freshly ground black pepper**
- **2 medium eggplants (about 1 pound), ends trimmed, cut into ½-inch cubes**
- **1½ cups Arborio rice**
- **½ cup freshly grated Parmigiano-Reggiano cheese, plus more for the table**
- **2 tablespoons minced fresh basil leaves**

1. Bring 6 cups water to a simmer in a medium saucepan. Keep it warm over low heat.

2. Heat the oil in a heavy-bottomed medium pot. Add the garlic and sauté over medium heat until golden, about 1 minute. Add the tomatoes and salt and pepper to taste, cover and cook until they soften, about 4 minutes.

3. Stir in the eggplant and cook, covered, until it softens, about 15 minutes. If it starts to stick to the bottom of the pot, add ¼ cup hot water and continue cooking.

4. Using a wooden spoon, stir in the rice and cook for 1 minute. Add ½ cup of the warm water and cook, stirring frequently, until the rice absorbs the liquid. Continue adding water in ½-cup increments, stirring, until the rice is creamy and soft but still a bit al dente, about 25 minutes. (Add more hot water if you run out.)

5. Remove the pot from the heat and vigorously stir in the ½ cup cheese and basil. Adjust the seasonings. Divide the risotto among individual soup bowls. Serve immediately with more grated cheese passed separately at the table.

Serving Suggestions

The eggplant makes this risotto quite substantial. Follow with a light green salad, such as Red Leaf Lettuce, Arugula and Fennel Salad (page 374) or Tender Green Salad with Pine Nuts and Yellow Raisins (page 375).

Lemon Risotto

SERVES 4

THIS LEMON-FLAVORED RISOTTO can be enriched with a little heavy cream. Although not necessary, the cream mellows some of the acidic edge.

- 6 cups Vegetable Stock (page 529) or 1 vegetable bouillon cube dissolved in 6 cups boiling water
- 1 tablespoon extra-virgin olive oil
- 3 tablespoons unsalted butter
- 1 medium onion, minced
- 1½ cups Arborio rice
- ½ cup dry white wine
- 1 teaspoon grated zest and 2 tablespoons juice from 1 large lemon
- 6 large fresh sage leaves, minced
- 2 tablespoons minced fresh parsley leaves
- ¼ cup freshly grated Parmigiano-Reggiano cheese, plus more for the table
- Salt and freshly ground black pepper
- 2 tablespoons heavy cream (optional)

1. Bring the stock to a simmer in a medium saucepan. Keep it warm over low heat.

2. Heat the oil and 2 tablespoons of the butter in a heavy-bottomed medium pot. Add the onion and sauté over medium heat until translucent, about 5 minutes. Using a wooden spoon, stir in the rice and cook for 1 minute. Add the wine and cook just until the alcohol aroma fades, 1 to 2 minutes.

3. Add ½ cup of the warm stock and cook, stirring frequently, until the rice absorbs the liquid. Continue adding stock in ½-cup increments, stirring. After about 15 minutes, stir in the lemon zest and sage.

4. Continue adding stock in ½-cup increments, stirring, until the rice is creamy and soft but still a bit al dente, about 10 minutes more. (Add hot water if you run out of stock.) Stir in the lemon juice and parsley and continue cooking until the lemon juice is absorbed, 1 to 2 minutes more.

5. Remove the pot from the heat and vigorously stir in the remaining 1 tablespoon butter and the ¼ cup cheese. Add salt and pepper to taste. Stir in the heavy cream, if using. Divide the risotto among individual soup bowls. Serve immediately with more grated cheese passed separately at the table.

SERVING SUGGESTIONS

I often serve this dish as part of an elegant spring dinner party. It might start with Crostini with Oven-Roasted Mushrooms (page 37) with the risotto followed by Roasted Asparagus with Olive Oil (page 330) or Artichokes Braised in White Wine with Garlic and Parsley (page 328).

Risotto with Peas and Plum Tomatoes

SERVES 4

THE TOMATOES FALL APART and turn the rice a bright red-orange color. Fresh peas are not necessary; frozen peas are fine.

- 6 cups Light Tomato Stock (page 530), Vegetable Stock (page 529) or water
- 2 tablespoons extra-virgin olive oil
- 1 medium onion, minced
- 2 medium garlic cloves, minced
- 5 medium, ripe plum tomatoes (about 1 pound), peeled, cored, seeded and cut into ½-inch cubes
- Salt and freshly ground black pepper
- 1½ cups Arborio rice
- 1 cup frozen peas, thawed
- 2 tablespoons minced fresh parsley leaves
- ½ cup freshly grated Parmigiano-Reggiano cheese, plus more for the table
- 1 tablespoon unsalted butter

1. Bring the stock or water to a simmer in a medium saucepan. Keep it warm over low heat.

2. Heat the oil in a heavy-bottomed medium pot. Add the onion and sauté over medium heat until translucent, about 5 minutes. Add the garlic and continue cooking for 1 to 2 minutes more.

3. Add the tomatoes and salt and pepper to taste. Cook, stirring occasionally, until they begin to lose their shape, about 7 minutes. Using a wooden spoon, stir in the rice and cook for 1 minute.

4. Add ½ cup of the warm stock or water and cook, stirring frequently, until the rice absorbs the liquid. Continue adding stock or water in ½-cup increments, stirring, until the rice is creamy and soft but still a bit al dente, about 25 minutes. (If you are using stock and run out of it, add hot water.) Stir in the peas and parsley and cook just until the peas are heated through, about 2 minutes.

5. Remove the pot from the heat and vigorously stir in the ½ cup cheese and the butter. Add salt and pepper to taste. Divide the risotto among individual soup bowls. Serve immediately with more grated cheese passed separately at the table.

Serving Suggestions

Start the meal with Crostini with Arugula and Ricotta Puree (page 30) and follow with a leafy salad or Fennel and Orange Salad (page 389).

Risotto with Spinach and Herbs

SERVES 4

FRESH SPINACH, PARSLEY AND BASIL give this risotto an herbal flavor. Nothing could be simpler or more satisfying.

- 6 cups Vegetable Stock (page 529) or water
- 2 cups packed fresh spinach leaves
- 2 tablespoons extra-virgin olive oil
- 2 medium shallots, minced
- 1½ cups Arborio rice
- ½ cup dry white wine
- ¼ cup minced fresh parsley leaves
- 2 tablespoons minced fresh basil leaves
- ½ cup freshly grated Parmigiano-Reggiano cheese, plus more for the table
- 1 tablespoon unsalted butter
- Salt and freshly ground black pepper

1. Bring the stock or water to a simmer in a medium saucepan. Keep it warm over low heat.

2. Remove and discard the stems from the spinach. Wash the leaves in successive bowls of cold water until grit no longer appears in the bottom of the bowl. Shake the leaves to remove excess water but do not dry them. Chop and set aside.

3. Heat the oil in a heavy-bottomed medium pot. Add the shallots and sauté over medium heat until golden, about 4 minutes. Using a wooden spoon, stir in the rice and cook for 1 minute. Add the wine and cook just until the alcohol aroma fades, 1 to 2 minutes.

4. Add ½ cup of the warm stock or water and cook, stirring frequently, until the rice absorbs the liquid. Continue adding stock in ½-cup increments, stirring, until the rice is almost fully cooked, about 20 minutes.

5. Stir in the spinach, parsley and basil and continue cooking, adding stock or water as needed, until the rice is creamy and soft but still a bit al dente, about 5 minutes.

6. Remove the pot from the heat and vigorously stir in the ½ cup cheese and butter. Add salt and pepper to taste. Divide the risotto among individual soup bowls. Serve immediately with more grated cheese passed separately at the table.

SERVING SUGGESTIONS

This dish should be followed by a colorful salad that does not contain any leafy greens. Fennel and Orange Salad (page 389) would be a good choice.

Risotto with Tomatoes, Parmesan and Basil

SERVES 4

SINCE THIS RECIPE CALLS FOR PLUM TOMATOES, it can be made at any time of the year. Choose ripe plum tomatoes that are still firm enough to be peeled by hand. Seed the tomatoes so that only the tomato meat goes into the risotto.

- 6 cups Light Tomato Stock (page 530), Vegetable Stock (page 529) or water
- 2 tablespoons extra-virgin olive oil
- 2 tablespoons unsalted butter
- 1 medium onion, minced
- 2 medium garlic cloves, minced
- 7 medium plum tomatoes (about 1½ pounds), peeled, cored, seeded and diced small
- Salt and freshly ground black pepper
- 1½ cups Arborio rice
- ½ cup dry white wine
- ½ cup freshly grated Parmigiano-Reggiano cheese, plus more for the table
- 10 large fresh basil leaves, cut into very thin strips

1. Bring the stock or water to a simmer in a medium saucepan. Keep it warm over low heat.

2. Heat the oil and 1 tablespoon of the butter in a heavy-bottomed medium pot. Add the onion and sauté over medium heat until translucent, about 5 minutes. Add the garlic and cook until lightly colored, about 1 minute. Add the tomatoes and salt and pepper to taste and cook until they soften, about 4 minutes.

3. Using a wooden spoon, stir in the rice and cook for 1 minute. Add the wine and cook until the alcohol aroma fades, 1 to 2 minutes. Add ½ cup of the warm stock or water and cook, stirring frequently, until the rice absorbs the liquid. Continue adding stock or water in ½-cup increments, stirring, until the rice is creamy and soft but still a bit al dente, about 25 minutes. (If you are using stock and run out of it, add hot water.)

4. Remove the pot from the heat and vigorously stir in the remaining 1 tablespoon butter, the ½ cup cheese and the basil. Adjust the seasonings. Divide the risotto among individual soup bowls. Serve immediately with more grated cheese passed separately at the table.

SERVING SUGGESTIONS

Follow this dish with something green, such as Sautéed Zucchini with Lemon and Mint (page 363), Wilted Spinach with Garlic (page 360) or a leafy salad.

Risotto with Zucchini, Tomatoes and Basil

SERVES 4

PEELED AND SEEDED TOMATOES form a thick, orange-red sauce that envelops the rice and zucchini. Tomato stock enhances the color and flavor of this dish, but regular vegetable stock or even water will produce good results.

- **6 cups Light Tomato Stock (page 530), Vegetable Stock (page 529) or water**
- **3 tablespoons extra-virgin olive oil**
- **1 medium onion, minced**
- **2 medium zucchini (about ¾ pound), scrubbed, ends trimmed, halved lengthwise and cut into thin half circles**
- **2 medium garlic cloves, minced**
- **Salt and freshly ground black pepper**
- **4 medium plum tomatoes (about ¾ pound), peeled, cored, seeded and diced small**
- **1½ cups Arborio rice**
- **½ cup freshly grated Parmigiano-Reggiano cheese, plus more for the table**
- **2 tablespoons minced fresh basil leaves**

1. Bring the stock or water to a simmer in a medium saucepan. Keep it warm over low heat.

2. Heat the oil in a heavy-bottomed medium pot. Add the onion and sauté over medium heat until translucent, about 5 minutes. Add the zucchini and cook, stirring often, until golden, 8 to 10 minutes. Add the garlic and salt and pepper to taste and cook for 1 to 2 minutes more. Add the tomatoes and cook just until they soften, about 4 minutes.

3. Using a wooden spoon, stir in the rice and cook for 1 minute. Add ½ cup of the warm stock or water and cook, stirring frequently, until the rice absorbs the liquid. Continue adding more stock or water in ½-cup increments, stirring, until the rice is creamy and soft but still a bit al dente, about 25 minutes. (If you are using stock and run out of it, add hot water.)

4. Remove the pot from the heat and vigorously stir in the ½ cup cheese and basil. Adjust the seasonings. Divide the risotto among individual soup bowls. Serve immediately with more grated cheese passed separately at the table.

SERVING SUGGESTIONS

This dish is a meal-in-one. But you could open with Crostini with Arugula and Ricotta Puree (page 30) and follow with a salad, such as Radicchio, Arugula and Endive Salad with Balsamic Vinaigrette (page 373) or Arugula Salad with Sliced Radishes and Carrots (page 371).

Risotto Cakes Stuffed with Mozzarella

SERVES 2 TO 3

WITH A MINIMUM OF EFFORT, leftover risotto can be transformed into crisp croquettes filled with cheese. Start with a risotto without large chunks of vegetables. Saffron Risotto (page 150) works best, but Risotto with Porcini Mushrooms (page 144) and Lemon Risotto (page 162) or Risotto with Spinach and Herbs (page 166) are also good choices. Croquettes are traditionally deep-fried, but baking them on a lightly greased cookie sheet at a high temperature makes them crisp with a minimum of fat.

1 tablespoon extra-virgin olive oil
2 cups leftover risotto, well chilled
2 large eggs
1 cup plain bread crumbs
2 ounces mozzarella cheese, cut into ½-inch cubes
Lemon wedges

1. Preheat the oven to 400 degrees F. Brush a large baking sheet with the oil and set it aside.

2. Combine the chilled risotto with one of the eggs. Beat the other egg in a shallow bowl. Place the bread crumbs in a second shallow bowl.

3. Gently shape 2 tablespoons of the rice mixture into a 2-inch oval. Make a slight depression in the oval and put in 1 or 2 cubes of cheese. Take another 2 tablespoons of the rice mixture and gently mold it over the cheese to cover it completely.

4. Dip the croquette into the beaten egg and then into the bread crumbs. Shake off the excess and place the croquette on the baking sheet. Repeat with the remaining rice mixture to form 8 or 9 croquettes.

5. Bake the croquettes, turning once, until golden brown, about 25 minutes. Serve immediately with the lemon wedges.

SERVING SUGGESTIONS

Serve with a substantial green salad, such as Tender Greens and Vegetables with Blood Orange Vinaigrette (page 376) or Mixed Greens with Tomatoes, Yellow Pepper and Fennel (page 377). Or accompany the croquettes with a lighter salad, such as Arugula Salad with Sliced Radishes and Carrots (page 371) or Red Leaf Lettuce, Arugula and Fennel Salad (page 374), and a vegetable side dish, such as Spicy Broccoli with Garlic (page 334) or Swiss Chard with Raisins and Almonds (page 340).

Boiled Arborio Rice with Mozzarella and Herbs

SERVES 4

ARBORIO RICE CAN BE COOKED LIKE PASTA until al dente, drained and tossed with a sauce or with cheese and herbs, as in this dish. Other fresh herbs (such as mint, chives or oregano) may also be used. The dish is much better with fresh mozzarella packed in water than with the shrink-wrapped kind.

- **1½ cups Arborio rice**
- **Salt**
- **4 ounces mozzarella cheese, shredded (about 1 cup)**
- **⅓ cup freshly grated Parmigiano-Reggiano cheese**
- **2 tablespoons unsalted butter, diced**
- **2 tablespoons minced fresh parsley leaves**
- **2 tablespoons minced fresh basil leaves**

1. Bring 4 quarts water to a boil in a medium saucepan. Add the rice and 2 teaspoons salt and boil, stirring occasionally, until al dente, 15 to 17 minutes.

2. Drain the rice and place it in a large bowl. Add the cheeses, butter and herbs and mix well until the mozzarella and butter melt, about 1 minute. Add salt to taste and serve immediately.

SERVING SUGGESTIONS

In spring or summer, serve this dish alongside Spring Vegetable Stew with Fennel, Carrots, Asparagus and Peas (page 322) or Baked Tomatoes Stuffed with Bread Crumbs, Parmesan and Herbs (page 310). It can also be paired with Sautéed Cherry Tomatoes with Garlic (page 362) and Spinach with Brown Butter and Pine Nuts (page 361) for a light meal.

Pesto Rice

SERVES 6

TO KEEP THE PESTO'S COLOR FROM FADING to a muddy brown when it hits the hot rice, add parsley to the basil. Walnuts or pine nuts are equally good in this pesto; it's a matter of cost and convenience.

- 1½ cups Arborio rice
- Salt
- 2 cups packed fresh basil leaves
- 1 cup packed fresh parsley leaves
- 3 tablespoons walnuts or pine nuts
- 2 small garlic cloves
- 6 tablespoons extra-virgin olive oil
- ¾ cup freshly grated Parmigiano-Reggiano cheese
- Freshly ground black pepper

1. Bring 4 quarts water to a boil in a medium saucepan. Add the rice and 2 teaspoons salt and boil, stirring occasionally, until al dente, 15 to 17 minutes.

2. While the rice is cooking, place the basil, parsley, nuts and garlic in the work bowl of a food processor. Process, scraping down the sides of the bowl once, until the ingredients are finely chopped. With the motor running, slowly pour the oil through the feed tube and process until the mixture is smooth. Scrape into a large serving bowl. Stir in the cheese and salt and pepper to taste. At this point, the pesto will be quite thick. When the rice is tender, use a ladle to remove ½ cup of the cooking liquid. Stir the liquid into the pesto to thin it.

3. Drain the rice and place it in the bowl with the pesto. Toss gently to evenly coat the grains with pesto. Serve immediately.

SERVING SUGGESTIONS

Serve this as a side dish or accompaniment with grilled vegetables. It's very nice with Grilled Portobello Mushrooms, Red Onions and Bell Peppers (page 320). The dish also works well with egg dishes, especially Zucchini Frittata with Parmesan (page 259) and Red Onion Frittata with Parmesan and Thyme (page 248). It can also be served as a main course for four along with a marinated tomato salad.

Summer Rice Salad with Tomatoes, Cucumber and Yellow Pepper

Serves 4 to 6

The slightly chewy texture of Arborio rice makes it a good choice for a summer salad. The warm rice is tossed with white wine vinegar and olive oil and allowed to cool to room temperature. Vegetables and herbs are added. The salad is best served right away.

- 1½ cups Arborio rice
- Salt
- 1 tablespoon white wine vinegar
- 1 medium garlic clove, minced
- Freshly ground black pepper
- 3 tablespoons extra-virgin olive oil
- 2 small, ripe tomatoes (about ½ pound), peeled, cored, seeded and diced
- 1 medium yellow bell pepper, cored, seeded and diced
- ½ medium cucumber, peeled, halved lengthwise, seeded and diced
- 10 large black olives, pitted and chopped
- 1 tablespoon minced fresh parsley leaves
- 1 tablespoon minced fresh basil leaves

1. Bring 4 quarts water to a boil in a medium saucepan. Add the rice and 2 teaspoons salt and boil, stirring occasionally, until al dente, 15 to 17 minutes.

2. Drain the rice and place it in a large bowl. Whisk the vinegar, garlic and salt and pepper to taste in a small bowl. Whisk in the oil until smooth. Drizzle the dressing over the rice and toss gently. Cool the rice to room temperature while you prepare the remaining ingredients.

3. Add the tomatoes, bell pepper, cucumber, olives, parsley and basil to the cooled rice. Mix thoroughly and adjust the seasonings. Serve immediately or set aside for up to 2 hours at room temperature

Serving Suggestions

This brightly colored rice salad makes a light main course for the dog days of summer. Serve it over a bed of lightly dressed salad greens along with some bread. The salad can also be included in a room-temperature meal with other salads and bruschetta or a frittata.

Baked Arborio Rice with Marinated Artichokes

SERVES 4 TO 6

THIS RECIPE COMES FROM APULIA via my friend and fellow food writer Lorna Sass. I have tinkered with it, replacing the long-grain rice in the original with Arborio. The rice comes out a bit creamier, more like risotto. If you prefer separate, fluffy grains, use long-grain rice instead. If your local Italian market marinates its own artichoke hearts, buy them. Otherwise, use one 11-ounce jar of imported marinated artichoke hearts.

- **2 tablespoons extra-virgin olive oil**
- **1 medium onion, minced**
- **3 medium garlic cloves, minced**
- **1½ cups Arborio rice**
- **1½ cups drained marinated artichoke hearts, chopped**
- **½ cup freshly grated Pecorino Romano cheese**
- **¼ cup minced fresh parsley leaves**
- **¾ teaspoon salt**
- **Freshly ground black pepper**

1. Preheat the oven to 375 degrees F. Bring 3 cups water to a boil in a small saucepan or tea kettle.

2. Heat the oil in a 4-quart flameproof casserole. Add the onion and sauté over medium heat until translucent, about 5 minutes. Stir in the garlic and cook until lightly colored, about 1 minute. Add the rice and cook, stirring constantly, just until the grains are coated with the oil, about 1 minute.

3. Stir in the artichoke hearts, cheese, parsley, boiling water, salt and pepper to taste. Mix well and cover the casserole.

4. Bake until the rice is tender and creamy and the liquid has been completely absorbed, 25 to 30 minutes. Remove the casserole from the oven and let stand, covered, for 5 minutes. Gently stir with a large spoon to distribute the artichokes and parsley evenly. Adjust the seasonings and serve immediately.

SERVING SUGGESTIONS

This dish can be served as either a main course or a side dish. With a leafy salad, such as Tender Green Salad with Pine Nuts and Yellow Raisins (page 375), and a loaf of bread, it will serve four. As a side dish with something like Onion and Mushroom Frittata (page 247) or Red Pepper Frittata with Mint (page 250), count on six servings.

POLENTA

POLENTA IS THE ITALIAN WORD FOR CORNMEAL as well as the name for a dish made by cooking the cornmeal in liquid, usually water, until it thickens to a soft, porridgelike consistency. A cousin to American grits, polenta is a staple in northern Italy, especially during the winter—hearty peasant fare that can be served in several ways.

With a sprinkling of fresh herbs and a drizzle of olive oil, or maybe a pat of butter and a dusting of grated cheese, polenta serves as a simple side dish. A soft mound of polenta can also be the base for cooked greens, mushrooms, cauliflower or almost any other vegetable.

Soft polenta can be spread on an oiled baking sheet or poured into an oiled loaf pan and cooled until firm. Then it is cut into squares or triangles and grilled (or broiled) or fried to make polenta crostini or thinly sliced and used to make a layered casserole.

Although polenta is remarkably simple—nothing more than cornmeal, water and salt—the dish has provoked a fair amount of debate about how it should be cooked. Italians approach polenta-making with lots of ritual and fanfare, much of which is both impractical for American cooks and just plain unnecessary. Traditionally, polenta is cooked in a heavy copper pot, called a *paiolo*, which is used specifically for the purpose. Although a heavy pot is essential, there is no need to buy a special piece of equipment.

Standard recipes rely on a technique that many modern cooks will find too time-consuming. The cornmeal is added to boiling water in a slow stream with one hand while the other hand stirs with a long-handled wooden spoon to create a vortex. The polenta is then stirred constantly for 30 to 40 minutes, or until it starts to pull away from the sides of the pan.

Frankly, I have never understood these directions. Polenta can start to pull away from the sides of the pan much earlier, as soon as five or ten minutes, and it certainly is not done at that point. It needs long cooking for the cornmeal to lose its raw flavor. Polenta is done when it tastes right—when the cornmeal has completely lost its gritty edge and, instead, tastes rich, buttery, even sweet.

SO WHAT'S THE BEST WAY TO GET PERFECT POLENTA? I have tried a number of methods, including using a double boiler and starting the cornmeal in cold water. To my mind, the simplest technique is very low heat and a cover. As long as the polenta is barely bubbling and a cover is holding in the moisture, it will not burn. The cooking time is still about 40 minutes, but instead of constant stirring, an occasional stir, every 10 minutes or so, is sufficient.

I make another minor adjustment to the classic technique and use a whisk rather than the traditional long wooden spoon to incorporate the cornmeal into the boiling water. Even with vigorous stirring, a spoon sometimes cannot prevent the formation of lumps. A whisk always does. Once the cornmeal has thickened, I switch to the long, wooden spoon for the occasional stirring.

There is also some confusion about what kind of cornmeal makes the best polenta. The first issue is the grind—whether fine, medium or coarse. Very fine cornmeal (with a texture like table salt) can become gummy when cooked. Most major brands of cornmeal sold in supermarkets (including Quaker and Goya) are finely ground. Medium-grind cornmeal cooks up soft and fluffy and is the better choice. (Coarse cornmeal is too gritty for polenta.) Since most packages are not labeled by the grind, you will have to feel the granules. Medium-grind cornmeal has a texture similar to granulated sugar.

The presence of germ and bran, both of which have a relatively high oil content, is just as important as the grind. For that reason, whole-grain cornmeal (called *polenta integra* in Italian) is perishable. To prolong its shelf life, manufacturers often remove the bran and germ, a process that also takes away a lot of the corn flavor.

Look for cornmeal that has light and dark specks from the germ and bran. Uniformly gold cornmeal has probably been degermed. Stone-ground cornmeal, usually sold in small paper bags near the flour in the baking aisle, generally contains some bran and germ and is usually the correct grind. Store whole-grain and stone-ground cornmeal in the refrigerator.

Packages of cornmeal imported from Italy (usually labeled "polenta") can be a good option (the grind is correct, and these products often contain some germ and bran), as long as they are fresh. However, I have opened many packages of Italian polenta only to find that they contain bugs. Given the perishability of whole-grain cornmeal, I prefer domestic products, which also are cheaper.

One imported product worth looking for is quick-cooking, or instant, polenta, a staple in Italian homes. It is prepared like regular polenta, but the cooking time is just five minutes. Although the instant version can be used for either soft or firm polenta, the flavor and texture of soft polenta are not nearly so good as in that made from regular cornmeal. For firm squares that will be grilled or broiled, though, instant polenta is fine.

Polenta

Basic Soft Polenta

SERVES 4

THIS IS POLENTA PLAIN AND SIMPLE. Traditional recipes call for 30 to 40 minutes of constant stirring, but I have found that cooking the polenta in a covered pan over very low heat delivers superior results with a minimum of fuss. An occasional stir, once every 10 minutes or so, is enough to keep the polenta from sticking. A heavy saucepan is essential.

Salt
1 cup medium-grind cornmeal
2 tablespoons unsalted butter

1. Pour 4 cups water into a medium, heavy saucepan set over high heat. When the water comes to a boil, add 1 teaspoon salt and lower the heat to medium. Whisk in the cornmeal in a slow, steady stream. This should take almost 1 minute. Make sure to whisk the cornmeal continuously to prevent lumps from forming. Continue whisking as the cornmeal comes back to a boil. Simmer, whisking constantly, until the polenta starts to thicken, 1 to 2 minutes.

2. Reduce the heat until the polenta is at the barest simmer. Cover the pot and cook very slowly, stirring with a long-handled wooden spoon every 10 minutes or so, until the cornmeal loses its raw flavor, 35 to 40 minutes.

3. Stir in the butter until melted and add more salt if needed. Transfer to a serving bowl and serve immediately.

SERVING SUGGESTIONS

There are numerous ways to embellish the dish (the following recipes are good examples), but when you want true corn flavor with just a little salt and butter, this is the best choice. Ladle stews, such as Spring Vegetable Stew with Fennel, Carrots, Asparagus and Peas (page 322), over mounds of polenta for a complete meal. Polenta also makes a good base for Mixed Roasted Vegetables with Rosemary and Garlic (page 318).

Polenta with Olive Oil and Fresh Herbs

SERVES 4

A DRIZZLE OF OLIVE OIL and a sprinkling of fresh herbs turn soft polenta into a side dish that can be served with grilled or roasted vegetables or any kind of beans. Fresh herbs are essential, so use whatever is on hand, including parsley, basil, sage, thyme or oregano. Use three tablespoons of milder herbs like parsley and basil, but only one to two tablespoons of more pungent herbs like sage, thyme and oregano.

1 cup medium-grind cornmeal
Salt
2 tablespoons extra-virgin olive oil, plus more for drizzling over the polenta
1-3 tablespoons minced fresh herbs, plus several whole leaves for garnish
Freshly ground black pepper

1. Cook the cornmeal in 4 cups simmering water with 1 teaspoon salt added as described in Steps 1 and 2 on page 181.

2. When the polenta has finished cooking, stir in the 2 tablespoons oil, the minced herbs and pepper to taste. Taste and adjust the seasonings if necessary. Transfer the polenta to a serving bowl. Drizzle with more oil to taste and garnish with several whole herb leaves. Serve immediately.

SERVING SUGGESTIONS

Serve with Roasted Fennel, Carrots and Red Onion (page 346), Grilled Vegetables with Thyme and Garlic (page 365) or Cannellini Beans with Tomatoes, Sage and Garlic (page 289).

Polenta with Gorgonzola

SERVES 4

A THIN SLICE OF CREAMY GORGONZOLA melts slowly over a bowl of piping hot polenta for an elegant but easy-to-prepare first course. The dish is also rich enough to make a light meal with a salad at its side. Look for a mild Gorgonzola at the market. Avoid aged types, which will be too salty, crumbly and pungent. Saga Blue is a good, if not authentic, substitute.

1 cup medium-grind cornmeal
1 teaspoon salt
2 tablespoons unsalted butter
4 ounces mild Gorgonzola *(dolcelatte)* cheese, cut into 4 slices

1. Cook the cornmeal in 4 cups simmering salted water as described in Steps 1 and 2 on page 181.

2. When the polenta has finished cooking, stir in the butter until melted. Divide the polenta among individual bowls. Top each portion with a slice of cheese and serve immediately.

SERVING SUGGESTIONS

When serving this dish as a first course, follow with Mixed Roasted Vegetables with Rosemary and Garlic (page 318). To make a meal of it, serve a salad dressed with lemon juice or some other citrus vinaigrette, like Spinach Salad with Orange Juice Vinaigrette and Toasted Walnuts (page 380).

Polenta with Parmesan and Butter

SERVES 4

THIS IS A FAVORITE SIDE DISH that I have eaten many times throughout northern Italy. Needless to say, really good Parmigiano-Reggiano makes all the difference in such a simple dish.

- **1 cup medium-grind cornmeal**
- **Salt**
- **3 tablespoons unsalted butter**
- **½ cup freshly grated Parmigiano-Reggiano cheese**

1. Cook the cornmeal in 4 cups simmering water with 1 teaspoon salt added as described in Steps 1 and 2 on page 181.

2. When the polenta has finished cooking, stir in the butter until melted. Remove the pan from the heat and stir in the cheese and more salt if needed. Transfer to a serving bowl and serve immediately.

SERVING SUGGESTIONS

This dish makes an elegant side dish or first course. Follow with a frittata and a vegetable side dish.

Polenta with Ricotta and Pecorino

SERVES 4

THE MILD, CREAMY RICOTTA is nicely offset by sharp Pecorino in this comforting dish. There is nothing flashy about it, but the flavors are perfectly matched.

2 cups medium-grind cornmeal
Salt
2 tablespoons unsalted butter
1 cup ricotta cheese, preferably homestyle
1 cup freshly grated Pecorino Romano or Parmigiano-Reggiano cheese

1. Cook the cornmeal in 8 cups simmering water with 1½ teaspoons salt added as described in Steps 1 and 2 on page 181.

2. When the polenta has finished cooking, stir in the butter until melted. Remove the pan from the heat. Stir in the ricotta and Pecorino or Parmesan cheeses and add more salt if needed. Transfer to a serving bowl and serve immediately.

SERVING SUGGESTIONS

You can serve this polenta as a main course along with a crunchy green vegetable, such as Steamed Green Beans with Tarragon (page 347) or Roasted Asparagus with Olive Oil (page 330). Add a leafy salad like Red Leaf Lettuce, Arugula and Fennel Salad (page 374).

Polenta with Mascarpone, Rosemary and Walnuts

SERVES 4

THIS DISH IS DECIDEDLY DECADENT. Rich Italian mascarpone, which is creamier and more flavorful than American cream cheese and less sweet, is spooned into each serving bowl. Hot polenta is ladled over it, and the dish is garnished with a rosemary-walnut sauce. As diners dig into the polenta, they will uncover the soft, creamy cheese. Look for mascarpone in Italian markets or gourmet stores; it is usually packaged in small plastic containers. American cream cheese is *not* a substitute.

- **2 teaspoons salt**
- **2 cups medium-grind cornmeal**
- **1 cup mascarpone cheese**
- **⅔ cup chopped walnuts**
- **2 tablespoons extra-virgin olive oil**
- **2 teaspoons minced fresh rosemary leaves**

1. Pour 8 cups water into a medium, heavy saucepan set over high heat. When the water comes to a boil, add the salt and lower the heat to medium. Whisk in the cornmeal in a slow, steady stream. This should take 1 to 2 minutes. Make sure to whisk the cornmeal continuously to prevent lumps from forming. Continue whisking as the cornmeal comes back to a boil. Simmer, whisking constantly, until the polenta starts to thicken, 1 to 2 minutes.

2. Reduce the heat until the polenta is at the barest simmer. Cover the pan and cook very slowly, stirring with a long-handled wooden spoon every 10 minutes or so, until the cornmeal loses its raw flavor, 35 to 40 minutes.

3. While the polenta is cooking, divide the mascarpone among 4 large bowls. Place the walnuts in a medium skillet set over medium heat. Toast, shaking the pan occasionally to turn the nuts, until fragrant, about 5 minutes. Transfer them to a small bowl. Add the oil and rosemary to the pan and sauté until the rosemary is tender and has infused the oil, about 2 minutes. Stir in the walnuts and cook for 1 to 2 minutes just to coat them with the oil and rosemary. Cover and keep warm until the polenta is ready.

4. Divide the polenta among the bowls containing the mascarpone. Spoon a little of the rosemary-walnut sauce over each portion and serve immediately.

Serving Suggestions

Serve this dish as a main course during the winter with a salad containing vegetables as well as leafy greens to follow. Possible choices include Red Leaf Lettuce, Arugula and Fennel Salad (page 374) and Tender Greens and Vegetables with Blood Orange Vinaigrette (page 376).

Polenta with Cauliflower and Onions

SERVES 4 TO 6

A MEDLEY OF CAULIFLOWER simmered slowly in a simple tomato sauce sweetened with tender onions is ladled over mounds of soft polenta and sprinkled liberally with grated Pecorino cheese. Parmesan would also be delicious.

- 2 cups medium-grind cornmeal
- Salt
- 1 medium cauliflower head (about 2 pounds)
- ¼ cup extra-virgin olive oil
- 2 medium onions, thinly sliced
- 1 28-ounce can whole tomatoes, drained and chopped, juice reserved
- Freshly ground black pepper
- 2 tablespoons unsalted butter
- Freshly grated Pecorino Romano or Parmigiano-Reggiano cheese

1. Cook the cornmeal in 8 cups simmering water with 2 teaspoons salt added as described in Steps 1 and 2 on page 181.

2. Meanwhile, bring several quarts water to a boil in a medium saucepan. Trim and discard the leaves from the cauliflower. Remove and discard the core and stalks and break the cauliflower into florets. Slice the florets into bite-size pieces. Add the cauliflower to the boiling water and cook until crisp-tender, about 4 minutes. Drain and set aside.

3. Heat the oil in a large sauté pan. Add the onions and cook over medium heat until tender and lightly colored, about 7 minutes. Add the tomatoes and their juice and simmer gently until they soften and the sauce thickens slightly, about 10 minutes.

4. Add the cauliflower and salt and pepper to taste. Cover and simmer, stirring occasionally, until the cauliflower is quite tender, 15 to 20 minutes.

5. When the polenta has finished cooking, stir in the butter and add more salt if needed. Divide the polenta among large individual bowls. Spoon some of the cauliflower sauce over each portion. Serve immediately with grated cheese passed separately at the table.

SERVING SUGGESTIONS

Tender Green Salad with Pine Nuts and Yellow Raisins (page 375) complements this dish.

Polenta with Summer Corn and Basil

SERVES 4

THIS DISH IS COMPLETELY INAUTHENTIC. Italians, like most Europeans, do not eat sweet summer corn. The corn they have is used as chicken feed and fodder. Nonetheless, my Italian grandmother loves this dish—which is all the blessing I need.

- **2 cups medium-grind cornmeal**
- **Salt**
- **4 medium ears fresh sweet corn**
- **2 tablespoons unsalted butter**
- **3 tablespoons minced fresh basil leaves**
- **½ cup freshly grated Parmigiano-Reggiano cheese**

1. Cook the cornmeal in 8 cups simmering water with 2 teaspoons salt added as described in Steps 1 and 2 on page 181.

2. While the polenta is cooking, shuck the corn. Use a sharp knife to cut the corn kernels from the cobs. (You should have about 3 cups.) Discard the cobs.

3. When the polenta has cooked for about 30 minutes, add the corn. Continue cooking over low heat, stirring occasionally, until the corn is tender, about 10 minutes.

4. Stir in the butter until melted. Remove the pan from the heat, stir in the basil and cheese and adjust the seasonings. Transfer to a serving bowl and serve immediately.

SERVING SUGGESTIONS

This dish is a favorite summer main course in my house. We especially like it with a tomato salad or Marinated Yellow Beans and Summer Tomato Salad (page 383).

Polenta with Portobello Mushrooms

SERVES 4 TO 6

LARGE, STURDY PORTOBELLO MUSHROOMS have the flavor and texture to stand up to the cornmeal in this dish. I particularly like this dish with *polenta taragna,* a blend of cornmeal and buckwheat flour that is popular in northern Italy. Look for this specialty polenta in Italian markets or gourmet shops.

2 cups medium-grind cornmeal or polenta taragna
Salt
¼ cup extra-virgin olive oil
4 medium garlic cloves, minced
1 teaspoon minced fresh rosemary leaves
8 medium portobello mushrooms (about 2 pounds), stems discarded and caps wiped clean and sliced into ½-inch-wide strips
Freshly ground black pepper
1 cup canned crushed tomatoes
½ cup red wine
2 tablespoons unsalted butter
Freshly grated Parmigiano-Reggiano cheese

1. Cook the cornmeal or *polenta taragna* in 8 cups simmering water with 2 teaspoons salt added as described in Steps 1 and 2 on page 181.

2. While the polenta is cooking, heat the oil in a large sauté pan. Add the garlic and rosemary and sauté over medium heat until the garlic is lightly colored, about 1 minute. Add the mushrooms and toss to coat them with the oil. Cook until they are nicely browned and tender, 5 to 7 minutes. Season with salt and pepper to taste.

3. Add the tomatoes and wine and bring to a boil. Reduce the heat to low and simmer until the tomatoes soften and the liquid in the pan reduces but does not completely evaporate, about 10 minutes. Adjust the seasonings.

4. When the polenta has finished cooking, stir in the butter and add more salt if needed. Divide the polenta among large individual bowls. Spoon some of the mushroom sauce over each portion. Serve immediately with grated cheese passed separately at the table.

SERVING SUGGESTIONS

This main-course dish should be served with an uncomplicated vegetable side dish, such as Gratinéed Asparagus with Parmesan (page 332), Wilted Escarole with Garlic and Lemon (page 343) or Wilted Spinach with Garlic (page 360), or followed by a green salad like Radicchio, Arugula and Endive Salad with Balsamic Vinaigrette (page 373).

Polenta with Garlicky Greens

SERVES 4 TO 6

COOKED-DOWN GREENS are ladled over polenta for this hearty main-course dish. Red-veined chard is my first choice, although white-veined chard can be used. Or prepare the dish with three pounds of flat-leaf spinach (the kind sold in bundles, not the curly leaves sold in bags) if you like. *See the photograph on page 193.*

- **2 cups medium-grind cornmeal**
- **Salt**
- **1½ pounds chard, preferably with red veins**
- **1½ pounds flat-leaf spinach**
- **¼ cup extra-virgin olive oil**
- **2 medium onions, thinly sliced**
- **6 medium garlic cloves, slivered**
- **Freshly ground black pepper**
- **2 tablespoons unsalted butter**

1. Cook the cornmeal in 8 cups simmering water with 2 teaspoons salt added as described in Steps 1 and 2 on page 181.

2. While the polenta is cooking, remove and discard the stems from the chard and spinach. Tear off the green portions from either side of the rib that runs down the center of each chard leaf. Discard the ribs. Tear any large chard and spinach leaves in half. Wash the leaves in successive bowls of cold water until grit no longer appears in the bottom of the bowl. Shake the leaves to remove excess water but do not dry them. Set aside.

3. Heat the oil in a large saucepan. Add the onions and sauté over medium heat until translucent, about 5 minutes. Stir in the garlic and cook until golden, about 2 minutes.

4. Add the greens to the pan. Stir to coat the leaves with the oil. Season with salt and pepper to taste. Cover and cook, stirring 2 or 3 times, until the greens are tender, 5 to 7 minutes. Remove the cover and simmer until some of the liquid evaporates, 2 to 3 minutes. The greens should be moist but not swimming in liquid.

5. When the polenta has finished cooking, stir in the butter and add more salt if needed. Divide the polenta among large individual bowls. Spoon some of the greens over each portion. Serve immediately.

SERVING SUGGESTIONS

Follow this main-course dish with Sautéed Button Mushrooms with Garlic and Herbs (page 351) or Mixed Bell Peppers with Onions, Tomatoes and Basil (page 354).

Marinated Black Olives (page 20), Marinated Bocconcini (page 23), Roasted Yellow Peppers (page 24), Crostini with Oven-Roasted Mushrooms (page 37)

Orecch[illegible] with Fava Beans, Plum Tomatoes and Ricotta Salata (page 94)

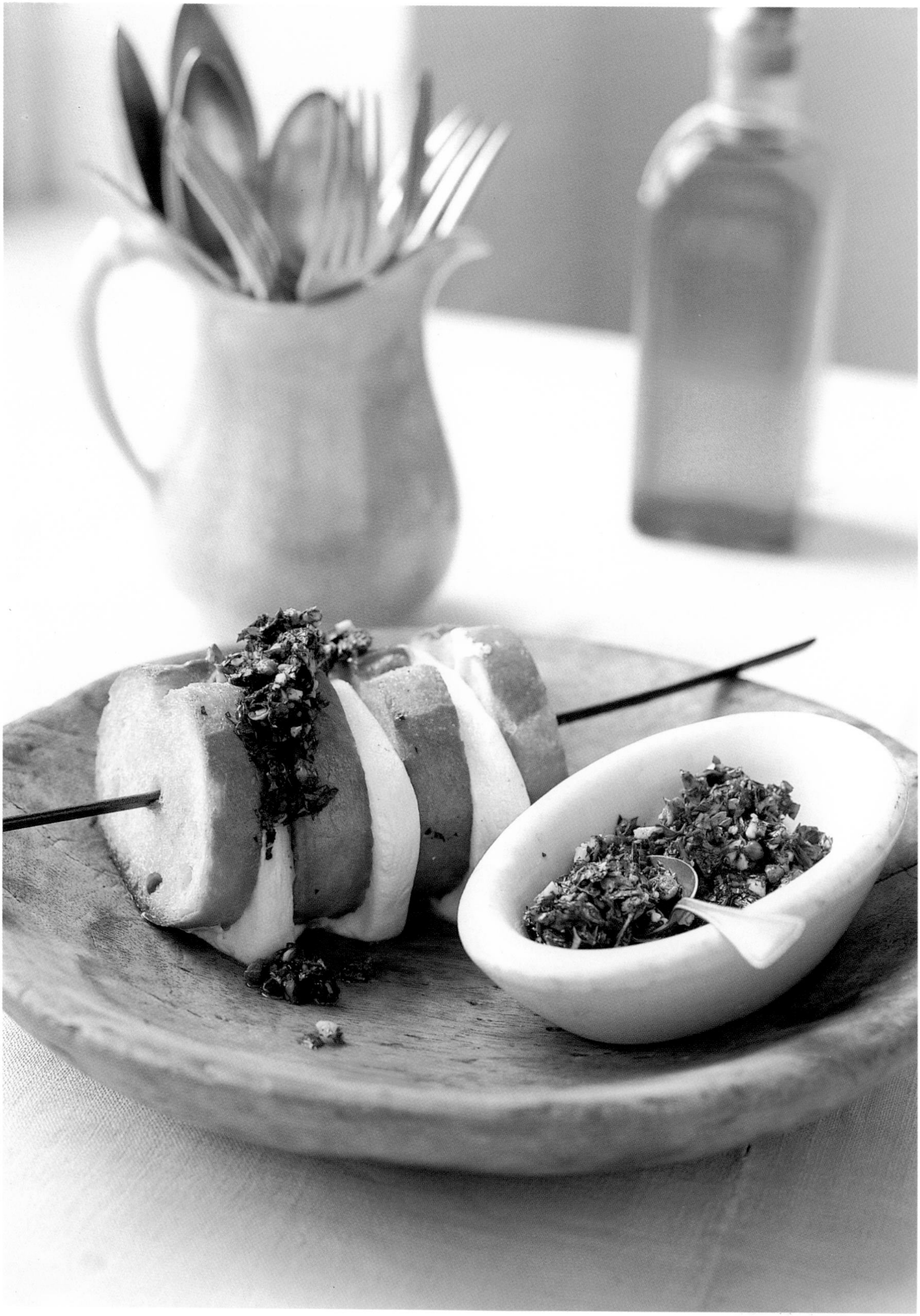

Mozzarella Spiedini with Lemon-Caper Sauce (page

Baked Red Peppers Stuffed with Saffron Risotto (page 303)

Polenta with Garlicky Greens (page 192)

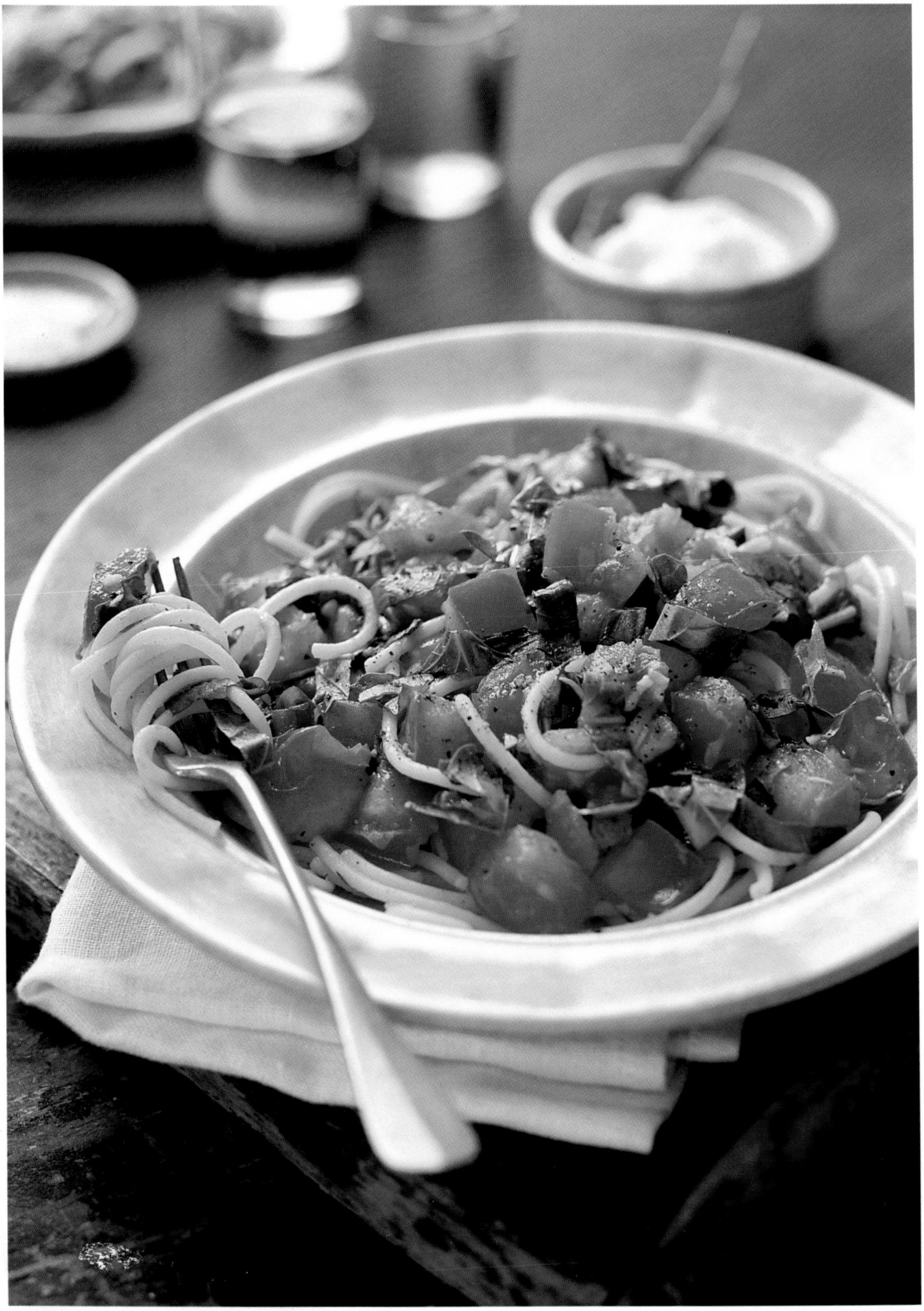

Summer Spaghetti with Raw Arugula and Tomatoes *(page 85)*

Potato Gnocchi with Tomato Sauce and Mint (page 224)

Baked Shells with Fontinc and Parmesan Bread Crumbs (page 116)

Asparagus Frittata with Basil, Shallots and Parmesan (page 245)

Fresh Tomato Tart with Basil-Garlic Crust (page 411)

Classic Minestrone with Pesto (page 60)

Potato, Arugula and Fontina Pizza (page 434)

Sicilian Chickpeas with Escarole and Caramelized Onions *(page 295)*

Risotto with Butternut Squash and Sage (page 148)

Peaches Poached in Chianti with Lemon and Fennel (page 495)

Blood Orange Sorbet *(page 512)*

Cappuccino Biscotti with Almonds and Chocolate *(page 500)*

Polenta with Lentils in Tomato Sauce

SERVES 4 TO 6

WITH BOTH LEGUMES AND STARCH, this dish is fit for winter. Remember that unlike other legumes, lentils do not require soaking. They become tender after about 25 minutes of cooking.

- 2 cups medium-grind cornmeal
- Salt
- ⅔ cup brown lentils
- 1 bay leaf
- 1 medium garlic clove
- 3 tablespoons extra-virgin olive oil
- 1 small onion, minced
- 1 medium carrot, peeled and diced small
- 1 celery rib, diced small
- 1½ cups chopped drained canned tomatoes
- 2 tablespoons minced fresh parsley leaves
- Freshly ground black pepper
- 2 tablespoons unsalted butter
- Freshly grated Parmigiano-Reggiano cheese

1. Cook the cornmeal in 8 cups simmering water with 2 teaspoons salt added as described in Steps 1 and 2 on page 181.

2. While the polenta is cooking, bring 8 cups water to a boil in a medium saucepan. Add the lentils, bay leaf and garlic and simmer over medium heat until the lentils are tender but still a bit firm, about 25 minutes. Drain, discard the bay leaf and garlic and set aside.

3. While the lentils are cooking, heat the oil in a large saucepan. Add the onion, carrot and celery and sauté over medium heat until the vegetables have softened, about 10 minutes.

4. Add the tomatoes. Simmer until the sauce thickens somewhat, about 10 minutes. Add the lentils and cook for 1 to 2 minutes to heat through. Stir in the parsley and season with salt and pepper to taste.

5. When the polenta has finished cooking, stir in the butter and add more salt if needed. Divide the polenta among large individual bowls. Spoon some of the lentils and sauce over each portion. Serve immediately with grated cheese passed separately at the table.

SERVING SUGGESTIONS

Follow with Fennel and Orange Salad (page 389), Spicy Broccoli Salad with Lemon (page 385) or another similarly refreshing salad.

Polenta with Grilled Radicchio

SERVES 4

LIGHTLY CHARRED RADICCHIO makes an unusual topping for a bowl of soft polenta. Grilling brings out some sweetness in the radicchio but still leaves plenty of its bitter notes. Balsamic vinegar drizzled over the radicchio just before serving heightens its flavor.

2 cups medium-grind cornmeal
Salt
2 medium radicchio heads (about 1¼ pounds)
¼ cup extra-virgin olive oil
Freshly ground black pepper
Aged balsamic vinegar

1. Cook the cornmeal in 8 cups simmering water with 2 teaspoons salt added as described in Steps 1 and 2 on page 181.

2. While the polenta is cooking, light the grill or preheat the broiler. Discard any limp or loose outer leaves from the radicchio. Quarter the radicchio through the stem end. Place the radicchio quarters in a large baking dish (flameproof if broiling) and brush them with the oil. Sprinkle with salt and pepper to taste.

3. Transfer the radicchio to the grill or place the baking dish under the broiler. Cook, turning the pieces twice so that each side spends some time directly facing the source of the heat. Cook the radicchio until it is lightly charred on all sides, about 8 minutes.

4. When the polenta has finished cooking, add more salt if needed. Divide the polenta among large individual bowls. Place 2 pieces of grilled radicchio over each serving. Drizzle vinegar to taste over the radicchio and serve immediately.

SERVING SUGGESTIONS

I like to serve fennel after this dish because its bracing sweetness complements the flavor of grilled radicchio. Either Roasted Fennel, Carrots and Red Onion (page 346) or Fennel and Orange Salad (page 389) would do.

Polenta with Kale

SERVES 4

IN MOST POLENTA RECIPES, the cornmeal is cooked in water and the polenta is used as a base for a sauce or vegetables. Here, the cornmeal is cooked with kale flavored with olive oil.

8 ounces kale
Salt
¼ cup extra-virgin olive oil
2 cups medium-grind cornmeal
Freshly grated Parmigiano-Reggiano cheese

1. Trim and discard the tough kale stems just below the base of the leaves. Tear off the tender, dark green leafy portion on either side of the center veins. Discard the veins. (You should have about 4 cups firmly packed leaves.) Wash the leaves in successive bowls of cold water until grit no longer appears in the bottom of the bowl. Shake the leaves to remove excess water and coarsely chop them.

2. Pour 9 cups water into a medium, heavy saucepan set over high heat. When the water comes to a boil, add 2 teaspoons salt and the oil. Stir in the kale, reduce the heat to medium and simmer until tender, about 10 minutes.

3. Whisk in the cornmeal in a slow, steady stream. This should take almost 1 minute. Make sure to whisk the cornmeal continuously to prevent lumps from forming. Continue whisking as the cornmeal comes back to a boil. Simmer, whisking constantly, until the polenta starts to thicken, 1 to 2 minutes.

4. Reduce the heat until the polenta is at the barest simmer. Cover the pan and cook very slowly, stirring with a long-handled wooden spoon every 10 minutes or so, until the cornmeal loses its raw flavor, 35 to 40 minutes.

5. Taste and add salt if needed. Divide the polenta among large individual bowls. Serve immediately with grated cheese passed separately at the table.

SERVING SUGGESTIONS

Follow this stewlike dish with a crisp salad of contrasting flavors, colors and textures. Roasted Beet Salad with Watercress, Walnuts and Fresh Pecorino (page 384) or Fennel and Orange Salad (page 389) would be good choices.

Polenta Crostini with Bell Peppers

SERVES 12

WHEN COOL AND FIRM, the polenta can be cut into squares, triangles or diamonds, toasted until crisp (this can be done either under the broiler or on the grill) and then topped with cooked vegetables and served as an antipasto. For crostini, I find that instant polenta is just fine. In addition to bell peppers, polenta crostini may be topped with Pesto, My Way (page 531) or Olivada (page 533).

Salt
1½ cups instant polenta
3 tablespoons extra-virgin olive oil, plus more for oiling the baking sheets
2 small onions, cut lengthwise in half and very thinly sliced
3 medium bell peppers (about 1¼ pounds), cored, seeded and cut into very thin strips
Freshly ground black pepper
2 tablespoons minced fresh basil leaves

1. Pour 5 cups water into a medium, heavy saucepan set over high heat. When the water comes to a boil, add 1½ teaspoons salt and lower the heat to medium. Whisk in the cornmeal in a slow, steady stream. This should take almost 1 minute. Make sure to whisk the cornmeal continuously to prevent lumps from forming.

2. Cook over medium-low heat, stirring constantly with a wooden spoon, until the polenta thickens and starts to pull away from the sides of the pan, about 5 minutes.

3. Lightly oil a 12-by-8-inch rimmed baking sheet. Spread the polenta out on the baking sheet. Cool for at least 30 minutes, or until firm. *(Wrap the baking sheet in plastic and refrigerate overnight if desired.)*

4. While the polenta is cooling, heat 2 tablespoons of the oil in a medium sauté pan. Add the onions and cook over medium heat until golden, about 10 minutes. If the onions start to brown, lower the heat.

5. Add the bell peppers and toss to coat them well with oil. Sprinkle with salt and pepper to taste. Cover the pan and cook, stirring occasionally, until the peppers are very tender, about 15 minutes. Stir in the basil, adjust the seasonings and turn off the heat. Cover the pan to keep the vegetables warm.

6. Preheat the broiler. Lightly oil a 10-by-15-inch baking sheet.

7. Place a large cutting board over the baking sheet with the cooled polenta and carefully invert the polenta onto the board. Cut the polenta into 2-inch squares, diamonds or triangles. Brush with the remaining 1 tablespoon oil and place them on the lightly oiled baking sheet.

8. Broil the polenta until crisp and just beginning to turn brown in spots, about 5 minutes. Turn and broil until crisp on the second side, about 5 minutes more. Divide the pepper mixture among the polenta crostini. Let cool slightly until just warm and serve.

SERVING SUGGESTIONS

This antipasto can be followed by almost any main-course vegetable dish, such as Roman-Style Stuffed Artichokes with Garlic and Mint (page 304) or Zucchini Stuffed with Ricotta and Herbs (page 308).

Polenta Lasagne with Mushroom Sauce and Parmesan

SERVES 8 TO 10

THIN SLICES OF COOLED POLENTA take the place of pasta in this hearty, layered casserole. Although this recipe may seem quite long, the preparation can be broken up into several parts. The sauce can be made several days in advance, and the polenta is fine if made a day ahead.

- 2¾ cups instant polenta
- Salt
- 1 ounce dried porcini mushrooms
- 3 tablespoons unsalted butter
- 1 small onion, diced
- 1 small carrot, diced
- 1 celery rib, diced
- 2 pounds white button mushrooms, wiped clean, stems trimmed, thinly sliced
- Freshly ground black pepper
- 2 cups canned crushed tomatoes
- 2 cups Classic Béchamel (page 527)
- 1 cup freshly grated Parmigiano-Reggiano cheese

1. Cook the cornmeal in 9 cups simmering water with 2 teaspoons salt added as directed in Steps 1 and 2 on page 181. Pour the polenta into 2 oiled loaf pans. Cool for at least 4 hours. *(The loaf pans can be wrapped in plastic and refrigerated overnight.)*

2. Place the porcini mushrooms in a small bowl and cover them with 1 cup hot water. Soak for 20 minutes. Carefully lift the mushrooms from the liquid and pick through to remove any foreign debris. Wash the mushrooms if they feel gritty. Chop them. Strain the soaking liquid through a sieve lined with a paper towel. Set aside the mushrooms and strained soaking liquid separately.

3. Heat the butter in a large sauté pan. Add the onion, carrot and celery and cook over medium heat, stirring occasionally, until the vegetables have softened, about 10 minutes.

4. Raise the heat to medium-high and add the button mushrooms to the pan. Cook, stirring often, until they release their juice, about 4 minutes. Sprinkle with 1 teaspoon salt and ¼ teaspoon pepper. Continue cooking until the liquid in the pan has evaporated, about 5 minutes more.

5. Add the chopped porcini mushrooms, their soaking liquid and the tomatoes. Reduce the heat to medium and simmer until the sauce thickens and is no longer liquid, about 20 minutes. Adjust the seasonings and set the sauce aside. *(The sauce can be refrigerated for 2 to 3 days. Bring it to room temperature before using.)*

6. Preheat the oven to 375 degrees F. Turn the loaves of polenta out onto a large cutting board. Cut the polenta into ¼-inch-thick slices.

7. Grease a 13-by-9-inch lasagne pan. Smear a few tablespoons of the béchamel across the bottom of the pan. Cover the bottom of the pan with a single layer of polenta slices. (You will need to cut some slices in order to make a single layer of slices that touch but do not overlap.) Spread one third of the mushroom sauce over the polenta. Drizzle ¼ cup béchamel over the mushroom sauce and then sprinkle with 3 tablespoons cheese. Repeat this process, making 2 more layers of polenta, mushroom sauce, béchamel and cheese. Make a fourth and final layer of polenta slices. Pour the remaining béchamel over this top layer. Use a spatula to spread the béchamel evenly over the polenta. Sprinkle with the remaining cheese. *(The polenta lasagne can be wrapped with foil and refrigerated up to one day in advance. Bring it back to room temperature before baking.)*

8. Bake the polenta lasagne until the top turns golden brown in spots, about 45 minutes. Remove the pan from the oven and let stand for 5 minutes. Cut the lasagne into squares and serve immediately.

SERVING SUGGESTIONS

This dish is substantial and calls for nothing more than a good salad, such as Red Leaf Lettuce, Arugula and Fennel Salad (page 374) or Radicchio, Arugula and Endive Salad with Balsamic Vinaigrette (page 373). You will have some polenta slices left over. Use them to make polenta croutons. Place the slices in an airtight container in the refrigerator, cut them into 1-inch squares and fry them for salads, such as Wilted Spinach Salad with Polenta Croutons (page 379).

Breakfast Polenta with Raisins and Almonds

SERVES 4

LIKE OTHER GRAINS, cornmeal makes an excellent hot cereal. In this breakfast dish, instant polenta is cooked in milk instead of water. Plump golden raisins, toasted almonds and a drizzle of maple syrup or honey add sweet and crunchy notes. Look for boxes of imported instant polenta in markets that carry a selection of Italian foods.

- ¼ cup sliced almonds
- 4 cups milk
- ½ cup raisins, preferably golden
- 1 cup instant polenta
- Maple syrup or honey

1. Place the almonds in a medium skillet set over medium heat. Toast, shaking the pan occasionally to turn the nuts, until fragrant, about 5 minutes. Transfer to a plate.

2. Place the milk and raisins in a medium, heavy saucepan. Bring the milk almost to a boil, turn off the heat and set aside until the raisins are soft and plump, about 5 minutes.

3. Use a slotted spoon to transfer the raisins to a small bowl. Bring the milk almost back to a boil and whisk in the cornmeal in a slow, steady stream. This should take almost 1 minute. Cook over medium-low heat, stirring constantly with a wooden spoon, until the polenta thickens and starts to pull away from the sides of the pan, about 5 minutes.

4. Stir in the raisins and divide the polenta among individual bowls. Sprinkle some of the toasted almonds over each portion and drizzle with maple syrup or honey to taste. Serve immediately.

SERVING SUGGESTIONS
Serve with a selection of fresh fruits for an Italian-style breakfast.

GNOCCHI AND FRITTERS

GNOCCHI, OR LITTLE DUMPLINGS, have been eaten since Roman times. Made from potatoes, ricotta or semolina, they are shaped by hand, boiled until tender, then sauced. Fritters, croquettes made of vegetables and cheese as well as flaked fish or ground meat, are breaded and deep-fried, pan-fried or baked until crisp. Gnocchi and fritters are prepared differently, but both make filling, satisfying vegetarian main courses.

The earliest recipe for gnocchi called for just flour and water. Today, gnocchi are commonly made with ricotta cheese and spinach; another regional specialty is made of a mixture of semolina, milk, butter, eggs and Parmesan. The most popular versions are made with potatoes, which gained wide culinary acceptance in Europe in the eighteenth century. But unlike potato dumplings from Germany and Central Europe, which are stick-to-your-ribs fare, well-made gnocchi are light, airy and fluffy.

The culprits behind leaden gnocchi are eggs (I never use any when making gnocchi with potatoes or ricotta) and too much flour. The potatoes need to be prepared so they require the least possible amount of flour to form a coherent dough. This means baking, not the boiling or steaming that some Italian authorities recommend. Baking dries out the potatoes and intensifies the potato flavor. Choose a russet, or baking, potato that will fluff up nicely when baked.

Peel the potatoes and put them through a ricer, which turns them into tiny bits. Mashing can leave behind lumps that will cause gnocchi to tear apart in the cooking water, while a food processor will make the potatoes gummy. If you care about gnocchi, spend $9 for an inexpensive ricer.

Ricotta gnocchi are quite similar to those made using potatoes, with ricotta and a little Parmigiano-Reggiano substituting for the potato. I find that supermarket ricotta is too watery, however. Drain it as described in the recipes that follow or, better yet, buy the firmer, drier homestyle ricotta you can find at an Italian market, gourmet store or cheese shop.

ROLL THE GNOCCHI DOUGH INTO LONG, THIN ROPES, cut them into short pieces and roll the pieces against a fork, butter paddle or meat mallet to create ridges. The ridges, as well as the indentation made on the opposite side when the dumpling is formed, trap the sauce.

Once all the gnocchi are made, start boiling and saucing them. Place each batch in a large serving bowl and top it with some of the sauce. Since gnocchi are cooked in batches, it helps to have two people for this operation: one to cook and scoop out the gnocchi, the other to sauce them and bring the bowls to the table. To keep gnocchi piping hot, warm the serving bowls in the oven briefly.

This chapter concludes with three recipes for fritters. Although such vegetable croquettes are traditionally deep-fried, I prefer to pan-fry them or bake them on a lightly oiled cookie sheet. Fritters should be served with a sauce of some sort. It can be as simple as a squirt of lemon juice or perhaps some Salsa Verde (page 532), Garlic Mayonnaise (page 534) or tomato sauce, depending on the flavors in the fritters.

Gnocchi

Fritters

Potato Gnocchi

Makes about 100 gnocchi

The hardest thing about making gnocchi is knowing how much flour to add—too little and the dumplings will be mushy when cooked, too much and they will be gummy. Since the moisture content in potatoes varies according to their age and variety, you will need to use some judgment here. Remember, you can always add more flour, but once you have put in too much, there is no turning back. See Steps 4 and 5 for two tests you can use to check the texture of the dough before shaping all the gnocchi.

2 pounds russet, or baking, potatoes, scrubbed
1¼ cups unbleached all-purpose flour, plus more as needed
Salt

1. Preheat the oven to 400 degrees F. Bake the potatoes until a metal skewer slides easily through them, about 50 minutes.

2. Wearing an oven mitt to hold the hot potatoes, use a vegetable peeler and your fingers to remove the skins. Place the peeled potatoes in a ricer, cutting them as needed, and rice them into a large bowl. Cool the potatoes for at least 20 minutes, or to room temperature.

3. Sprinkle 1¼ cups flour and 1 teaspoon salt over the cooled potatoes. Using your hands, work the mixture into a soft, smooth dough. If the dough is sticky (which is usually the case), add flour as needed, up to ¼ cup more. Do not overwork or knead the dough; just incorporate the flour into the potatoes.

4. Break off a piece of the dough and roll it out into a long rope about ¾ inch thick. If the rope won't hold together, return it to the bowl with the rest of the dough and work in more flour as needed.

5. The dough sometimes comes together before there is enough flour to prevent the gnocchi from being mushy. Before shaping all the gnocchi, break off a small piece of dough, shape it into 2 gnocchi and drop them into boiling water. Scoop up the gnocchi when they float and taste them. If they seem too mushy, work in more flour and proceed with the recipe. Once you become experienced making gnocchi, you can skip this step.

6. Slice the dough rope into ¾-inch lengths. Hold a fork, butter paddle or meat mallet in one hand and press 1 piece of the dough against the ridged surface with the index finger of your other hand to make an indentation in the center. Flip and roll the dough off the ridges and allow it to drop onto the work surface below. The gnocchi should look like slept-on pillows on one side with several thin grooves on the other. Repeat the rolling, cutting and shaping process with the remaining dough. *(The gnocchi can be placed in a single layer on a baking sheet and refrigerated for several hours. The baking sheet can also be placed in the freezer for about 1 hour. Transfer the partially frozen gnocchi to a plastic bag or container, seal and freeze for up to 1 month.)*

7. Bring 4 quarts water to a medium boil in a large pot. Avoid cooking the gnocchi at a rolling boil, since violently churning water makes it difficult to determine when they are floating. Add 2 teaspoons salt, or to taste. Add about one third of the gnocchi and cook until they float to the surface, 1½ to 2 minutes for fresh gnocchi. Do not thaw frozen gnocchi before cooking. Cook them for about 3 minutes, or until they float. (Bubbles may cause the gnocchi to bob temporarily to the surface and then sink again. The gnocchi are done when they float and not before.)

8. Scoop up the gnocchi with a slotted spoon and transfer them to a warm, shallow serving bowl or platter with as little cooking liquid as possible. While you boil the next batch of gnocchi, top the cooked gnocchi with sauce (see the recipes that follow). When the last batch has been added to the serving dish, toss gently and either bring the bowl or platter to the table or divide the gnocchi among individual warm pasta bowls. Serve immediately.

Serving Suggestions

Sauced gnocchi make a substantial meal. Follow with a salad or a vegetable side dish.

Potato Gnocchi with Butter, Sage and Parmesan

SERVES 6

ALTHOUGH SAGE IS THE CLASSIC HERB CHOICE in this preparation, other intensely flavored herbs, such as oregano, thyme, chives or marjoram, could be used in its place.

- 1 recipe Potato Gnocchi (page 220)
- 6 tablespoons (¾ stick) unsalted butter
- 12 large fresh sage leaves, cut into thin strips
- ½ cup freshly grated Parmigiano-Reggiano cheese, plus more for the table

1. Prepare the gnocchi through Step 6 of the master recipe. Bring the water to a boil for cooking the gnocchi as directed in Step 7.

2. Meanwhile, melt the butter in a small skillet. When the butter foams, add the sage. Remove the pan from the heat to prevent the butter from browning. Keep warm.

3. Cook the gnocchi in batches as directed in Step 7 of the master recipe. Scoop up the gnocchi with a slotted spoon and transfer them to a warm platter. Drizzle some of the sage butter over the gnocchi and sprinkle with some of the cheese. Repeat with the remaining batches of cooked gnocchi. When the last batch has been sauced, serve immediately with more grated cheese passed separately at the table.

SERVING SUGGESTIONS

This dish is filling, so follow it with something light. A simple tossed salad is fine. Tender Greens and Vegetables with Blood Orange Vinaigrette (page 376) would complete a winter or an early-spring dinner.

Potato Gnocchi with Pesto

SERVES 6

THE PESTO RECIPE MAKES A LITTLE LESS THAN ONE CUP OF SAUCE. Use an equal amount of your favorite pesto to sauce a full recipe of gnocchi.

1 recipe Potato Gnocchi (page 220)

1 recipe Pesto, My Way (page 531), made with ¼ cup cheese

1. Prepare the gnocchi through Step 6 of the master recipe. Bring the water to a boil for cooking the gnocchi as directed in Step 7.

2. Cook the gnocchi in batches as directed in Step 7 of the master recipe. Scoop up the gnocchi with a slotted spoon and transfer them to a warm platter. Gently toss the gnocchi with some pesto. Repeat with the remaining batches of cooked gnocchi. When the last batch has been sauced, serve immediately.

SERVING SUGGESTIONS

The pesto sauce in this dish is best followed by something crisp and cool, like Fennel and Orange Salad (page 389) or Red Leaf Lettuce, Arugula and Fennel Salad (page 374).

Potato Gnocchi with Tomato Sauce and Mint

Serves 6

This sauce goes particularly well with gnocchi because it has a fresh garden flavor. It is also low in fat. The sauce is pureed after it has cooked so that it will cling to the tiny crevices on the gnocchi. *See the photograph on page 195.*

- **1 recipe Potato Gnocchi (page 220)**
- **2 tablespoons extra-virgin olive oil**
- **3 tablespoons peeled and chopped carrot**
- **3 tablespoons chopped celery**
- **2 tablespoons chopped onion**
- **1 28-ounce can crushed tomatoes**
- **8 large fresh mint leaves**
- **Salt**
- **Freshly grated Parmigiano-Reggiano cheese**

1. Prepare the gnocchi through Step 6 of the master recipe.

2. Heat the oil in a medium saucepan. Add the carrot, celery and onion and cook over medium heat until the vegetables soften slightly, about 8 minutes.

3. Add the tomatoes, mint and salt to taste. Simmer until the sauce thickens and the vegetables soften completely, about 30 minutes. Puree the sauce in a food processor or blender. Adjust the seasonings and keep warm.

4. Bring the water to a boil for cooking the gnocchi as directed in Step 7 of the master recipe. Cook the gnocchi in batches. Scoop up the gnocchi with a slotted spoon and transfer them to a warm platter. Gently toss the gnocchi with some tomato sauce. Repeat with the remaining batches of cooked gnocchi. When the last batch has been sauced, serve immediately with grated cheese passed separately at the table.

Serving Suggestions

The carrots and onions make this tomato sauce faintly sweet. To offset that sweetness, serve a salad of bitter greens, such as Radicchio, Arugula and Endive Salad with Balsamic Vinaigrette (page 373) or Arugula, Pine Nut and Parmesan Salad (page 370). Serve bread with the gnocchi to sop up any sauce remaining in the bowls.

Potato Gnocchi Gratinéed with Fontina Cheese

SERVES 6

THESE GNOCCHI ARE SO SUMPTUOUS, you might consider serving small portions as an appetizer for a fancy dinner party. Tossed with melted butter and sprinkled with cheese, they are run under the broiler until crisp in spots. One cup of freshly grated Parmigiano-Reggiano can be substituted for the fontina cheese.

1 recipe Potato Gnocchi (page 220)
5 tablespoons unsalted butter
4 ounces Italian fontina cheese, shredded (about 1 cup)

1. Prepare the gnocchi through Step 6 of the master recipe. Bring the water to a boil for cooking the gnocchi as directed in Step 7.

2. Preheat the broiler. Smear a flameproof gratin dish large enough to hold the gnocchi in a single layer with 2 tablespoons of the butter (or use 2 dishes if necessary). Melt the remaining 3 tablespoons butter in a small skillet and set aside.

3. Cook the gnocchi in batches according to Step 7 of the master recipe. Scoop up the gnocchi with a slotted spoon and transfer them to the buttered dish. When the last batch has been added to the dish, toss the gnocchi with the melted butter and then sprinkle evenly with the cheese.

4. Broil the gnocchi about 4 inches from the source of the heat until the cheese melts and just begins to turn golden brown in spots, no more than 3 to 4 minutes. Remove the dish from the oven and serve immediately.

SERVING SUGGESTIONS

If serving the gnocchi as a first course, follow with a vegetable main course, such as Roman-Style Stuffed Artichokes with Garlic and Mint (page 304) or Eggplant Stuffed with Bread Crumbs, Olives, Lemon and Herbs (page 306). The gnocchi can also be the main course. In that case, a tossed salad is all that is needed to complete the meal.

Potato-Spinach Gnocchi

MAKES ABOUT 100 GNOCCHI

CHOPPED COOKED SPINACH mixed with potatoes creates bright green gnocchi. The secret to success is to squeeze every last drop of liquid from the spinach before adding it to the riced potatoes. Even a small amount of water can make the gnocchi gummy. I chop the cooled spinach on a large cutting board and press the spinach against the board to press out most of the cooking liquid. As a final step, I take the chopped spinach in my hand, a little at a time, and squeeze it as tight as I can over the sink. One pound of stemmed white swiss chard (ribs removed) may be used in place of the spinach if desired.

- **2 pounds russet, or baking, potatoes, scrubbed**
- **1 10-ounce package frozen spinach**
- **1¼ cups unbleached all-purpose flour, plus more as needed**
- **Salt**

1. Preheat the oven to 400 degrees F. Bake the potatoes until a metal skewer slides easily through them, about 50 minutes.

2. Wearing an oven mitt to hold the hot potatoes, use a vegetable peeler and your fingers to remove the skins. Place the peeled potatoes in a ricer, cutting them as needed, and rice them into a large bowl. Cool the potatoes for at least 20 minutes, or to room temperature.

3. Bring 1 quart water to a boil in a small saucepan. Add the spinach and cook until tender, about 5 minutes. Drain and cool. Squeeze out every drop of moisture from the spinach. Finely chop it, squeeze it again and stir it into the cooled potatoes. Mix well with your hands to work the spinach into the potatoes.

4. Sprinkle 1¼ cups flour and 1 teaspoon salt over the potato-spinach mixture. Using your hands, work the mixture into a soft, smooth dough. If the dough is sticky (which is usually the case), add flour as needed, up to ¼ cup more. Do not overwork or knead the dough; just incorporate the flour into the potatoes.

5. Break off a piece of the dough and roll it out into a long rope about ¾ inch thick. If the rope won't hold together, return it to the bowl with the rest of the dough and work in more flour as needed. Check the texture of the gnocchi as described in Step 5 on page 220 if desired.

6. Slice the dough rope into ¾-inch lengths. Hold a fork, butter paddle or meat mallet in one hand and press 1 piece of the dough against the ridged surface with the index finger of your other hand to make an indentation in the center. Flip and roll the dough off the ridges and allow it to drop onto the work surface below. The gnocchi should look like slept-on pillows on one side with several thin grooves on the other. Repeat the rolling, cutting and shaping process with the remaining dough. *(The gnocchi can be placed in a single layer on a baking sheet and refrigerated for several hours. The baking sheet can also be placed in the freezer for about 1 hour. Transfer the partially frozen gnocchi to a plastic bag or container, seal and freeze for up to 1 month.)*

7. Bring 4 quarts water to a medium boil in a large pot. Avoid cooking the gnocchi at a rolling boil, since violently churning water makes it difficult to determine when they are floating. Add 2 teaspoons salt, or to taste. Add about one third of the gnocchi and cook until they float to the surface, 1½ to 2 minutes for fresh gnocchi. Do not thaw frozen gnocchi before cooking. Cook them for about 3 minutes, or until they float. (Bubbles may cause the gnocchi to bob temporarily to the surface and then sink again. The gnocchi are done when they float and not before.)

8. Scoop up the gnocchi with a slotted spoon and transfer them to a warm, shallow serving bowl or platter with as little cooking liquid as possible. While you boil the next batch of gnocchi, top the cooked gnocchi with sauce (see the recipes that follow). When the last batch has been added to the serving dish, toss gently and either bring the bowl or platter to the table or divide the gnocchi among individual warm pasta bowls. Serve immediately.

SERVING SUGGESTIONS

These gnocchi have enough flavor to stand up to a Gorgonzola sauce or pesto (see the recipes that follow). They are equally delicious when sauced simply with melted butter and a sprinkling of Parmigiano-Reggiano.

Potato-Spinach Gnocchi with Gorgonzola Sauce

SERVES 6

THIS DISH IS BOTH RICH (because of the cheese sauce) and light (because of the texture of the gnocchi). A mild Gorgonzola is preferable to a sharp aged one.

- **1 recipe Potato-Spinach Gnocchi (page 226)**
- **4 ounces mild Gorgonzola *(dolcelatte)* cheese (about ⅔ cup crumbled)**
- **¼ cup milk**
- **2 tablespoons unsalted butter**

1. Prepare the gnocchi through Step 6 of the master recipe. Bring the water to a boil for cooking the gnocchi as directed in Step 7.

2. Place the cheese, milk and butter in a small saucepan. Bring the mixture to a simmer, mashing the cheese with a large spoon to break apart the pieces. When the sauce is creamy and thick, turn off the heat and cover the pan to keep the sauce warm.

3. Cook the gnocchi in batches as directed in Step 7 of the master recipe. Scoop up the gnocchi with a slotted spoon and transfer them to a warm platter. Gently toss the gnocchi with some Gorgonzola sauce. Repeat with the remaining batches of cooked gnocchi. When the last batch has been sauced, serve immediately.

SERVING SUGGESTIONS

A leafy salad with vegetables that does not contain rich elements like nuts or cheese but has a nicely acidic dressing is a good follow-up to this dish. Good choices include Red Leaf Lettuce, Arugula and Fennel Salad (page 374) and Tender Greens and Vegetables with Blood Orange Vinaigrette (page 376).

Potato-Spinach Gnocchi with Pesto

SERVES 6

IDEALLY, THE SAUCE FOR THIS DISH is Pesto, My Way (page 531) made with ¼ cup cheese, since the pesto must be fairly runny to coat the gnocchi properly. You can use your own recipe, but stir in an extra tablespoon or two of oil if the pesto seems thick.

1 recipe Potato-Spinach Gnocchi (page 226)
1 recipe Pesto, My Way (page 531)

1. Prepare the gnocchi through Step 6 of the master recipe. Bring the water to a boil for cooking the gnocchi as directed in Step 7.

2. Cook the gnocchi in batches as directed in Step 7 of the master recipe. Scoop up the gnocchi with a slotted spoon and transfer them to a warm platter. Gently toss the gnocchi with some pesto. Repeat with the remaining batches of cooked gnocchi. When the last batch has been sauced, serve immediately.

SERVING SUGGESTIONS

During high tomato season, I follow this dish with a refreshing Marinated Tomato and Red Onion Salad (page 395) or Tomato Salad with Black Olives, Capers and Herbs (page 394). Either Asparagus with Lemon-Shallot Vinaigrette (page 331) or Fennel and Orange Salad (page 389) is an appropriate match at other times of the year.

Ricotta-Herb Gnocchi

MAKES 100 GNOCCHI

SINCE THERE IS NO PRECOOKING OF INGREDIENTS, these gnocchi can be prepared rather quickly. If possible, buy smooth, creamy ricotta cheese from a local Italian delicatessen or gourmet shop. Skim-milk ricotta is fine, but try to avoid supermarket brands. Feel free to adapt the herb combination as desired.

- **3 cups ricotta cheese, preferably homestyle**
- **¾ cup freshly grated Parmigiano-Reggiano cheese**
- **¾ cup finely minced fresh parsley leaves**
- **¼ cup finely minced fresh basil leaves**
- **3 tablespoons finely minced fresh mint leaves**
- **Salt**
- **1½ cups unbleached all-purpose flour, plus more as needed**

1. If using supermarket ricotta, line a large colander or mesh sieve with several layers of paper towels. Spread the cheese over the towels and let drain until thickened and creamy, about 1 hour. Remove the cheese from the colander and discard the paper towels; they should be quite moist. (Homestyle ricotta does not need to be drained.)

2. Combine the ricotta, Parmigiano-Reggiano, parsley, basil, mint and 1 teaspoon salt in a large bowl. Sprinkle 1½ cups flour over the cheese-herb mixture. Using your hands, work the mixture into a soft, smooth dough. If the dough is sticky, add flour as needed, up to ¼ cup more. Do not overwork or knead the dough; just incorporate the flour into the cheese mixture.

3. Lightly flour a work surface. Break off a piece of the dough and roll it out into a long rope about ¾ inch thick. If the rope won't hold together, return it to the bowl with the rest of the dough and work in more flour as needed. Check the texture of the gnocchi as described in Step 5 on page 220 if desired.

4. Slice the dough rope into ¾-inch lengths. Hold a fork, butter paddle or meat mallet in one hand and press 1 piece of the dough against the ridged surface with the index finger of your other hand to make an indentation in the center. Flip and roll the dough off the ridges and allow it to drop onto the work surface below. The gnocchi should look like slept-on pillows on one side with several thin grooves on the other. Repeat the rolling, cutting and shaping process with the remaining dough. *(The gnocchi can be placed in a single layer on a baking sheet and refrigerated for several hours. The baking sheet can also be placed in the freezer for about 1 hour. Transfer the partially frozen gnocchi to a plastic bag or container, seal and freeze for up to 1 month.)*

5. Bring 4 quarts water to a medium boil in a large pot. Avoid cooking the gnocchi at a rolling boil, since violently churning water makes it difficult to determine when they are floating. Add 2 teaspoons salt, or to taste. Add about one third of the gnocchi and cook until they float to the surface, 2 to 3 minutes for fresh gnocchi. Do not thaw frozen gnocchi before cooking. Cook them for about 3 minutes, or until they float. (Bubbles may cause the gnocchi to bob temporarily to the surface and then sink again. The gnocchi are done when they float and not before.)

6. Scoop up the gnocchi with a slotted spoon and transfer them to a warm, shallow serving bowl or platter with as little cooking liquid as possible. While you boil the next batch of gnocchi, top the cooked gnocchi with sauce (see the recipes that follow). When the last batch has been added to the serving dish, toss gently and either bring the bowl or platter to the table or divide the gnocchi among individual warm pasta bowls. Serve immediately.

Serving Suggestions

These gnocchi have a strong herb flavor, so top them with a neutral sauce.

Ricotta-Herb Gnocchi with Butter and Parmesan

Serves 6

The butter and Parmesan allow the flavors of the herbs to shine through. The gnocchi themselves are soft and pillowy, but the butter and grated cheese make this main course quite filling.

- **1 recipe Ricotta-Herb Gnocchi (page 230)**
- **4 tablespoons (½ stick) unsalted butter**
- **Freshly grated Parmigiano-Reggiano cheese**

1. Prepare the gnocchi through Step 4 of the master recipe. Bring the water to a boil for cooking the gnocchi as directed in Step 5.

2. Melt the butter in a small skillet. Remove the pan from the heat and keep warm.

3. Cook the gnocchi in batches as directed in Step 5 of the master recipe. Scoop up the gnocchi with a slotted spoon and transfer them to a warm platter. Drizzle some of the butter over the cooked gnocchi. Repeat with the remaining batches of cooked gnocchi. When the last batch has been sauced, serve immediately with grated cheese passed separately at the table.

Serving Suggestions

Serve with crusty bread and follow with a tossed salad, such as Tender Green Salad with Pine Nuts and Yellow Raisins (page 375) or Arugula, Tomato and Black Olive Salad (page 372).

Ricotta-Herb Gnocchi with Tomato Sauce

SERVES 6

A PLAIN TOMATO SAUCE IS ENRICHED with a little butter so that it can play off the creamy gnocchi.

- 1 recipe Ricotta-Herb Gnocchi (page 230)
- 2 tablespoons extra-virgin olive oil
- 2 medium garlic cloves, minced
- 1 28-ounce can crushed tomatoes
- 2 tablespoons unsalted butter
- Salt
- Freshly grated Parmigiano-Reggiano cheese

1. Prepare the gnocchi through Step 4 of the master recipe. Bring the water to a boil for cooking the gnocchi as directed in Step 5.

2. Heat the oil in a medium saucepan. Add the garlic and sauté over medium heat until golden, about 2 minutes. Add the tomatoes and simmer until the sauce thickens considerably, 10 to 15 minutes. Swirl in the butter and add salt to taste. Remove the pan from the heat and keep warm.

3. Cook the gnocchi in batches as directed in Step 5 of the master recipe. Scoop up the gnocchi with a slotted spoon and transfer them to a warm platter. Gently toss the gnocchi with some tomato sauce. Repeat with the remaining batches of cooked gnocchi. When the last batch has been sauced, serve immediately with grated cheese passed separately at the table.

SERVING SUGGESTIONS

Serve something light after this dish. A leafy salad or a vegetable side dish, such as Roasted Asparagus with Olive Oil (page 330), Spicy Broccoli with Garlic (page 334) or Pan-Roasted Leeks (page 350), is a good choice.

Spicy Eggplant Fritters with Basil

SERVES 2 TO 6

THESE FRITTERS ARE SURPRISINGLY MEATY. The wide range of the portions reflects the two ways they can be served. Sometimes I offer them with drinks as an hors d'oeuvre. In that case, I make 15 or so small patties, about two inches across, enough for four to six people with drinks. Sometimes I serve slightly larger fritters (see the directions below) as a supper for two or three.

- 1 large eggplant (about 1¼ pounds)
- 3 medium garlic cloves
- ¼ cup fresh basil leaves
- ½ teaspoon dried hot red pepper flakes, or more to taste
- 1 cup plain bread crumbs, plus more as needed
- ½ cup freshly grated Pecorino Romano cheese
- 1 large egg, lightly beaten
- Salt
- Olive oil for pan-frying
- Lemon wedges

1. Preheat the oven to 425 degrees F. Place the eggplant on a small baking sheet. Bake until soft and collapsed, about 40 minutes. Cool.

2. Trim and discard the stem of the eggplant and then peel away the skin. Place the eggplant flesh in a strainer set over a bowl and mash gently with a fork, picking out and discarding any large clumps of seeds. Drain for 15 minutes.

3. Place the garlic, basil and hot red pepper flakes in the work bowl of a food processor. Process, scraping down the sides of the bowl as needed, until the ingredients are finely chopped. Add the drained eggplant; process until smooth.

4. Scrape the eggplant mixture into a large bowl. Add ½ cup bread crumbs, the cheese and egg and mix well. If the mixture seems sticky, stir in more bread crumbs. Add salt to taste.

5. Spread the remaining bread crumbs on a large plate. Heat about ¼ inch oil over medium-high heat in a large skillet.

6. Take 2 generous tablespoons of the eggplant mixture and shape it into a 2½-inch flat patty. Coat both sides with bread crumbs and shake off the excess. Place the patty on a large platter and repeat with the remaining eggplant mixture and bread crumbs. You should have about 12 fritters. Turn on the oven to 200 degrees F.

7. To test the oil, dip the edge of a fritter into the pan. If it sizzles, the oil is ready. If the oil starts to smoke at any time, lower the heat. Add as many fritters as will fit comfortably in the pan. Fry until the bottoms are a rich golden brown, about 4 minutes. Carefully turn the fritters and continue to fry until the second side is also rich golden brown, another 4 minutes.

8. Transfer the cooked fritters to a baking sheet and keep them warm in the oven while you fry the remaining fritters When finished, divide among individual plates and serve with lemon wedges.

SERVING SUGGESTIONS

If you serve the fritters for supper, accompany them with a tossed green salad.

Spinach and Mushroom Cakes with Salsa Verde

SERVES 4

THESE TENDER, SAVORY CAKES are baked instead of fried to keep the fat content in check. Baking also allows the cook more flexibility. The cakes may be shaped and breaded hours in advance and then slipped into the oven when guests arrive, making this dish a good choice for entertaining.

- 3 tablespoons extra-virgin olive oil
- 2 medium shallots, minced
- 8 ounces cremini or white button mushrooms, wiped clean, stems trimmed, diced
- Salt and freshly ground black pepper
- 1 large bunch flat-leaf spinach (about 1 pound)
- 1 cup ricotta cheese, homestyle or supermarket
- 2 large eggs, separated
- ½ cup unbleached all-purpose flour
- 1 cup plain bread crumbs
- 1 recipe Salsa Verde (page 532)

1. Heat 2 tablespoons of the oil in a large, deep saucepan. Add the shallots and sauté over medium heat until golden, about 3 minutes. Add the mushrooms and cook, stirring often, until they are golden brown and any liquid in the pan has evaporated, about 9 minutes. Add salt and pepper to taste and scrape the mixture into a large bowl.

2. Preheat the oven to 425 degrees F. Brush a large baking sheet with the remaining 1 tablespoon oil and set aside.

3. Remove and discard the stems from the spinach. Wash the leaves in successive bowls of cold water until grit no longer appears in the bottom of the bowl. Shake the leaves to remove excess water but do not dry them.

4. Add the damp spinach leaves to the empty saucepan and stir to coat them evenly with the oil left in the pan. Sprinkle with salt to taste. Cover and cook over medium heat, stirring occasionally, until wilted, about 5 minutes. Transfer the spinach to a colander. Cool. Finely chop the spinach, pressing out any excess liquid.

5. Add the spinach, ricotta and egg yolks to the bowl with the mushrooms. Mix well. Stir in the flour and adjust the seasonings.

6. Place the egg whites in a shallow bowl and beat lightly with a fork. Spread the bread crumbs on a large plate. Take ¼ cup of the spinach-mushroom mixture and shape it into a 3-inch cake. Dip the cake into the egg whites and then coat it with the bread crumbs. Place the cake on the oiled baking sheet. Repeat with the remaining spinach-mushroom mixture. You should have 12 cakes. *(The baking sheet may be loosely covered with plastic and refrigerated for several hours. Remove the pan from the refrigerator about 20 minutes before baking.)*

7. Bake, turning once, until golden brown on both sides, about 30 minutes. Divide the cakes among individual plates. Serve immediately with the Salsa Verde passed separately at the table.

Serving Suggestions

Don't compete with the piquant flavors in the Salsa Verde when assembling a meal. Sautéed Cherry Tomatoes with Garlic (page 362) and a salad, such as Tender Green Salad with Pine Nuts and Yellow Raisins (page 375), make good partners for this dish.

Zucchini and Ricotta Fritters with Lemon

SERVES 4 TO 6

LEMON ZEST PERFUMES THESE TENDER FRITTERS, which are served with lemon wedges as well. The ricotta makes the fritters creamy, moist and rich. Depending on the appetites of your family or friends, figure on two to four fritters for a main course.

- ½ cup ricotta cheese, homestyle or supermarket
- 2 large eggs, lightly beaten
- 2 tablespoons minced fresh parsley leaves
- 2 medium garlic cloves, minced
- ½ teaspoon grated lemon zest
- 3 medium zucchini (about 1¼ pounds), scrubbed and ends trimmed
- Salt and freshly ground black pepper
- 1¾ cups plain bread crumbs
- Vegetable oil for pan-frying
- Lemon wedges

1. Combine the ricotta, eggs, parsley, garlic and lemon zest in a large bowl.

2. Shred the zucchini, using the shredding disk on a food processor or the large holes on a hand grater. Wrap the shredded zucchini in a kitchen towel or paper towels and squeeze out as much moisture as possible. Add the zucchini to the ricotta mixture. Add salt and pepper to taste. Stir well. Add enough bread crumbs (about 1 cup) so that the mixture is no longer sticky.

3. Spread the remaining bread crumbs on a large plate. Heat about ½ inch oil in a large skillet over medium-high heat.

4. Take about ⅓ cup of the zucchini mixture and shape it into a 3-inch patty. Coat both sides with the bread crumbs. Place the patty on a platter and repeat with the remaining zucchini mixture and bread crumbs. You should have about 15 fritters. Turn on the oven to 200 degrees F.

5. To test the oil, dip the edge of a fritter into the pan. If it sizzles, the oil is ready. If the oil starts to smoke at any time, lower the heat. Add as many fritters as will fit comfortably in the pan. Fry until the bottoms are a rich golden brown, about 4 minutes. Carefully turn the fritters and continue to fry until the second side is also rich golden brown, another 4 minutes.

6. Transfer the cooked fritters to a baking sheet and keep them warm in the oven while you fry the remaining fritters When finished, divide among individual plates and serve with lemon wedges.

Serving Suggestions

These fritters need only a leafy salad to complete the meal. Radicchio, Arugula and Endive Salad with Balsamic Vinaigrette (page 373), Arugula, Tomato and Black Olive Salad (page 372) or Spinach Salad with Orange Juice Vinaigrette and Toasted Walnuts (page 380) would all be suitable.

Eggs

Eggs play an important role in the Italian kitchen, in fresh pastas, fritters and tarts. They can also stand on their own, especially in a frittata, Italy's answer to the omelette. Unlike its French cousin, though, the frittata requires no deft folding or flipping. At its simplest, lightly beaten eggs flavored with herbs and cheese are poured into a large skillet, cooked until set and then inverted or placed under the broiler to brown the top. (I prefer to use a flameproof skillet and run it under the broiler.)

To keep any vegetables in the frittata from sticking to the pan, Italian cooks (including my grandmother) sauté them, then scrape them out of the pan into the bowl with the beaten eggs, herbs and cheese. Adding a little more oil to the pan, they pour the eggs and vegetables back in.

Nonstick cookware simplifies the process and reduces the amount of oil needed. Once the vegetables are cooked, I usually add the beaten eggs to the pan, stir gently with a fork to combine everything and wait patiently for the frittata to set. Keep the heat fairly low; you don't want the bottom to burn. To ensure that the frittata will release easily from the pan when it is done, occasionally run a spatula around the edges as the eggs set. When all but a thin layer of egg has set, transfer the pan to the broiler and finish cooking the top for a minute or two. Stick close to the stove when broiling; a frittata can go from golden brown to burned very quickly.

The frittata is the basic workaday dish of the Italian kitchen. It may be eaten hot, warm or at room temperature, for breakfast, lunch or dinner. Some roasted potatoes, spicy broccoli or a leafy salad can be served alongside to complete the meal. Depending on the time of day and the accompaniments, one frittata can serve two to four people as a main course.

The frittata may also be cooled, sliced into thin wedges and served as part of an antipasto course. For instance, a potato frittata can be cut into at least 16 slices and offered with some marinated olives for eight or more. Leftovers can be refrigerated for a sandwich filling. Slide a few strips into a crusty roll and add some leafy greens and garlic mayonnaise or even pesto for a quick lunch.

LIKE THE FRENCH, Italians also make soufflés and crepelike pancakes called *crespelle*. Soufflés resemble French versions, except that the flavorings are typically Italian, featuring Parmesan cheese rather than Gruyère, for example, and vegetables like artichokes and cauliflower. The soufflé may be enjoyed plain or embellished with a tomato-cream sauce.

The *sformato*, a Tuscan specialty, looks a bit like a fallen soufflé. Made with whole eggs, it is cooked in a springform pan in a waterbath. As a result, its texture is custardy, like an ethereal flan—comfort food at its best.

Like crepes, crespelle with savory fillings are usually baked in a gratin dish and served as a first course in place of pasta or rice, though they can be substantial enough for a main course. Traditionally, they are filled with cream-enriched vegetables, meat, chicken or seafood, covered with béchamel and baked into a rich, bubbling casserole. It's possible to use lighter fillings (ricotta cheese works wonderfully) and to omit the béchamel topping in favor of a light dusting of cheese and a few dots of butter.

Frittatas

Soufflés and Vegetable Puddings

Crespelle

Arugula Frittata

SERVES 2 TO 4

THIS FRITTATA IS AS SIMPLE AS IT GETS. Garlic is cooked in a little oil, then eggs and arugula are added. The arugula is blanched first to soften its sharp punch. Other bitter greens, especially dandelion, work well in this recipe.

6 cups packed stemmed arugula leaves, washed
Salt
6 large eggs
Freshly ground black pepper
1 tablespoon extra-virgin olive oil
2 medium garlic cloves, minced

1. Bring several quarts water to a boil in a large saucepan. Add the arugula and salt to taste and cook until tender, about 2 minutes. Drain the arugula and allow it to cool slightly. Press out the excess water and finely chop the arugula. Set aside.

2. Use a fork to lightly beat the eggs and salt and pepper to taste in a large bowl. Beat in the arugula.

3. Preheat the broiler. Heat the oil in a 10-inch nonstick skillet with an ovenproof handle. Swirl the oil to coat the bottom of the pan evenly. Add the garlic and sauté over medium heat until golden, about 2 minutes. Add the egg mixture and stir gently with a fork to incorporate the garlic. Cook over medium-low heat, occasionally sliding a spatula around the edges of the pan to loosen the frittata as it sets. Continue cooking until the frittata is set, except for the top, about 8 minutes.

4. Place the pan directly under the broiler and cook just until the top is golden brown and set, 1 to 2 minutes. Do not let the frittata burn.

5. Invert the frittata onto a large platter. Cut it into wedges and serve. The frittata may also be cooled to room temperature and then cut and served.

SERVING SUGGESTIONS

This simple frittata is a superb choice as a sandwich filling, perhaps moistened with a little Garlic Mayonnaise (page 534). It turns into a light dinner when served with Oven-Roasted Portobello Mushrooms (page 353).

Asparagus Frittata with Basil, Shallots and Parmesan

SERVES 2 TO 4

THIN ASPARAGUS, NO THICKER THAN YOUR PINKIE, often have more flavor and better texture than larger asparagus. If you must use large spears, slice them in half lengthwise and then on the bias so that the pieces are not too thick. *See the photograph on page 197.*

- **1 pound thin asparagus**
- **Salt**
- **2 tablespoons extra-virgin olive oil**
- **3 medium shallots, minced**
- **6 large eggs**
- **½ cup freshly grated Parmigiano-Reggiano cheese**
- **¼ cup shredded fresh basil leaves**
- **Freshly ground black pepper**

1. Bring several quarts water to a boil in a medium saucepan. Snap and discard the tough ends from the asparagus. Slice the asparagus on the bias into 1-inch-long pieces. Add the asparagus and salt to taste to the boiling water and cook until almost tender, about 1½ minutes. Drain and set aside.

2. Preheat the broiler. Heat the oil in a 10-inch nonstick skillet with an ovenproof handle. Swirl the oil to coat the bottom of the pan evenly. Add the shallots and sauté over medium heat until translucent, about 3 minutes. Add the asparagus and cook for 30 seconds.

3. Use a fork to lightly beat the eggs, cheese, basil and salt and pepper to taste in a medium bowl. Add the egg mixture to the pan and stir gently with a fork to incorporate the vegetables. Cook over medium-low heat, occasionally sliding a spatula around the edges of the pan to loosen the frittata as it sets. Continue cooking until the frittata is set, except for the top, about 8 minutes.

4. Place the pan directly under the broiler and cook just until the top is golden brown and set, 1 to 2 minutes. Do not let the frittata burn.

5. Invert the frittata onto a large platter. Cut it into wedges and serve. The frittata may also be cooled to room temperature and then cut and served.

SERVING SUGGESTIONS

This is a favorite Sunday brunch dish at my house. For supper, serve it with Roasted New Potatoes with Garlic and Herbs (page 357) and a salad.

Cauliflower Frittata with Parsley and Pecorino

SERVES 2 TO 4

CAULIFLOWER CUT INTO VERY SMALL FLORETS makes an excellent addition to a frittata. Half a cauliflower head is all that is needed for this recipe.

- 3 cups small cauliflower florets (½ head)
- Salt
- 2 tablespoons extra-virgin olive oil
- 1 medium onion, minced
- 6 large eggs
- ¼ cup freshly grated Pecorino Romano cheese
- 2 tablespoons minced fresh parsley leaves
- Freshly ground black pepper

1. Bring 2 quarts water to a boil in a medium saucepan. Add the cauliflower and salt to taste and simmer until tender, about 5 minutes. Drain and set aside.

2. Preheat the broiler. Heat the oil in a 10-inch nonstick skillet with an ovenproof handle. Swirl the oil to coat the bottom of the pan evenly. Add the onion and sauté over medium heat until translucent, about 5 minutes. Add the cauliflower and stir-cook just until well coated with oil and onions, about 30 seconds.

3. Use a fork to lightly beat the eggs, cheese, parsley and salt and pepper to taste in a medium bowl. Add the egg mixture to the pan and stir gently with a fork to incorporate the vegetables. Cook over medium-low heat, occasionally sliding a spatula around the edges of the pan to loosen the frittata as it sets. Continue cooking until the frittata is set, except for the top, about 8 minutes.

4. Place the pan directly under the broiler and cook just until the top is golden brown and set, 1 to 2 minutes. Do not let the frittata burn.

5. Invert the frittata onto a large platter. Cut it into wedges and serve. The frittata may also be cooled to room temperature and then cut and served.

SERVING SUGGESTIONS

This frittata should be served with a green vegetable or salad, such as Swiss Chard with Raisins and Almonds (page 340) or Spinach Salad with Orange Juice Vinaigrette and Toasted Walnuts (page 380).

Onion and Mushroom Frittata

Serves 2 to 4

Any type of mushroom can be used in this recipe, including the common white buttons. However, more flavorful types will deliver superior results.

- **2 tablespoons extra-virgin olive oil**
- **1 medium onion, cut into ½-inch dice**
- **½ pound wild, cremini or white button mushrooms, wiped clean, stems trimmed, thinly sliced**
- **Salt and freshly ground black pepper**
- **6 large eggs**
- **3 tablespoons freshly grated Parmigiano-Reggiano cheese**
- **2 tablespoons minced fresh parsley leaves**

1. Heat the oil in a 10-inch nonstick skillet with an ovenproof handle. Swirl the oil to coat the bottom of the pan evenly. Add the onion and sauté over medium heat until translucent, about 5 minutes.

2. Add the mushrooms and sauté until they turn golden brown and the liquid has evaporated, about 8 minutes. Add salt and pepper to taste.

3. Preheat the broiler. Use a fork to lightly beat the eggs, cheese and parsley in a medium bowl. Add the egg mixture to the pan and stir gently with a fork to incorporate the vegetables. Cook over medium-low heat, occasionally sliding a spatula around the edges of the pan to loosen the frittata as it sets. Continue cooking until the frittata is set, except for the top, about 8 minutes.

4. Place the pan directly under the broiler and cook just until the top is golden brown and set, 1 to 2 minutes. Do not let the frittata burn.

5. Invert the frittata onto a large platter. Cut it into wedges and serve. The frittata may also be cooled to room temperature and then cut and served.

Serving Suggestions

This hearty frittata is a favorite for breakfast but is equally suitable for dinner. As with any frittata, this one can be cooled, sliced and then sandwiched into a roll for a portable lunch. Brush the roll with a little rosemary oil or oil made from another herb.

Red Onion Frittata with Parmesan and Thyme

SERVES 2 TO 4

LIGHTLY CARAMELIZED RED ONIONS give this frittata a hint of sweetness. You can use fresh oregano instead of the thyme.

- 2 tablespoons extra-virgin olive oil
- 2 medium red onions, thinly sliced
- 6 large eggs
- ⅓ cup freshly grated Parmigiano-Reggiano cheese
- 1 teaspoon whole fresh thyme leaves
- Salt and freshly ground black pepper

1. Heat the oil in a 10-inch nonstick skillet with an ovenproof handle. Swirl the oil to coat the bottom of the pan evenly. Add the onions and sauté over medium heat until lightly browned, about 10 minutes.

2. Preheat the broiler. Use a fork to lightly beat the eggs, cheese, thyme and salt and pepper to taste in a medium bowl. Add the egg mixture to the pan and stir gently with a fork to incorporate the onions. Cook over medium-low heat, occasionally sliding a spatula around the edges of the pan to loosen the frittata as it sets. Continue cooking until the frittata is set, except for the top, about 8 minutes.

3. Place the pan directly under the broiler and cook just until the top is golden brown and set, 1 to 2 minutes. Do not let the frittata burn.

4. Invert the frittata onto a large platter. Cut it into wedges and serve. The frittata may also be cooled to room temperature and then cut and served.

SERVING SUGGESTIONS

Accompany with Roasted Potato Salad with Herbs and Red Wine Vinegar (page 391). Or serve the frittata with a green salad, such as Spinach Salad with Orange Juice Vinaigrette and Toasted Walnuts (page 380), or any green vegetable.

Parsley and Shallot Frittata

SERVES 2 TO 4

THIS THIN FRITTATA IS GOOD FOR A LIGHT MEAL or as a sandwich filling.

- 2 tablespoons extra-virgin olive oil
- 3 medium shallots, minced
- 6 large eggs
- ½ cup whole fresh flat-leaf parsley leaves
- ¼ cup freshly grated Parmigiano-Reggiano cheese
- Salt and freshly ground black pepper

1. Preheat the broiler. Heat the oil in a 10-inch nonstick skillet with an oven-proof handle. Swirl the oil to coat the bottom of the pan evenly. Add the shallots and sauté over medium heat until translucent, about 3 minutes.

2. Use a fork to lightly beat the eggs, parsley, cheese and salt and pepper to taste in a medium bowl. Add the egg mixture to the pan and stir gently with a fork to incorporate the shallots. Cook over medium-low heat, occasionally sliding a spatula around the edges of the pan to loosen the frittata as it sets. Continue cooking until the frittata is set, except for the top, about 8 minutes.

3. Place the pan directly under the broiler and cook just until the top is golden brown and set, 1 to 2 minutes. Do not let the frittata burn.

4. Invert the frittata onto a large platter. Cut it into wedges and serve. The frittata may also be cooled to room temperature and then cut and served.

SERVING SUGGESTIONS

This frittata is especially good when cut into wedges and used as a sandwich filling along with Garlic Mayonnaise (page 534).

Red Pepper Frittata with Mint

SERVES 2 TO 4

SLOW-COOKED ONIONS AND RED BELL PEPPER give this frittata a pleasant sweetness. Mint adds a welcome note, but basil or parsley may be substituted.

- 2 tablespoons extra-virgin olive oil
- 1 medium onion, very thinly sliced
- 1 medium red bell pepper, cored, seeded and cut into ¼-inch-wide strips
- 6 large eggs
- ¼ cup shredded fresh mint leaves
- ¼ cup freshly grated Parmigiano-Reggiano cheese
- Salt and freshly ground black pepper

1. Heat the oil in a 10-inch nonstick skillet with an ovenproof handle. Swirl the oil to coat the bottom of the pan evenly. Add the onion and sauté over medium heat until translucent, about 5 minutes. Add the red pepper, cover and cook until tender, about 12 minutes more.

2. Preheat the broiler. Use a fork to lightly beat the eggs, mint, cheese and salt and pepper to taste in a medium bowl. Add the egg mixture to the pan and stir gently with a fork to incorporate the vegetables. Cook over medium-low heat, occasionally sliding a spatula around the edges of the pan to loosen the frittata as it sets. Continue cooking until the frittata is set, except for the top, about 8 minutes.

3. Place the pan directly under the broiler and cook just until the top is golden brown and set, 1 to 2 minutes. Do not let the frittata burn.

4. Invert the frittata onto a large platter. Cut it into wedges and serve. The frittata may also be cooled to room temperature and then cut and served.

SERVING SUGGESTIONS

Serve this frittata with Roasted New Potatoes with Garlic and Herbs (page 357). It's also good with Swiss Chard with Raisins and Almonds (page 340) as well as other leafy vegetables.

Frittata with Scallions and Ricotta Salata

SERVES 2 TO 4

THIS SOUTHERN ITALIAN FRITTATA combines strong-flavored ricotta salata with scallions and a little parsley. The combination is simple and gutsy.

- **2 tablespoons extra-virgin olive oil**
- **4 medium scallions, white and light green parts only, thinly sliced**
- **6 large eggs**
- **½ cup grated ricotta salata cheese**
- **2 tablespoons minced fresh parsley leaves**
- **Salt and freshly ground black pepper**

1. Preheat the broiler. Heat the oil in a 10-inch nonstick skillet with an oven-proof handle. Swirl the oil to coat the bottom of the pan evenly. Add the scallions and sauté over medium heat until tender, about 3 minutes.

2. Use a fork to lightly beat the eggs, cheese, parsley and salt and pepper to taste in a medium bowl. Use salt sparingly, since the cheese is fairly salty. Add the egg mixture to the pan and stir gently with a fork to incorporate the scallions. Cook over medium-low heat, occasionally sliding a spatula around the edges of the pan to loosen the frittata as it sets. Continue cooking until the frittata is set, except for the top, about 8 minutes.

3. Place the pan directly under the broiler and cook just until the top is golden brown and set, 1 to 2 minutes. Do not let the frittata burn.

4. Invert the frittata onto a large platter. Cut it into wedges and serve. The frittata may also be cooled to room temperature and then cut and served.

SERVING SUGGESTIONS

This frittata makes a substantial meal when served with Roasted New Potatoes with Garlic and Herbs (page 357) and Mixed Bell Peppers with Onions, Tomatoes and Basil (page 354). Since its flavors stand out, it is particularly good served at room temperature, cut into thin slices as part of an antipasto spread.

Frittata with Swiss Chard and Roasted Garlic

SERVES 2 TO 4

TO ROAST GARLIC, I usually enclose the whole heads in foil pouches and bake them. When I need just a few cloves, however, I separate them and dry-roast them, still in their skins, in a skillet until soft and light brown.

- 4 cups packed stemmed swiss chard leaves, washed
- 8 large garlic cloves, unpeeled
- 6 large eggs
- ¼ cup freshly grated Parmigiano-Reggiano cheese
- Salt and freshly ground black pepper
- 1 tablespoon extra-virgin olive oil

1. Bring several quarts water to a boil in a medium saucepan. Add the swiss chard and cook just until tender, about 3 minutes. Drain and set aside to cool. Press out the excess liquid and finely chop the chard. Set aside.

2. Place the unpeeled garlic cloves in a 10-inch nonstick skillet with an ovenproof handle. Roast the garlic over medium heat, shaking the pan occasionally to turn the cloves, until they soften and the skins turn light brown, about 20 minutes. Do not let the skins burn. Transfer the garlic to a cutting board and cool slightly. Peel the cloves.

3. Preheat the broiler. Use a fork to lightly beat the eggs, chard, garlic, cheese and salt and pepper to taste in a medium bowl.

4. Heat the oil in the same skillet used to roast the garlic. Swirl the hot oil to coat the bottom of the pan evenly. Add the egg mixture to the pan. Cook over medium-low heat, occasionally sliding a spatula around the edges of the pan to loosen the frittata as it sets. Continue cooking until the frittata is set, except for the top, about 8 minutes.

5. Place the pan directly under the broiler and cook just until the top is golden brown and set, 1 to 2 minutes. Do not let the frittata burn.

6. Invert the frittata onto a large platter. Cut it into wedges and serve. The frittata may also be cooled to room temperature and then cut and served.

SERVING SUGGESTIONS

Choose a vegetable side dish that has enough presence to stand up to the garlic and chard. Possible choices include something sweet, like Roasted Beets with Balsamic Vinegar and Parsley (page 333), Slow-Browned Carrots with Butter (page 335) or Roasted Fennel, Carrots and Red Onion (page 346).

Frittata with Cremini Mushrooms and Spinach

SERVES 2 TO 4

ALTHOUGH WHITE BUTTON MUSHROOMS MAY BE USED IN THIS FRITTATA, the combination of the stronger-tasting cremini and spinach is especially pleasing.

- 2 tablespoons extra-virgin olive oil
- 1 medium onion, minced
- 8 ounces cremini or white button mushrooms, wiped clean, stems trimmed, thinly sliced
- 2 medium garlic cloves, minced
- Salt and freshly ground black pepper
- 2 cups packed spinach leaves
- 6 large eggs
- ¼ cup freshly grated Parmigiano-Reggiano cheese

1. Heat the oil in a 10-inch nonstick skillet with an ovenproof handle. Swirl the oil to coat the bottom of the pan evenly. Add the onion and sauté over medium heat until translucent, about 5 minutes. Add the mushrooms and sauté until they turn golden brown and the liquid in the pan has evaporated, about 7 minutes more. Add the garlic, season generously with salt and pepper to taste and cook for 1 minute more.

2. Preheat the broiler. Remove and discard the stems from the spinach. Wash the leaves in successive bowls of cold water until grit no longer appears in the bottom of the bowl. Shake the leaves to remove excess water but do not dry them. Add the damp spinach to the pan, stirring often, until it has wilted, 2 to 3 minutes.

3. Use a fork to lightly beat the eggs and cheese in a medium bowl. Add the egg mixture to the pan and stir gently with a fork to incorporate the vegetables. Cook over medium-low heat, occasionally sliding a spatula around the edges of the pan to loosen the frittata as it sets. Continue cooking until the frittata is set, except for the top, about 8 minutes.

4. Place the pan directly under the broiler and cook just until the top is golden brown and set, 1 to 2 minutes. Do not let the frittata burn.

5. Invert the frittata onto a large platter. Cut it into wedges and serve. The frittata may also be cooled to room temperature and then cut and served.

SERVING SUGGESTIONS

Pan-Roasted Leeks (page 350) makes a good accompaniment to this frittata, as does Roasted Asparagus with Olive Oil (page 330).

Frittata with Potatoes, Onions and Thyme

SERVES 2 TO 4

THIS FRITTATA PAIRS NEW POTATOES AND ONION with thyme, a classic combination. An equal amount of sage may be used in place of the thyme.

- **4 small new potatoes (about ½ pound), scrubbed and cut into ½-inch dice**
- **Salt**
- **3 tablespoons extra-virgin olive oil**
- **1 medium onion, thinly sliced**
- **Freshly ground black pepper**
- **6 large eggs**
- **1 teaspoon minced fresh thyme leaves**

1. Bring 1 quart water to a boil in a small saucepan. Add the potatoes and salt to taste and simmer until they are tender but not mushy or falling apart, about 10 minutes. Drain and set aside.

2. Heat 2 tablespoons of the oil in a 10-inch nonstick skillet with an ovenproof handle. Add the onion and sauté over medium heat until it starts to soften, about 3 minutes. Add the potatoes and continue cooking, stirring often, until the potatoes and onion are just starting to brown, about 8 minutes more. Season with salt and pepper to taste and set aside to cool slightly.

3. Preheat the broiler. Use a fork to lightly beat the eggs and thyme in a medium bowl. Stir in the potatoes and onion and adjust the seasonings.

4. Wipe out the skillet used to cook the potatoes and heat the remaining 1 tablespoon oil in it. Swirl the oil to coat the bottom of the pan evenly. Add the egg mixture to the pan. Cook over medium-low heat, occasionally sliding a spatula around the edges of the pan to loosen the frittata as it sets. Continue cooking until the frittata is set, except for the top, about 8 minutes.

5. Place the pan directly under the broiler and cook just until the top is golden brown and set, 1 to 2 minutes. Do not let the frittata burn.

6. Invert the frittata onto a large platter. Cut it into wedges and serve. The frittata may also be cooled to room temperature and then cut and served.

SERVING SUGGESTIONS

Served with a green salad, such as Arugula, Pine Nut and Parmesan Salad (page 370), this frittata makes a meal. Or cool the frittata to room temperature, cut it into thin wedges and serve it as an antipasto.

Sun-Dried Tomato Frittata with Basil and Garlic

SERVES 2 TO 4

THIS FRITTATA HAS PLENTY OF FLAVOR. Be sure to cut the sun-dried tomatoes into thin strips so they don't overpower the eggs. You can also use Oven-Dried Tomatoes (page 525) if you have any on hand.

- 1½ tablespoons extra-virgin olive oil
- 2 medium garlic cloves, minced
- 6 sun-dried tomatoes packed in oil, drained and cut into thin strips
- 6 large eggs
- ¼ cup shredded fresh basil leaves
- ¼ cup freshly grated Parmigiano-Reggiano cheese
- Salt and freshly ground black pepper

1. Preheat the broiler. Heat the oil in a 10-inch nonstick skillet with an oven-proof handle. Swirl the oil to coat the bottom of the pan evenly. Add the garlic and sauté over medium heat until golden, about 2 minutes. Add the sun-dried tomatoes and cook, stirring to coat them well with the garlic and oil, for 1 to 2 minutes more.

2. Use a fork to lightly beat the eggs, basil, cheese and salt and pepper to taste in a medium bowl. Add the egg mixture to the pan and stir gently with a fork to incorporate the garlic and sun-dried tomatoes. Cook over medium-low heat, occasionally sliding a spatula around the edges of the pan to loosen the frittata as it sets. Continue cooking until the frittata is set, except for the top, about 8 minutes.

3. Place the pan directly under the broiler and cook just until the top is golden brown and set, 1 to 2 minutes. Do not let the frittata burn.

4. Invert the frittata onto a large platter. Cut it into wedges and serve. The frittata may also be cooled to room temperature and then cut and served.

SERVING SUGGESTIONS

With sun-dried tomatoes, this frittata can be served as a reminder of summer when vine-ripened tomatoes are no longer available. Accompany it with Roasted Fennel, Carrots and Red Onion (page 346) or Red Leaf Lettuce, Arugula and Fennel Salad (page 374).

Zucchini Frittata with Parmesan

SERVES 2 TO 4

SHREDDED ZUCCHINI makes a quick summer frittata. Blotting the zucchini dry removes excess moisture that might make the frittata watery. Cook a shredded carrot along with the zucchini if you like.

- **4 medium zucchini (about 1½ pounds), scrubbed and ends trimmed**
- **3 tablespoons extra-virgin olive oil**
- **2 medium garlic cloves, minced**
- **2 tablespoons minced fresh basil or mint leaves**
- **Salt and freshly ground black pepper**
- **6 large eggs**
- **¼ cup freshly grated Parmigiano-Reggiano cheese**

1. Shred the zucchini, using the large holes on a box grater or the shredding disk on a food processor. Wrap the shredded zucchini in a kitchen towel and squeeze gently. Continue squeezing until the zucchini is fairly dry.

2. Preheat the broiler. Heat the oil in a 10-inch nonstick skillet with an ovenproof handle. Add the zucchini and garlic and cook over medium-high heat, stirring occasionally, until the zucchini is tender, about 7 minutes. Stir in the basil or mint and salt and pepper to taste.

3. Use a fork to lightly beat the eggs and cheese in a medium bowl. Add the egg mixture to the pan and stir gently with a fork to incorporate the zucchini. Cook over medium-low heat, occasionally sliding a spatula around the edges of the pan to loosen the frittata as it sets. Continue cooking until the frittata is set, except for the top, about 8 minutes.

4. Place the pan directly under the broiler and cook just until the top is golden brown and set, 1 to 2 minutes. Do not let the frittata burn.

5. Invert the frittata onto a large platter. Cut it into wedges and serve. The frittata may also be cooled to room temperature and then cut and served.

SERVING SUGGESTIONS

This frittata makes a light summer dinner with a marinated tomato salad or a simple bruschetta, such as Bruschetta with Tomatoes and Basil (page 476) or Bruschetta with Fresh Herbs (page 477). If serving with the tomato bruschetta, use mint in the frittata.

Parmesan and Basil Frittata

SERVES 2 TO 4

THIS FRITTATA COMBINES TWO FAVORITE INGREDIENTS, basil and Parmesan. Top-quality cheese is a must in this dish, which can be served as part of a light meal or used in sandwiches.

- 2 tablespoons extra-virgin olive oil
- 1 medium onion, minced
- 6 large eggs
- ½ cup freshly grated Parmigiano-Reggiano cheese
- ⅓ cup shredded fresh basil leaves
- Salt and freshly ground black pepper

1. Preheat the broiler. Heat the oil in a 10-inch nonstick skillet with an oven-proof handle. Swirl the oil to coat the bottom of the pan evenly. Add the onion and sauté over medium heat until translucent, about 5 minutes.

2. Use a fork to lightly beat the eggs, cheese, basil and salt and pepper to taste in a medium bowl. Add the egg mixture to the pan and stir gently with a fork to incorporate the onion. Cook over medium-low heat, occasionally sliding a spatula around the edges of the pan to loosen the frittata as it sets. Continue cooking until the frittata is set, except for the top, about 8 minutes.

3. Place the pan directly under the broiler and cook just until the top is golden brown and set, 1 to 2 minutes. Do not let the frittata burn.

4. Invert the frittata onto a large platter. Cut it into wedges and serve. The frittata may also be cooled to room temperature and then cut and served.

SERVING SUGGESTIONS

This frittata goes well with a tomato salad. Marinated Tomato and Red Onion Salad (page 395) is a good choice. A green vegetable, such as Roasted Asparagus with Olive Oil (page 330) or Swiss Chard with Raisins and Almonds (page 340), is also an inspired match. If you use the frittata for a sandwich filling, you may want to spread the bread with Garlic Mayonnaise (page 534).

Frittata with Ricotta and Mint

SERVES 2 TO 4

RICOTTA CHEESE MAKES THIS FRITTATA especially light and fluffy. Basil or parsley would work in place of the mint.

- **2 tablespoons extra-virgin olive oil**
- **2 medium shallots, minced**
- **6 large eggs**
- **1 cup ricotta cheese, homestyle or supermarket**
- **2 tablespoons shredded fresh mint leaves**
- **Salt and freshly ground black pepper**

1. Preheat the broiler. Heat the oil in a 10-inch nonstick skillet with an ovenproof handle. Swirl the oil to coat the bottom of the pan evenly. Add the shallots and sauté over medium heat until translucent, about 3 minutes.

2. Use a fork to lightly beat the eggs, cheese, mint and salt and pepper to taste in a medium bowl. Add the egg mixture to the pan and stir gently with a fork to incorporate the shallots. Cook over medium-low heat, occasionally sliding a spatula around the edges of the pan to loosen the frittata as it sets. Continue cooking until the frittata is set, except for the top, about 8 minutes.

3. Place the pan directly under the broiler and cook just until the top is golden brown and set, 1 to 2 minutes. Do not let the frittata burn.

4. Invert the frittata onto a large platter. Cut it into wedges and serve. The frittata may also be cooled to room temperature and then cut and served.

SERVING SUGGESTIONS

The ricotta makes this frittata a little sweet, so I serve it for brunch (rather than dinner) along with Roasted New Potatoes with Garlic and Herbs (page 357) or Mashed Potatoes with Oven-Dried Tomatoes (page 356).

Frittata with Penne, Zucchini and Plum Tomato Sauce

SERVES 4

THIS FRITTATA, WHICH TURNS OUT LIKE AN EGGY BAKED PASTA DISH, is very hearty. Leftover pasta may be used. (If the leftover pasta has been coated with oil, omit the oil in Step 1.)

- 5 ounces uncooked penne or other short tubular-shaped pasta or 2 cups cooked
- Salt
- 5 tablespoons extra-virgin olive oil
- 4 small zucchini (about 1 pound), scrubbed, ends trimmed, halved lengthwise and cut into thin half circles
- 2 large garlic cloves, minced
- Freshly ground black pepper
- 5 medium plum tomatoes (about 1 pound), cored and cut into ½-inch dice
- 8 large fresh basil leaves, shredded
- 7 large eggs
- ¼ cup freshly grated Parmigiano-Reggiano cheese

1. If using uncooked pasta, bring 4 quarts water to a boil in a large pot. Add the pasta and salt to taste and cook until al dente. Drain and transfer to a large bowl. Drizzle 1 tablespoon of the oil over the cooked pasta and toss gently to coat the pieces to keep them from sticking together. Set aside to cool to room temperature. If using leftover cooked pasta, remove it from the refrigerator and bring to room temperature.

2. Heat 2 tablespoons oil in a large skillet. Add the zucchini and sauté over medium-high heat until it starts to brown, 8 to 10 minutes. Stir in half the garlic and salt and pepper to taste. Cook for 1 minute more. Set aside to cool to room temperature.

3. While waiting for the pasta and zucchini to cool, make the tomato sauce. Heat 1 tablespoon oil in a medium skillet. Add the remaining garlic and sauté over medium heat until lightly colored, about 1 minute. Add the tomatoes and basil and cook until the tomatoes soften a bit, about 4 minutes. Add salt and pepper to taste. Keep the sauce warm and reheat if needed at serving time.

4. Preheat the broiler. Use a fork to lightly beat the eggs, cheese and salt and pepper to taste in a medium bowl. Pour the egg mixture over the pasta, add the zucchini and mix well.

5. Heat the remaining 1 tablespoon oil in a 10-inch nonstick skillet with an oven-proof handle. Swirl the oil to coat the bottom of the pan evenly. Add the egg mixture. Cook over medium-low heat, occasionally sliding a spatula around the edges of the pan to loosen the frittata as it sets. Cook until the bottom appears golden brown when lifted, about 8 minutes. (The top of the frittata will be pasta, so you won't be able to see how much the eggs have set.)

6. Place the pan directly under the broiler and cook just until the top is golden brown and set, 1 to 2 minutes. Do not let the frittata burn.

7. Invert the frittata onto a large platter. Cut it into wedges and serve with the tomato sauce. The frittata may also be cooled to room temperature and then cut and served with hot tomato sauce.

SERVING SUGGESTIONS

This is really a one-dish meal. Serve it with bread if you like.

Frittata with Spaghetti and Herbs

SERVES 4

THERE ARE FEW GOOD USES FOR LEFTOVER SPAGHETTI. That said, I often toss mine with a little oil and save it to prepare this dish. The eggs thoroughly coat the strands of pasta, and the mixture cooks up into a firm, chewy cake. If the leftover pasta has been coated with oil, omit the oil in Step 1.

- 8 ounces uncooked spaghetti or 3 cups cooked
- Salt
- 3 tablespoons extra-virgin olive oil
- 7 large eggs
- ¼ cup freshly grated Parmigiano-Reggiano cheese
- 2 tablespoons minced fresh basil leaves
- 2 tablespoons minced fresh parsley leaves
- Freshly ground black pepper

1. If using uncooked spaghetti, bring 4 quarts water to a boil in a large pot. Add the spaghetti and salt to taste and cook until al dente. Drain and transfer to a large bowl. Drizzle 2 tablespoons of the oil over the cooked spaghetti and toss gently to coat the strands to keep them from sticking together. Set aside to cool to room temperature. If using leftover cooked spaghetti, remove it from the refrigerator and bring to room temperature.

2. Preheat the broiler. Use a fork to lightly beat the eggs, cheese, basil, parsley and salt and pepper to taste in a medium bowl. Pour the egg mixture over the spaghetti and mix well.

3. Heat the remaining 1 tablespoon oil in a 10-inch nonstick skillet with an oven-proof handle. Swirl the oil to coat the bottom of the pan evenly. Add the egg mixture. Cook over medium-low heat, occasionally sliding a spatula around the edges of the pan to loosen the frittata as it sets. Cook until the bottom appears golden brown when lifted, about 8 minutes. (The top of the frittata will be pasta, so you won't be able to see how much the eggs have set.)

4. Place the pan directly under the broiler and cook just until the top is golden brown and set, 1 to 2 minutes. Do not let the frittata burn.

5. Invert the frittata onto a large platter. Cut it into wedges and serve. The frittata may also be cooled to room temperature and then cut and served.

SERVING SUGGESTIONS

This frittata is heartier and thicker than most, so it should serve four people for dinner along with a salad or green vegetable. This dish is also a great late-night snack, especially when made with leftover cooked spaghetti.

Parmesan Soufflé

SERVES 4

THIS IS A CLASSIC CHEESE SOUFFLÉ made with the king of Italian cheeses, Parmigiano-Reggiano. Since there are no vegetables in this soufflé, it is quicker to prepare than the others in this chapter.

- **5 tablespoons unsalted butter, plus more for buttering the dish**
- **3 tablespoons plain bread crumbs**
- **2 cups milk**
- **¼ cup unbleached all-purpose flour**
- **½ teaspoon salt**
- **Pinch of freshly ground white pepper**
- **Pinch of freshly grated nutmeg**
- **5 large egg yolks**
- **1 cup freshly grated Parmigiano-Reggiano cheese**
- **6 large egg whites**

1. Preheat the oven to 400 degrees F. Generously butter a 2-quart ceramic soufflé dish about 7 inches in diameter. Sprinkle the bread crumbs into the dish and shake to coat the bottom and sides. Shake out the excess.

2. Gently heat the milk in a small pan until it is hot but not scalded or boiling. Meanwhile, melt the 5 tablespoons butter in a medium skillet. When it is foamy, whisk in the flour until smooth. Stir-cook for 2 minutes over medium heat. Do not let the flour brown.

3. Add several tablespoons hot milk to the butter and flour and whisk vigorously. Continue adding milk in small increments, whisking until it is incorporated. Eventually, you will be able to add milk in larger amounts until it has all been incorporated into the sauce.

4. Add the salt, pepper and nutmeg and cook over medium-low heat, stirring often, until the sauce thickens to the consistency of heavy cream, about 3 minutes.

5. Remove the pan from the heat to prevent further thickening. Whisk in the egg yolks, one at a time. Scrape the contents of the pan into a large bowl and stir in the cheese.

6. In another large bowl, which is completely free of grease, beat the egg whites to stiff peaks. Use a rubber spatula to stir one quarter of the beaten whites into the bowl with the cheese and yolks. Gently fold in the remaining whites. Scrape the soufflé mixture into the prepared dish.

7. Bake until the soufflé has risen and is golden brown, about 25 minutes. The top should be firm. Remove the dish from the oven and serve immediately.

SERVING SUGGESTIONS

Serve with a salad, such as Mixed Greens with Tomatoes, Yellow Pepper and Fennel (page 377) or Spinach Salad with Orange Juice Vinaigrette and Toasted Walnuts (page 380). Add a vegetable, such as Roasted Asparagus with Olive Oil (page 330) or Slow-Browned Carrots with Butter (page 335), to make an even more substantial meal.

Artichoke Soufflé

SERVES 4

BRIEFLY COOKED ARTICHOKES are folded into a standard béchamel enriched with a little Parmesan. The process of cleaning the artichokes is fairly lengthy (working with fresh artichokes always is), but the result is a soufflé with a forthright flavor.

- **1 lemon, halved**
- **4 medium artichokes (about 1¾ pounds)**
- **6 tablespoons (¾ stick) unsalted butter, plus more for buttering the dish**
- **2 medium garlic cloves, minced**
- **Salt and freshly ground black pepper**
- **3 tablespoons plain bread crumbs**
- **1½ cups milk**
- **3 tablespoons unbleached all-purpose flour**
- **5 large egg yolks**
- **⅓ cup freshly grated Parmigiano-Reggiano cheese**
- **6 large egg whites**

1. Bring several quarts water to a boil in a medium saucepan.

2. Squeeze the lemon halves into a large bowl of cold water and add the lemon to the bowl. Working with 1 artichoke at a time, bend back and snap off the tough outer leaves. Remove several layers until you reach the leaves that are mostly pale green or yellow except for the tips. With a sharp knife, slice off the dark green pointed tip of the artichoke. Trim the end of the stem and use a vegetable peeler to peel the outer layer. Use the peeler to remove any dark green leaf bases that may surround the top of the stem. Quarter the artichoke lengthwise, leaving a part of the stem attached to each piece. Slide a small, sharp knife under the fuzzy choke and cut toward the leaf tips to remove it. Drop the cleaned quarters into the bowl of cold lemon water. Repeat with the remaining artichokes.

3. Drain the artichokes, discarding the lemon, and add them to the boiling water. Simmer until quite tender, about 15 minutes. Drain and cool. Finely chop the artichokes.

4. Heat 2 tablespoons of the butter in a medium skillet. Add the garlic and sauté over medium heat until golden, about 2 minutes. Add the artichokes and cook, stirring often, until they are completely dry and coated with the butter and garlic, about 2 minutes. Season with salt and pepper to taste and scrape the artichoke mixture into a large bowl. *(The mixture can be covered and set aside at room temperature for several hours.)*

5. Preheat the oven to 400 degrees F. Generously butter a 2-quart ceramic soufflé dish about 7 inches in diameter. Sprinkle the bread crumbs into the dish and shake to coat the bottom and sides. Shake out the excess.

6. Gently heat the milk in a small pan until it is hot but not scalded or boiling. Meanwhile, melt the remaining 4 tablespoons butter in a medium skillet. When it is foamy, whisk in the flour until smooth. Stir-cook for 2 minutes over medium heat. Do not let the flour brown.

7. Add several tablespoons hot milk to the butter and flour and whisk vigorously. Continue adding milk in small increments, whisking until it is incorporated. Eventually, you will be able to add milk in larger amounts until it has all been incorporated into the sauce. Cook over medium-low heat, stirring often, until the sauce thickens to the consistency of heavy cream, about 3 minutes.

8. Remove the pan from the heat to prevent further thickening. Whisk in the egg yolks, one at a time. Scrape the contents of the pan into the bowl with the artichokes. Stir in the cheese and adjust the seasonings.

9. In another large bowl, which is completely free of grease, beat the egg whites to stiff peaks. Use a rubber spatula to stir one quarter of the beaten whites into the bowl with the artichokes and yolks. Gently fold in the remaining whites. Scrape the soufflé mixture into the prepared dish.

10. Bake until the soufflé has risen and is golden brown, about 30 minutes. The top should be firm. Remove the dish from the oven and serve immediately.

Serving Suggestions

Save this soufflé for a special meal. Start with Crostini with Sun-Dried Tomato and Black Olive Puree (page 34) or Bruschetta with Fresh Herbs (page 477). After the main course, offer a substantial salad, such as Fava Bean and Asparagus Salad with Basil Toasts (page 382) or Tomato Salad with Black Olives, Capers and Herbs (page 394).

Cauliflower Soufflé with Pink Tomato Sauce

SERVES 4

GARLICKY CAULIFLOWER flavors this impressive soufflé. Although the soufflé itself is not complicated, the tomato sauce does require extra work. However, it is a must.

- ¾ medium cauliflower head (about 1½ pounds)
- 6 tablespoons (¾ stick) unsalted butter, plus more for buttering the dish
- 2 medium garlic cloves, minced
- 2 tablespoons minced fresh parsley leaves
- Salt and freshly ground black pepper
- 3 tablespoons plain bread crumbs
- 1½ cups milk
- 3 tablespoons unbleached all-purpose flour
- 5 large egg yolks
- ⅓ cup freshly grated Parmigiano-Reggiano cheese
- 6 large egg whites
- 1 recipe Mom's Favorite Pink Tomato Sauce (page 524)

1. Bring several quarts water to a boil in a medium saucepan. Trim and discard the leaves and stems from the cauliflower and cut it into small florets. (You should have about 4 cups florets.) Add the cauliflower to the boiling water and simmer until quite tender, about 10 minutes. Drain and cool. Very finely chop the cauliflower.

2. Heat 2 tablespoons of the butter in a medium skillet. Add the garlic and sauté over medium heat until golden, about 2 minutes. Add the florets and cook, stirring often, until they are completely dry and coated with the butter and garlic, about 2 minutes. Stir in the parsley and salt and pepper to taste and scrape the cauliflower mixture into a large bowl. *(The mixture can be covered and set aside at room temperature for several hours.)*

3. Preheat the oven to 400 degrees F. Generously butter a 2-quart ceramic soufflé dish about 7 inches in diameter. Sprinkle the bread crumbs into the dish and shake to coat the bottom and sides. Shake out the excess.

4. Gently heat the milk in a small pan until it is hot but not scalded or boiling. Meanwhile, melt the remaining 4 tablespoons butter in a medium skillet. When it is foamy, whisk in the flour until smooth. Stir-cook for 2 minutes over medium heat. Do not let the flour brown.

5. Add several tablespoons hot milk to the butter and flour and whisk vigorously. Continue adding milk in small increments, whisking until it is incorporated. Eventually, you will be able to add milk in larger amounts until it has all been incorporated into the sauce. Cook over medium-low heat, stirring often, until the sauce thickens to the consistency of heavy cream, about 3 minutes.

6. Remove the pan from the heat to prevent further thickening. Whisk in the egg yolks, one at a time. Scrape the contents of the pan into the bowl with the cauliflower. Stir in the cheese and adjust the seasonings.

7. In another large bowl, which is completely free of grease, beat the egg whites to stiff peaks. Use a rubber spatula to stir one quarter of the beaten whites into the bowl with the cauliflower and yolks. Gently fold in the remaining whites. Scrape the soufflé mixture into the prepared dish.

8. Bake until the soufflé has risen and is golden brown, about 30 minutes. The top should be firm. Remove the dish from the oven and serve immediately with the tomato sauce passed separately at the table.

SERVING SUGGESTIONS

This dish requires a fair amount of work, so keep the rest of the meal simple. A green salad or green vegetable can round out the meal. Good choices include Roasted Asparagus with Olive Oil (page 330), Sautéed Zucchini with Lemon and Mint (page 363) and Spinach Salad with Orange Juice Vinaigrette and Toasted Walnuts (page 380).

Cauliflower Sformato

SERVES 4 TO 6

A SFORMATO is a cross between a vegetable pudding and a soufflé. Not as dense as a pudding, not as airy as a soufflé, a sformato should be light on the tongue but creamy, like a good custard. Though this dish is often cooked in a ring mold, I prefer to use a springform pan and bake it in a waterbath, which produces a slightly softer result. In Tuscany, where this dish is especially popular, it is often served with tomato sauce alongside. You may do the same (Mom's Favorite Pink Tomato Sauce on page 524 would be my first choice), or you can serve it plain, as in this recipe.

- **1 medium cauliflower head (about 2 pounds)**
- **4 tablespoons (½ stick) unsalted butter, plus more for buttering the pan**
- **¼ cup plain bread crumbs**
- **1 cup milk**
- **Salt and freshly ground black pepper**
- **4 large eggs**
- **½ cup freshly grated Parmigiano-Reggiano cheese**
- **2 tablespoons unbleached all-purpose flour**

1. Bring several quarts water to a boil in a medium saucepan. Trim and discard the leaves and stems from the cauliflower and cut it into small florets. (You should have about 5 cups florets.) Add the cauliflower to the boiling water and simmer until tender, about 10 minutes. Drain.

2. While the cauliflower is cooking, preheat the oven to 375 degrees F. Generously butter a 9-inch springform pan. Sprinkle the bread crumbs into the pan and shake to coat the bottom and sides. Shake out the excess.

3. Gently heat the milk in a small pan until it is hot but not scalded or boiling. Meanwhile, melt 2 tablespoons of the butter in a large skillet. Add the cauliflower and cook, stirring often, until golden, about 5 minutes. Season with salt and pepper to taste and scrape it into a large bowl. (Set aside the skillet.) Mash the cauliflower with a potato masher or a large fork into a coarse puree. Beat in the eggs, one at a time. Stir in the cheese. Set aside.

4. Put a filled tea kettle on to boil.

5. Melt the remaining 2 tablespoons butter in the skillet used to cook the cauliflower. When the butter is foamy, whisk in the flour until smooth. Stir-cook for 1 minute over medium heat. Do not let the flour brown. Add several tablespoons hot milk to the butter and flour and whisk vigorously. Continue adding milk in small increments, whisking until it is all incorporated. Cook over medium-low heat, stirring often, until the sauce thickens to the consistency of heavy cream, about 2 minutes.

6. Scrape the contents of the skillet into the bowl with the cauliflower mixture. Adjust the seasonings. Pour the mixture into the prepared pan. Place the springform pan in a large roasting pan. Add enough boiling water to come halfway up the sides of the springform pan.

7. Bake until the top of the sformato is firm and a knife inserted into the center comes out clean, about 30 minutes. Remove the springform pan from the oven and cool it on a rack for 10 minutes. Unmold the sformato and cut it into slices. Serve immediately.

SERVING SUGGESTIONS

I usually serve the sformato with some bread and a green salad. Choices include Red Leaf Lettuce, Arugula and Fennel Salad (page 374), Mixed Greens with Tomatoes, Yellow Pepper and Fennel (page 377), Tender Greens and Vegetables with Blood Orange Vinaigrette (page 376) and Spinach Salad with Orange Juice Vinaigrette and Toasted Walnuts (page 380).

Potato and Spinach Pudding

SERVES 4

THIS HEARTY VEGETABLE PUDDING is similar to a soufflé but much less airy, since the egg whites are not beaten separately to add volume.

3 medium baking potatoes (about 1½ pounds), peeled and cut into 1-inch chunks
Salt
8 ounces spinach
4 tablespoons (½ stick) unsalted butter, plus more for buttering the baking dish
2 medium garlic cloves, minced
Freshly ground black pepper
1 cup milk
½ cup freshly grated Parmigiano-Reggiano cheese
3 large eggs, lightly beaten
2 tablespoons plain bread crumbs

1. Bring several quarts water to a boil in a medium saucepan. Add the potatoes and salt to taste. Cook until the potatoes are tender, about 15 minutes.

2. While the potatoes are cooking, remove and discard the stems from the spinach. Wash the leaves in successive bowls of cold water until grit no longer appears in the bottom of the bowl. Shake the leaves to remove excess water but do not dry them. Coarsely chop the leaves and set aside.

3. Melt 2 tablespoons of the butter in a large saucepan. Add the garlic and sauté over medium heat until golden, about 2 minutes. Add the spinach and cook, stirring often, until it has wilted completely, about 5 minutes. Season with salt and pepper to taste and set aside.

4. Drain the potatoes and mash them with the remaining 2 tablespoons butter in a large bowl. Stir in the milk, ¼ cup at a time, until the mixture is smooth. Stir in the cheese. Stir in the eggs and the spinach mixture. Adjust the seasonings. *(The mixture can be covered and refrigerated for several hours.)*

5. Preheat the oven to 375 degrees F. Generously butter a 2-quart soufflé dish. Sprinkle the bread crumbs into the dish and shake to coat the bottom and sides. Shake out the excess.

6. Pour the potato mixture into the prepared dish. Bake until the center of the pudding is firm and the top has turned golden brown in spots, about 40 minutes. Spoon portions onto individual plates and serve immediately.

SERVING SUGGESTIONS

This dish makes an excellent main course for a cold-weather supper. Serve with a vegetable, such as Roasted Fennel, Carrots and Red Onion (page 346). Or accompany with bread and a leafy salad, such as Tender Green Salad with Pine Nuts and Yellow Raisins (page 375).

Crespelle

MAKES ABOUT 16 THIN PANCAKES

CRESPELLE ARE THIN, EGGY PANCAKES. They are made with a little less butter than French crepes, but otherwise, they are quite similar. Italians generally use them as wrappers for savory items. Often, they drizzle the filled crespelle with béchamel sauce, sprinkle them with cheese and bake until golden. Making crespelle is easy; the batter takes only two minutes to prepare. Use a nonstick pan to keep the crespelle from sticking. I find it helpful to pour the batter for each pancake (two tablespoons) into a ¼-cup measuring cup, then pour all of the batter into the pan at once.

- **¾ cup unbleached all-purpose flour**
- **¼ teaspoon salt**
- **2 large eggs**
- **1 cup milk**
- **1 tablespoon unsalted butter, melted**

1. Whisk the flour and salt together in a medium bowl until well mixed. Beat the eggs with a fork in a separate bowl. Beat the milk into the eggs. Slowly pour the liquid ingredients over the dry ingredients, whisking until the batter is smooth and free of lumps.

2. Set a 7- or 8-inch nonstick skillet over medium heat. When the pan is hot, brush it lightly with melted butter. Pour 2 tablespoons of the batter into the pan and swirl to coat the bottom of the pan evenly. Cook until the bottom is light golden brown, about 1 minute. Carefully flip with a spatula and continue cooking until it is light golden brown in spots on the second side, about 45 seconds.

3. Transfer to a platter. Brush the pan lightly with more butter. Repeat this process until the batter has all been used. Use the crespelle immediately or layer them with sheets of plastic wrap when cooled. *(The crespelle can be refrigerated in an airtight container for up to 2 days.)*

Mushroom Crespelle

SERVES 4

THIS RECIPE IS MUCH LIGHTER than Spinach Crespelle (page 280), since it contains no béchamel. Instead, the sautéed mushrooms are flavored with white wine and heavy cream, which also provide some moisture for the filling, and the filled crespelle are dusted with Parmesan and dotted with butter.

- **5 tablespoons unsalted butter**
- **1 medium onion, minced**
- **1¼ pounds white button mushrooms, wiped clean, stems trimmed, chopped**
- **Salt and freshly ground black pepper**
- **½ cup dry white wine**
- **2 tablespoons minced fresh parsley leaves**
- **¼ cup heavy cream**
- **¾ cup freshly grated Parmigiano-Reggiano cheese**
- **1 recipe Crespelle (page 276)**

1. Heat 2 tablespoons of the butter in a large skillet. Add the onion and sauté over medium heat until translucent, about 5 minutes. Add the mushrooms and raise the heat to medium-high. Cook, stirring often, until the liquid has evaporated and the mushrooms turn golden brown, about 8 minutes more.

2. Season the mushrooms with salt and pepper to taste. Add the wine and simmer until the alcohol aroma evaporates, about 2 minutes.

3. Stir in the parsley and cream. Simmer until the cream reduces and thickens, 1 to 2 minutes. Scrape the mixture into a medium bowl. Stir in ¼ cup of the cheese and adjust the seasonings.

4. Preheat the oven to 450 degrees F. Use 1 tablespoon butter to grease a 13-by-9-inch baking dish. Lay 1 crespelle on a work surface. Spread 2 tablespoons of the mushroom filling in a fairly thin line going almost from the top to the bottom, about 2 inches in from the left edge. Fold the left edge over the filling and roll up the crespelle. Place it, seam side down, in the baking dish. Repeat this process with the remaining crespelle and filling. The crespelle should fit in a single layer.

5. Sprinkle the remaining ½ cup cheese over the crespelle. Cut the remaining 2 tablespoons butter into small pieces and dot the crespelle with them.

6. Bake until golden brown, about 12 minutes. Remove from the oven and serve immediately.

Serving Suggestions

This dish makes a wonderful meal with a green vegetable and/or salad, such as Roasted Asparagus with Olive Oil (page 330), Swiss Chard with Raisins and Almonds (page 340), Mixed Greens with Tomatoes, Yellow Pepper and Fennel (page 377) or Tender Greens and Vegetables with Blood Orange Vinaigrette (page 376).

Spinach Crespelle

SERVES 4

SPINACH IS THE BASE FOR A SAVORY FILLING for these crespelle. They are covered with béchamel sauce and cheese and baked until golden.

1 large bunch flat-leaf spinach (about 1 pound)
Salt
5 tablespoons unsalted butter
1 medium onion, minced
1 cup Classic Béchamel (page 527) or Low-Fat Béchamel (page 528)
1 cup freshly grated Parmigiano-Reggiano cheese
1 recipe Crespelle (page 276)

1. Remove and discard the stems from the spinach. Wash the leaves in successive bowls of cold water until grit no longer appears in the bottom of the bowl. Shake the leaves to remove excess water but do not dry them.

2. Place the spinach leaves and salt to taste in a deep pot set over medium heat. Cook, stirring often, until the spinach is completely wilted and tender, about 5 minutes. Drain the spinach and cool it slightly. Press out any excess moisture. Finely chop the leaves.

3. Heat 3 tablespoons of the butter in a large skillet. Add the onion and sauté over medium heat until golden, about 6 minutes. Stir in the spinach and cook, stirring often, until it is well flavored with butter and onion, about 2 minutes.

4. Scrape the spinach into a large bowl. Stir in ½ cup of the béchamel and ½ cup of the cheese. Add salt to taste.

5. Preheat the oven to 450 degrees F. Use 1 tablespoon butter to grease a 13-by-9-inch baking dish. Lay 1 crespelle on a work surface. Spread 1 generous tablespoon of the spinach filling in a fairly thin line going almost from the top to the bottom, about 2 inches in from the left edge. Fold the left edge over the filling and roll up the crespelle. Place it, seam side down, in the baking dish. Repeat this process with the remaining crespelle and filling. The crespelle should fit in a single layer.

6. Spread the remaining ½ cup béchamel over the crespelle with the back of a spoon or a rubber spatula. Sprinkle the remaining ½ cup cheese over the béchamel. Cut the remaining 1 tablespoon butter into small pieces and dot the top with them.

7. Bake until golden brown, 12 to 15 minutes. Remove from the oven and allow to stand for a few minutes before serving. Serve hot.

SERVING SUGGESTIONS

Follow with something substantial but not creamy or buttery. You may want to serve a vegetable and then a salad to round out a special meal. Good choices include Sautéed Button Mushrooms with Garlic and Herbs (page 351) or Oven-Roasted Portobello Mushrooms (page 353), followed by Arugula Salad with Sliced Radishes and Carrots (page 371) or Fava Bean and Asparagus Salad with Basil Toasts (page 382).

Ricotta and Basil Crespelle

SERVES 4

HOMESTYLE RICOTTA, which has a creamy texture and a sweet, rich flavor, makes all the difference in the filling for these thin crepes. Since the filling is not cooked, this recipe is quick.

2 cups ricotta cheese, preferably homestyle
3 tablespoons unsalted butter
¾ cup freshly grated Parmigiano-Reggiano cheese
⅓ cup minced fresh basil leaves
¼ cup heavy cream
Salt and freshly ground black pepper
1 recipe Crespelle (page 276)

1. If using supermarket ricotta, line a colander or mesh sieve with several layers of paper towels. Spread the cheese over the towels and let drain until thickened and creamy, about 1 hour. Remove the cheese from the colander and discard the paper towels; they should be quite moist. (Homestyle ricotta does not need to be drained.)

2. Preheat the oven to 450 degrees F. Use 1 tablespoon of the butter to grease a 13-by-9-inch baking dish and set aside.

3. Combine the ricotta, ¼ cup of the Parmigiano-Reggiano, the basil, cream and salt and pepper to taste in a medium bowl.

4. Lay 1 crespelle on a work surface. Spread 2 tablespoons of the ricotta filling in a fairly thin line going almost from the top to the bottom, about 2 inches in from the left edge. Fold the left edge over the filling and roll up the crespelle. Place it, seam side down, in the baking dish. Repeat this process with the remaining crespelle and filling. The crespelle should fit in a single layer.

5. Sprinkle the remaining ½ cup Parmigiano-Reggiano over the crespelle. Cut the remaining 2 tablespoons butter into small pieces and dot the crespelle with them.

6. Bake until golden brown, about 12 minutes. Remove from the oven and serve immediately.

SERVING SUGGESTIONS

For a summer main course, serve this dish with a tomato salad, such as Marinated Tomato and Red Onion Salad (page 395) or Arugula, Tomato and Black Olive Salad (page 372). Sautéed Cherry Tomatoes with Garlic (page 362), made with mint instead of basil, also makes a good partner.

LEGUMES

BEANS ARE IMPORTANT in some regions of Italy, particularly in Tuscany, where the residents are mockingly referred to by other Italians as bean-eaters because of their fondness for cannellini beans. Such derision ignores the fact that beans are delicious and nutritious fare, perfect for the cold winters in the mountains and valleys of Tuscany.

While cannellini, or white kidney, beans are popular in the north, chickpeas are commonly used in southern Italy. Both kinds are best cooked from scratch. Canned versions are often mushy and usually very salty. They can be used in many of the recipes in this chapter, but the results will not be the same. (For more information, see page 284.)

Cooking your own beans is simple. Soak the beans for at least eight hours in several inches of water to cover. If you have forgotten to soak them overnight or all day, use the quick-soak method. Place the cleaned beans and water to cover in a large saucepan. Bring to a boil, reduce the heat to low and simmer for two minutes. Turn off the heat, cover the pan and set aside for one hour.

Whether you use the eight-hour soak or the quick-soak, drain the beans, then simmer them in fresh water with aromatics (bay leaves, garlic, sage leaves and sprigs of thyme are some of the possible choices). Have the water at a slow simmer to keep the bean skins from splitting. Because freshness among dried beans varies greatly, some batches are done in 40 minutes, while others might take an hour or more. Longer soaking will shorten the cooking time.

Whatever you do, add salt only when the beans are mostly cooked. If you put salt in at the start of cooking, it can prevent the beans from softening properly. Cool the beans right in their cooking liquid so that they continue to drink in the flavorful cooking liquid; the liquid also seems to prevent the skins from splitting. Pour the beans and liquid into airtight containers and refrigerate for several days. In some recipes, the cooking liquid is used in a sauce.

If you've made a large batch, freeze small portions of cooled beans and cooking liquid. They will keep for several months in the freezer. Defrost them on the counter or in a microwave set to medium power.

This chapter concludes with two recipes for legumes that do not require soaking. Dried split fava beans are a specialty item available in some Italian markets and gourmet stores. They have a unique buttery flavor and are well worth seeking out. Lentils, readily available in supermarkets, often cook in less than 30 minutes.

Buying and Using Canned Beans

I'M NOT A BIG FAN OF CANNED BEANS, which tend to be mushy and salty. Since I work at home, I find that canned beans really aren't much of a convenience. Soaking and cooking dried beans takes less than five minutes of hands-on work. They do, however, require some planning ahead.

If soaking and simmering don't fit with your lifestyle, be sure to shop carefully. I find that except for Green Giant, organic brands sold in natural-foods stores and some supermarkets are much firmer than most supermarket brands. I have had good luck with Eden and Westbrae. Organic brands are also remarkably less salty than all others, including Green Giant. While organic beans may not taste great straight from the can (they are bland), you can add your own seasonings. They are firm enough to withstand a little cooking. None, however, are sturdy enough to cook for any length of time.

If you like, use canned beans in any of the recipes in this chapter that call for cooked beans. You may want to shave several minutes off the cooking time to keep them from falling apart. Use Vegetable Stock (page 529) or water in place of any bean-cooking liquid called for in recipes. The packing liquid that surrounds canned beans is unusable and should be thoroughly rinsed off. Place the beans in a colander under gently running cold water before using them.

Legumes

Basic Cannellini Beans

MAKES 7½ CUPS

LARGE WHITE KIDNEY BEANS—CALLED CANNELLINI in Italy and increasingly in this country—are especially popular in Tuscany. Their creaminess makes them an excellent choice for main courses, side dishes and salads. Great Northern or navy beans, which are similar, may be substituted.

- **1 pound dried cannellini beans (2½ cups)**
- **3 large garlic cloves**
- **2 bay leaves**
- **Salt**

1. Pick through the beans to remove any stones or shriveled beans. Place the beans in a large bowl and add enough cold water to cover by several inches. Soak for at least 8 hours or overnight. Or bring the cleaned beans and water to cover to a boil in a large saucepan. Reduce the heat to low and simmer for 2 minutes, turn off the heat, cover and set aside for 1 hour.

2. Drain the beans and place them in a large saucepan with enough cold water to cover by several inches. Add the garlic and bay leaves and bring to a boil. Reduce the heat to low and simmer gently for 30 minutes.

3. Add salt to taste (at least 1 or 2 teaspoons) and continue cooking until the beans are still a little firm, tender but not falling apart, 5 to 30 minutes more, depending on the freshness of the beans and how long they were soaked. Turn off the heat and allow the beans to cool in their cooking liquid. *(The cooled beans and cooking liquid may be poured into a large airtight container and refrigerated for up to 3 days. Or divide the cooled beans and cooking liquid among several smaller airtight containers and freeze for up to several months. Thaw before using.)*

4. Drain the beans, discarding the bay leaves and garlic, and use in recipes or season as desired.

Summer White Bean Salad with Tomatoes, Basil and Olive Oil

SERVES 4

RIPE SUMMER TOMATOES, a little shredded fresh basil and a drizzle of fine extra-virgin olive oil transform basic white beans into a wonderful main course for a warm night. Cook the beans in the morning and refrigerate them in their cooking liquid all day. (This can also be done a day or two in advance.) At dinnertime, drain and add the remaining ingredients.

4 cups drained Basic Cannellini Beans (page 286)
3 medium, ripe tomatoes (about 1¼ pounds), cored and cut into ½-inch cubes
12 large fresh basil leaves, cut into thin strips
¼ cup extra-virgin olive oil, plus more for drizzling over the beans
Salt and freshly ground black pepper

1. Place the beans, tomatoes and basil in a large bowl. Drizzle with the ¼ cup oil and season with salt and pepper to taste.

2. Divide the bean mixture among large individual bowls. Drizzle with more oil to taste and serve immediately.

SERVING SUGGESTIONS

Make sure to serve some crusty bread to soak up the liquid, a flavorful combination of tomato juice, bean broth and olive oil. Serve with a leafy green salad. Good choices include Tender Green Salad with Pine Nuts and Yellow Raisins (page 375), Red Leaf Lettuce, Arugula and Fennel Salad (page 374) and Spinach Salad with Orange Juice Vinaigrette and Toasted Walnuts (page 380).

Cannellini Beans and Spicy Broccoli Rabe

SERVES 4

MILD CANNELLINI BEANS ARE A GOOD MATCH for the pungent flavors of broccoli rabe, garlic and hot red pepper flakes. Broccoli rabe is a nonheading variety of broccoli, but it tastes more like assertive leafy greens, such as collards or kale, than broccoli.

1 medium bunch broccoli rabe (about 1¼ pounds)
Salt
¼ cup extra-virgin olive oil
4 medium garlic cloves, minced
½ teaspoon dried hot red pepper flakes, plus more to taste
4 cups drained Basic Cannellini Beans (page 286)
Salt

1. Bring several quarts water to a boil in a large saucepan. Discard the tough, thick stems from the broccoli rabe. Tear large leaves in half and break large florets into pieces. Rinse the broccoli rabe under cold running water.

2. Add the broccoli rabe and salt to taste to the boiling water and cook until tender, about 3 minutes. Drain and set aside.

3. Heat the oil in a large sauté pan. Add the garlic and sauté over medium heat until golden, 1 to 2 minutes. Add the hot red pepper flakes and cook for 20 seconds.

4. Add the broccoli rabe and stir well to coat with the oil. Add the beans and cook, stirring several times, just until everything is heated through. Add salt to taste and more hot pepper if desired. Serve immediately.

SERVING SUGGESTIONS

This dish makes a good main course. Serve with bread to soak up the pan juices. The dish should be followed by something light and a little sweet, such as Roasted Fennel, Carrots and Red Onion (page 346) or Fennel and Orange Salad (page 389).

Cannellini Beans with Tomatoes, Sage and Garlic

SERVES 4

WINTERS IN TUSCANY are not particularly snowy, but they can be cold and damp. Hearty dishes like this help take off the chill from even the wettest day. Other beans, especially tiny navy beans, may be used instead of the cannellini.

- 2 tablespoons extra-virgin olive oil, plus more for the table
- 4 medium garlic cloves, minced
- 5 large fresh sage leaves, minced
- 1¼ cups crushed canned tomatoes
- 5 cups drained Basic Cannellini Beans (page 286), 1 cup cooking liquid reserved
- Salt and freshly ground black pepper

1. Heat the 2 tablespoons oil in a large sauté pan. Add the garlic and sauté over medium heat until golden, 1 to 2 minutes. Add the sage and cook for 30 seconds.

2. Add the tomatoes, beans and ½ cup of the bean-cooking liquid to the pan. Simmer gently until the sauce thickens and the flavors meld, about 10 minutes.

3. Add more bean-cooking liquid to thin the sauce if desired. The beans should be thick enough to eat with a fork but still moist enough that bread can be used to sop up the extra sauce. Season with salt and pepper to taste. Serve immediately with olive oil passed separately at the table.

SERVING SUGGESTIONS

This dish calls for some crusty country bread to soak up the sauce. Otherwise, a salad of bitter greens is all that is needed to round out the meal. Good choices include Arugula, Pine Nut and Parmesan Salad (page 370) and Radicchio, Arugula and Endive Salad with Balsamic Vinaigrette (page 373).

Cannellini Beans with Thyme and Sage

SERVES 6 TO 8

IN THIS DISH, the beans are flavored with onion, cloves, thyme and sage in addition to garlic and bay leaves as they cook. Top-quality olive oil and fresh herbs are added just before serving. Cannellini beans are traditional, but smaller navy beans will work too.

- 2½ cups dried cannellini beans or small white beans (1 pound)
- 1 small onion
- 2 whole cloves
- 4 medium garlic cloves, lightly smashed
- 2 bay leaves
- Several sprigs of fresh thyme, plus 2 tablespoons whole leaves for garnish
- Several sprigs of fresh sage, plus 6 whole leaves for garnish
- Salt
- ⅓ cup extra-virgin olive oil
- Freshly ground black pepper

1. Pick through the beans to remove any stones or shriveled beans. Place the beans in a large bowl and add enough cold water to cover by several inches. Soak for at least 8 hours or overnight. Or bring the cleaned beans and water to cover to a boil in a large saucepan. Reduce the heat to low and simmer for 2 minutes, turn off the heat, cover and set aside for 1 hour.

2. Drain the beans and place them in a large saucepan with enough cold water to cover by several inches. Peel the onion and cut in half. Stick 1 clove into each onion half and add to the pot. Add the garlic, bay leaves and sprigs of fresh thyme and sage.

3. Bring the beans to a boil. Reduce the heat to low and simmer gently for 30 minutes. Add 1½ teaspoons salt and continue cooking until the beans are quite tender but not mushy, 15 to 30 minutes more.

4. Drain the beans and discard the onion, garlic, bay leaves and herb sprigs. Place the beans in a large serving bowl and drizzle with oil. Add the whole thyme and sage leaves and pepper to taste. Toss gently and adjust the seasonings. The beans may be served hot, warm or at room temperature. *(The beans may be refrigerated for 2 days. Bring to room temperature before serving.)*

SERVING SUGGESTIONS

Serve the beans hot for supper with a salad and bread. Or serve them at room temperature as part of an antipasto spread or buffet meal. They go well with garden-ripe tomatoes drizzled with oil and balsamic vinegar.

Tuscan-Style Baked Cannellini Beans with Rosemary and Garlic

Serves 4

When I lived in Florence, I did as the locals did and ate a lot of beans. Baking them in a covered dish in slow oven heat allows them to soften without their skins puckering and separating. By the time they are done, the flavors of rosemary, garlic and olive oil will have penetrated deeply into the beans.

2½ cups dried cannellini beans or small white beans (1 pound)
¼ cup extra-virgin olive oil, plus more for the table
3 tablespoons fresh rosemary leaves
3 large garlic cloves, minced
Salt and freshly ground black pepper

1. Pick through the beans to remove any stones or shriveled beans. Place the beans in a large bowl and add enough cold water to cover by several inches. Soak for at least 8 hours or overnight. Or bring the cleaned beans and water to cover to a boil in a large saucepan. Reduce the heat to low and simmer for 2 minutes, turn off the heat, cover and set aside for 1 hour.

2. Preheat the oven to 375 degrees F. Drain the beans and place them in a large casserole dish with a lid. Add the ¼ cup oil, rosemary, garlic and enough cold water (about 1 cup) to just cover the beans.

3. Cover the casserole dish and bake, stirring once or twice, until the beans are tender, about 1½ hours. If the liquid in the casserole has been absorbed before they are tender, add more hot water as needed. When the beans are tender, a little creamy white sauce should have formed around them.

4. Season the beans with salt and pepper to taste and serve with more oil for drizzling at the table. *(Leftover beans can be refrigerated for 2 days and reheated in the microwave as is or on top of the stove with a little water added.)*

Serving Suggestions

Serve these beans as a main course with dense country white bread. Follow with a simple vegetable dish, such as Roasted Asparagus with Olive Oil (page 330), Gratinéed Asparagus with Parmesan (page 332), Roasted Fennel, Carrots and Red Onion (page 346) or Swiss Chard with Raisins and Almonds (page 340).

Mashed Borlotti Beans with Parmesan

SERVES 4 TO 6

A LITTLE SMALLER THAN CANNELLINI BEANS, borlotti beans are mottled with magenta and tan. When cooked, they turn a rich brown, and their flavor is warm and earthy, with chestnut undertones. Cranberry beans, another speckled red and white variety popular in Italy, can be used with similar results. Look for these beans in Italian markets or natural-food stores. Cannellini beans may be prepared in the same fashion, but their flavor is sweeter and not quite as intense. I don't mind little pieces of bean skin in the puree, so I mash the beans and potatoes by hand. The result is a rustic, homey puree. If you want a smoother puree, push the beans through the fine disk of a food mill. Do not puree them in the food processor, or they will be gummy.

10 ounces dried borlotti or cranberry beans (1½ cups)
3 medium garlic cloves
4 whole fresh sage leaves
2 bay leaves
1 large baking potato (about 10 ounces), peeled and cut into 1-inch chunks
2 tablespoons unsalted butter
½ cup freshly grated Parmigiano-Reggiano cheese
Salt and freshly ground black pepper

1. Pick through the beans to remove any stones or shriveled beans. Place the beans in a large bowl and add enough cold water to cover by several inches. Soak for at least 8 hours or overnight. Or bring the cleaned beans and water to cover to a boil in a large saucepan. Reduce the heat to low and simmer for 2 minutes, turn off the heat, cover and set aside for 1 hour.

2. Drain the beans and place them in a large saucepan with enough cold water to cover by several inches. Add the garlic, sage and bay leaves and bring to a boil. Reduce the heat to low and simmer gently for 35 minutes.

3. Add the potato and simmer until the beans and potato are quite tender, 20 to 30 minutes more. Drain well, discarding the bay and sage leaves.

4. Return the beans, potato and garlic to the pan and mash until fairly smooth. Beat in the butter and stir in the cheese. Season with salt and pepper to taste and serve immediately.

SERVING SUGGESTIONS

These beans make an intriguing alternative to mashed potatoes. Serve them as a side dish with a frittata. Or serve them with Roasted Fennel, Carrots and Red Onion (page 346) and a green salad.

Basic Chickpeas

MAKES ABOUT 6½ CUPS

WHILE CANNELLINI BEANS ARE THE PREFERRED LEGUME in northern Italy, southern Italians use chickpeas in many of their bean dishes. The soaking and simmering methods for both legumes are similar, although the cooking times for chickpeas seem to be much more variable, depending on their freshness. Chickpeas, especially those you cook yourself, have an earthy, almost nutty flavor that can tolerate more robust seasonings than the milder, sweeter white beans.

1 pound dried chickpeas (2½ cups)
3 large garlic cloves
2 bay leaves
Salt

1. Pick through the chickpeas to remove any stones or shriveled beans. Place the chickpeas in a large bowl and add enough cold water to cover by several inches. Soak for at least 8 hours or overnight. Or bring the cleaned chickpeas and water to cover to a boil in a large saucepan. Reduce the heat to low and simmer for 2 minutes, turn off the heat, cover and set aside for 1 hour.

2. Drain the chickpeas and place them in a large saucepan with enough cold water to cover by several inches. Add the garlic and bay leaves and bring to a boil. Reduce the heat to low and simmer until the chickpeas are still a little firm, tender but not falling apart, 35 to 60 minutes, depending on the freshness of the chickpeas and how long they were soaked.

3. Add salt to taste, turn off the heat and allow the chickpeas to cool in their cooking liquid. *(The cooled chickpeas and cooking liquid may be poured into a large airtight container and refrigerated for up to 3 days. Or divide the cooled beans and cooking liquid among several smaller airtight containers and freeze for up to several months. Thaw before using.)*

4. Drain the chickpeas, discarding the garlic and bay leaves, and use in recipes or season as desired.

Chickpea Salad with Sun-Dried Tomato Vinaigrette

SERVES 4 TO 6

PLAIN ARUGULA MAKES A NICE BED FOR THE SALAD, as does a mix of salad greens or mesclun. Although 30 minutes is enough time to allow some of the dressing to soak into the chickpeas in this colorful salad, they will taste even better after a few hours.

- 5 large sun-dried tomatoes packed in oil, drained
- 1 small garlic clove
- 1 tablespoon red wine vinegar
- ¼ cup extra-virgin olive oil
- Salt and freshly ground black pepper
- 3 cups drained Basic Chickpeas (page 293)
- 2 tablespoons minced fresh basil or parsley leaves

1. Place the sun-dried tomatoes, garlic and vinegar in the work bowl of a food processor. Process, scraping down the sides of the bowl as needed, until the ingredients are minced. Add the oil and process until smooth. Scrape the dressing into a large serving bowl. Stir in salt and pepper to taste.

2. Add the chickpeas and basil or parsley and toss to coat the chickpeas well with the dressing. Marinate at room temperature for at least 30 minutes or up to 3 hours. Adjust the seasonings and serve.

SERVING SUGGESTIONS

These beans can be eaten as a side dish with sandwiches or egg dishes, especially Bel Paese Sandwiches with Baby Spinach (page 466) and Frittata with Scallions and Ricotta Salata (page 251).

Sicilian Chickpeas with Escarole and Caramelized Onions

SERVES 4

WITH THEIR SLIGHT HINT OF BITTERNESS, tender escarole leaves can stand up to caramelized onions and creamy, nutty-tasting chickpeas. Dark raisins give this dish a Sicilian character. *See the photograph on page 205.*

- **1 large escarole head (about 1½ pounds)**
- **¼ cup extra-virgin olive oil**
- **2 medium onions, halved and thinly sliced**
- **2 teaspoons sugar**
- **¼ cup dark raisins**
- **Salt and freshly ground black pepper**
- **3 cups drained Basic Chickpeas (page 293), ⅓ cup cooking liquid reserved**

1. Discard any dry or tough outer leaves from the escarole. Trim and discard the core and any tough stems. Wash the leaves in a large bowl of cold water, changing the water several times until no sand appears in the bottom of the bowl. Tear the leaves into large pieces and set aside.

2. Heat the oil in a large sauté pan. Add the onions and cook, stirring often, over medium heat until golden, about 15 minutes. Stir in the sugar and continue cooking until the onions are golden brown, about 5 minutes. Do not let the onions burn; lower the heat if necessary.

3. Add the raisins and the escarole to the pan. Cook, turning the escarole occasionally, until the leaves are tender and the stem ends are just a little crunchy, about 6 minutes. Season with salt and pepper to taste.

4. Stir in the chickpeas and cooking liquid. Simmer, stirring occasionally, until the flavors have blended, about 3 minutes. Adjust the seasonings and serve immediately.

SERVING SUGGESTIONS

With greens and beans, this can be a one-dish meal. Follow with Fennel and Orange Salad (page 389) for a more elaborate southern Italian dinner.

Chickpeas Simmered with Tomatoes and Rosemary

SERVES 4

MANY ROMAN RESTAURANTS SERVE CHICKPEAS that have been simmered in a simple tomato sauce flavored with herbs and hot red pepper. Feel free to use thyme, oregano or marjoram instead of rosemary.

2 tablespoons extra-virgin olive oil
4 medium garlic cloves, minced
2 teaspoons minced fresh rosemary leaves
½ teaspoon dried hot red pepper flakes, or to taste
2 cups canned crushed tomatoes
Salt
1 recipe drained Basic Chickpeas (page 293)
2 tablespoons minced fresh parsley leaves

1. Heat the oil in a large saucepan. Add the garlic and sauté over medium heat until lightly colored, about 1 minute. Stir in the rosemary and hot red pepper flakes and cook for 30 seconds.

2. Add the tomatoes and salt to taste and simmer just until sauce thickens a bit, about 5 minutes. Stir in the chickpeas and parsley and simmer just until the flavors have blended, about 10 minutes. Adjust the seasonings and serve immediately.

SERVING SUGGESTIONS

Serve the chickpeas with crusty peasant bread to soak up the extra sauce and a leafy green salad, such as Red Leaf Lettuce, Arugula and Fennel Salad (page 374), Tender Greens and Vegetables with Blood Orange Vinaigrette (page 376) or Radicchio, Arugula and Endive with Balsamic Vinaigrette (page 373).

Spicy Lentils with Tomatoes and Aromatic Vegetables

SERVES 4 TO 6

THIS IS THE BASIC LENTIL DISH AT MY HOUSE. It's delicious and fast, since the lentils do not require any soaking. A jolt of cayenne gives this dish an edge. If you have fresh basil on hand, try it instead of the parsley.

- 2 tablespoons extra-virgin olive oil
- 1 medium onion, minced
- 1 medium carrot, peeled and minced
- 1 celery rib, minced
- 2 medium garlic cloves, minced
- 1½ cups drained canned whole tomatoes, chopped
- 1½ cups brown lentils (about 10 ounces)
- Pinch of cayenne
- 2 tablespoons minced fresh parsley leaves
- Salt

1. Heat the oil in a large saucepan. Add the onion, carrot and celery and sauté over medium heat until softened, about 10 minutes. Stir in the garlic and cook for 1 minute more until slightly softened.

2. Add the tomatoes, lentils, cayenne and 4 cups water. Bring to a boil, reduce the heat to low and simmer gently, stirring occasionally, until the lentils are tender and the liquid in the pan has evaporated, about 30 minutes.

3. Stir in the parsley and salt to taste and serve immediately. *(Leftover lentils can be refrigerated for several days and reheated as needed. You may need to add a little water when reheating them.)*

SERVING SUGGESTIONS

As a side dish, the lentils work well with most frittatas. Serve large portions of this dish as a simple main course, with bread and salad. Or mix the lentils with steamed white rice for an Italian-style rice-and-bean dinner or thin the lentils with stock or water and use them as a pasta sauce.

Mashed Fava Beans and Potatoes with Greens

SERVES 4

FOR THIS APULIAN DISH, dried split fava beans are mashed together with potatoes. If you use Yukon Gold potatoes, the favas will reinforce their pale yellow color. Choose yellow split favas that have already been peeled; they can be cooked like split peas or lentils without any soaking. They are available in Italian and Middle Eastern markets or see page 554 for a mail-order source.

Do not buy brown, puffy whole dried favas. They need to be soaked and peeled, which is a long, tedious process. Other bitter greens, such as chicory or dandelion or even milder chard or spinach, can be substituted for arugula. Use only the finest olive oil, preferably something very fruity.

8 ounces dried split fava beans (1½ cups)
2 medium Yukon Gold or baking potatoes (about 1 pound), peeled and cut into 1-inch cubes
¾ pound arugula or other bitter greens
¼ cup extra-virgin olive oil, plus more to taste
Salt

1. Place the fava beans in a large saucepan. Add 6 cups cold water and bring to a boil. Reduce the heat to low and simmer for 10 minutes. Add the potatoes and simmer until the favas and potatoes are tender and falling apart, about 25 minutes. If the pot starts to run dry before the beans and potatoes are fully cooked, add more water as needed. There should be just a little water, no more than ¼ cup in the pot, when the beans and potatoes are done.

2. Meanwhile, bring several quarts water to a boil in a medium saucepan. Remove and discard the stems from the arugula or other greens. Wash the arugula and shake off the excess water. Wash the leaves of other greens in successive bowls of cold water until grit no longer appears in the bottom of the bowl. Add the arugula or other greens to the boiling water and cook until tender, about 3 minutes for arugula, longer for other greens. Drain and cool. Chop the leaves and squeeze out as much liquid as possible.

3. When the potatoes and favas are cooked, mash them in the pot with any remaining cooking liquid. They should be smooth and fluffy and resemble mashed potatoes. Beat in 2 tablespoons of the oil and salt to taste. Stir in the cooked arugula or other greens and adjust the seasoning.

4. Divide the fava puree among large individual bowls. Drizzle ½ tablespoon oil over each portion and serve immediately, with more olive oil passed at the table if desired.

Serving Suggestions

Because it contains beans, potatoes and greens, this dish makes an excellent main course. Follow with an acidic, brightly colored salad, such as Fennel and Orange Salad (page 389) or Tomato Salad with Black Olives, Capers and Herbs (page 394).

VEGETABLE MAIN COURSES

ITALIANS LOOK AT VEGETABLE ENTRÉES as a way of celebrating seasonal ingredients. Why not turn a large tomato into a lunch with the addition of pesto and mozzarella or stuff red bell peppers with saffron risotto to make an elegant but light supper?

Italians employ a number of techniques to turn vegetables into main attractions. One tactic, popular throughout the Mediterranean, is to stuff them with filling like bread crumbs or rice and/or cheese. Many stuffed vegetables are served at room temperature, making them especially good for summer cooking. Tomatoes, eggplants, zucchini, artichokes and bell peppers are all sufficiently large and tasty to stuff. With the exception of artichokes, which require the addition of some liquid to cook the leaves, they are all juicy enough to keep a filling moist.

When stuffing a vegetable, don't go overboard—you don't want it to crack or explode because you pushed too much filling into it. In order to keep tomatoes, zucchini and other vegetables with a high water content from becoming watery or mushy during cooking, bake them uncovered with no added liquid.

Hearty lasagnelike casseroles can be made by layering several vegetables in a pan and baking them. Potatoes make a good base because they are substantial enough to satisfy hungry appetites and don't lose their shape in the oven. The layers can be alternated with tomatoes and sprinkled with herbs, olives or cheese.

A third method for turning vegetables into a main course is to combine enough of them so that the sheer abundance and selection satisfies even the most ardent meat eater. For example, meaty portobello mushrooms can anchor vegetable brochettes that are grilled and served with rice or another starch. Roasted root vegetables together with butternut squash, portobellos and endive are an equally flavorful meal.

A final all-vegetable option is a stew. Unlike meat stews, which improve with very long cooking or reheating, vegetable stews should be simmered only until the vegetables are tender and served soon after. Otherwise, their textures will be mushy, and their bright colors and flavors will fade.

Vegetable Main Courses

Baked Red Peppers Stuffed with Saffron Risotto

SERVES 6

THIS ELEGANT AND BEAUTIFUL DISH is easy to prepare and makes an impressive vegetarian main course suitable for entertaining. The risotto can be prepared a few hours in advance, stuffed into red bell peppers and baked just before serving. *See the photograph on page 202.*

- **6 medium red bell peppers (each about 6 ounces)**
- **1 tablespoon unsalted butter**
- **1 recipe Saffron Risotto (page 150)**
- **¼ cup freshly grated Parmigiano-Reggiano cheese**

1. Preheat the oven to 400 degrees F. Cut off and discard a ½-inch-thick slice from the top of each pepper, which should include the stem and most of the seeds. Scrape out any remaining seeds and white pith from the inside of each pepper.

2. Smear the butter over a baking dish large enough to hold the peppers in a single layer. Place the peppers in the dish, cut side up. Mound a portion of risotto into each pepper. Sprinkle with cheese.

3. Bake until the peppers are tender and the risotto has turned golden brown in spots, about 40 minutes. Serve immediately.

SERVING SUGGESTIONS

Follow this dish with a green vegetable, such as Artichokes Braised in White Wine with Garlic and Parsley (page 328) or Roasted Asparagus with Olive Oil (page 330) and/or a leafy green salad, such as Radicchio, Arugula and Endive Salad with Balsamic Vinaigrette (page 373) or Tender Green Salad with Pine Nuts and Yellow Raisins (page 375).

Roman-Style Stuffed Artichokes with Garlic and Mint

SERVES 4

THIS ELEGANT MAIN COURSE is popular in trattorias in Rome. The artichokes may be served warm but are just as good at room temperature. Let your guests know that the entire artichoke is edible when prepared in this fashion.

- **1 lemon, halved**
- **4 large artichokes (each about ¾ pound)**
- **6 tablespoons plain bread crumbs**
- **6 medium garlic cloves, minced**
- **¼ cup minced fresh mint leaves**
- **¼ cup minced fresh parsley leaves, with stems reserved**
- **6 tablespoons extra-virgin olive oil**
- **¾ teaspoon salt**

1. Squeeze the lemon halves into a large bowl of cold water and add the lemon to the bowl. Working with 1 artichoke at a time, bend back and snap off the tough outer leaves. Remove several layers until you reach the leaves that are mostly pale green or yellow except for the tips. With a sharp knife, slice off the dark green pointed tip of the artichoke. Trim the end of the stem and use a vegetable peeler to peel the outer layer. Use the peeler to remove any dark green leaf bases that may surround the top of the stem. Gently spread apart the outer leaves and use a grapefruit knife or small spoon to loosen and remove the spiky inner leaves and the fuzzy choke. Rinse the artichoke under cold running water to flush out any remaining choke hairs and drop it into the bowl of cold lemon water. Repeat with the remaining artichokes. Set aside.

2. Combine the bread crumbs, garlic, mint, parsley leaves, 4 tablespoons of the oil and salt in a small bowl and mix well. Taste and adjust the seasonings.

3. Drain the artichokes, reserving the lemon halves. Gently spread apart the outer leaves and fill each artichoke with about ¼ cup stuffing. Place the stuffed artichokes on their sides in a deep pot that is just wide enough to hold all of them in a single layer. Add the lemon halves and the reserved parsley stems. Pour in enough water so that most of the stem on each artichoke is submerged and the water level is just below the cavity that holds the stuffing. Drizzle the remaining 2 tablespoons oil over the artichokes.

4. Bring to a boil. Lower the heat, cover and simmer, turning the artichokes once, until they are tender but still a bit firm, 35 to 40 minutes. To check for doneness, slide a knife into the artichoke heart. It should meet with just a little resistance.

5. Use a slotted spoon to transfer the artichokes to a shallow platter or individual bowls. Remove and discard the lemon halves and parsley stalks. Simmer the liquid in the pot for a few minutes, or until thickened. Pour the sauce over the artichokes and serve immediately or at room temperature. *(The artichokes and sauce can be covered and kept at room temperature for several hours.)*

SERVING SUGGESTIONS

This main course must be served with plenty of bread to sop up the extra sauce. Finish off with a substantial salad that has a sweet element, such as Tender Greens and Vegetables with Blood Orange Vinaigrette (page 376) or Roasted Beet Salad with Watercress, Walnuts and Fresh Pecorino (page 384).

Eggplant Stuffed with Bread Crumbs, Olives, Lemon and Herbs

SERVES 4

EGGPLANT MAKES A GOOD MAIN COURSE, especially during the summer when it is so plentiful and inexpensive. Many recipes start by removing the flesh and then combining it with flavorful ingredients. Here, the eggplant is slashed and a well-seasoned bread-crumb mixture is stuffed into it. The remaining stuffing is patted over the surface—altogether much easier than other versions.

- 2 large eggplants (about 2 pounds)
- Salt and freshly ground black pepper
- 1 cup plain bread crumbs
- 4 medium garlic cloves, minced
- 1 teaspoon grated zest and 3 tablespoons juice from 1 large lemon
- ¼ cup minced fresh parsley leaves
- 2 teaspoons minced fresh thyme or oregano leaves
- 20 large green olives, pitted and minced
- 2 teaspoons minced drained and rinsed capers
- 2-3 tablespoons extra-virgin olive oil

1. Preheat the oven to 400 degrees F. Trim the green tops from the eggplants. Cut the eggplants in half lengthwise. Use a small, sharp knife to make deep slashes across the flesh of each half, starting about ½ inch in from 1 side and ending about ½ inch from the other side. Make the slashes fairly deep but do not puncture the skin. Make another slash down the center from the stem end almost to the base. Sprinkle with salt and pepper to taste and set aside.

2. Combine the bread crumbs, garlic, lemon zest and juice, parsley, thyme or oregano, olives and capers in a small bowl. Add as much of the oil as needed to work the mixture into a wet paste with your hands.

3. Use your fingers to open the slashes in the eggplants and fill them with the stuffing. Pat the remaining stuffing over the eggplants to cover them completely. Place the stuffed eggplants on a large baking sheet.

4. Bake until the eggplants are tender and the bread-crumb mixture is golden brown, about 45 minutes. Serve hot or warm.

SERVING SUGGESTIONS

This dish calls for a tomato salad, such as Marinated Tomato and Red Onion Salad (page 395). Together, these two dishes make a light but satisfying meal.

Zucchini Stuffed with Ricotta and Herbs

SERVES 4

HOLLOWED-OUT ZUCCHINI SHELLS are a good vehicle for a creamy filling made with ricotta cheese. The light sprinkling of bread crumbs on top absorbs excess moisture and gives this dish a pleasant crunch. Although Parmesan will work fine, I prefer the sharper taste of Pecorino with the mild ricotta.

- 4 medium-large zucchini (about 2 pounds), scrubbed
- Salt
- 3 tablespoons extra-virgin olive oil
- 1 medium onion, minced
- 2 medium garlic cloves, minced
- 1 cup ricotta cheese, homestyle or supermarket
- ¼ cup freshly grated Pecorino Romano cheese
- 2 teaspoons minced fresh thyme or oregano leaves
- 1 large egg, lightly beaten
- Freshly ground black pepper
- 3 tablespoons plain bread crumbs

1. Bring several quarts water to a boil in a large saucepan. Add the zucchini and salt to taste and simmer until the zucchini offer just a little resistance when pierced with a skewer, about 6 minutes. Drain the zucchini and cool to room temperature. Trim the ends and slice the zucchini in half lengthwise. Scoop out the seeds and some of the surrounding flesh, taking care not to puncture the skin. The hollowed-out zucchini should still be about ½ inch thick in most places.

2. Preheat the oven to 375 degrees F. Heat 2 tablespoons of the oil in a small skillet. Add the onion and sauté over medium heat until translucent, about 5 minutes. Stir in the garlic and cook until golden, about 2 minutes.

3. Scrape the onion mixture into a large bowl. Stir in the ricotta and Pecorino cheeses, thyme or oregano, egg and salt and pepper to taste. Divide the filling among the hollowed-out zucchini.

4. Use the remaining 1 tablespoon oil to lightly grease a baking dish large enough to hold the zucchini in a single layer. Arrange the zucchini in the dish and sprinkle the bread crumbs over the filling.

5. Bake until the filling is golden, 45 to 50 minutes. Serve hot or warm. *(The zucchini can be covered and kept at room temperature for a few hours. Reheat just prior to serving.)*

Serving Suggestions

This dish is good for summer, since it can be served warm or made several hours in advance and reheated as needed. Serve something acidic after it, either Tomato Salad with Black Olives, Capers and Herbs (page 394) or Marinated Tomato and Red Onion Salad (page 395). A leafy green salad and a loaf of bread or some Bruschetta with Fresh Herbs (page 477) can round out the meal.

Baked Tomatoes Stuffed with Bread Crumbs, Parmesan and Herbs

SERVES 4

LARGE SUMMER TOMATOES can be stuffed with many different kinds of ingredients for a light main course. Here, the filling consists of bread crumbs, Parmesan cheese, garlic, parsley and basil. Be sure to choose tomatoes that are ripe but still firm for stuffing. Soft tomatoes will be difficult to hollow out and may fall apart in the oven. A demitasse spoon or baby spoon is the best tool for seeding the tomatoes. You may also gently squeeze the tomatoes to bring some of the seeds and surrounding liquid to the surface, but do not let the tomatoes lose their shape.

- 4 large, ripe but firm tomatoes (about 2 pounds)
- 1 cup plain bread crumbs
- 1 cup freshly grated Parmigiano-Reggiano cheese
- 6 tablespoons minced fresh parsley leaves
- 3 tablespoons minced fresh basil leaves
- 2 medium garlic cloves, minced
- 5 tablespoons extra-virgin olive oil
- ¾ teaspoon salt
- Freshly ground black pepper

1. Preheat the oven to 375 degrees F. Cut off and discard a ½-inch-thick slice from the top of each tomato. Use a small spoon to scoop out and discard any remaining parts of the core as well as the seeds. Reach down into the tomatoes to pull up as much liquid matter as possible. Be careful not to puncture the skin as you work. Set aside.

2. Combine the bread crumbs, cheese, parsley, basil, garlic, 3 tablespoons of the oil, the salt and pepper to taste in a small bowl. Use your fingers or a small spoon to stuff the tomatoes with this mixture, making sure that the filling reaches into all the hollowed-out areas. Mound the filling a little above the top of each tomato and pat the filling gently to compact it.

3. Use ½ tablespoon oil to lightly grease a baking dish just large enough to hold the tomatoes in a single layer. Place the tomatoes in the dish. Drizzle the remaining 1½ tablespoons oil over the tomatoes.

4. Bake until the stuffing turns golden brown and the tomatoes are soft but not falling apart, 25 to 30 minutes. Allow the tomatoes to cool for at least 15 minutes. Serve warm or at room temperature. *(The tomatoes can be kept at room temperature for several hours.)*

Serving Suggestions

These tomatoes make an especially good main course in summer. Finish the meal with a leafy green salad, such as Red Leaf Lettuce, Arugula and Fennel Salad (page 374) or Spinach Salad with Orange Juice Vinaigrette and Toasted Walnuts (page 380). For a more substantial meal, start with a bowl of chilled soup, such as Chilled Potato and Zucchini Soup with Fresh Tomato Garnish (page 55), and end with a leafy salad.

Baked Tomatoes Stuffed with Rice and Mozzarella

SERVES 4

LIKE OTHER BAKED-TOMATO RECIPES, this one can be prepared several hours in advance of serving. Although I prefer Arborio rice in this recipe (it retains some chew even after boiling and baking), regular long-grain can be used as well. The boiling time for long-grain will be several minutes less, and the rice will be much softer after baking.

- ½ cup Arborio rice
- Salt
- 4 large, ripe but firm tomatoes (about 2 pounds)
- 4 ounces mozzarella cheese, shredded (about 1 cup)
- 10 large black olives, pitted and chopped
- ¼ cup minced fresh parsley leaves
- 2 medium garlic cloves, minced
- 2 tablespoons extra-virgin olive oil
- Freshly ground black pepper

1. Bring 1 quart water to a boil in a medium saucepan. Add the rice and salt to taste and simmer until al dente, 15 to 17 minutes. Drain and place the rice in a large bowl. Cool to room temperature.

2. Preheat the oven to 375 degrees F. Cut off and discard a ½-inch-thick slice from the top of each tomato. Use a small spoon to scoop out and discard any remaining parts of the core as well as the seeds. Reach down into the tomatoes to pull up as much liquid matter as possible. Be careful not to puncture the skin as you work. Set aside.

3. Add the cheese, olives, parsley, garlic and 1½ tablespoons of the oil to the cooled rice. Mix well and add salt and pepper to taste. Use your fingers or a small spoon to stuff the tomatoes with the rice mixture, making sure that the filling reaches into all the hollowed-out areas. Mound the filling a little above the top of each tomato and pat the filling gently to compact it.

4. Use the remaining ½ tablespoon oil to lightly grease a baking dish just large enough to hold the tomatoes in a single layer. Place the tomatoes in the dish.

5. Bake until the tomatoes are soft but not falling apart and the top layer of rice has become a little crisp, 25 to 30 minutes. Allow the tomatoes to cool for at least 15 minutes. Serve warm or at room temperature. *(The tomatoes can be kept at room temperature for several hours.)*

SERVING SUGGESTIONS

Serve these tomatoes on a bed of lightly dressed baby arugula or spinach. A marinated vegetable salad, such as Marinated Cauliflower Salad with Olives (page 388) or Marinated Zucchini Salad with Lemon and Thyme (page 396), can complete this meal. For a more substantial dinner, start with a first course of pizza or bruschetta, such as a Pesto Pizza (page 432) or Bruschetta with Grilled Portobello Mushrooms (page 482).

Baked Tomatoes Stuffed with Pesto and Mozzarella

SERVES 4

THIS STUFFED-TOMATO RECIPE IS VERY SIMPLE. Pesto is used to flavor shredded mozzarella, and bread crumbs are added to absorb excess moisture.

- **4 large, ripe but firm tomatoes (about 2 pounds)**
- **½ cup Pesto, My Way (page 531)**
- **5 ounces mozzarella cheese, shredded (about 1¼ cups)**
- **⅓ cup plain bread crumbs**
- **Salt and freshly ground black pepper**

1. Preheat the oven to 375 degrees F. Cut off and discard a ½-inch-thick slice from the top of each tomato. Use a small spoon to scoop out and discard any remaining parts of the core as well as the seeds. Reach down into the tomatoes to pull up as much liquid matter as possible. Be careful not to puncture the skin as you work. Set aside.

2. Combine the pesto, cheese, bread crumbs and salt and pepper to taste in a small bowl until well mixed. Taste and adjust the seasonings. Use your fingers or a small spoon to stuff the tomatoes with the pesto-mozzarella mixture, making sure that the filling reaches into all the hollowed-out areas. Mound the filling a little above the top of each tomato and pat the filling gently to compact it. Place the tomatoes in a lightly greased baking dish just large enough to hold them.

3. Bake until the tomatoes are soft but not falling apart and the cheese is bubbling and turning golden brown in spots, 25 to 30 minutes. Allow the tomatoes to cool for at least 15 minutes. Serve warm or at room temperature. *(The tomatoes can be kept at room temperature for several hours.)*

SERVING SUGGESTIONS

These tomatoes may be served as an all-in-one summer luncheon or a light dinner. Add a salad, such as Red Leaf Lettuce, Arugula and Fennel Salad (page 374) or Wilted Spinach Salad with Polenta Croutons (page 379), to complete the meal.

Baked Potato Casserole with Tomatoes and Mozzarella

SERVES 4 TO 6

IN THIS CASSEROLE, THE POTATOES are layered with mozzarella cheese and plum tomatoes. Slicing the potatoes no thicker than ⅛ inch is essential. A sharp chef's knife will do the job, although a mandoline or the slicing blade of a food processor will get the potatoes even thinner.

- **¼ cup extra-virgin olive oil**
- **1 tablespoon minced fresh rosemary leaves**
- **1 teaspoon salt**
- **Freshly ground black pepper**
- **3 large baking potatoes (about 2 pounds), scrubbed and sliced crosswise into ⅛-inch-thick rounds**
- **6 ounces mozzarella cheese, shredded (about 1½ cups)**
- **6 medium plum tomatoes (about 1¼ pounds), peeled, cored, seeded and diced**

1. Preheat the oven to 400 degrees F. Brush 1 tablespoon of the oil over a 13-by-9-inch baking dish. Set aside.

2. Combine the remaining 3 tablespoons oil with the rosemary, salt and pepper to taste in a small bowl. Place the potatoes in a large bowl. Drizzle the rosemary mixture over the potatoes and toss gently with your hands to coat them evenly.

3. Line the bottom of the baking dish with one third of the potatoes, overlapping the slices slightly. Sprinkle half the mozzarella over the potatoes and half of the tomatoes over the cheese. Repeat the layering of potatoes, cheese and tomatoes one more time. Use the remaining potatoes to make a third and final layer. *(The casserole may be covered tightly and refrigerated overnight. Bring to room temperature before baking.)*

4. Bake until the top layer of potatoes is golden brown, about 1 hour. Cool for 5 minutes and serve hot.

SERVING SUGGESTIONS

Serve the casserole with a green salad, such as Spinach Salad with Orange Juice Vinaigrette and Toasted Walnuts (page 380) or Tender Greens and Vegetables with Blood Orange Vinaigrette (page 376). It can be followed by a green vegetable, such as Spicy Broccoli with Garlic (page 334) or Wilted Spinach with Garlic (page 360).

Potato and Tomato Casserole with Olives and Herbs

SERVES 6

THIS CASSEROLE comes from southern Italy. It's like a vegetable lasagne. Slices of potato and tomato are layered with chopped black olives and a pungent herb paste. The flavors meld in the oven.

- **½ cup fresh basil leaves**
- **¼ cup fresh oregano leaves**
- **¼ cup fresh mint leaves**
- **3 large garlic cloves**
- **¼ cup extra-virgin olive oil**
- **1½ teaspoons salt**
- **¼ teaspoon freshly ground black pepper**
- **½ cup plain bread crumbs**
- **4 medium baking potatoes (about 2 pounds), peeled and sliced crosswise into ¼-inch-thick rounds**
- **10 large black olives, pitted and chopped**
- **6 small, ripe but firm tomatoes (about 1½ pounds), cored and sliced crosswise into ⅛-inch-thick rounds**

1. Preheat the oven to 400 degrees F. Place the herbs and garlic in the work bowl of a food processor or blender. Pulse, scraping down the sides of the bowl as needed, until the ingredients are finely chopped. With the motor running, slowly add 2 tablespoons of the oil to form a thick paste. Scrape the herb paste into a small bowl and stir in the salt and pepper.

2. Place the bread crumbs in a small bowl and drizzle 1 tablespoon oil over them. Mix just until the crumbs are moistened.

3. Brush a 13-by-9-inch baking dish with the remaining 1 tablespoon oil. Cover the bottom of the pan with one half of the potatoes, overlapping the slices slightly. Sprinkle half the olives over the potatoes. Cover with a layer of half of the tomato slices and then dot each tomato with a tiny bit of the herb paste. Repeat the layering of potatoes, olives, tomatoes and herb paste. Sprinkle the crumbs over the top.

4. Cover the pan with aluminum foil and bake for 40 minutes. Remove the foil and bake until the juices are bubbling and the bread crumbs are lightly browned, about 25 minutes more.

5. Let the casserole cool on a rack for 10 minutes so the layers solidify. Cut into squares and serve immediately.

SERVING SUGGESTIONS

Serve with a loaf of crusty bread and simple salad, such as Tender Green Salad with Pine Nuts and Yellow Raisins (page 375). The raisins and nuts echo the southern Italian theme.

Mixed Roasted Vegetables with Rosemary and Garlic

SERVES 4

THIS MEDLEY OF ROASTED VEGETABLES makes a splendid main course for winter. To allow for their different cooking times, the vegetables are cooked in stages, butternut squash and new potatoes first, followed by the onions, mushrooms and endive.

- 1 small butternut squash (about 1½ pounds), halved lengthwise, stringy pulp and seeds discarded, peeled and cut into 1½-inch chunks
- 4 medium red new potatoes (about ¾ pound), scrubbed and quartered
- 2 medium red onions (about ¾ pound), cut through root ends into 8 wedges
- 2 medium portobello mushrooms (about 8 ounces), stems discarded, caps wiped clean and sliced into 1-inch-wide strips
- 1 medium belgian endive, quartered lengthwise
- ⅓ cup extra-virgin olive oil
- 6 medium garlic cloves, minced
- 1 tablespoon minced fresh rosemary leaves
- Salt and freshly ground black pepper

1. Preheat the oven to 450 degrees F. Place the squash and potatoes in a large roasting pan. Place the onions, mushrooms and endive in a second large roasting pan. The vegetables should fit in each pan in a single layer without crowding.

2. Combine the oil, garlic, rosemary and salt and pepper to taste in a small bowl. Drizzle this mixture over the vegetables in both pans, turning to coat them well.

3. Place the pan with the squash and potatoes in the oven and roast, turning once, for 30 minutes. Place the second pan in the oven and roast, turning at least once, until tender and golden brown, about 30 minutes longer. (If the squash and potatoes seem to be ready before the other vegetables, remove the pan from the oven and cover with foil to keep warm.) Adjust the seasonings and serve immediately.

SERVING SUGGESTIONS Serve these vegetables as is, followed by a large green salad, such as Arugula, Pine Nut and Parmesan Salad (page 370), Red Leaf Lettuce, Arugula and Fennel Salad (page 374) or Spinach Salad with Orange Juice Vinaigrette and Toasted Walnuts (page 380). You may also serve the vegetables over Basic Soft Polenta (page 181) for a more substantial meal. Or serve the vegetables as side dish for a large party of six or more, perhaps with Three-Cheese Pizza (page 439) or Frittata with Ricotta and Mint (page 261).

Grilled Portobello Mushrooms, Red Onions and Bell Peppers

Serves 4

If you don't have metal skewers, wooden ones are fine, but remember that they must be soaked in cold water for about 30 minutes before using on the grill. Wear an oven mitt or use a pair of long tongs to turn the skewers. Squeeze grilled lemon wedges over the brochettes at the table.

- **¼ cup extra-virgin olive oil**
- **2 tablespoons lemon juice, plus 1 lemon cut into 8 wedges**
- **2 medium garlic cloves, minced**
- **1 tablespoon minced fresh mint leaves**
- **1 tablespoon minced fresh oregano leaves**
- **Salt and freshly ground black pepper**
- **4 medium portobello mushrooms (about 1 pound)**
- **4 small red onions (about 1¼ pounds)**
- **2 large red bell peppers (about 1 pound)**

1. Whisk together the oil, lemon juice, garlic, mint, oregano and salt and pepper to taste in a small bowl. Set aside.

2. Remove and discard the stems from the mushrooms. With a towel, wipe any dirt from the caps. Cut them into 1-inch chunks. Peel the onions and cut them lengthwise into ¾-inch-thick pieces. Trim the top and bottom from the peppers and cut them in half lengthwise. Lightly press each half with the back of a knife so that it lies flat on the cutting board. Slide a knife along the inside of each half to cut away the white pith, seeds and top layer of translucent flesh. Cut the cleaned halves into 1-inch-wide lengthwise strips.

3. Thread the mushroom, onion and pepper pieces alternately on 8 skewers. Thread a lemon wedge on the end of each skewer. Place the skewers in a deep baking dish and brush with the oil mixture. Marinate at room temperature for about 30 minutes.

4. Light the grill or make a charcoal fire. Place the skewers on the rack and brush with any marinade left in the baking dish. Grill, turning the skewers once or twice, until the vegetables are marked with dark stripes, about 10 minutes. Remove from the grill and serve.

SERVING SUGGESTIONS

Serve with Boiled Arborio Rice with Mozzarella and Herbs (page 173) or Panzanella (page 399).

Spring Vegetable Stew with Fennel, Carrots, Asparagus and Peas

SERVES 4

THIS STEW IS THE PERFECT WAY TO CELEBRATE the arrival of spring. The vegetables are added at different times, since some need longer to cook than others, and the light orange-red broth thickens as they soften. A small amount of butter is beaten into the stew at the end to thicken the sauce even further. I find this method preferable to using flour or cornstarch, both of which weigh down delicate stews.

- 1 medium fennel bulb (about 1¼ pounds)
- 2 tablespoons extra-virgin olive oil
- 3 medium shallots, minced
- 5 medium plum tomatoes (about 1 pound), peeled, cored, seeded and diced
- Salt and freshly ground black pepper
- 3 cups Vegetable Stock (page 529) or water
- 25 baby carrots, peeled (about 5 ounces)
- 1 pound medium asparagus, tough ends snapped off, cut on the bias into 1½-inch pieces
- 1 cup fresh or frozen peas, thawed
- 2 tablespoons unsalted butter
- Freshly grated Parmigiano-Reggiano cheese

1. Trim the stems and fronds from the fennel. Discard the stems. Mince 1 tablespoon of the fronds and set aside. Trim a thin slice from the base of the bulb and remove any tough or blemished outer layers. Cut the bulb in half through the base and use a small, sharp knife to remove the triangular piece of the core from each half. With the flat side of the fennel bulb down and your knife parallel to the work surface, slice each fennel half crosswise to yield several ½-inch-thick slices. Cut the slices lengthwise to yield long strips about ¼ inch thick.

2. Heat the oil in a large saucepan. Add the shallots and sauté over medium heat until golden, about 3 minutes. Add the tomatoes and salt and pepper to taste and simmer just until the tomatoes soften, about 5 minutes.

3. Add the fennel strips and cook, stirring often, until softened slightly, about 10 minutes. If the fennel starts to stick or burn, lower the heat.

4. Add the stock or water and bring to a boil. Add the carrots and simmer for 15 minutes. Add the asparagus and fresh peas, if using, and simmer for 10 minutes more.

5. Stir in the reserved fennel fronds and thawed frozen peas, if using, and cook for 1 to 2 minutes more. Add the butter and stir vigorously until it melts and the sauce thickens a bit, about 1 minute. Adjust the seasonings.

6. Ladle the stew into shallow bowls. Serve immediately with grated cheese passed separately at the table.

Serving Suggestions

This stew is a meal in itself. Serve it with crusty bread or Bruschetta with Fresh Herbs (page 477) to soak up the juices or, for a heartier meal, ladle the stew over Garlic Mashed Potatoes with Rosemary and Olive Oil (page 355), Mashed Potatoes with Oven-Dried Tomatoes (page 356) or Basic Soft Polenta (page 181).

VEGETABLE SIDE DISHES

THE VEGETABLE COURSE IS CALLED *contorno* in Italian, literally translated as "contour." By reminding us of the season and its flavors, vegetables give shape to a meal. A few roasted asparagus in spring, grilled eggplants in summer or some braised fennel in the winter round out a dinner.

The flavors in a contorno should not be too aggressive; they should complement the vegetable, not overwhelm it. For this reason, Italians are more likely to mash their potatoes with a little olive oil than a stick of butter and a cup of cream, which add undeniable richness but also obscure the natural potato taste. Likewise, they might toss asparagus with olive oil and roast it in a hot oven to intensify its flavor, rather than drowning it in a heavy sauce like hollandaise.

Because you are relying on the taste of the vegetables themselves, they should be at the peak of freshness. Buying those that are in season is key. Choosing the proper cooking technique to show the vegetable at its best is also important.

Braising—cooking in a covered pan with a small amount of liquid—is a preferred method for hard vegetables like artichokes or fennel that can withstand long, gentle heat. As the vegetable cooks in the covered pan, it absorbs the flavors of the braising liquid. Canned tomatoes packed in juice, wine and vegetable stock all make good liquids for braising.

Two quicker cooking methods that also add moisture are boiling and steaming. These methods are generally interchangeable, although I prefer to steam vegetables like green beans that are easily overcooked. Both techniques are fast (broccoli, peas and cauliflower can be ready in minutes), but neither adds flavor.

One way to supply flavor is to dress cooked vegetables as soon as they are drained. For instance, you might toss boiled cauliflower with a pungent green herb sauce (see page 338), or sprinkle asparagus with lemon-shallot vinaigrette or drizzle green beans with olive oil and tarragon. Another way to add flavor is to sauté partially cooked vegetables in a seasoned oil. Broccoli sautéed in olive oil infused with garlic and hot red pepper flakes (page 334) is a good example of this technique.

WHILE BRAISING, BOILING AND STEAMING all require liquid as a cooking medium, other cooking techniques rely on dry heat. By cooking off the excess liquid in the vegetables, roasting, grilling and sautéing concentrate flavors. All three methods rely on high heat to caramelize the vegetables' natural sugars, highlighting sweetness. Quick-cooking vegetables like mushrooms and zucchini, which have a high moisture content, respond best to grilling and sautéing. Denser root vegetables like beets, carrots, potatoes and squash take especially well to roasting.

In Italy, vegetable side dishes are traditionally served with the second course—a plate of crisp-roasted potatoes, slow-browned carrots or spicy wilted spinach accompanying meat, poultry or fish. In a vegetarian meal, side dishes function somewhat differently. If eggs are the main course, I generally serve the vegetables on the same plate. With rice or pasta, on the other hand, I often offer vegetables after the main course, in place of (or before) salad. Follow your own instincts, but consider how things will work together on the plate when you plan a vegetarian meal.

Vegetable Side Dishes

Artichokes Braised in White Wine with Garlic and Parsley

SERVES 4

ACCORDING TO SOME EXPERTS, artichokes clash with white wine. However, when simmered slowly in a covered pan, the artichoke quarters absorb the flavors of the wine, and the result is a harmonious marriage of tender vegetable and good wine. Choose a fairly light, not overly oaky wine, perhaps a sauvignon blanc or pinot grigio.

- **1 lemon, halved**
- **3 large artichokes (about 2 pounds)**
- **3 tablespoons extra-virgin olive oil**
- **3 medium garlic cloves, minced**
- **¾ teaspoon salt**
- **1⅓ cups dry white wine**
- **2 tablespoons minced fresh parsley leaves**

1. Squeeze the lemon halves into a large bowl of cold water and add the lemon to the bowl. Working with 1 artichoke at a time, bend back and snap off the tough outer leaves. Remove several layers until you reach the leaves that are mostly pale green or yellow except for the tips. With a sharp knife, slice off the dark green pointed tip of the artichoke. Trim the end of the stem and use a vegetable peeler to peel the outer layer. Use the peeler to remove any dark green leaf bases that may surround the top of the stem. Quarter the artichoke lengthwise, leaving a part of the stem attached to each piece. Slide a small, sharp knife under the fuzzy choke and cut toward the leaf tips to remove it. Drop the cleaned quarters into the bowl of cold lemon water. Repeat with the remaining artichokes. Set aside.

2. Heat the oil in a large sauté pan. Add the garlic and sauté over medium heat until golden, about 2 minutes. Drain the artichokes and add them to the pan along with 1 lemon half. (Discard the other lemon half.) Sprinkle the salt over the artichokes and stir to coat them with the oil.

3. Add the wine and bring to a boil. Reduce the heat, cover and simmer, turning the artichokes occasionally, until they are quite tender, 35 to 40 minutes. There should be a few tablespoons of liquid still left in the pan. Stir in the parsley and adjust the seasonings. Serve immediately.

Serving Suggestions

Serve the artichokes with Lemon Risotto (page 162), Sun-Dried Tomato Frittata with Basil and Garlic (page 258) or Onion and Mushroom Frittata (page 247).

Roasted Asparagus with Olive Oil

SERVES 4

ROASTING CONCENTRATES THE FLAVORS in asparagus and imparts a sweetness not apparent when the vegetable is steamed or boiled. Medium-thick spears work best in this recipe. Very thin ones may burn in the hot oven, while thicker asparagus may fail to cook through by the time the exterior browns. In any case, watch carefully; the asparagus can go from tender and nicely caramelized to burned in just a few minutes.

1½ pounds medium asparagus
2½ tablespoons extra-virgin olive oil
Salt

1. Preheat the oven to 450 degrees F. Snap the tough ends from the asparagus. Place the asparagus on a shallow, rimmed baking sheet large enough to hold them in a single layer. Drizzle the oil over and sprinkle with salt to taste. Toss the asparagus, making sure that each spear is coated with oil.

2. Bake until the spears are lightly browned and tender, about 10 minutes. Serve immediately.

SERVING SUGGESTIONS

Serve with egg dishes, such as Onion and Mushroom Frittata (page 247) or Parmesan Soufflé (page 266), or with Saffron Risotto (page 150).

Asparagus with Lemon-Shallot Vinaigrette

SERVES 4

IN FRANCE, A DISH OF BOILED ASPARAGUS is often dressed with a sauce containing mustard and vinegar, whereas in Italy, lemon vinaigrette is preferred. Serve this dish warm or at room temperature.

- **1½ pounds medium asparagus**
- **1 teaspoon grated zest and 2 tablespoons juice from 1 large lemon**
- **1 medium shallot, minced**
- **Salt and freshly ground black pepper**
- **¼ cup extra-virgin olive oil**

1. Bring several quarts water to a boil in a large saucepan. Snap the tough ends from the asparagus. Set the asparagus aside.

2. Whisk together the lemon zest and juice, shallot and salt and pepper to taste in a medium bowl. Slowly whisk in the oil until smooth. Adjust the seasonings and set aside.

3. Add the asparagus and salt to taste to the boiling water. Cook until the spears are tender but not limp, about 4 minutes.

4. Drain the asparagus and place in a single layer on a large platter. Whisk the dressing again and drizzle it over the asparagus. Let cool for 10 minutes. Serve warm or at room temperature. *(The asparagus can be kept at room temperature for 1 hour.)*

SERVING SUGGESTIONS

This dish is superb with Fresh Tomato Pizza with Oregano (page 437) and with Risotto with Porcini Mushrooms (page 144).

Gratinéed Asparagus with Parmesan

SERVES 4

THIS FAIRLY RICH DISH IS SIMPLE BUT ELEGANT. Use only the finest Parmigiano-Reggiano cheese.

- **1½ pounds medium asparagus**
- **1 teaspoon salt**
- **2 tablespoons unsalted butter**
- **⅓ cup freshly grated Parmigiano-Reggiano cheese**

1. Bring several quarts water to a boil in a large saucepan. Snap the tough ends from the asparagus. Add the asparagus and salt to the boiling water. Cook until the spears are tender but not limp, about 4 minutes. Drain the asparagus and set aside to cool briefly.

2. Preheat the broiler. Grease a shallow 13-by-9-inch flameproof baking dish with 1 tablespoon of the butter.

3. Place the asparagus in a single layer in the baking dish. Cut the remaining 1 tablespoon butter into small bits. Dot the asparagus with the butter and sprinkle the cheese evenly over the asparagus.

4. Slide the baking dish under the broiler and cook, watching carefully, until the cheese is golden brown and bubbling, about 3 minutes. Serve immediately.

SERVING SUGGESTIONS

This dish is good after Polenta with Portobello Mushrooms (page 190) or almost any egg dish.

Roasted Beets with Balsamic Vinegar and Parsley

SERVES 4 TO 6

BALSAMIC VINEGAR ACCENTUATES THE SWEETNESS of oven-roasted beets. A syrupy, aged vinegar (see page 549) is good here. Some beets come with plenty of healthy-looking leaves, others with none. Therefore, I have specified their trimmed weight. Save the leaves and substitute them in any of the spinach or swiss chard recipes.

6 medium beets (about 1½ pounds without greens), scrubbed
2 teaspoons aged balsamic vinegar
2 tablespoons extra-virgin olive oil
1 tablespoon minced fresh parsley leaves
Salt

1. Preheat the oven to 400 degrees F. Trim all but the last inch or so of the stems from the beets. Trim any long dangling roots. Wrap the beets in a large piece of aluminum foil.

2. Bake until the beets are tender, about 1½ hours, or until a metal skewer glides through them easily. Unwrap and let cool slightly.

3. Use a paper towel to lift off and discard the skins from the warm beets. Cut the beets into ½-inch-thick slices and arrange them on a large platter. Drizzle the vinegar and oil over them. Sprinkle with the parsley and salt to taste. Serve immediately or at room temperature.

SERVING SUGGESTIONS

Roasted beets make a good foil to a main course that has bitter greens or other strong flavors, such as Frittata with Swiss Chard and Roasted Garlic (page 252), Potato, Arugula and Fontina Pizza (page 434) or Grilled Smoked Mozzarella and Arugula Panini (page 473).

Spicy Broccoli with Garlic

SERVES 4

AS LONG AS YOU PEEL THEM, broccoli stalks are tender and delicious. Cut off and discard the tough bottom portion, separate the broccoli into long spears and peel the outer skin from each piece. This is an attractive way to serve broccoli.

1 medium bunch broccoli (about 1½ pounds)
Salt
2 tablespoons extra-virgin olive oil
3 medium garlic cloves, minced
½ teaspoon dried hot red pepper flakes, or to taste

1. Bring several quarts water to a boil in a large saucepan. Trim all but the last 3 inches from the broccoli stalks. Break the broccoli into fairly large spears and peel away the tough outer layer from the stalks. Add the broccoli and salt to taste to the boiling water. Cook until the broccoli is crisp-tender, 4 to 5 minutes. Drain well. *(The broccoli may be set aside for up to 1 hour.)*

2. Heat the oil in a large skillet set over medium heat. Add the garlic and hot red pepper flakes and cook until the garlic is golden, about 2 minutes. Add the broccoli and stir to coat well with the flavored oil, cooking for 1 to 2 minutes. Add salt to taste and serve immediately.

SERVING SUGGESTIONS

Partner this dish with a tomato-based pizza or tart, such as Pizza with Tomatoes, Mozzarella and Basil (page 438) or Fresh Tomato Tart with Basil-Garlic Crust (page 411). It is also good with egg dishes, such as Red Pepper Frittata with Mint (page 250), as well as pasta dishes, such as Linguine with Grilled Plum Tomato Sauce (page 106).

Slow-Browned Carrots with Butter

SERVES 4

THIS DISH IS SO BASIC—carrots, butter and salt—that you may think, "Who needs a recipe?" But slow-cooking the carrots in a little butter intensifies their flavor and makes them incredibly sweet. For extra richness, sprinkle the cooked carrots generously with grated Parmigiano-Reggiano cheese.

5 large carrots (about 1¼ pounds)
3 tablespoons unsalted butter
Salt

1. Peel and cut the carrots on the bias into ¼-inch-thick ovals.

2. Place the carrots and butter in a large skillet. Turn the heat to medium-low and cook, stirring often, until the carrots shrink and start to brown, 1¼ to 1½ hours. Season with salt to taste and serve immediately.

SERVING SUGGESTIONS

This side dish is buttery and should be served with a light main course, such as Asparagus Frittata with Basil, Shallots and Parmesan (page 245). In that case, or whenever you plan to serve the dish after a main course with cheese, do not add the Parmesan to the carrots.

Carrots with Two Vinegars and Oregano

SERVES 4 TO 6

RED WINE VINEGAR HELPS BALANCE THE SWEETNESS of the carrots and shallots, while a little balsamic vinegar creates a light glaze. Thyme or parsley may be used in place of the oregano.

- **8 large carrots (about 2 pounds)**
- **Salt**
- **2 tablespoons extra-virgin olive oil**
- **3 medium shallots, minced**
- **¼ cup red wine vinegar**
- **2 tablespoons aged balsamic vinegar**
- **2 teaspoons minced fresh oregano leaves**
- **½ teaspoon sugar (optional)**

1. Bring several quarts water to a boil in a large saucepan. Peel and cut the carrots on the bias into ⅜-inch-thick ovals. Add the carrots and salt to taste to the boiling water. Cook until the carrots are a little underdone, about 8 minutes. Drain and set aside.

2. Heat the oil in a large skillet. Add the shallots and sauté over medium heat until golden, about 3 minutes. Add the carrots and stir to coat them well with the oil. Cook for about 1 minute.

3. Add the red wine vinegar, balsamic vinegar and oregano to the skillet. Simmer, stirring occasionally, over high heat until the vinegar evaporates, about 5 minutes. Add salt to taste. If the carrots were not particularly sweet, stir in the sugar and cook for 1 to 2 minutes more. The carrots may be served immediately or at room temperature.

SERVING SUGGESTIONS

Serve these carrots at room temperature as part of a buffet with egg dishes, tarts and other vegetables.

Spicy Cauliflower Simmered in Red Wine

SERVES 6

THIS SICILIAN-STYLE SIDE DISH calls for a number of heady ingredients, including green olives, capers and hot red pepper flakes. Simmered in red wine until tender, the cauliflower florets take on a lovely purplish hue.

1 medium cauliflower head (about 2 pounds)
3 tablespoons extra-virgin olive oil
1 medium onion, thinly sliced
8 large green olives, pitted and chopped (about ½ cup)
¾ cup fruity red wine, such as merlot or zinfandel
½ teaspoon dried hot red pepper flakes
2 tablespoons minced fresh parsley leaves
1 tablespoon drained capers, rinsed
Salt

1. Trim the leaves and stems from the cauliflower and cut it into small florets. Set aside.

2. Heat the oil in a large sauté pan. Add the onion and cook over medium heat until golden, about 8 minutes.

3. Add the cauliflower, olives, wine and hot red pepper flakes. Bring to a simmer, reduce the heat to medium-low and cover. Cook, stirring occasionally, until the cauliflower has absorbed the liquid in the pan and is tender but still offers some resistance to the bite, about 35 minutes.

4. Stir in the parsley and capers. Taste for salt and add if necessary. Serve immediately or let cool to room temperature.

SERVING SUGGESTIONS

Serve it hot with a tomato-based pizza, such as Pizza with Tomatoes, Mozzarella and Basil (page 438). Serve it at room temperature with Mozzarella and Tomato Panini with Pesto (page 469) for a hearty lunch.

Cauliflower in Green Sauce

SERVES 6

A LIVELY SAUCE MADE WITH PARSLEY, basil, capers, lemon juice and olive oil adds plenty of flavor to mild boiled cauliflower.

- ⅓ cup minced fresh parsley leaves
- 2 tablespoons minced fresh basil leaves
- 2 tablespoons drained capers, rinsed and minced
- 1 tablespoon lemon juice
- 3 tablespoons extra-virgin olive oil
- Salt
- 1 medium cauliflower head (about 2 pounds)

1. Combine the parsley, basil, capers, lemon juice, oil and salt to taste in a medium bowl. Taste and adjust the seasonings.

2. Bring several quarts water to a boil in a large saucepan. Trim the leaves and stems from the cauliflower and cut it into small florets. Add the cauliflower and salt to taste to the boiling water. Cook until the florets are tender, about 7 minutes.

3. Drain the cauliflower and toss with the herb sauce in a large bowl. Serve immediately.

SERVING SUGGESTIONS

The herb sauce makes this dish a good companion to eggs or a bread-based dish. Serve it with Onion and Mushroom Frittata (page 247) or mozzarella sandwiches made with Focaccia with Sun-Dried Tomatoes and Garlic (page 454).

Braised Celery with Onions and Tomatoes

SERVES 4

MOST AMERICANS DO NOT THINK OF SERVING COOKED CELERY as a side dish, but in many parts of Europe, including Italy, its mild sweet flavor is much appreciated. Choose celery with leaves attached and peel the ribs to remove any stringy fibers.

- **8 medium celery ribs with leaves (about 1 pound)**
- **3 tablespoons extra-virgin olive oil**
- **1 medium onion, minced**
- **1 cup drained canned whole tomatoes, chopped**
- **Salt**

1. Mince the celery leaves and set aside. Trim and discard any tough portions from the bottom and top of each rib. Peel the outside to remove the stringy fibers. Cut the ribs into 2-inch-long pieces and set aside.

2. Heat the oil in a large sauté pan. Add the onion and sauté over medium heat until translucent, about 5 minutes. Add the celery and cook until slightly softened, about 8 minutes.

3. Add the tomatoes, celery leaves and salt to taste. Reduce the heat to medium-low, cover and simmer, stirring occasionally, until the celery is tender and the tomatoes have cooked down, about 20 minutes. Adjust the seasonings and serve hot or warm.

SERVING SUGGESTIONS

Match with an egg dish, such as Arugula Frittata (page 244), or a pizza without tomatoes, such as Three-Cheese Pizza (page 439).

Swiss Chard with Raisins and Almonds

SERVES 4

MANY VERSIONS OF THIS DISH are made throughout Italy. Sometimes currants and pine nuts are used; in some cases, chopped olives are added. In many northern regions, butter takes the place of oil. Feel free to adapt the recipe as you like. As long as you follow the general technique of wilting the slightly damp greens in a large open pot, the results will be fine. Other leafy greens, including spinach, dandelion and beet greens, may be used in place of the chard.

- 3 tablespoons sliced almonds
- 2 pounds swiss chard
- 3 tablespoons extra-virgin olive oil
- 1 medium onion, minced
- 1 medium garlic clove, minced
- 2 tablespoons dark or golden raisins
- Salt and freshly ground black pepper

1. Place the almonds in a small skillet set over medium heat. Toast, shaking the pan occasionally to turn the almonds, until golden, about 5 minutes. Set aside.

2. Remove and discard the stems from the swiss chard. Tear off the green portions from either side of the rib that runs down the center of each leaf. Discard the ribs. Wash the leaves in successive bowls of cold water until grit no longer appears in the bottom of the bowl. Shake off as much excess water as possible but do not dry the leaves.

3. Heat the oil in a deep pot. Add the onion and sauté over medium heat until translucent, about 5 minutes. Add the garlic and cook until golden, about 1 minute.

4. Add the damp swiss chard to the pot. Cook, stirring occasionally to bring up leaves from the bottom of the pot, until the leaves have completely wilted and all the liquid in the pan has evaporated, about 5 minutes.

5. Stir in the almonds, raisins and salt and pepper to taste. Cook for 1 to 2 minutes more. Adjust the seasonings and serve immediately.

SERVING SUGGESTIONS

Serve this side dish with any frittata that does not contain leafy greens or after something spicy, such as Penne with Oven-Dried Tomatoes, Olives and Herbs (page 80). It can also follow a dish with bitter notes, such as Risotto with Radicchio (page 146).

Grilled Eggplant with Garlic and Herbs

SERVES 4

WHEN THE GRILL IS GOING, I like to cook as many things as possible over hot coals. Eggplant becomes meltingly tender when cooked this way and takes on a smoky flavor. Oregano, thyme, mint and tarragon, or a combination, are good with eggplant.

- **3 tablespoons extra-virgin olive oil**
- **3 medium garlic cloves, minced**
- **1 tablespoon minced fresh herbs (see above)**
- **Salt and freshly ground black pepper**
- **4 medium eggplants (about 1¾ pounds), washed**

1. Light the grill or make a charcoal fire. Combine the oil, garlic, herbs and salt and pepper to taste in a small bowl.

2. Trim and discard the ends from the eggplants and cut the eggplants lengthwise into ½-inch-thick pieces. Peel the outer slices. Lay the slices on a large baking sheet or platter. Brush them with the oil mixture.

3. Grill the eggplant over a medium-hot fire, turning once, until marked with dark stripes, about 10 minutes. Transfer to a large platter and serve immediately.

SERVING SUGGESTIONS

Serve this dish after a summery pasta with tomatoes, such as Summer Spaghetti with Raw Arugula and Tomatoes (page 85) or Linguine with Grilled Plum Tomato Sauce (page 106).

Oven-Roasted Endive with Parmesan

SERVES 4 TO 6

ENDIVE TAKES JUST AS WELL TO COOKING as it does to the salad bowl. It may be grilled, braised or sautéed, or quickly roasted under a light topping of Parmesan cheese, as in this recipe.

- **4 medium-large belgian endives (about 1½ pounds)**
- **2 tablespoons unsalted butter**
- **Salt and freshly ground black pepper**
- **½ cup freshly grated Parmigiano-Reggiano cheese**

1. Preheat the oven to 425 degrees F. Remove any limp outer leaves from the endives. Slice the endives in half lengthwise.

2. Grease a baking dish just large enough to hold the endives in a single layer with 1 tablespoon of the butter. Place the endives in the dish, cut side down. Cut the remaining 1 tablespoon butter into small pieces and scatter over the endives. Season with salt and pepper to taste and sprinkle with the cheese.

3. Bake until the endives are tender and golden brown, about 20 minutes. Serve immediately.

SERVING SUGGESTIONS

This dish goes well with egg dishes, such as Red Pepper Frittata with Mint (page 250). Or serve it after a pasta dish, such as Penne with Cauliflower, Onions and Saffron (page 90) or Fusilli with Tomato and Porcini Sauce (page 76).

Wilted Escarole with Garlic and Lemon

SERVES 4

ALTHOUGH AMERICANS tend to think of escarole as a salad green, Italians add this lettucelike vegetable to soups, rice dishes and pasta sauces. They also prepare it as a side dish. Escarole leaves are similar to spinach or swiss chard in that they can be wilted in a pot without first being blanched. Unlike spinach and chard, however, these greens will retain a little crunch when cooked.

- **1 large escarole head (about 1¼ pounds)**
- **2 tablespoons extra-virgin olive oil**
- **2 large garlic cloves, cut into thin slivers**
- **½ teaspoon grated lemon zest**
- **Salt and freshly ground black pepper**

1. Discard any dry or tough outer leaves from the escarole. Trim and discard the core and tough stems. Wash the leaves in successive bowls of cold water until grit no longer appears in the bottom of the bowl. Shake the leaves to remove excess water but do not dry them. Set aside.

2. Heat the oil in a deep pot. Add the garlic and sauté over medium heat until golden, about 2 minutes. Add the lemon zest and cook for 30 seconds.

3. Add the escarole to the pot. Cook, turning occasionally, until the leaves are tender and the stem ends are just a little crunchy, about 6 minutes. Season with salt and pepper to taste and serve immediately.

SERVING SUGGESTIONS

This dish goes well with nearly any egg dish and with pizzas. It is especially good after Frittata with Potatoes, Onions and Thyme (page 256) or Three-Cheese Pizza (page 439).

Braised Fennel with Parmesan and White Wine

SERVES 4

WHILE SAUTÉING FENNEL EMPHASIZES ITS SWEETNESS, braising it in butter and wine highlights the dense, almost unctuous texture of this versatile vegetable. A dusting of Parmesan complements the rich flavors in this dish.

- **2 medium fennel bulbs (about 2 pounds)**
- **3 tablespoons unsalted butter**
- **Salt and freshly ground black pepper**
- **⅓ cup dry white wine**
- **¼ cup freshly grated Parmigiano-Reggiano cheese**

1. Trim and discard the stems and fronds from the fennel bulbs. Trim a very thin slice from the base of each bulb and remove any tough or blemished outer layers. Slice the bulbs through the base into ½-inch-thick pieces that resemble fans. Do not remove the core.

2. Melt the butter in a sauté pan large enough to hold the fennel in a single layer. Add the fennel and sprinkle with salt and pepper to taste. Add the wine, cover, and simmer over medium heat for 15 minutes. Turn the fennel and continue to simmer, covered, until it is quite tender and has absorbed most of the liquid in the pan, about 10 minutes.

3. Sprinkle the fennel with the cheese. Transfer to a platter or individual plates and serve immediately.

SERVING SUGGESTIONS

Serve this dish after Asparagus Frittata with Basil, Shallots and Parmesan (page 249) or Spinach Crespelle (page 279).

Sautéed Fennel with Garlic

Serves 4

Sautéing causes the fennel's anise flavor to fade but concentrates its natural sugars.

- **2 medium fennel bulbs (about 2 pounds)**
- **3 tablespoons extra-virgin olive oil**
- **4 medium garlic cloves, minced**
- **Salt and freshly ground black pepper**
- **2 tablespoons minced fresh parsley leaves**

1. Trim the stems and fronds from the fennel bulbs. Discard the stems. Mince and reserve 1 tablespoon of the fronds. Trim a very thin slice from the base of each bulb and remove any tough or blemished outer layers. Cut the bulbs in half through the base and use a small, sharp knife to remove the triangular piece of the core from each half. With the flat side of the fennel bulb down and your knife parallel to the work surface, slice each fennel half crosswise to yield several ½-inch-thick slices. Cut the slices lengthwise to yield long strips about ½ inch thick.

2. Heat the oil in a large skillet. Add the garlic and sauté over medium heat until golden, about 1 minute. Add the fennel strips and toss to coat them with oil. Cook, stirring often, until they have softened considerably but still offer some resistance, about 15 minutes.

3. Season generously with salt and pepper to taste. Stir in the minced fennel fronds and parsley. Serve immediately.

Serving Suggestions

Serve with a vegetable pizza, such as Fresh Tomato Pizza with Oregano (page 437) or Pizza with Tomatoes, Mozzarella and Basil (page 438). This dish also goes well with assertively seasoned egg dishes, such as Sun-Dried Tomato Frittata with Basil and Garlic (page 258).

Roasted Fennel, Carrots and Red Onion

SERVES 4

A TABLESPOON OF BALSAMIC VINEGAR drizzled over the vegetables during the last minutes of roasting heightens their sweetness.

- **1 large fennel bulb (about 1½ pounds)**
- **1 medium red onion, cut into 8 wedges**
- **2 medium carrots, peeled, halved lengthwise and cut into 2-inch lengths**
- **2 tablespoons extra-virgin olive oil**
- **Salt**
- **1 tablespoon aged balsamic vinegar**

1. Preheat the oven to 425 degrees F. Trim and discard the stems and fronds from the fennel. Trim a very thin slice from the base of the bulb and remove any tough or blemished outer layers. Cut the bulb in half through the base and use a small, sharp knife to remove the triangular piece of the core from each half. With the flat side of the fennel bulb down and your knife parallel to the work surface, slice each fennel half crosswise to yield several ½-inch-thick slices. Cut the slices lengthwise to yield long strips about ½ inch thick.

2. Toss the fennel, onion and carrots in a large roasting pan with the oil. Season generously with salt. Roast for 30 minutes, turning once after 20 minutes.

3. Drizzle the vinegar over the vegetables and toss gently. Continue roasting until the vegetables are richly colored and tender, about 5 minutes more. Adjust the seasonings. Serve hot or at room temperature.

SERVING SUGGESTIONS

Serve the vegetables after Polenta with Olive Oil and Fresh Herbs (page 182) or Frittata with Swiss Chard and Roasted Garlic (page 252).

Steamed Green Beans with Tarragon

SERVES 4

THE ANISE FLAVOR OF TARRAGON complements fresh green beans. Only a small amount of olive oil is needed, although you can use more. This is one dish where quality is more important than quantity. If possible, choose an oil that is full-bodied and fruity rather than sharp or peppery.

1 pound green beans, ends snapped off
4 teaspoons extra-virgin olive oil
1 tablespoon minced fresh tarragon leaves
Salt and freshly ground black pepper

1. Bring 1 to 2 inches water to a boil in a deep, wide pan. Arrange the beans in a steamer basket and carefully place the basket over the boiling water. Cook until the beans are tender but not mushy, about 5 minutes.

2. Remove the basket from the water and shake several times to remove all traces of water. Turn the beans into a large serving dish. Drizzle with oil immediately. Sprinkle with tarragon and salt and pepper to taste. Toss gently and serve immediately.

SERVING SUGGESTIONS

Serve this dish after Polenta with Ricotta and Pecorino (page 185) or an egg dish, such as Red Onion Frittata with Parmesan and Thyme (page 248), Frittata with Spaghetti and Herbs (page 264) or Frittata with Ricotta and Mint (page 261).

Green Beans Braised in Tomatoes

SERVES 4

SLOW-COOKING GREEN BEANS causes them to lose some of their bright color, but on the other hand, it infuses them with the flavors of onions and tomatoes.

- 2 tablespoons extra-virgin olive oil
- 1 medium onion, diced
- 1 cup drained canned whole tomatoes, chopped
- 1 pound green beans, ends snapped off
- Salt and freshly ground black pepper
- 1 tablespoon minced fresh tarragon leaves

1. Heat the oil in a large sauté pan. Add the onion and cook over medium heat until translucent, about 5 minutes. Add the tomatoes and simmer until the juices thicken, about 5 minutes.

2. Add the green beans, ½ teaspoon salt and pepper to taste. Stir well, reduce the heat to medium-low and cover. Cook, stirring occasionally, until the beans are tender but still offer some resistance to the bite, 30 to 35 minutes.

3. Stir in the tarragon and adjust the seasonings. Serve immediately.

SERVING SUGGESTIONS

This is a good accompaniment for egg dishes, such as Zucchini Frittata with Parmesan (page 259) or Frittata with Swiss Chard and Roasted Garlic (page 252).

Green Beans and Potatoes with Pesto

SERVES 6

THE CITY OF GENOA IS KNOWN THE WORLD OVER for its pesto sauce. In many homes in that city, boiled green beans and potatoes are tossed with pesto and served with pasta or as a side dish. For this recipe, I prefer a pesto made without cheese. However, it's fine to substitute a scant ½ cup of pesto with cheese, made your way or mine (see page 531). Leave a little water dripping from the vegetables after draining them to thin and spread the pesto. Walnuts may be used in place of the pine nuts if desired.

- **2 cups loosely packed fresh basil leaves**
- **2 tablespoons pine nuts**
- **1 medium garlic clove**
- **¼ cup extra-virgin olive oil**
- **Salt and freshly ground black pepper**
- **1 pound small new potatoes, scrubbed and cut into 1-inch cubes**
- **¾ pound green beans, ends snapped off**

1. Place the basil, pine nuts and garlic in the work bowl of a food processor. Grind the ingredients into a rough puree, stopping once or twice to scrape down the sides of the bowl. With the motor running, slowly pour the oil through the feed tube and process until the pesto comes together. Scrape it into a large serving bowl. Season generously with salt and pepper to taste and set aside.

2. Bring 3 quarts water to a boil in a large saucepan. Add the potatoes and 1 teaspoon salt. Cook until a skewer slides easily through them, about 8 minutes. The potatoes should still be fairly firm, not falling apart or mushy.

3. Add the green beans to the pot and continue cooking until they are tender, about 5 minutes. Drain the potatoes and beans, leaving a little moisture dripping from them, and transfer to the bowl with the pesto. Toss and serve immediately.

SERVING SUGGESTIONS

Serve with an egg dish, such as Onion and Mushroom Frittata (page 247), or as a side dish with Scrambled Egg Sandwiches with Red Peppers and Onions (page 474).

Pan-Roasted Leeks

SERVES 4

ITALIANS OFTEN SERVE LEEKS as a side dish, especially during the winter and early spring, when other green vegetables are not yet in season. Parboiling shortens the cooking time but can cause the layers to separate. A better option is to turn off the heat once the water comes to a boil, add the leeks, cover the pot and allow the residual heat to soften them. Then the leeks pan-roast in a little olive oil. A fresh herb, such as basil, tarragon or parsley, may be added, but the leeks are fine as is.

8 small leeks (about 2½ pounds)
Salt
3 tablespoons extra-virgin olive oil
Freshly ground black pepper

1. Bring several quarts water to a boil in a large saucepan. Trim and discard the dark green tops and tough outer leaves from the leeks. Remove the roots along with a very thin slice of the nearby white part. Halve the leeks lengthwise and wash them under cold running water. Gently spread apart but do not separate the inner layers to remove all traces of soil. If the leeks are particularly sandy, soak them in several changes of clean water.

2. When the water comes to a boil, turn off the heat, add the leeks and salt to taste, cover the pot and let stand until the leeks are tender, about 10 minutes. Carefully remove the leeks from the water with a slotted spoon and transfer them to a platter lined with several layers of paper towels. Cool slightly and then blot dry with more paper towels.

3. Heat the oil in a skillet large enough to hold the leeks in a single layer. Add the leeks and cook over medium-high heat, turning once, until they are golden brown in spots, 10 to 12 minutes. Season with salt and pepper to taste. Serve immediately or at room temperature.

SERVING SUGGESTIONS

Leeks make a good accompaniment to egg dishes, such as Cauliflower Frittata with Parsley and Pecorino (page 246) or Frittata with Ricotta and Mint (page 261). The dish is also good after a pizza, such as Fresh Tomato Pizza with Oregano (page 437) or Three-Cheese Pizza (page 439).

Sautéed Button Mushrooms with Garlic and Herbs

SERVES 4 TO 6

GARLIC AND AN ASSORTMENT OF FRESH HERBS add life to plain button mushrooms. Of course, this dish can be made with cremini mushrooms, but to my mind, these potent flavorings work best with the bland white ones. The key to cooking them is fairly high heat. The mushrooms need to brown and shed most of their moisture. As for herbs, sage, oregano, thyme, marjoram, basil, parsley and chives can be used. Use smaller amounts of stronger herbs like sage or oregano, and balance them with milder herbs like basil and parsley.

- **1½ pounds white button mushrooms, wiped clean, stems trimmed**
- **3 tablespoons extra-virgin olive oil**
- **3 medium garlic cloves, minced**
- **Salt and freshly ground black pepper**
- **¼ cup minced fresh herbs**

1. Halve small mushrooms and quarter larger ones. Set aside.

2. Heat the oil in a large skillet. Add the garlic and sauté over medium heat until golden, about 1 minute. Add the mushrooms and raise the heat to medium-high. Cook, stirring often, until the mushrooms are golden brown and the liquid in the pan has mostly evaporated, about 8 minutes.

3. Add salt and pepper to taste and stir in the herbs. Cook for 1 to 2 minutes just until the pan is dry. Serve immediately.

SERVING SUGGESTIONS

These mushrooms are very good with egg dishes, such as Parsley and Shallot Frittata (page 249) or Zucchini Frittata with Parmesan (page 259). Or serve them after a rich tart or torta with a leafy green vegetable, such as spinach or swiss chard.

Sautéed Button Mushrooms with Onions and Balsamic Vinegar

SERVES 4 TO 6

ONIONS AND A LITTLE BALSAMIC VINEGAR give mushrooms some sweetness, reinforcing the effect of cooking them in a very hot pan.

- 1¼ pounds white button mushrooms, wiped clean, stems trimmed
- 3 tablespoons extra-virgin olive oil
- 1 medium onion, chopped
- Salt and freshly ground black pepper
- 2 teaspoons aged balsamic vinegar

1. Halve small mushrooms and quarter larger ones. Set aside.

2. Heat the oil in a large skillet. Add the onion and sauté over medium heat until it starts to soften, about 3 minutes. Add the mushrooms and raise the heat to medium-high. Cook, stirring often, until the mushrooms are golden brown and the liquid in the pan has mostly evaporated, about 8 minutes.

3. Stir in salt and pepper to taste and the vinegar. Cook just until the mushrooms have absorbed the vinegar, about 1 minute. Serve immediately.

SERVING SUGGESTIONS

The mushrooms go well with egg and spinach dishes, such as Spinach Crespelle (page 279), or with any frittata that does not contain mushrooms.

Oven-Roasted Portobello Mushrooms

SERVES 4

ROASTING PORTOBELLO MUSHROOMS concentrates their flavor while caramelizing the surfaces. The mushrooms are roasted upside down to keep their juices from oozing out. To serve, invert them onto a platter.

- **4 medium portobello mushrooms (about 1¼ pounds)**
- **2 tablespoons extra-virgin olive oil**
- **2 large garlic cloves, cut into thin slivers**
- **1 teaspoon minced fresh thyme or oregano leaves**
- **Salt and freshly ground black pepper**

1. Preheat the oven to 450 degrees F. Remove and discard the mushroom stems. (They may be saved for making stock.) Wipe the caps clean with a paper towel.

2. Grease a small baking sheet with ½ tablespoon of the oil. Place the mushrooms, gill sides up, on the baking sheet. Gently slip the garlic slivers into the gills, taking care not to break the mushrooms. (It's fine if some of the garlic slivers stick out of the mushrooms.) Sprinkle with the thyme or oregano, drizzle with the remaining 1½ tablespoons oil and season with salt and pepper to taste.

3. Bake until the mushrooms begin to turn golden brown around the edges, about 12 minutes. Invert the mushrooms onto a platter and serve immediately.

SERVING SUGGESTIONS

As a side dish, this recipe is a good way to "beef" up a light main course. Serve with any frittata that does not contain mushrooms or with a sandwich, such as Grilled Eggplant and Red Pepper Sandwiches with Olivada (page 471). Or serve it after a simple rice dish, such as Saffron Risotto (page 150).

Mixed Bell Peppers with Onions, Tomatoes and Basil

SERVES 6

PEPPERS RESPOND WELL TO BEING COOKED in a covered pan over low heat; they soften without browning. The result is a tender texture and sweet flavor.

- 2 large red bell peppers
- 2 large yellow bell peppers
- 3 tablespoons extra-virgin olive oil
- 2 medium onions, thinly sliced
- 2 medium plum tomatoes, peeled, cored, seeded and diced
- 10 large fresh basil leaves, cut into very thin strips
- Salt and freshly ground black pepper

1. Core, halve and seed the red and yellow bell peppers. Slice into 1-inch-wide strips.

2. Heat the oil in a large sauté pan set over medium-high heat. Add the peppers and onions and cook, stirring constantly to coat with the oil, for 1 minute. Cover and lower the heat to medium-low. You should hear a gentle hiss from the pan. Cook until the vegetables are soft, about 15 minutes.

3. Uncover and add the tomatoes, basil and salt and pepper to taste. Continue cooking until the tomatoes soften, about 4 minutes. Adjust the seasonings and serve. *(This dish can be cooled to room temperature, covered and served several hours later.)*

SERVING SUGGESTIONS

This dish goes with just about any frittata. Especially good choices are Parsley and Shallot Frittata (page 249) and Zucchini Frittata with Parmesan (page 259).

Garlic Mashed Potatoes with Rosemary and Olive Oil

SERVES 4

ITALIAN-STYLE MASHED POTATOES are enriched with extra-virgin olive oil, not butter and cream. The result is a clearer potato flavor, as opposed to an over-the-top dairy richness. Boiling the garlic along with the potatoes mellows its punch. Thyme or oregano would be fine instead of rosemary. If you can, use Yukon Gold potatoes. Their yellow color and buttery flavor are a plus when making mashed potatoes.

4 medium baking potatoes (about 2 pounds), peeled and cut into 1-inch chunks
4 large garlic cloves
1 sprig fresh rosemary
4-6 tablespoons extra-virgin olive oil
Salt

1. Place the potatoes, garlic and rosemary in a medium saucepan. Add cold water to cover by several inches. Bring to a boil and simmer until the potatoes are tender, about 20 minutes.

2. Drain the potatoes and garlic well and discard the rosemary sprig. (Most of the rosemary leaves will probably have fallen off. Mash them with the potatoes and garlic.)

3. Return the potatoes and garlic to the saucepan and mash until smooth. Drizzle 4 tablespoons of the oil over the potatoes and beat in until smooth. For added richness, beat in up to 2 tablespoons more oil. Add salt to taste and serve immediately.

SERVING SUGGESTIONS

Serve these mashed potatoes with a frittata, such as Frittata with Cremini Mushrooms and Spinach (page 254) or Onion and Mushroom Frittata (page 247). Or make a light dinner out of the potatoes and another vegetable dish, such as Roasted Asparagus with Olive Oil (page 330) or Roasted Fennel, Carrots and Red Onion (page 346).

Mashed Potatoes with Oven-Dried Tomatoes

SERVES 4

THIS RECIPE MAY SOUND LIKE AN ODD COMBINATION, but it has become a favorite in my home. It is based on a side dish served at New York's famed Union Square Cafe. My version eliminates the butter and cream and adds garlic and high-quality olive oil to the mashed potatoes. Oven-dried tomatoes are pureed with a bit more olive oil and beaten into the potatoes. The result is a rosy puree that tastes of both potatoes and tomatoes, with garlic and rosemary in the background.

4 medium baking potatoes (about 2 pounds), peeled and cut into 1-inch chunks
4 large garlic cloves
1 sprig fresh rosemary
¾ cup Oven-Dried Tomatoes (page 525)
6 tablespoons extra-virgin olive oil
Salt

1. Place the potatoes, garlic and rosemary in a medium saucepan. Add cold water to cover by several inches. Bring to a boil and simmer until the potatoes are tender, about 20 minutes.

2. Meanwhile, puree the tomatoes with 2 tablespoons of the oil in a food processor or blender until smooth. Set aside.

3. Drain the potatoes and garlic well and discard the rosemary sprig. (Most of the rosemary leaves will probably have fallen off. Mash them with the potatoes and garlic.)

4. Return the potatoes and garlic to the saucepan and mash until smooth. Drizzle the remaining 4 tablespoons oil over the potatoes and beat in until smooth.

5. Stir the tomato puree into the mashed potatoes and add salt to taste. Serve immediately.

SERVING SUGGESTIONS

Serve these potatoes with Spring Vegetable Stew with Fennel, Carrots, Asparagus and Peas (page 322).

Roasted New Potatoes with Garlic and Herbs

SERVES 4

SOAKING CUBED POTATOES in cold water helps them retain more moisture during roasting and prevents them from sticking to the baking dish. Garlic and herbs are added halfway through the roasting process so that they do not burn. Thyme and/or oregano could be used in place of the combination of rosemary and sage.

- **1½ pounds new potatoes, scrubbed**
- **¼ cup extra-virgin olive oil**
- **3 medium garlic cloves, minced**
- **6 large sage leaves, minced**
- **1 teaspoon minced fresh rosemary leaves**
- **1 teaspoon salt**

1. Preheat the oven to 425 degrees F. Cut the potatoes into 1-inch cubes and place them in a large bowl. Cover with cold water and set aside for 10 minutes.

2. Drain the potatoes (do not blot dry) and place them in a baking dish large enough to hold them in a single layer. Drizzle with 2 tablespoons of the oil and toss to coat evenly. Roast, turning once, for 30 minutes.

3. Combine the remaining 2 tablespoons oil, garlic, sage, rosemary and salt in a small bowl. Drizzle over the partially roasted potatoes. Toss gently to distribute the seasonings. Continue roasting, turning the potatoes occasionally, until golden brown, 25 to 30 minutes more. Serve immediately.

SERVING SUGGESTIONS

These crisp, garlicky potatoes make an excellent accompaniment to any egg dish, including all of the frittatas. They can also team up with most pizzas and sandwiches.

Grilled New Potatoes with Herbs

SERVES 4 TO 6

THE KEY TO GRILLING POTATOES without precooking them is to choose small new potatoes (about the size of a whole walnut) and use medium-low heat. After half an hour, the potatoes will be toasty on the outside and tender in the center. Unless the grids on your grill are very closely spaced, use a nonstick vegetable grid to keep the potatoes from falling onto the coals. (You can buy such a grid at a hardware store or kitchenware shop that sells grilling equipment; for a mail-order source, see page 554.)

2 pounds small new potatoes, scrubbed and halved
6 tablespoons extra-virgin olive oil
Salt and freshly ground black pepper
1½ tablespoons red wine vinegar
¼ cup minced fresh parsley leaves
2 tablespoons minced fresh chives or scallions

1. Light the grill or make a charcoal fire. Place the potatoes in a large bowl, drizzle with 2 tablespoons of the oil and toss to coat. Sprinkle with salt and pepper to taste.

2. Place a vegetable grid over a medium-low fire and heat for several minutes. Spread the potatoes out over the grid in a single layer. Grill, turning once, until the potatoes are browned on both sides and tender throughout, about 30 minutes. Place the grilled potatoes in a large bowl and cool slightly.

3. Meanwhile, combine the vinegar and salt and pepper to taste in a small bowl. Slowly whisk in the remaining 4 tablespoons oil until smooth. Whisk in the parsley and chives or scallions and adjust the seasonings.

4. Pour the dressing over the warm potatoes. Toss gently to coat them with the dressing. Serve warm or at room temperature. *(The potatoes can be covered and kept at room temperature for several hours.)*

SERVING SUGGESTIONS

Serve this dish with other grilled dishes, such as Grilled Portobello Mushrooms, Red Onions and Bell Peppers (page 320), or with Baked Tomatoes Stuffed with Pesto and Mozzarella (page 314).

Grilled Radicchio

SERVES 4 TO 6

GRILLING CAUSES THE EDGES OF THE RADICCHIO TO CARAMELIZE and helps balance the bitter flavor of the inner leaves with some sweetness.

3 medium radicchio heads (about 1½ pounds)
⅓ cup extra-virgin olive oil
Salt and freshly ground black pepper

1. Light the grill or make a charcoal fire. Discard any limp outer leaves from the radicchio. Quarter the radicchio through the stem end. Place the pieces in a large baking dish and brush with the oil. Sprinkle with salt and pepper to taste.

2. Grill the radicchio, turning it twice, until it is lightly charred on all sides, about 8 minutes. Transfer to a platter and serve immediately.

SERVING SUGGESTIONS

For a summer meal from the grill, start with a simple bruschetta and serve Grilled Portobello Mushrooms, Red Onions and Bell Peppers (page 320) as the main course with the radicchio on the side.

Wilted Spinach with Garlic

Serves 4

This is among the simplest of Italian vegetable side dishes as well as one of the most popular. Just make sure there is some moisture on the spinach leaves when they go into the pot, but not so much that the spinach becomes watery. Flat-leaf spinach has much more flavor and a better texture than the curly variety sold in plastic bags.

2 pounds spinach, preferably flat-leaf
2 tablespoons extra-virgin olive oil
3 medium garlic cloves, minced
Salt

1. Remove and discard the stems from the spinach. Wash the leaves in successive bowls of cold water until grit no longer appears in the bottom of the bowl. Shake the leaves to remove excess water but do not dry them.

2. Heat the oil in a large saucepan or stockpot. Add the garlic and sauté over medium heat until golden, about 1 minute. Add the spinach leaves and stir to coat evenly with the oil. Sprinkle with salt to taste.

3. Cover and cook, stirring occasionally, until the spinach is wilted, about 5 minutes. If there is any liquid in the pot, use a slotted spoon to transfer the spinach to a serving bowl. Adjust the seasonings and serve immediately.

Serving Suggestions
This basic side dish goes with any egg dish, pizza or pasta, especially Parmesan and Basil Frittata (page 260), Three-Cheese Pizza (page 439) and Orecchiette with Two Mushrooms and Rosemary (page 100).

Spinach with Brown Butter and Pine Nuts

SERVES 4

COOKING BUTTER UNTIL THE SOLIDS BECOME GOLDEN BROWN gives it an intense dairy flavor and aroma. Spinach is briefly sautéed in the brown butter to infuse it with flavor. Swiss chard may also be treated in the same manner.

2 pounds spinach, preferably flat-leaf
Salt
3 tablespoons pine nuts
3 tablespoons unsalted butter

1. Bring 4 quarts water to a boil in a large saucepan. Remove and discard the stems from the spinach. Wash the leaves in successive bowls of cold water until grit no longer appears in the bottom of the bowl.

2. Add the spinach and 2 teaspoons salt to the boiling water and cook, stirring to submerge all the leaves, until tender, about 2 minutes. Drain and set aside. *(The spinach can be set aside at room temperature for up to 1 hour.)*

3. Place the pine nuts in a medium skillet set over medium heat. Toast, shaking the pan occasionally to turn the nuts, until golden, about 5 minutes. Transfer to a plate.

4. Reduce the heat to medium-low and add the butter to the empty skillet. Cook, swirling the pan occasionally, until the butter turns golden brown, about 4 minutes. Stir in the toasted nuts and the spinach. Use 2 forks to pull apart the spinach leaves and coat them evenly with the butter and add salt to taste. Serve immediately.

SERVING SUGGESTIONS

Since it contains both nuts and butter, this preparation is an indulgence. Serve it after an equally rich dish, such as Squash Ravioli with Sage and Parmesan (page 126) or Polenta with Ricotta and Pecorino (page 185).

Sautéed Cherry Tomatoes with Garlic

SERVES 4

RIPE CHERRY TOMATOES make a simple summer dish when sautéed in olive oil flavored with garlic. Add shredded basil or mint to finish the dish. Parsley or tarragon would also be good.

2 tablespoons extra-virgin olive oil
3 medium garlic cloves, cut into very thin slivers
24 medium, ripe cherry tomatoes (about 1½ pounds), stemmed
Salt and freshly ground black pepper
10 large fresh basil or mint leaves, cut into thin strips

1. Heat the oil in a skillet large enough to hold the tomatoes in a single layer. Add the garlic and sauté over medium heat until lightly colored, about 1 minute.

2. Add the tomatoes and cook, stirring often, just until the skins start to blister in spots, about 3 minutes. Season generously with salt and pepper to taste. Stir in the basil or mint and serve immediately.

SERVING SUGGESTIONS

Serve after any main course that does not contain tomatoes, such as Zucchini Frittata with Parmesan (page 259), Whole Wheat Spaghetti with Spicy Broccoli and Pecorino (page 89) or Orecchiette with Peas, Ricotta and Parmesan (page 102).

Sautéed Zucchini with Lemon and Mint

SERVES 4

WHEN SAUTÉED, sliced zucchini releases a lot of moisture, which prevents browning. Salting the zucchini before cooking removes much of its juice. Cut the zucchini into ¼-inch-thick slices. Thinner slices will fall apart during cooking, while thicker slices require longer salting.

4 medium zucchini (about 1½ pounds), scrubbed and ends trimmed
2 teaspoons salt, plus more to taste
3 tablespoons extra-virgin olive oil
1 small onion or 2 large shallots, minced
1 teaspoon grated zest and 1 tablespoon juice from 1 medium lemon
2 tablespoons minced fresh mint leaves
Freshly ground black pepper

1. Slice the zucchini into ¼-inch-thick rounds. Place them in a colander and sprinkle with the 2 teaspoons salt. Set the colander in the sink or on a plate for 30 minutes. Rinse and thoroughly dry the zucchini with paper towels or a kitchen towel.

2. Heat the oil in a large skillet. Add the onion or shallots and sauté over medium heat until slightly translucent, about 3 minutes. Add the zucchini and lemon zest. Raise the heat to medium-high and cook, stirring occasionally, until the zucchini is golden brown, about 10 minutes.

3. Stir in the lemon juice, mint and pepper to taste. Toss the ingredients and cook for 1 to 2 minutes to heat through. Adjust the seasonings and serve immediately or at room temperature.

SERVING SUGGESTIONS

Serve at room temperature with sandwiches, such as Mozzarella Panini with Black Olive Paste (page 465) or Grilled Eggplant and Red Pepper Sandwiches with Olivada (page 471). Or serve it hot or warm with any egg dish or after a pasta with tomatoes, such as Summer Spaghetti with Raw Arugula and Tomatoes (page 85).

Shredded Zucchini with Garlic and Herbs

SERVES 4

UNLESS IT IS GRILLED or salted to draw off its excess moisture, zucchini is hopelessly bland. One time-saving way to draw off moisture is to shred the zucchini and then press it dry with a towel. Use any fresh herb on hand, varying the amount depending on its intensity. For instance, use two tablespoons of basil, parsley or chives, but just one tablespoon of oregano, thyme or tarragon. To add color, replace one zucchini with two shredded carrots.

4 medium zucchini (about 1½ pounds), scrubbed and ends trimmed
3 tablespoons extra-virgin olive oil
2 medium garlic cloves, minced
1-2 tablespoons minced fresh herb leaves
Salt and freshly ground black pepper

1. Shred the zucchini using the large holes on a box grater or the shredding disk on a food processor. Wrap the shredded zucchini in a kitchen towel and squeeze gently. Continue squeezing, using new towels if necessary, until the zucchini is fairly dry.

2. Heat the oil in a large skillet set over medium-high heat. Add the zucchini and garlic and cook, stirring occasionally, until the zucchini is tender, about 7 minutes. Stir in the herbs and salt and pepper to taste. Serve immediately.

SERVING SUGGESTIONS

Serve this simple summer side dish with a frittata, especially Frittata with Scallions and Ricotta Salata (page 251) or Arugula Frittata (page 244), to make a light meal. It's also wonderful with any pizza that contains tomatoes or alongside baked tomatoes or a tomato tart.

Grilled Vegetables with Thyme and Garlic

SERVES 6

ZUCCHINI, EGGPLANTS, RED PEPPER AND RED ONIONS, brushed with flavored olive oil, can be grilled until nicely caramelized. Unless the grids on your grill are very closely spaced, use a vegetable grid (see page 552) to keep the onions from falling onto the coals.

- **⅓ cup extra-virgin olive oil**
- **3 medium garlic cloves, minced**
- **1 tablespoon minced fresh thyme leaves, plus several sprigs for garnish**
- **Salt and freshly ground black pepper**
- **3 medium zucchini (about 1¼ pounds), scrubbed**
- **2 medium eggplants (about 1 pound), washed**
- **2 large red onions (about 1 pound)**
- **1 large red bell pepper**

1. Light the grill or make a charcoal fire. Combine the oil, garlic, minced thyme and salt and pepper to taste in a small bowl. Set aside.

2. Trim and discard the ends from the zucchini and eggplants and cut the vegetables lengthwise into ½-inch-thick pieces. Peel the outer slices. Peel and cut the onions crosswise into ½-inch-thick slices and separate the slices into rings. Core, seed and cut the pepper into large wedges. Lay the vegetables on a large baking sheet or platter and brush them with the flavored oil.

3. Place a vegetable grid over a medium-hot fire and heat for several minutes. Spread the onions on the grid in a single layer. Place the remaining vegetables on the open parts of the grill. If necessary, grill the vegetables in batches.

4. Grill, turning the onions several times but the other vegetables just once, until everything is marked with dark stripes, about 6 minutes for the onions and 10 minutes for the zucchini, eggplants and peppers.

5. As each vegetable looks done, transfer it to a large platter. Garnish the platter with thyme sprigs and serve the vegetables hot, warm or at room temperature. *(The vegetables can be covered and kept at room temperature for several hours.)*

SERVING SUGGESTIONS

Serve the vegetables with a pasta dish, such as Linguine with Grilled Plum Tomato Sauce (page 106) or Summer Spaghetti with Raw Arugula and Tomatoes (page 85).

Salads

Although the Italian side of my family has adopted many American customs over the years, we still abide by the tradition of serving salad after the main course rather than as a first course. I have a theory about why most Americans do it the other way round. Bland greens like iceberg lettuce are better suited to calming hunger pangs (which, after all, is a main function for a first course) than cleansing the palate. The more strongly flavored greens that Italians have always favored in their salads are bracing and refreshing, especially if eaten in small quantities after a large meal, and the dressing also helps clear away heavy flavors and prepare the appetite for fruit or dessert.

Most of the leafy salads in this chapter, made with greens like spinach and lettuce as well as arugula, radicchio and endive, are dressed with oil and vinegar (or lemon juice) and are intended to be served in the Italian fashion. The dressing can be made in one of two ways, depending on the desired effect. The greens may be sprinkled with salt and pepper, drizzled with vinegar, then oil, and tossed. This method relies more on tasting as you go than on an exact formula—a sure sign that it is rooted in Italian home cooking. Drizzling the vinegar and oil on separately also allows their flavors to stand out more clearly. Because salads made in this way have a strong acidic punch, be sure to choose only the best vinegars for them. Likewise, use the finest extra-virgin olive oil.

The second method, whisking oil and vinegar or citrus juice together in a vinaigrette, is common practice. It creates a thicker dressing with a mellower flavor, since the tiny vinegar droplets are coated with oil. It also makes it possible to add herbs, garlic and other ingredients to the dressing.

This chapter also contains a number of nonleafy salads. Some are made with raw vegetables like tomatoes, fennel or zucchini, while in others, the vegetables are cooked and cooled. They generally are dressed with oil and sometimes an acid. Many are marinated. These salads are especially welcome in the summer or at any time when, say, a bowl of steaming-hot broccoli would seem out of place but a room-temperature broccoli salad with lemon and tomatoes would be just right. They can also act like condiments alongside a sandwich, pizza or focaccia, or several can be grouped together for a meal. And because the salads are served at room temperature, they give the cook some flexibility when it comes to timing the various other components of a meal.

The chapter concludes with salads made from softened day-old bread or couscous, which are by definition substantial. These salads can stand alone as a light meal or be paired with other salads, either leafy or vegetable, for a summer meal or picnic.

Leafy Salads

Vegetable Salads

Bread and Grain Salads

Arugula, Pine Nut and Parmesan Salad

SERVES 4

THIS SALAD IS BOTH LIGHT (there are only three main ingredients) and rich, due to the nuts and cheese. Although pine nuts are traditional, walnuts would be equally good. Use a vegetable peeler to remove long, thin curls from a piece of Parmigiano-Reggiano. The recipe calls for ½ cup of cheese shavings, but you can add as much or as little as you like.

- **⅓ cup pine nuts**
- **6 cups stemmed arugula leaves (2 large bunches), washed and thoroughly dried**
- **½ cup Parmigiano-Reggiano cheese shavings**
- **Salt**
- **1 tablespoon red wine vinegar**
- **3 tablespoons extra-virgin olive oil**

1. Place the pine nuts in a medium skillet set over medium heat. Toast, shaking the pan occasionally to turn the nuts, until golden, about 5 minutes. Transfer to a plate.

2. Place the arugula, pine nuts and cheese in a large salad bowl. Sprinkle lightly with salt to taste and drizzle with the vinegar. Toss to mix the ingredients.

3. Drizzle the oil over the salad and toss again. Divide among individual plates and serve immediately.

SERVING SUGGESTIONS

Serve this salad after a main course that does not contain much cheese.

Arugula Salad with Sliced Radishes and Carrots

SERVES 4

THIN DISKS OF RADISHES AND CARROTS bring color and contrasting flavors to this arugula salad. The salad is strongly flavored, so I do not use any vinegar, just a light sprinkling of salt and a drizzle of fine olive oil.

5 cups stemmed arugula leaves (2 bunches), washed and thoroughly dried
6 small radishes, ends trimmed, very thinly sliced
2 medium carrots
Salt
3 tablespoons extra-virgin olive oil

1. Place the arugula in a large salad bowl. Add the radish slices. Peel and trim the ends from the carrots and slice them very thinly on the bias. Add the carrots to the bowl.

2. Sprinkle salt to taste over the salad and toss. Drizzle the oil over the salad. Toss again and adjust the seasoning. Divide among individual plates and serve immediately.

SERVING SUGGESTIONS

This salad is good after a rich main course, such as Potato Gnocchi with Butter, Sage and Parmesan (page 222) or Mushroom Tortellini with Brown Butter and Pine Nuts (page 128).

Arugula, Tomato and Black Olive Salad

SERVES 4

IF YOU CAN GET YELLOW TOMATOES, which are sometimes available at gourmet markets and farm stands, use one yellow and one red tomato in this recipe.

- **4 cups stemmed arugula leaves (2 bunches), washed and thoroughly dried**
- **2 medium, ripe tomatoes (about 1 pound), cored and cut into ¾-inch wedges**
- **20 small black olives, pitted**
- **Salt and freshly ground black pepper**
- **2 teaspoons red wine vinegar**
- **2 tablespoons extra-virgin olive oil**

1. Place the arugula, tomatoes and olives in a large salad bowl. Lightly sprinkle with salt and pepper to taste.

2. Drizzle the vinegar and then the oil over the salad. Toss and adjust the seasonings. Divide among individual plates and serve immediately.

SERVING SUGGESTIONS

Serve this salad after egg dishes, pizzas, sandwiches and pastas, such as Zucchini Frittata with Parmesan (page 259), Three-Cheese Pizza (page 439), Scrambled Egg Sandwiches with Red Peppers and Onions (page 474) or Fettuccine with Zucchini, Lemon and Mint (page 112).

Radicchio, Arugula and Endive Salad with Balsamic Vinaigrette

SERVES 4 TO 6

THE COMBINATION OF BITTER GREENS with a lightly sweet balsamic vinaigrette is a classic, and rightly so. Unfortunately, many cooks go overboard with the balsamic vinegar, which is really too strong and sweet to use straight in a salad dressing. It's better to blend it with red wine vinegar.

- **3 cups torn radicchio leaves (1 small head), washed and thoroughly dried**
- **3 cups stemmed arugula leaves (1 large bunch), washed and thoroughly dried**
- **2 cups sliced belgian endive leaves (2 heads), washed and thoroughly dried**
- **2 teaspoons red wine vinegar**
- **1½ teaspoons aged balsamic vinegar**
- **Salt and freshly ground black pepper**
- **¼ cup extra-virgin olive oil**

1. Place the radicchio, arugula and endive in a large salad bowl. Combine the red wine and balsamic vinegars and salt and pepper to taste in a small bowl. Slowly whisk in the oil until the dressing is smooth.

2. Drizzle the dressing over the salad greens and toss. Divide among individual plates and serve immediately.

SERVING SUGGESTIONS

Serve this salad after a main course with some sweetness, such as Potato Gnocchi with Tomato Sauce and Mint (page 224) or Fettuccine with Mascarpone, Toasted Walnuts and Basil (page 84).

Red Leaf Lettuce, Arugula and Fennel Salad

SERVES 4

THE FLAVORS IN THIS SALAD complement each other well. The light dressing of lemon juice and olive oil does not overwhelm the greens or fennel and allows their individual tastes to come through.

1 small fennel bulb (about ¾ pound)
3 cups torn red leaf lettuce, washed and thoroughly dried
3 cups stemmed arugula leaves (1 large bunch), washed and thoroughly dried
1½ tablespoons lemon juice
Salt and freshly ground black pepper
3 tablespoons extra-virgin olive oil

1. Trim and discard the stems and fronds from the fennel. Trim a thick slice from the base of the bulb and remove any tough or blemished outer layers. Cut the bulb in half through the base and use a small, sharp knife to remove the triangular piece of the core from each half. Lay the halves flat side down on a cutting board and slice crosswise as thin as possible. Place the fennel, lettuce and arugula in a large salad bowl.

2. Combine the lemon juice and salt and pepper to taste in a small bowl. Slowly whisk in the oil until the dressing is smooth.

3. Drizzle the dressing over the salad and toss. Divide among individual plates and serve immediately.

SERVING SUGGESTIONS

Serve this versatile salad after a rich main course that contains cheese, eggs, cream and/or butter.

Tender Green Salad with Pine Nuts and Yellow Raisins

SERVES 4 TO 6

ANY TENDER YOUNG LETTUCES ARE APPROPRIATE FOR THIS SALAD, preferably a mixture of some of the following: red leaf lettuce, escarole, watercress, young arugula, frisée, mizuna and tatsoi. Create your own combination or use the prewashed mesclun sold in many markets.

2 tablespoons pine nuts
8 cups tender lettuces and baby greens, washed and thoroughly dried
2 tablespoons yellow raisins
1½ tablespoons lemon juice
Salt and freshly ground black pepper
3 tablespoons extra-virgin olive oil

1. Place the pine nuts in a medium skillet set over medium heat. Toast, shaking the pan occasionally to turn the nuts, until golden, about 5 minutes. Transfer to a plate.

2. Place the greens, pine nuts and raisins in a large salad bowl.

3. Whisk together the lemon juice and salt and pepper to taste in a small bowl. Whisk in the oil until smooth.

4. Drizzle the dressing over the salad and toss. Divide among individual plates and serve immediately.

SERVING SUGGESTIONS

This basic salad should follow a complex main course that does not contain an acidic component. For example, the lemon dressing is a tart foil for the richness of Baked Shells with Fontina and Parmesan Bread Crumbs (page 116).

Tender Greens and Vegetables with Blood Orange Vinaigrette

SERVES 6

THE VINAIGRETTE FOR THIS SALAD is flavored with the zest and juice of a blood orange. A regular orange may be substituted but lacks the complex taste of a blood orange. Regular green beans may be used instead of the thin haricots verts. Increase the cooking time for regular green beans to four to six minutes, depending on their size and freshness.

6 ounces haricots verts
8 cups mixed tender greens, washed and thoroughly dried
1 large yellow bell pepper, cored, seeded and thinly sliced
1 teaspoon grated zest and 2 tablespoons juice from 1 blood orange
1 tablespoon white wine vinegar
Salt and freshly ground black pepper
¼ cup extra-virgin olive oil

1. Bring 1 quart water to a boil in a small saucepan. Snap the ends from the haricots verts. (If using ordinary green beans, cut any long ones in half.) Add the beans to the boiling water and cook for 2 minutes. Drain and refresh in a bowl of cold water. Drain again and dry thoroughly.

2. Place the haricots verts, greens and bell pepper in a large salad bowl.

3. Whisk together the orange zest and juice, vinegar and salt and pepper to taste in a small bowl. Slowly whisk in the oil until the dressing is smooth.

4. Drizzle the dressing over the salad and toss. Divide among individual plates and serve immediately.

SERVING SUGGESTIONS

Serve this substantial salad with almost any frittata or after a rich polenta or pasta dish that contains cheese, especially Polenta with Mascarpone, Rosemary and Walnuts (page 186) or Baked Shells with Fontina and Parmesan Bread Crumbs (page 116).

Mixed Greens with Tomatoes, Yellow Pepper and Fennel

SERVES 8 TO 10

THIS FRESH COMBINATION is among my favorite summer salads. The vegetables add color and flavor to an assortment of greens. You can use mesclun or another salad mix if you like. Aged balsamic vinegar gives the dressing a little sweetness.

- **10 cups mixed greens, washed and thoroughly dried**
- **1 large yellow bell pepper**
- **1 small fennel bulb (about ¾ pound)**
- **2 medium, ripe tomatoes (about ¾ pound), cored and cut into very thin wedges**
- **1 tablespoon red wine vinegar**
- **1½ teaspoons aged balsamic vinegar**
- **Salt and freshly ground black pepper**
- **4½ tablespoons extra-virgin olive oil**

1. Place the greens in a large salad bowl. Core, halve and seed the pepper. Cut the pepper halves crosswise in half then cut them into very thin strips about 2 inches long. Add the pepper to the greens.

2. Trim and discard the stems and fronds from the fennel. Trim a thick slice from the base of the bulb and remove any tough or blemished outer layers. Cut the bulb in half through the base and use a small, sharp knife to remove the triangular piece of the core from each half. Lay the halves, flat side down, on a cutting board and slice crosswise as thin as possible. Add the fennel strips and tomatoes to the greens and pepper.

3. Whisk the red wine and balsamic vinegars and salt and pepper to taste in a small bowl. Whisk in the oil until the dressing is smooth.

4. Drizzle the dressing over the salad and toss. Divide among individual plates and serve immediately.

SERVING SUGGESTIONS

This salad is a festive way to end a summer meal. Serve it after Grilled Portobello Mushrooms, Red Onions and Bell Peppers (page 320) or Zucchini Stuffed with Ricotta and Herbs (page 308).

Romaine Lettuce Salad with Gorgonzola and Walnuts

SERVES 4 TO 6

ROMAINE LETTUCE CAN STAND UP TO CHEESE AND NUTS. Do not try to use a more tender green. I prefer a mild, creamy Gorgonzola, called *dolcelatte,* for this dish. Add salt sparingly to the dressing, because the cheese is fairly salty.

½ cup walnut halves
1 medium romaine lettuce head (about 1 pound)
3 ounces mild Gorgonzola *(dolcelatte)* cheese, crumbled (scant ½ cup)
1 tablespoon red wine vinegar
Salt and freshly ground black pepper
¼ cup extra-virgin olive oil

1. Place the walnuts in a medium skillet set over medium heat. Toast, shaking the pan occasionally to turn the nuts, until fragrant, about 5 minutes. Transfer to a plate.

2. Remove and discard the tough outer leaves from the lettuce and detach the remaining leaves from the core. Wash the leaves in successive bowls of cold water until grit no longer appears in the bottom of the bowl. Thoroughly dry the lettuce. Tear the leaves into bite-size pieces and place them in a large salad bowl. *(The lettuce can be covered with plastic and refrigerated for several hours.)*

3. Scatter the cheese and nuts over the lettuce. Whisk the vinegar and salt and pepper to taste in a small bowl. Slowly whisk in the oil until the dressing is smooth.

4. Drizzle the dressing over the salad and toss until the leaves are evenly coated. Divide among individual plates and serve immediately.

SERVING SUGGESTIONS

This salad can be served for four as a light lunch or for six as an after-dinner salad. For lunch, add a simple bruschetta or focaccia, such as Focaccia with Onions (page 448) or bread. For dinner, start with a frittata, such as Asparagus Frittata with Basil, Shallots and Parmesan (page 245) or Onion and Mushroom Frittata (page 247). The salad is a good choice before a dessert of fresh fruit, especially ripe autumn pears.

Wilted Spinach Salad with Polenta Croutons

SERVES 2 TO 4

LEFTOVER POLENTA can be cut into small croutons, fried and used to garnish a spinach salad. Fresh mushrooms and a warm lemon-garlic dressing round out this dish. I prefer to use young spinach leaves, but larger spinach leaves can be stemmed and torn into bite-size pieces.

You can use leftovers from Polenta Lasagne with Mushroom Sauce and Parmesan (see Serving Suggestions, page 215) or from leftover Basic Soft Polenta (page 181) that has been cooled until firm.

- 6 cups packed baby spinach leaves
- 4 ounces cremini or white button mushrooms, wiped clean, stems trimmed, thinly sliced
- ¼ cup extra-virgin olive oil
- Polenta croutons, cut into 1-inch squares (see above)
- 1 small garlic clove, minced
- ¾ teaspoon salt
- ¼ teaspoon freshly ground black pepper
- 2 tablespoons lemon juice

1. Wash the spinach leaves in successive bowls of cold water until grit no longer appears in the bottom of the bowl. Shake the leaves to remove excess water and dry them thoroughly. Place the spinach in a large bowl. Add the mushrooms and set aside.

2. Heat the oil in a medium skillet. When it is hot, add the polenta croutons. Fry over medium-high heat until they are crisp and a rich golden color on the bottom, about 5 minutes. Carefully flip them and continue cooking until they are crisp on the second side, 3 to 4 minutes. Use a slotted spatula to transfer the croutons to a platter lined with paper towels. Remove the pan from the heat.

3. Let the oil cool in the skillet until no longer hot but still quite warm, about 1 minute. If necessary, return the pan to low heat. Add the garlic and cook until golden, about 2 minutes.

4. Whisk the salt, pepper and lemon juice into the pan. Add the croutons to the salad. Pour the warm dressing over and toss gently. Divide among individual plates and serve immediately.

SERVING SUGGESTIONS

This is a perfect lunch for two or a substantial first course for four. If serving as a first course, follow with Mixed Roasted Vegetables with Rosemary and Garlic (page 318) or baked stuffed tomatoes (pages 310 to 314).

Spinach Salad with Orange Juice Vinaigrette and Toasted Walnuts

SERVES 4

WALNUT OIL COMPLEMENTS THE TOASTED NUTS IN THIS SALAD and works well with the fresh orange juice and zest in the dressing. Look for the oil in better supermarkets, gourmet shops or natural-food stores. Walnut oil is highly perishable, so store it in the refrigerator.

- **⅓ cup walnut halves**
- **1 pound flat-leaf spinach**
- **1 teaspoon grated zest and 2 tablespoons juice from 1 orange**
- **1 teaspoon finely minced shallot**
- **Salt and freshly ground black pepper**
- **2 tablespoons walnut oil**

1. Place the walnuts in a medium skillet set over medium heat. Toast, shaking the pan occasionally to turn the nuts, until fragrant, about 5 minutes. Transfer to a plate.

2. Remove and discard the stems from the spinach. Wash the leaves in successive bowls of cold water until grit no longer appears in the bottom of the bowl. Shake the leaves to remove excess water and dry thoroughly. Place the spinach in a large salad bowl.

3. Combine the orange zest and juice, shallot and salt and pepper to taste in a small bowl. Slowly whisk in the oil until the dressing is smooth. Adjust the seasonings.

4. Add the walnuts to the bowl with the spinach. Drizzle the dressing over the salad and toss gently. Divide among individual plates and serve immediately.

SERVING SUGGESTIONS

This salad complements egg dishes, such as Onion and Mushroom Frittata (page 247) or Red Pepper Frittata with Mint (page 250), and pasta dishes, such as Fusilli with Spicy Tomato Sauce and Ricotta Salata (page 78) or Penne with Oven-Dried Tomatoes, Olives and Herbs (page 80).

Radicchio and Cannellini Bean Salad

SERVES 6

STRIPS OF BITTER RADICCHIO contrast with creamy cannellini beans. The radicchio and beans are dressed with a little oil and served over a bed of arugula. Due to the sharpness of the greens, there is no vinegar in this salad.

3 cups stemmed arugula leaves (1 large bunch), washed and thoroughly dried
5 cups torn radicchio leaves (1 large head), washed and thoroughly dried
1½ cups Basic Cannellini Beans (page 286)
¼ cup extra-virgin olive oil
Salt and freshly ground black pepper

1. Divide the arugula among 6 salad plates. Set aside.

2. Remove the core from the radicchio with a small, sharp knife. Cut the radicchio in half through the core end. Lay the halves, flat side down, on a cutting board and cut them crosswise into very thin strips. Place the radicchio in a large bowl. Add the beans and toss.

3. Drizzle the oil over the radicchio and beans. Sprinkle with salt and pepper to taste and toss again. Adjust the seasonings. Spoon some of the salad over the arugula on each plate and serve immediately.

SERVING SUGGESTIONS

Serve this salad with sandwiches, especially Tomato Panini with Basil Mayonnaise (page 468), Grilled Eggplant and Red Pepper Sandwiches with Olivada (page 471) or Panini with Marinated Artichokes, Fontina and Basil (page 472).

Fava Bean and Asparagus Salad with Basil Toasts

SERVES 4

THIS SPRING SALAD brings together fava beans and asparagus. Parmesan is shaved over the lightly dressed vegetables, which are served with toast.

- 1 pound fresh fava beans in pods
- 1¼ pounds medium asparagus
- Salt
- 2 tablespoons extra-virgin olive oil, plus more to taste
- 1 tablespoon minced fresh basil leaves
- 4 ½-inch-thick slices Italian bread (each about 3 inches across)
- 1 medium lemon, halved
- Large piece of Parmigiano-Reggiano cheese, enough for about 12 thin shavings

1. Bring 1 quart water to a boil in a medium saucepan. Shell the fava beans. There should be about 1 cup shelled beans. Add the beans to the boiling water and simmer for 2 minutes. Drain the beans, refresh them in cold water and drain again. Use your fingers to scrape away part of the outer light green skin on each fava. Squeeze the skin to pop out the dark green beans. Set aside.

2. Bring 2 quarts water to a boil in a medium saucepan. Snap off the tough ends from the asparagus. Add the asparagus and salt to taste to the boiling water. Cook until the spears are tender, about 4 minutes. Drain, refresh in cold water and drain again. Set aside.

3. Combine the 2 tablespoons oil, basil and salt to taste in a small bowl and set aside. Toast the bread until golden brown on both sides. Brush 1 side of each bread slice with the basil oil.

4. Arrange the cooked fava beans and asparagus on individual salad plates. Squeeze lemon juice to taste over the vegetables and drizzle with olive oil to taste. Place 1 toast, oiled side up, on each plate and use a vegetable peeler to shave several thin cheese slices over each plate. Serve immediately.

SERVING SUGGESTIONS

This fairly substantial salad can be served as a first course, before a frittata or risotto, or it can conclude the meal. It's good after a main course that does not contain many vegetables, such as Lemon Risotto (page 162).

Marinated Yellow Beans and Summer Tomato Salad

SERVES 4

I MAKE THIS DISH when local yellow string beans, also called wax beans, are at my farmers' market. The juice of summer tomatoes and good-quality red wine vinegar give the beans a wonderful flavor. The dish can be made with green beans, but they cannot be marinated for more than 30 minutes without discoloring.

1 pound yellow string beans, ends snapped off
Salt
1½ tablespoons red wine vinegar
1 medium shallot, minced
Freshly ground black pepper
4½ tablespoons extra-virgin olive oil
3 small, ripe tomatoes (about ¾ pound), cored and cut into ¾-inch cubes

1. Bring several quarts water to a boil in a medium pan. Add the beans and salt to taste. Simmer until almost tender, about 5 minutes. Drain and let cool to room temperature.

2. Whisk together the vinegar, shallot and salt and pepper to taste in a large serving bowl. Whisk in the oil. Add the tomatoes and toss to coat them with the dressing. Let stand for 5 minutes to blend the flavors.

3. Add the cooled beans and toss again. Marinate for at least 30 minutes. *(The salad may be covered and kept at room temperature for up to 2 hours.)* Adjust the seasonings and serve.

SERVING SUGGESTIONS

Serve this salad with a pasta dish, such as Fettuccine with Zucchini, Lemon and Mint (page 112), or a rice dish, such as Boiled Arborio Rice with Mozzarella and Herbs (page 173). Or make a meal of it with another vegetable salad, such as Raw Zucchini Salad with Lemon and Basil (page 397), and a loaf of bread and some cheese.

Roasted Beet Salad with Watercress, Walnuts and Fresh Pecorino

SERVES 4

IN THIS SALAD, warm roasted beets are served on a bed of watercress with strips of fresh Pecorino cheese. Fresh Pecorino is a mild semisoft sheep's milk cheese with a texture akin to Bel Paese or Italian fontina, either of which can be used as a substitute.

- 3 medium beets (about ¾ pound without greens), scrubbed
- ½ cup walnuts
- 1 bunch watercress (about 6 ounces)
- 2 teaspoons aged balsamic vinegar
- 2 teaspoons red wine vinegar
- Salt and freshly ground black pepper
- 3 tablespoons extra-virgin olive oil
- 2 ounces fresh Pecorino cheese, cut into very thin strips

1. Preheat the oven to 400 degrees F. Trim all but the last inch of the beet stems, saving the leaves for another purpose. Trim any long dangling roots. Wrap the beets in aluminum foil. Bake until the beets are tender, 1 to 1¼ hours, or until a metal skewer glides through them easily. Unwrap and let cool.

2. While the beets cool, place the walnuts in a medium skillet set over medium heat. Toast, shaking the pan occasionally to turn the nuts, until fragrant, about 5 minutes. Transfer to a plate.

3. Trim the stems of the watercress about ½ inch below the leaves. Wash and thoroughly dry the watercress. Divide among individual salad plates.

4. Place the balsamic and red wine vinegars and salt and pepper to taste in a small bowl. Slowly whisk in the oil until smooth. Set aside.

5. Use a paper towel to lift off and discard the skins from the warm beets. Cut the beets into ¼-inch-thick slices.

6. Arrange the beet slices over the watercress and drizzle with the dressing. Garnish with toasted walnuts and cheese shavings. Serve immediately.

SERVING SUGGESTIONS

This dish makes an elegant first course, or it can be served after a main course like Spaghetti with Spicy Spinach and Toasted Bread Crumbs (page 104) or Risotto with Fennel (page 142). It can also be served as lunch for two.

Spicy Broccoli Salad with Lemon

SERVES 4 TO 6

SINCE LEMON JUICE will discolor cooked broccoli if it is added while the florets are still hot, dress the drained broccoli with the olive oil, allow it to cool to room temperature and stir in the lemon juice just before serving. I like this dish spicy, but you can use less red pepper for a milder version.

1 large bunch broccoli (about 1¾ pounds)
Salt
3 tablespoons extra-virgin olive oil
½ teaspoon dried hot red pepper flakes
1 tablespoon lemon juice

1. Bring several quarts water to a boil in a large saucepan. Remove and discard all but ½ to 1 inch of the broccoli stalks. Cut the florets and the remaining portion of the stalks into 2-inch pieces.

2. Add the broccoli and salt to taste to the boiling water. Cook until the broccoli is tender, about 6 minutes. Drain well and transfer to a serving bowl. Drizzle the oil over and sprinkle with the hot red pepper flakes. Mix to coat the florets evenly. Set aside to cool to room temperature.

3. Drizzle the lemon juice over the broccoli and mix well. Add salt to taste and serve immediately.

SERVING SUGGESTIONS

Add this salad to a meal that includes a room-temperature frittata or pasta dish, such as Frittata with Scallions and Ricotta Salata (page 251) or Linguine with Grilled Plum Tomato Sauce (page 106).

Broccoli and Tomato Salad with Lemon-Basil Dressing

SERVES 4 TO 6

THIS SALAD PAIRS BROCCOLI SPEARS with slices of summer tomatoes. The dressing gives both vegetables a clean, fresh flavor.

1 medium bunch broccoli (about 1½ pounds)
Salt
2 medium, ripe tomatoes (about ¾ pound), cored and cut crosswise into ½-inch-thick slices
1 tablespoon lemon juice
1 small garlic clove, finely minced
Freshly ground black pepper
3 tablespoons extra-virgin olive oil
1 tablespoon minced fresh basil leaves

1. Bring several quarts water to a boil in a large saucepan. Trim all but the last 3 inches from the broccoli stalks. Break the broccoli into fairly large spears and peel away the tough outer layer from the stalks. Add the broccoli and salt to taste to the boiling water. Cook until the broccoli is tender, 5 to 6 minutes. Drain and refresh under cold running water. Drain well and blot dry with paper towels.

2. Arrange the broccoli on a large platter, alternating with tomato slices. *(The platter may be covered and set aside at room temperature for 1 hour.)*

3. Whisk together the lemon juice, garlic and salt and pepper to taste in a small bowl. Whisk in the oil until the dressing is smooth. Stir in the basil and adjust the seasonings.

4. Drizzle the dressing over the vegetables and serve immediately.

SERVING SUGGESTIONS

This salad can follow a pizza without tomatoes, such as Pizza with Mozzarella, Onions and Olives (page 431) or Three-Cheese Pizza (page 439). Or serve it with Boiled Arborio Rice with Mozzarella and Herbs (page 173).

Grated Carrot Salad with Lemon and Currants

SERVES 4

ITALIANS SHRED CARROTS and dress them with a little lemon juice, salt and, of course, good-quality olive oil. I like currants in the salad (they add a sweet note), but they can be omitted if desired.

2 tablespoons dried currants
8 medium carrots (about 1 pound), peeled and trimmed
4 teaspoons lemon juice
3 tablespoons extra-virgin olive oil
Salt

1. Place the currants in a small bowl. Cover them with boiling water and soak for 15 minutes, or until softened.

2. Grate the carrots using the largest holes on a hand grater or the shredding disk on a food processor. Place the carrots in a large serving bowl.

3. Drain the currants and add them to the bowl with the carrots. Drizzle with lemon juice and mix. Drizzle with oil and sprinkle with salt to taste. Toss and adjust the seasonings. Serve immediately.

SERVING SUGGESTIONS

This slawlike salad is an accompaniment rather than a stand-alone dish. Serve it with an egg dish, such as Zucchini Frittata with Parmesan (page 259), or a sandwich, such as Tomato Panini with Basil Mayonnaise (page 468). It can also be part of an antipasto spread.

Marinated Cauliflower Salad with Olives

SERVES 4

IN THIS SICILIAN DISH, cauliflower is dressed with olives and a vinaigrette seasoned with parsley. I prefer small olives, such as niçoise, here. They are usually less salty than large black olives and do not overwhelm the other flavors.

1 medium cauliflower head (about 2 pounds), stems removed, cut into bite-size florets
Salt
1 tablespoon white wine vinegar
2 tablespoons minced fresh parsley leaves
Freshly ground black pepper
3 tablespoons extra-virgin olive oil
⅓ cup small black olives, pitted

1. Bring several quarts water to a boil in a medium saucepan. Add the cauliflower and salt to taste. Cook until the cauliflower is just tender, 5 to 6 minutes. Drain and set aside to cool to room temperature.

2. Whisk together the vinegar, parsley and salt and pepper to taste in a large serving bowl. Slowly whisk in the oil until the dressing is smooth. Adjust the seasonings.

3. Add the cauliflower and olives and toss. Marinate at room temperature for at least 1 hour. *(The salad can be kept at room temperature for up to 6 hours.)*

SERVING SUGGESTIONS

This dish would go well with most summer meals. I particularly like it with any fresh-tomato pizza.

Fennel and Orange Salad

SERVES 4

THIS SALAD IS POPULAR IN SOUTHERN ITALY, where fennel is much appreciated because it is so refreshing. Use small black olives in brine, such as niçoise or gaeta. Although mint is the classic herbal garnish, chopped parsley can be substituted.

2 large seedless oranges
1 medium fennel bulb (about 1¼ pounds)
⅓ cup small black olives
12 large fresh mint leaves, cut into thin strips
Salt and freshly ground black pepper
2 tablespoons extra-virgin olive oil

1. Trim thick slices from the ends of the oranges so they sit flat on the cutting board. Slice downward around the oranges to remove the peel and white pith. Slice the oranges crosswise into ½-inch-thick circles. Place the orange slices and any juice they have given off in a large bowl.

2. Trim and discard the stems and fronds from the fennel. Trim a thick slice from the base of the bulb and remove any tough or blemished outer layers. Cut the bulb in half through the base and use a small, sharp knife to remove the triangular piece of the core from each half. With the flat side of the fennel bulb down and your knife parallel to the work surface, slice each fennel half crosswise to yield several ½-inch-thick slices. Cut the slices lengthwise to yield long strips about ¼ inch thick.

3. Add the fennel, olives and mint to the bowl with the oranges. Season with salt and pepper to taste. Drizzle with the oil and toss. Serve immediately.

SERVING SUGGESTIONS

Serve this crisp, refreshing salad after a main course with lots of butter, cheese or eggs, such as Potato Gnocchi Gratinéed with Fontina Cheese (page 225) or Orecchiette with Peas, Ricotta and Parmesan (page 102).

Grilled Portobello Mushroom Salad with Red Peppers and Garlic Croutons

SERVES 4

I LIKE TO SERVE THIS GRILLED SALAD at room temperature. Since the croutons become soggy fairly quickly, I don't add them until the last minute.

5 tablespoons extra-virgin olive oil
2 medium garlic cloves, minced
1 teaspoon grated zest and 1 tablespoon juice from 1 lemon
Salt and freshly ground black pepper
2 large portobello mushrooms (about 1 pound)
1 large red bell pepper
4 ½-inch-thick slices country white bread
3 tablespoons minced fresh parsley leaves

1. Light the grill or make a charcoal fire. Combine 4 tablespoons of the oil with the garlic, lemon zest and salt and pepper to taste in a small bowl. Set aside.

2. Remove and discard the mushroom stems. (They may be saved for making stock.) Wipe the caps clean with a paper towel. Core, seed and cut the pepper into large wedges. Place the mushrooms, pepper and bread slices on a large platter and brush them generously with the flavored oil.

3. Place the vegetables and bread over a medium-hot fire, making sure that the mushrooms are gill side up. Grill, turning the pepper and bread once but leaving the mushrooms as is, until they are streaked with dark grill stripes, about 2 minutes for the bread and 10 minutes for the mushrooms and pepper.

4. Transfer the vegetables and bread to a cutting board. Cut the mushrooms in half and then into ½-inch-wide strips. Cut the pepper into ¼-inch-wide strips. Cut the bread into ½-inch croutons.

5. Toss the vegetables in a large serving bowl with the remaining 1 tablespoon oil, the lemon juice and parsley. Adjust the seasonings. *(The vegetables can be covered and kept at room temperature for 1 hour.)* Stir in the croutons and serve immediately.

SERVING SUGGESTIONS
Serve as a side dish with eggs, especially Frittata with Ricotta and Mint (page 261) or Arugula Frittata (page 244).

Roasted Potato Salad with Herbs and Red Wine Vinegar

SERVES 6

IN THIS POTATO SALAD, roasting rather than the conventional boiling intensifies the flavor of the potatoes. Although any baking potatoes will do, small white ones about the length of one finger and the width of three work best.

- **2 pounds small white potatoes, scrubbed and cut into 1-inch cubes**
- **5 tablespoons extra-virgin olive oil**
- **Salt**
- **3 medium garlic cloves, minced**
- **4 teaspoons red wine vinegar**
- **15 large fresh basil leaves, cut into thin strips**
- **1 teaspoon whole fresh thyme leaves**
- **Freshly ground black pepper**

1. Preheat the oven to 425 degrees F. Place the potatoes in a baking dish large enough to hold them in a single layer. Drizzle 3 tablespoons of the oil over the potatoes and sprinkle with ½ teaspoon salt. Mix to coat evenly.

2. Bake the potatoes, turning once, for 30 minutes. Sprinkle with the garlic, drizzle with another 1 tablespoon oil and turn again. Continue baking until the potatoes are golden brown, about 30 minutes more.

3. Transfer the potatoes to a large serving bowl. Drizzle with the vinegar and toss. Add the remaining 1 tablespoon oil, the basil, thyme and pepper to taste and toss again. Serve warm or at room temperature. *(The potato salad will keep at room temperature for several hours.)*

SERVING SUGGESTIONS

Serve this dish with Steamed Green Beans with Tarragon (page 347), a plate of impeccably ripe sliced tomatoes and a frittata, especially Red Pepper Frittata with Mint (page 250) or Red Onion Frittata with Parmesan and Thyme (page 248). The beans and frittata can be served slightly warm or at room temperature.

Grilled Potato Salad with Red Pepper and Onion

SERVES 4 TO 6

GRILLED NEW POTATOES, RED BELL PEPPER AND RED ONION seasoned with garlic and oregano are drizzled with a little white wine vinegar and oil. The potatoes will cook more evenly if parboiled before grilling.

- **2 pounds small new potatoes, scrubbed**
- **Salt**
- **1 medium red bell pepper, cored, seeded and cut into 1-inch-wide strips**
- **1 large red onion, sliced crosswise into ½-inch-thick rings**
- **¼ cup extra-virgin olive oil**
- **2 medium garlic cloves, minced**
- **2 teaspoons minced fresh oregano or thyme leaves**
- **Freshly ground black pepper**
- **1 tablespoon white wine vinegar**

1. Bring several quarts water to a boil in a large saucepan. Add the potatoes and salt to taste. Simmer until a skewer slides through the potatoes with just a little resistance, about 12 minutes. Drain and cool to room temperature.

2. Light the grill or make a charcoal fire. Cut small potatoes in half or quarter large ones. Place the potatoes, red pepper and onion in a large dish. Combine 3 tablespoons of the oil with the garlic, oregano or thyme and salt and pepper to taste in a small bowl. Brush over the vegetables.

3. If the grates on your grill are widely spaced, place a vegetable grid (see page 552) over a medium-hot fire and heat it for several minutes. Place the onion, potatoes and pepper on the grid. (If necessary, grill the vegetables in batches.)

4. Grill, turning once, until the vegetables are marked with dark stripes, about 8 minutes for the pepper and onion and 10 minutes for the potatoes. As each vegetable looks done, transfer it to a large bowl.

5. When all the vegetables are cooked, drizzle with vinegar and toss. Drizzle the remaining 1 tablespoon oil over and adjust the seasonings. Serve warm or at room temperature. *(The salad can be covered and kept at room temperature for several hours.)*

SERVING SUGGESTIONS

Serve this dish with any meal from the grill. In summer, accompany it with Grilled Zucchini and Eggplant Salad with Tomatoes and Balsamic Vinegar (page 398), a loaf of bread and some cheese. The dish can also double as a main course for four if the salad is spooned over lightly dressed mixed greens.

Tomato Salad with Black Olives, Capers and Herbs

SERVES 4

RIPE SUMMER TOMATOES need little to make a memorable salad, but in this dish, they are embellished with olives and capers.

- 4 medium, ripe tomatoes (about 1½ pounds), cored and cut crosswise into ½-inch-thick slices
- 10 large black olives, pitted and sliced (about ¼ cup)
- 1 teaspoon drained capers, rinsed
- 8 large fresh basil leaves, cut into thin strips
- 1 teaspoon minced fresh oregano leaves
- Salt and freshly ground black pepper
- 2 tablespoons extra-virgin olive oil

1. Arrange the tomato slices on a large serving platter. Scatter the olives, capers, basil and oregano over the tomatoes. *(The platter can be covered and kept at room temperature for up to 1 hour.)*

2. Lightly sprinkle the tomatoes with salt and pepper to taste, since the olives and capers are salty. Drizzle with oil and serve immediately.

SERVING SUGGESTIONS

This dish can be served as an antipasto or a salad. As an antipasto, serve it with grilled bread. As a salad, serve it after an egg dish, tart, rice dish or pasta that does not contain tomatoes.

Marinated Tomato and Red Onion Salad

SERVES 2 TO 4

THIS SALAD IS ONE OF MY FAVORITES for peak-season tomatoes. The dressing contains red wine vinegar for acidity and balsamic vinegar for sweetness. A high-quality aged balsamic will shine in this dish. Mint or parsley can be substituted for the basil. This recipe yields four small servings if served with other salads or two generous servings if it is the only vegetable on the table.

4 small, ripe tomatoes (about 1 pound), cored and cut into ¾-inch-thick wedges
½ small red onion, diced (about ¼ cup)
8 large fresh basil leaves, cut into thin strips
1 teaspoon red wine vinegar
1 teaspoon aged balsamic vinegar
Salt and freshly ground black pepper
2 tablespoons extra-virgin olive oil

1. Place the tomatoes, onion and basil in a large serving bowl.

2. Whisk together the red wine and balsamic vinegars and salt and pepper to taste in a small bowl. Whisk in the oil until the dressing is smooth. Pour the dressing over the salad and toss.

3. Cover and set aside at room temperature for at least 30 minutes, but not more than 2 hours. Just before serving, toss again and adjust the seasonings.

SERVING SUGGESTIONS

This salad can be served at any summer meal; it is especially good with sandwiches or with pizza, pasta or rice dishes that do not contain tomatoes, such as Three-Cheese Pizza (page 439), Grilled Smoked Mozzarella and Arugula Panini (page 473) or Risotto with Spinach and Herbs (page 166).

Marinated Zucchini Salad with Lemon and Thyme

SERVES 4 TO 6

BLANCHED ZUCCHINI ARE MARINATED in a dressing of lemon juice, garlic, thyme and olive oil. The zucchini gives off some liquid as it cools, so lifting it out of the dressing before serving makes for a neater presentation.

2 tablespoons lemon juice
2 medium garlic cloves, minced
1 teaspoon minced fresh thyme leaves
Salt and freshly ground black pepper
¼ cup extra-virgin olive oil
6 small zucchini (about 1½ pounds), scrubbed and ends trimmed

1. Whisk together the lemon juice, garlic, thyme and salt and pepper to taste in a large bowl. Whisk in the oil until smooth and adjust the seasonings. Set aside.

2. Bring several quarts water to a boil in a large saucepan for cooking the zucchini.

3. Cut the zucchini into ½-inch-thick strips about 3 inches long. Add the zucchini and salt to taste to the boiling water and simmer until crisp-tender, about 2 minutes.

4. Drain the zucchini well and place it in the bowl with the dressing. Toss to coat evenly. Cool to room temperature, stirring occasionally. *(The zucchini can be kept at room temperature for up to 2 hours.)* When ready to serve, use a slotted spoon or large fork to lift the zucchini onto a platter or individual plates.

SERVING SUGGESTIONS

Serve after a pasta or rice dish with tomatoes, such as Linguine with Grilled Plum Tomato Sauce (page 106) or Risotto with Tomatoes, Parmesan and Basil (page 168).

Raw Zucchini Salad with Lemon and Basil

SERVES 4

FOR THIS SALAD, you need to slice the zucchini transparently thin. Use a mandoline, if possible, or the slicing blade of a food processor or a very sharp chef's knife. Chill the zucchini and dress it just before serving to prevent wilting.

- **4 medium zucchini (about 1½ pounds), scrubbed and ends trimmed**
- **3 tablespoons extra-virgin olive oil**
- **1 tablespoon lemon juice**
- **Salt**
- **10 large fresh basil leaves, cut into very thin strips**

1. Slice the zucchini as thin as possible. Place in a large bowl and refrigerate until well chilled. *(The zucchini may be refrigerated for several hours.)*

2. When ready to serve, whisk together the oil, lemon juice and salt to taste in a small bowl. Drizzle the dressing over the zucchini and sprinkle with the shredded basil leaves. Toss and adjust the seasonings. Serve immediately.

SERVING SUGGESTIONS

Serve this refreshing salad after a simple pasta or rice dish with tomatoes, such as Summer Spaghetti with Raw Arugula and Tomatoes (page 85) or Risotto with Peas and Plum Tomatoes (page 164).

Grilled Zucchini and Eggplant Salad with Tomatoes and Balsamic Vinegar

SERVES 6

THIS SALAD is served at room temperature and so can be made several hours in advance. Although the delicate flavor of small eggplants (either white or purple) makes this dish very special, large eggplants can be used—just slice them into ½-inch-thick rounds for grilling. You can substitute an equal amount of parsley or half as much oregano, thyme or mint for the basil.

- **3 medium zucchini (about 1¼ pounds), scrubbed and ends trimmed**
- **2 medium eggplants (about 1 pound), washed and ends trimmed**
- **¼ cup extra-virgin olive oil**
- **Salt and freshly ground black pepper**
- **1½ tablespoons aged balsamic vinegar**
- **2 medium, ripe tomatoes (about ¾ pound)**
- **¼ cup minced fresh basil leaves**

1. Light the grill or make a charcoal fire.

2. Trim the ends from the zucchini and eggplants and cut them lengthwise into ½-inch-thick strips. Remove the peel from the outer slices so that they match the others. Lay the strips on a baking sheet and brush both sides lightly with 2 tablespoons of the oil. Season generously with salt and pepper.

3. Grill the zucchini and eggplant until dark grill marks are visible on both sides, about 5 minutes per side. Remove from the grill and cool to room temperature.

4. Whisk the remaining 2 tablespoons oil with the vinegar, ½ teaspoon salt and ¼ teaspoon pepper in a large serving bowl. Core the tomatoes and cut each into 12 wedges. Toss the tomatoes and basil with the dressing.

5. Cut the grilled vegetables into 2-inch pieces. Add them to the tomatoes and mix. Serve at once or cover and set aside at room temperature for up to 3 hours.

SERVING SUGGESTIONS

Serve the salad as part of a summer meal with an egg dish or a sandwich or after a pasta or rice dish. Since it is hearty, it can make a meal out of something that might seem too light on its own for dinner, such as Pesto Rice (page 174) or Mozzarella Panini with Black Olive Paste (page 465).

Panzanella

SERVES 4 TO 6

THRIFTY TUSCANS PUT DAY-OLD BREAD TO GOOD USE in dishes like this tomato-and-bread salad. The bread cubes absorb juices from the tomatoes and red wine vinegar and take on a rosy hue. This dish is best made with country white bread or sourdough bread that is a day or two old. Save rock-hard bread for crumb-making.

- **4 cups day-old country white bread, cut into 1-inch cubes**
- **3 large, ripe tomatoes (about 1½ pounds), cored and cut into ½-inch cubes**
- **½ small red onion, thinly sliced**
- **½ cucumber, peeled, halved lengthwise, seeded and diced small**
- **6 large green olives, pitted and coarsely chopped**
- **8 large fresh basil leaves, cut into thin strips**
- **1 teaspoon minced fresh oregano leaves**
- **Salt and freshly ground black pepper**
- **1½ tablespoons red wine vinegar**
- **3 tablespoons extra-virgin olive oil**

1. Place the bread, tomatoes, onion, cucumber, olives, basil and oregano in a large bowl. Sprinkle with salt and pepper to taste and toss.

2. Drizzle the vinegar and then the oil over the salad. Mix and set aside at room temperature until the bread softens somewhat but is not mushy, about 30 minutes. *(If the bread is quite stale, you may need to set aside the salad for 1 to 2 hours at room temperature.)* Adjust the seasonings and serve immediately.

SERVING SUGGESTIONS

Because this salad is dressed in advance of serving, it is a favorite for picnics. Serve it with other marinated vegetable salads, especially Grilled Potato Salad with Red Pepper and Onion (page 392) and Marinated Zucchini Salad with Lemon and Thyme (page 396). Or line four large plates with lightly dressed arugula or leaf lettuce and divide the bread mixture among the plates for a summer lunch.

Bread Salad with Roasted Peppers and Black Olives

SERVES 4 TO 6

IN THIS BREAD SALAD, the juice of roasted red bell peppers helps moisten the bread. Be sure to work over a bowl when peeling and seeding the peppers.

- 2 large red bell peppers (about 1 pound)
- 8 large black olives, pitted and chopped
- 1 celery rib, minced
- 1 medium scallion, white and light green parts only, thinly sliced
- 1 tablespoon chopped fresh basil leaves
- 4 cups day-old bread, cut into 1-inch cubes
- Salt and freshly ground black pepper
- 1½ tablespoons white wine vinegar
- 3 tablespoons extra-virgin olive oil

1. Roast and peel the peppers as directed on page 526, working over a bowl to catch the juice. Core and seed the peppers and cut them into ½-inch-wide strips.

2. Place the peppers and juice in a large serving bowl. Add the olives, celery, scallion, basil and bread. Sprinkle with salt and pepper to taste and toss.

3. Drizzle the vinegar and then the oil over the salad. Mix and set aside at room temperature until the bread softens somewhat but is not mushy, about 30 minutes. *(If the bread is quite stale, you may need to set aside the salad for 1 to 2 hours at room temperature.)* Adjust the seasonings and serve immediately.

SERVING SUGGESTIONS

If spooned over salad greens, this dish makes a light lunch. It can also be served as part of a room-temperature summer meal, with grilled vegetables or marinated vegetable salads.

Whole Wheat Bread Salad with Arugula, Fennel and Tomatoes

SERVES 4

WHOLE WHEAT COUNTRY BREAD makes this salad particularly hearty. If possible, use one red and one yellow tomato.

1 small fennel bulb (about ¾ pound)
4 cups day-old whole wheat bread, cut into 1-inch cubes
3 large, ripe tomatoes (about 1½ pounds), cored and cut into ½-inch cubes
12 large black olives, pitted and coarsely chopped
8 large fresh basil leaves, cut into thin strips
Salt and freshly ground black pepper
2 tablespoons lemon juice
3 tablespoons extra-virgin olive oil
3 cups stemmed arugula leaves (1 large bunch), washed and thoroughly dried

1. Trim the stems and fronds from the fennel. Discard the stems; mince and reserve 2 tablespoons of the fronds. Trim a thick slice from the base of the bulb and remove any tough or blemished outer layers. Cut the bulb in half through the base and use a small, sharp knife to remove the triangular piece of the core from each half. Lay the halves, flat side down, on a cutting board and slice crosswise as thin as possible.

2. Place the fennel and minced fronds in a large serving bowl. Add the bread, tomatoes, olives and basil. Sprinkle with salt and pepper to taste and toss.

3. Drizzle the lemon juice and then the oil over the salad. Mix and set aside at room temperature until the bread softens somewhat but is not mushy, about 30 minutes. *(If the bread is quite stale, you may need to set aside the salad for 1 to 2 hours at room temperature.)*

4. Divide the arugula among 4 large dinner plates. Adjust the seasonings in the bread salad. Spoon a portion of bread salad over the arugula on each plate and serve immediately.

SERVING SUGGESTIONS

This dish makes an excellent light main course for lunch, with a granita or sorbet for dessert.

Couscous Salad with Cherry Tomatoes, Cucumber and Mint

SERVES 4

THIS CHILLED PASTA SALAD calls for cherry tomatoes, which are generally sweet but not too juicy, and cucumber. The couscous is mixed with the vegetables while hot, causing them to soften just a bit. Basil may be substituted for the mint.

- ½ medium cucumber, peeled, halved lengthwise, seeded and cut into ½-inch dice
- 10 cherry tomatoes, stemmed and cut into wedges
- 2 tablespoons thinly sliced fresh mint leaves
- 3 tablespoons extra-virgin olive oil
- 1 tablespoon lemon juice
- Salt and freshly ground black pepper
- 1 cup couscous

1. Place the cucumber, tomatoes and mint in a large serving bowl. Drizzle with oil and lemon juice and sprinkle with salt and pepper to taste. Toss and set aside.

2. Bring 1½ cups water to a boil in a medium saucepan. Stir in 1 teaspoon salt and the couscous. Remove from the heat, cover and set aside for 5 minutes.

3. Fluff the couscous with a fork. Turn it into the bowl with the vegetables and toss to mix. Adjust the seasonings. Refrigerate for at least 1 hour or up to 6 hours. Serve cold.

SERVING SUGGESTIONS

Make a summer meal by adding another salad or two, such as Grilled Zucchini and Eggplant Salad with Tomatoes and Balsamic Vinegar (page 398) or Roasted Peppers Marinated in Garlic Oil (page 25), as well as bread or Bruschetta with Fresh Herbs (page 477).

SAVORY TARTS AND TORTAS

TARTS AND TORTAS make excellent vegetarian main courses; they can also be served as a first course or as part of an antipasto spread. Tarts, which are made with pastry dough, have quichelike fillings and are generally thin and delicate. Fillings range from the simple—sliced ripe tomatoes and mozzarella cheese—to such complex combinations as porcini mushrooms, onion, herbs, eggs and Parmesan cheese.

The definition of torta is more nebulous. The word can be used to describe almost any casserolelike dish, but I prefer to reserve the term for a crustless tart. (In some cases, a thin layer of bread crumbs forms the bottom layer, but this is more to absorb moisture than to act as a crust.)

There are several kinds of tortas. Ricotta tortas are like savory cheesecakes—rich, thick and substantial. They are served at room temperature, at which point the filling has firmed and they can be cut into wedges. Because ricotta tortas are baked in advance, they are an excellent addition to picnics or other summer meals. A second kind of torta contains vegetables and cheese baked into a cakelike crustless pie. Tortas are baked in a springform pan; the sides of the pan are removed, and the torta can be easily sliced.

Because tarts involve pastry, they are somewhat more time-consuming than tortas, but making the dough is easy, especially in a food processor. Although you can cut the butter into the dry ingredients with your fingertips or a wire pastry blender, it's much quicker in the processor.

Once the dough is made, it must be refrigerated before rolling out. Chilling prevents the dough from sticking. Plan on refrigerating it for at least one hour. Many times, I make tart dough in advance and refrigerate it for several days or freeze it for a month. Tarts are best baked in a fluted metal pan with a removable bottom. A ceramic dish may look nice, but the sides make it difficult to get the slices out neatly.

For most tarts, I prefer an all-butter dough. Butter gives pastry a rich flavor that olive oil or vegetable shortening cannot duplicate. I have also included an olive-oil dough, which is traditional in many parts of Italy. It goes particularly well with Swiss Chard and Parmesan Tart, because of its rich filling. If you are concerned about saturated fat, use this dough for any of the tarts in this chapter.

In addition, you can choose from two other butter-based variations, one made with whole wheat pastry flour and the other flavored with basil and garlic. The four tart doughs can be used interchangeably, although I have made recommendations as to which ones I think work best with each filling.

Tarts

Tortas

Artichoke and Sun-Dried Tomato Tart

SERVES 4 TO 6

THIS TART MAKES AN IMPRESSIVE MAIN COURSE for dinner or a substantial lunch. Although the artichokes will continue to cook in the oven, they should be almost tender before they are added to the filling. If you have them, you can use Oven-Dried Tomatoes (page 525) in place of the sun-dried.

- 1 recipe Basic Tart Dough (page 413) or Whole Wheat Tart Dough (page 414)
- 1 lemon, halved
- 3 medium artichokes (about 1½ pounds)
- 3 tablespoons extra-virgin olive oil
- 1 medium onion, minced
- 2 medium garlic cloves, minced
- Salt and freshly ground black pepper
- 1¾ cups ricotta cheese, homestyle or supermarket
- ½ cup freshly grated Parmigiano-Reggiano cheese
- 3 large eggs, lightly beaten
- 2 teaspoons minced fresh thyme or oregano leaves
- 4 sun-dried tomatoes packed in oil, drained and cut into thin slivers

1. Prepare the dough and fit it into a 10-inch tart pan with a removable bottom. Refrigerate for at least 30 minutes.

2. Preheat the oven to 375 degrees F. Prick the dough with a fork in several places and line with a piece of aluminum foil. Fill with dried beans or pie weights. Bake for 15 minutes. Remove the foil and beans or weights and continue baking just until the dough starts to color, about 10 minutes. If it starts to puff, prick it with a fork. Remove from the oven and set aside. Leave the oven on.

3. While the tart shell is baking, squeeze the lemon halves into a large bowl of cold water and add the lemon to the bowl. Working with 1 artichoke at a time, bend back and snap off the tough outer leaves. Remove several layers until you reach the leaves that are mostly pale green or yellow except for the tips. With a sharp knife, slice off the dark green pointed tip of the artichoke. Trim the end of the stem and use a vegetable peeler to peel the outer layer from the stem. Use the peeler to remove any dark green leaf bases that may surround the top of the stem. Quarter the artichoke lengthwise, leaving a part of the stem attached to each piece. Slide a small, sharp knife under the fuzzy choke and cut toward the leaf tips to remove it. Slice the cleaned quarters into ¼-inch-thick wedges and drop them into the bowl of cold lemon water. Repeat with the remaining artichokes. Set aside.

4. Heat the oil in a large sauté pan. Add the onion and sauté over medium heat until translucent, about 5 minutes. Add the garlic and cook for 1 minute more.

5. Drain the artichokes and discard the lemon halves. Add the artichoke pieces to the pan and cook, stirring often, for 5 minutes. Add ½ cup water, cover and simmer over medium-low heat until the artichokes are almost tender, about 20 minutes. Raise the heat and simmer, uncovered, for 1 to 2 minutes to cook off any liquid in the pan. Season with salt and pepper to taste and set aside to cool slightly.

6. Combine the ricotta and Parmigiano-Reggiano cheeses, eggs and thyme or oregano in a large bowl. Stir in the artichoke mixture and mix well. Adjust the seasonings and pour the filling into the prebaked crust. Scatter the sun-dried tomato slivers on top. Bake until the filling is set in the center and is golden brown in spots, 40 to 45 minutes.

7. Cool on a rack. Serve warm or at room temperature, sliced into wedges.

Serving Suggestions

Follow with a leafy salad, such as Radicchio, Arugula and Endive Salad with Balsamic Vinaigrette (page 373), Red Leaf Lettuce, Arugula and Fennel Salad (page 374) or Fennel and Orange Salad (page 389). For a fancier meal, start with a bowl of Chickpea Soup with Fennel and Orange Zest (page 64).

Porcini Mushroom Tart

SERVES 4 TO 8

THIS DISH SHOWS OFF PORCINI MUSHROOMS at their best in a cheese filling delicately accented with onion and parsley.

- 1 recipe Basic Tart Dough (page 413) or Whole Wheat Tart Dough (page 414)
- 2 ounces dried porcini mushrooms
- 1½ tablespoons extra-virgin olive oil
- 1½ tablespoons unsalted butter
- 1 medium onion, minced
- 2 tablespoons minced fresh parsley leaves
- Salt and freshly ground black pepper
- 3 large eggs, lightly beaten
- ½ cup freshly grated Parmigiano-Reggiano cheese

1. Prepare the dough and fit it into a 10-inch tart pan with a removable bottom. Refrigerate for at least 30 minutes.

2. Preheat the oven to 375 degrees F. Prick the dough with a fork in several places and line with a piece of aluminum foil. Fill with dried beans or pie weights. Bake for 15 minutes. Remove the foil and beans or weights and continue baking just until the dough starts to color, about 10 minutes. If it starts to puff, prick it with a fork. Remove from the oven and set aside. Leave the oven on.

3. While the tart shell is baking, place the porcini mushrooms in a small bowl and cover with 2¼ cups hot water. Soak until softened, about 20 minutes. Carefully lift the mushrooms from the liquid and pick through them to remove any foreign debris. Wash them if they feel gritty. Chop them. Strain the soaking liquid through a sieve lined with a paper towel. Set aside the mushrooms and strained soaking liquid separately.

4. Heat the oil and butter in a large sauté pan. Add the onion and sauté over medium heat until golden, about 7 minutes. Add the mushrooms and parsley to the pan and cook for 1 minute more. Season the mushrooms with salt and pepper to taste.

5. Add the reserved soaking liquid. Simmer until the sauce has thickened and mostly evaporated, about 10 minutes. Place in a large bowl and set aside to cool slightly.

6. Stir the eggs and cheese into the mushroom mixture. Adjust the seasonings. Pour the mushroom mixture into the prebaked crust. Bake until the filling is set, about 25 minutes.

7. Cool on a rack. Serve warm or at room temperature, sliced into wedges.

SERVING SUGGESTIONS

As a first course, cut the tart into small wedges and follow it with Potato Gnocchi with Tomato Sauce and Mint (page 224) or Orecchiette with Fava Beans, Plum Tomatoes and Ricotta Salata (page 94). As a light main course, follow with Tender Greens and Vegetables with Blood Orange Vinaigrette (page 376).

Swiss Chard and Parmesan Tart

SERVES 8 AS AN APPETIZER

THIS DISH IS A CROSS BETWEEN A FRITTATA AND A TART, since the filling is quite dense and does not rise. Spinach could be used in place of swiss chard if desired.

- **1 recipe Basic Tart Dough (page 413) or Olive Oil Tart Dough (page 416)**
- **1 pound swiss chard**
- **1 tablespoon extra-virgin olive oil**
- **2 medium garlic cloves, minced**
- **Salt and freshly ground black pepper**
- **4 large eggs**
- **1¼ cups freshly grated Parmigiano-Reggiano cheese**

1. Prepare the dough and fit it into a 10-inch tart pan with a removable bottom. Refrigerate while preparing the filling. *(The tart shell can be refrigerated for several hours if desired.)*

2. Preheat the oven to 350 degrees F. Remove and discard the stems from the swiss chard. Tear off the green portions from either side of the rib that runs down the center of each leaf. Discard the ribs. Wash, dry and coarsely chop the leaves. Set aside.

3. Heat the oil in a large saucepan. Add the garlic and sauté over medium heat until golden, about 2 minutes. Add the chard and cook, stirring often, until the leaves have completely wilted and all the liquid in the pan has evaporated, about 5 minutes. Set aside to cool slightly. Add salt and pepper to taste.

4. Beat the eggs in a large bowl with a fork. Stir in the cheese and the chard mixture. Carefully pour the mixture into the prepared tart pan.

5. Bake until the filling is set in the center and turns golden brown in spots, 40 to 45 minutes. Let cool for 5 minutes and cut into thin strips. *(The tart can be completely cooled, set aside at room temperature for several hours and sliced just before serving.)*

SERVING SUGGESTIONS

Serve slivers of tart with drinks before an elegant meal, along with Marinated Black Olives with Rosemary and Lemon Zest (page 20).

Fresh Tomato Tart with Basil-Garlic Crust

SERVES 4 TO 6

THE BRILLIANT GREEN SHELL OF THIS TART is not prebaked, making it quick to assemble and put on the table. If you make this tart with Basic Tart Dough (page 413), sprinkle a tablespoon or two of minced basil between the cheese and tomato layers. *See the photograph on page 198.*

- **1 recipe Basil and Garlic Tart Dough (page 415)**
- **8 ounces mozzarella cheese, very thinly sliced**
- **2 large, ripe tomatoes (about 1 pound), cored and cut crosswise into thin slices**
- **Salt and freshly ground black pepper**
- **1 tablespoon extra-virgin olive oil**

1. Prepare the dough and fit it into a 10-inch tart pan with a removable bottom. *(The tart shell can be refrigerated for several hours if desired.)*

2. Preheat the oven to 375 degrees F. Line the bottom of the tart shell with the slices of cheese. Arrange the tomatoes over the cheese in a ring around the edge of the tart and a second ring in the center, slightly overlapping the slices. Sprinkle with salt and pepper to taste and drizzle with the oil.

3. Bake until the crust is golden brown and the cheese has started to brown in spots, 35 to 40 minutes. Cool on a rack for at least 5 minutes before slicing. Serve hot, warm or at room temperature. *(The tart may be covered and kept at room temperature for 6 hours.)*

SERVING SUGGESTIONS

Serve the tart as a light main course for four, followed by a green salad, such as Spicy Broccoli Salad with Lemon (page 385) or Marinated Zucchini Salad with Lemon and Thyme (page 396). Or start with Roasted Yellow Pepper Soup (page 53) and follow with a leafy salad.

Ricotta and Basil Tart

SERVES 6 TO 8

THE KEY TO THIS RECIPE is mincing the fresh basil fine so it almost melts into the filling. You can mince the basil and garlic together in a food processor. Parmesan may be used instead of Pecorino Romano if desired.

- 1 recipe Basic Tart Dough (page 413)
- 2½ cups ricotta cheese, homestyle or supermarket
- ½ cup freshly grated Pecorino Romano cheese
- ½ cup minced fresh basil leaves
- 1 medium garlic clove, minced
- 2 large eggs, lightly beaten
- Salt and freshly ground black pepper

1. Prepare the dough and fit it into a 10-inch tart pan with a removable bottom. Refrigerate for 30 minutes.

2. Preheat the oven to 375 degrees F. Prick the dough with a fork in several places and line with a piece of aluminum foil. Fill with dried beans or pie weights. Bake for 15 minutes. Remove the foil and beans or weights and continue baking just until the dough starts to color, about 10 minutes. If it starts to puff, prick it with a fork. Remove from the oven and set aside. Leave the oven on.

3. While the tart shell is baking, combine the ricotta and Pecorino Romano cheeses, the basil, garlic, eggs and salt and pepper to taste in a large bowl. Scrape this mixture into the prebaked crust.

4. Bake until the filling has puffed slightly and the top is set, 35 to 40 minutes.

5. Cool on a rack. Serve warm or at room temperature, sliced into wedges.

SERVING SUGGESTIONS

Serve the tart as a first course, followed by something light, such as Linguine with Grilled Plum Tomato Sauce (page 106) or Fusilli with Summer Tomatoes and Olivada (page 107). As a main course, serve it with a vegetable salad, such as Tomato Salad with Black Olives, Capers and Herbs (page 394), Fennel and Orange Salad (page 389) or Spicy Broccoli Salad with Lemon (page 385).

Basic Tart Dough

MAKES ONE 10-INCH TART SHELL

A FOOD PROCESSOR IS THE BEST and easiest tool to work butter into flour. If you want to make the dough by hand, place the flour and salt in a large bowl and cut the butter into small bits. Work the butter into the dry ingredients with a pastry blender or rub the butter in with your fingers until the mixture resembles pea-size crumbs. Stirring quickly with a fork, mix in the ice water until the dough comes together. Continue with Steps 4 and 5.

1¼ cups unbleached all-purpose flour
½ teaspoon kosher salt
8 tablespoons (1 stick) unsalted butter, chilled and cut into 8 to 10 pieces
4-5 tablespoons ice water

1. Place the flour and salt in the work bowl of a food processor. Pulse several times to combine.

2. Place the butter in the work bowl. Pulse about 10 times, or until the mixture resembles pea-size crumbs.

3. Add the water, 1 tablespoon at a time, pulsing several times after each addition. After 4 tablespoons water have been added, process the dough for several seconds to see if it is coming together into a ball. If not, add the remaining 1 tablespoon water. Once the dough seems to be coming together, continue processing until it comes together into a ball. Remove the dough from the food processor.

4. Flatten the dough into a 5-inch disk. Wrap it in plastic and refrigerate for at least 1 hour. *(The dough can be placed in a zipper-lock plastic bag and refrigerated for several days or frozen for 1 month. If frozen, defrost the dough in the refrigerator.)*

5. Remove the dough from the refrigerator and roll it out on a lightly floured surface into a 12-inch circle. Lay the dough over the tart pan and press it into the pan. Trim the dough and proceed with the tart recipe as directed.

Whole Wheat Tart Dough

MAKES ONE 10-INCH TART SHELL

THIS RECIPE IS SIMILAR TO BASIC TART DOUGH, except that a blend of all-purpose flour and whole wheat pastry flour is used. Regular whole wheat flour is not suitable for tart dough; it is best used in bread. Soft whole wheat pastry flour, available at natural-food stores and gourmet shops, is what you want. To mix the dough by hand, see the directions on page 413.

- **¾ cup unbleached all-purpose flour**
- **½ cup whole wheat pastry flour**
- **½ teaspoon kosher salt**
- **8 tablespoons (1 stick) unsalted butter, chilled and cut into8 to 10 pieces**
- **4-5 tablespoons ice water**

1. Place the all-purpose and whole wheat pastry flours and salt in the work bowl of a food processor. Pulse several times to combine.

2. Place the butter in the work bowl. Pulse about 10 times, or until the mixture resembles pea-size crumbs.

3. Add the water, 1 tablespoon at a time, pulsing several times after each addition. After 4 tablespoons water have been added, process the dough for several seconds to see if it is coming together into a ball. If not, add the remaining 1 tablespoon water. Once the dough seems to be coming together, continue processing until it comes together into a ball. Remove the dough from the food processor.

4. Flatten the dough into a 5-inch disk. Wrap it in plastic and refrigerate for at least 1 hour. *(The dough can be placed in a zipper-lock plastic bag and refrigerated for several days or frozen for 1 month. If frozen, defrost the dough in the refrigerator.)*

5. Remove the dough from the refrigerator and roll it out on a lightly floured surface into a 12-inch circle. Lay the dough over the tart pan and press it into the pan. Trim the dough and proceed with the tart recipe as directed.

Basil and Garlic Tart Dough

MAKES ONE 10-INCH TART SHELL

THIS LIGHT GREEN TART DOUGH is very flavorful and works especially well with tomato-based fillings. To mix the dough by hand, see the directions on page 413.

- **⅓ cup fresh basil leaves**
- **1 medium garlic clove**
- **1¼ cups unbleached all-purpose flour**
- **½ teaspoon kosher salt**
- **8 tablespoons (1 stick) unsalted butter, chilled and cut into8 to 10 pieces**
- **4-5 tablespoons ice water**

1. Place the basil and garlic in the work bowl of a food processor. Process, scraping down the sides of the bowl as needed, until finely chopped. Add the flour and salt and pulse several times to combine.

2. Place the butter in the work bowl. Pulse about 10 times, or until the mixture resembles pea-size crumbs.

3. Add the water, 1 tablespoon at a time, pulsing several times after each addition. After 4 tablespoons water have been added, process the dough for several seconds to see if it is coming together into a ball. If not, add the remaining 1 tablespoon water. Once the dough seems to be coming together, continue processing until it comes together into a ball. Remove the dough from the food processor.

4. Flatten the dough into a 5-inch disk. Wrap it in plastic and refrigerate for at least 1 hour. *(The dough can be placed in a zipper-lock plastic bag and refrigerated for several days or frozen for 1 month. If frozen, defrost the dough in the refrigerator.)*

5. Remove the dough from the refrigerator and roll it out on a lightly floured surface into a 12-inch circle. Lay the dough over the tart pan and press it into the pan. Trim the dough and proceed with the tart recipe as directed.

Olive Oil Tart Dough

MAKES ONE 10-INCH TART SHELL

OLIVE OIL CAN BE USED IN PLACE OF BUTTER to make a crisp, flaky tart shell. This dough is best made in a bowl with a fork to combine the ingredients. The dough is quite crumbly and cannot be rolled out. Use your fingers to press it into the tart pan.

- **1¼ cups unbleached all-purpose flour**
- **½ teaspoon kosher salt**
- **⅓ cup extra-virgin olive oil**
- **2 tablespoons ice water**

1. Stir the flour and salt together in a medium bowl with a fork. Add the oil in a slow, steady stream, mixing with the fork as you pour the oil over the dry ingredients. The mixture should resemble pea-size crumbs when all the oil has been incorporated.

2. Add the water, 1 tablespoon at a time, until the dough comes together. Knead briefly with your hands to form the dough into a large ball.

3. Flatten the dough into a disk and place it in a 10-inch tart pan with a removable bottom. With your fingers, press the dough into the pan and up the sides. Fill the tart immediately or set aside at room temperature for several hours.

Ricotta Torta with Herbs

SERVES 6

BEATEN EGG WHITES cause this rich cheese torta to puff up in the oven, and they make the texture light and airy. Any pairing of milder and stronger herbs is fine, just as long as you adhere to the basic ratio of four parts mild herbs to one part strong herbs. For instance, try ¼ cup basil and 1½ teaspoons each oregano and thyme.

1 tablespoon unsalted butter
¼ cup plain bread crumbs
4 cups ricotta cheese, homestyle or supermarket
½ cup freshly grated Parmigiano-Reggiano cheese
3 large eggs, separated
¼ cup minced fresh parsley leaves
2 teaspoons minced fresh sage leaves
1 teaspoon minced fresh rosemary leaves
Salt and freshly ground black pepper

1. Preheat the oven to 375 degrees F. Butter a 9-inch springform pan. Sprinkle the bread crumbs into the buttered pan. Working over the sink, turn the pan to distribute the crumbs around the bottom and sides. Shake out the excess crumbs.

2. Combine the ricotta and Parmigiano-Reggiano cheeses, the egg yolks, parsley, sage, rosemary and salt and pepper to taste in a large bowl. Use a spatula to incorporate the ingredients evenly.

3. In another large bowl, which is completely free of grease, beat the egg whites until they hold stiff peaks. Fold the beaten whites into the cheese mixture. Scrape the mixture into the prepared pan, leveling the top with the spatula.

4. Bake until the top of the torta is firm to the touch and golden brown, about 1 hour. Cool to room temperature on a rack. Remove the sides of the pan and cut the torta into wedges. *(The cooled torta may be wrapped and refrigerated overnight if desired. Bring to room temperature before slicing.)*

SERVING SUGGESTIONS

This torta is perfect picnic food. For dinner, serve a wedge of the torta along with a substantial salad, such as Tender Greens and Vegetables with Blood Orange Vinaigrette (page 376) or Mixed Greens with Tomatoes, Yellow Pepper and Fennel (page 377).

Double Ricotta Torta with Black Olives and Thyme

SERVES 6

THIS RUSTIC TORTA contains both fresh and salted ricotta cheese. The fresh ricotta gives the torta its creamy texture and mild flavor; the ricotta salata adds depth. Black olives and thyme are used in this recipe, but other herbs, green olives or sun-dried tomatoes would also be appropriate. The torta rises like a soufflé in the oven but falls a bit as it cools.

1 tablespoon unsalted butter
¼ cup plain bread crumbs
4 cups ricotta cheese, homestyle or supermarket
½ cup grated ricotta salata
4 large eggs, lightly beaten
10 large black olives, pitted and coarsely chopped
1½ teaspoons minced fresh thyme leaves
Salt and freshly ground black pepper

1. Preheat the oven to 350 degrees F. Butter a 9-inch springform pan. Sprinkle the bread crumbs into the buttered pan. Working over the sink, turn the pan to distribute the crumbs around the bottom and sides. Shake out the excess crumbs.

2. Combine the ricotta and ricotta salata, the eggs, olives, thyme and salt and pepper to taste in a large bowl. Be careful with the salt, since the ricotta salata and olives may be rather salty. Use a spatula to incorporate the ingredients evenly. Scrape the mixture into the prepared pan, leveling the top with the spatula.

3. Bake until the top of the torta is firm to the touch and golden brown, about 1 hour and 10 minutes. Cool to room temperature on a rack. Remove the sides of the pan and cut the torta into wedges. *(The cooled torta may be wrapped and refrigerated overnight if desired. Bring to room temperature before slicing.)*

SERVING SUGGESTIONS

Since this dish can be served at room temperature and transports particularly well, it is ideal for a picnic. It can be served as a main course for six or as an appetizer for ten to twelve. If serving as a main course, follow with a leafy green salad, such as Tender Green Salad with Pine Nuts and Yellow Raisins (page 375) or Spinach Salad with Orange Juice Vinaigrette and Toasted Walnuts (page 380).

Roasted Zucchini Torta with Tomatoes and Mozzarella

SERVES 6

LAYERS OF ZUCCHINI AND MOZZARELLA meld in the oven to form a cakelike main-course torta, bursting with the flavors of summer. I prefer this torta when it is slightly warm.

- **6 medium zucchini, scrubbed (about 2¼ pounds)**
- **5 tablespoons extra-virgin olive oil**
- **Salt and freshly ground black pepper**
- **2 medium garlic cloves, minced**
- **1¾ cups canned crushed tomatoes**
- **2 tablespoons minced fresh basil leaves**
- **10 ounces mozzarella cheese, shredded (about 2½ cups)**
- **¼ cup freshly grated Parmigiano-Reggiano cheese**

1. Preheat the oven to 400 degrees F. Trim the ends from the zucchini. Cut the zucchini lengthwise into ¼-inch-thick slices. Lay the zucchini slices on 2 large baking sheets. Brush both sides with 3 tablespoons of the oil and sprinkle with salt and pepper to taste. Bake just until the zucchini slices start to brown around the edges, about 25 minutes. Remove from the oven, leaving it on. Cool the zucchini.

2. While the zucchini is in the oven, heat 1 tablespoon oil in a medium saucepan. Add the garlic and sauté over medium heat until golden, 1 to 2 minutes. Add the tomatoes and simmer until the sauce becomes fairly thick and reduces to about 1⅓ cups, about 15 minutes. Stir in the basil and salt and pepper to taste. Set aside.

3. Brush the bottom and sides of a 9-inch springform pan with the remaining 1 tablespoon oil. Line the bottom of the pan with a layer of zucchini slices, cutting the pieces if necessary to cover the pan completely. Do not overlap the slices. Spoon ⅓ cup of the tomato sauce over the zucchini and sprinkle with a generous ½ cup mozzarella and 1 tablespoon Parmigiano-Reggiano. Repeat the process, making 3 more layers of zucchini, tomato sauce and cheese. *(The torta can be wrapped tightly and refrigerated overnight. Unwrap, transfer directly to the oven and increase the baking time by 5 to 10 minutes.)*

4. Bake until the top of the torta is golden brown in spots and the sauce is bubbling, about 30 minutes. Remove from the oven and cool on a rack for at least 15 minutes. Remove the sides of the pan and cut the torta into wedges. The torta may also be cooled to room temperature and then sliced.

Serving Suggestions

Serve the torta with a salad, such as Radicchio, Arugula and Endive Salad with Balsamic Vinaigrette (page 373) or Red Leaf Lettuce, Arugula and Fennel Salad (page 374), and bread or Bruschetta with Fresh Herbs (page 477).

Pizza, Calzone and Focaccia

Perhaps no Italian food (with the possible exception of pasta) has had a greater impact on American eating habits than pizza. This simple, quick flatbread has become a favorite snack and meal on both sides of the Atlantic. Calzone, stuffed pizza dough, has become almost as popular. Focaccia, another flatbread that is a close culinary cousin to pizza, is also becoming better known.

Both pizza and focaccia are made with water, oil, yeast, flour and salt. Pizza generally has less yeast and rises for less time and is therefore thinner when rolled out. When baked, the crust should be thin and crisp. Focaccia contains more yeast and rises a bit longer. The texture when baked is chewier, almost spongy. There are other differences as well. Pizza crust is really a vehicle for other ingredients—tomatoes, cheese, vegetables. Focaccia is topped more lightly, perhaps with just fresh herbs and salt.

For baking pizza, I cannot emphasize enough the value of a baking stone. If you want to make really good pizza (or any kind of bread, for that matter) at home, spend $20 on the largest stone that will fit in your oven. Crusts will cook faster and be crisper when slid onto a preheated stone. The pizzas in this chapter were tested on a stone in an oven that is capable of maintaining 500 degrees. If you bake pizza on a baking sheet, add two to three minutes to the cooking time. If your oven loses heat easily, your pizzas may need more cooking time than indicated in the recipes.

A batch of dough makes enough for two 12-inch pizzas. I find that one pizza feeds two or maybe three if there are plenty of vegetable or salad accompaniments. Freeze the second ball of dough for later use. For a large crowd, bake one pizza after the other.

Focaccia dates back thousands of years to the time when flatbreads were baked on open hearths. In fact, the name derives from the Latin word *focus*, meaning hearth. Nowadays, the bread is baked on a baking sheet in the oven. A dark jelly-roll pan (as opposed to a shiny one) will promote browning of the bottom crust. Avoid insulated jelly-roll pans, which are great for making cakes, since they inhibit browning, but are not designed for bread-baking.

Before the focaccia dough is baked, it is "dimpled" by pressing the forefinger into it at regular intervals. These indentations should be large enough to hold small pieces of tomato or onion as well as pools of olive oil. It is imperative that you use olive oil (a focaccia made with canola oil is just not the same), and preferably one of high quality. A sprinkling of coarse salt is also important for flavor.

A SIMPLE FOCACCIA WITH SAGE OR ROSEMARY is best served as a snack or as bread with dinner. One large rectangular focaccia will yield at least six servings. Focaccia may also be cut into squares and split horizontally for use as sandwich bread. In Italy, mozzarella and prosciutto are common choices for fillings, but use your imagination. Marinated artichoke hearts, grilled vegetables, arugula with black olive paste or garlicky sautéed spinach work nicely. Focaccia can also be used for the sandwiches in the next chapter.

Serve more substantial focaccia with vegetable toppings as accompaniments to a main course or as a light meal in themselves, perhaps with a salad. Alongside a meal, a focaccia will easily yield six servings. As a lunch or light dinner, one rectangular focaccia will be enough for four generous servings.

Pizza and Calzone

Focaccia

Garlic and Rosemary Pizza

MAKES ONE 12-INCH PIZZA

THIS BASIC PIZZA, called *pizza bianca* (white pizza) in Italy, is a favorite late-afternoon snack.

- ½ recipe Basic Pizza Dough (page 420) or Whole Wheat Pizza Dough (page 442)
- 2 tablespoons extra-virgin olive oil
- 3 medium garlic cloves, minced
- 2 teaspoons chopped fresh rosemary leaves
- Salt and freshly ground black pepper
- Cornmeal for sprinkling

1. Prepare the dough through Step 2 of the dough recipe. If using a baking stone, place it in the oven. Preheat the oven to 500 degrees F for 30 minutes.

2. Combine the oil, garlic, rosemary and salt and pepper to taste in a small bowl.

3. Sprinkle a pizza peel or large rimless baking sheet with cornmeal and stretch the dough into a 12-inch circle as directed in the dough recipe. Brush the oil mixture evenly over the dough and prick it all over with a fork.

4. If using a stone, slide the pizza from the peel or baking sheet onto the preheated stone. Otherwise, place the baking sheet in the oven and bake until the crust starts to brown in spots, 8 to 10 minutes.

5. Remove the pizza from the oven. Cut into wedges and serve immediately.

SERVING SUGGESTIONS

Serve this pizza as a snack, an appetizer or a special bread with dinner or with a soup, such as Chilled Potato and Zucchini Soup with Fresh Tomato Garnish (page 55), Lentil and Tomato Soup with Escarole (page 68) or Kale and White Bean Soup (page 66).

Artichoke Pizza with Garlicky Bread Crumbs

MAKES ONE 12-INCH PIZZA

THIS UNUSUAL PIZZA TOPPING starts with thinly sliced baby artichokes. Tiny artichokes that do not have fuzzy chokes and are small enough to cook through when sautéed are necessary for this recipe.

- ½ recipe Basic Pizza Dough (page 440) or Whole Wheat Pizza Dough (page 442)
- 1 lemon, halved
- 5 baby artichokes (about 10 ounces)
- ½ cup coarse homemade bread crumbs (see page 538)
- 5 tablespoons extra-virgin olive oil
- 3 medium garlic cloves, minced
- ½ teaspoon salt
- Cornmeal for sprinkling

1. Prepare the dough through Step 2 of the dough recipe. If using a baking stone, place it in the oven. Preheat the oven to 500 degrees F for 30 minutes.

2. Squeeze the lemon halves into a large bowl of cold water and add the lemon to the bowl. Working with 1 artichoke at a time, bend back and snap off the tough outer leaves. Remove several layers until you reach the leaves that are mostly pale green or yellow except for the tips. With a sharp knife, slice off the dark green pointed tip of the artichoke. Trim the end of the stem and use a vegetable peeler to peel the outer layer. Use the peeler to remove any dark green leaf bases that may surround the top of the stem. Cut the artichoke lengthwise into thin slices and drop them into the bowl of cold lemon water. Repeat with the remaining artichokes. Set aside.

3. Place the bread crumbs in a large skillet over medium heat. Toast, shaking the pan occasionally, until the crumbs are golden brown, about 4 minutes. Set aside in a small bowl.

4. Add 4 tablespoons of the oil and the garlic to the skillet. Sauté just until the garlic starts to color, no more than 30 seconds. Drain the artichokes and add them to the skillet. Cook, turning often, until they start to soften, 4 to 5 minutes. Turn off the heat and sprinkle the salt and bread crumbs over the artichokes. Stir to combine.

5. Sprinkle a pizza peel or large rimless baking sheet with cornmeal and stretch the dough into a 12-inch circle as directed in the dough recipe. Evenly distribute the artichoke mixture over the dough, leaving a ½-inch border around the edge. Drizzle the remaining 1 tablespoon oil over the artichokes.

6. If using a stone, slide the pizza from the peel or baking sheet onto the preheated stone. Otherwise, place the baking sheet in the oven and bake until the crust starts to brown in spots, 8 to 10 minutes.

7. Remove the pizza from the oven. Cut into wedges and serve immediately.

Serving Suggestions

Serve this pizza as an appetizer for a multicourse spring meal. One pizza will be enough for four people. Follow with Orecchiette with Fava Beans, Plum Tomatoes and Ricotta Salata (page 94) or Orecchiette with Peas, Ricotta and Parmesan (page 102). Or serve the pizza as a light dinner for two with a leafy salad, such as Mixed Greens with Tomatoes, Yellow Pepper and Fennel (page 377).

Pizza with Eggplant, Ricotta and Basil

MAKES ONE 12-INCH PIZZA

BASIL AND GARLIC flavor a mixture of ricotta and Pecorino Romano cheese in this pizza. The cheese is spread over the dough, and when the pizza is almost done, slices of broiled eggplant are laid on top, then the pizza is returned to the oven for several minutes. If you have the grill going, grill the eggplant instead of broiling it.

- ½ recipe Basic Pizza Dough (page 440) or Whole Wheat Pizza Dough (page 442)
- 1 cup ricotta cheese, preferably homestyle
- 1 medium eggplant (about ¾ pound)
- 2 tablespoons extra-virgin olive oil
- Salt and freshly ground black pepper
- ¼ cup freshly grated Pecorino Romano or Parmigiano-Reggiano cheese
- 2 medium garlic cloves, minced
- 2 tablespoons minced fresh basil leaves
- Cornmeal for sprinkling

1. Prepare the dough through Step 2 of the dough recipe.

2. If using supermarket ricotta, line a small colander or mesh sieve with several layers of paper towels. Spread the cheese over the towels and let drain until thickened and creamy, about 1 hour. Remove the cheese from the colander and discard the paper towels; they should be quite moist. (Homestyle ricotta does not need to be drained.)

3. Preheat the broiler. Trim the ends from the eggplant and cut it lengthwise into ¼-inch-thick slices. Brush the eggplant with the oil and season with salt and pepper to taste. Broil, turning once, until golden brown, about 10 minutes. Set aside.

4. If using a baking stone, place it in the oven. Preheat the oven to 500 degrees F for 30 minutes.

5. Combine the ricotta and Pecorino Romano or Parmigiano-Reggiano cheese, the garlic, basil and salt and pepper to taste in a medium bowl.

6. Sprinkle a pizza peel or large rimless baking sheet with cornmeal and stretch the dough into a 12-inch circle as directed in the dough recipe. Spread the ricotta mixture over the dough, leaving a ½-inch border around the edge.

7. If using a stone, slide the pizza from the peel or baking sheet onto the preheated stone. Otherwise, place the baking sheet in the oven and bake for 8 minutes. Quickly lay the eggplant slices in a circle on top of the cheese, overlapping them somewhat in a flowerlike design. Continue baking until the crust starts to brown in spots, 3 to 4 minutes.

8. Remove the pizza from the oven. Cool for 1 to 2 minutes to allow the cheese to solidify. Cut into wedges and serve immediately.

Serving Suggestions

Mixed Greens with Tomatoes, Yellow Pepper and Fennel (page 377) is the perfect accompaniment to this pizza. Also suitable is a tomato salad, such as Marinated Tomato and Red Onion Salad (page 395) or Tomato Salad with Black Olives, Capers and Herbs (page 394).

Pizza with Mozzarella, Artichoke Hearts and Cremini Mushrooms

MAKES ONE 12-INCH PIZZA

THE TOPPINGS FOR THIS PIZZA do not require precooking, and so it's a good choice when you are pressed for time. Cremini mushrooms are a must. White button mushrooms contain a lot of liquid and will make the crust soggy unless they are precooked.

½ recipe Basic Pizza Dough (page 440) or Whole Wheat Pizza Dough (page 442)
Cornmeal for sprinkling
4 ounces mozzarella cheese, shredded (about 1 cup)
1 six-ounce jar marinated quartered artichoke hearts, drained
4 ounces cremini mushrooms, wiped clean, stems trimmed, cut into ¼-inch-thick slices

1. Prepare the dough through Step 2 of the dough recipe. If using a baking stone, place it in the oven. Preheat the oven to 500 degrees F for 30 minutes.

2. Sprinkle a pizza peel or large rimless baking sheet with cornmeal and stretch the dough into a 12-inch circle as directed in the dough recipe. Evenly distribute the cheese over the dough, leaving a ½-inch border around the edge. Scatter the artichokes and mushrooms over the cheese.

3. If using a stone, slide the pizza from the peel or baking sheet onto the preheated stone. Otherwise, place the baking sheet in the oven and bake until the crust starts to brown and the cheese turns golden brown in spots, 10 to 12 minutes.

4. Remove the pizza from the oven. Cut into wedges and serve immediately.

SERVING SUGGESTIONS

Serve with a simple green salad, such as Radicchio, Arugula and Endive Salad with Balsamic Vinaigrette (page 373), or a vegetable side dish with tomatoes, such as Marinated Tomato and Red Onion Salad (page 395) or Sautéed Cherry Tomatoes with Garlic (page 362).

Pizza with Mozzarella, Onions and Olives

MAKES ONE 12-INCH PIZZA

A LAYER OF MOZZARELLA conceals a mélange of onions and olives. Since the onions continue to cook in the oven, take care that they don't brown in the skillet.

- ½ recipe Basic Pizza Dough (page 440) or Whole Wheat Pizza Dough (page 442)
- 2 tablespoons extra-virgin olive oil
- 1 medium onion, thinly sliced
- 12 large black olives, pitted and chopped
- 2 teaspoons minced fresh oregano leaves
- Cornmeal for sprinkling
- 4 ounces mozzarella cheese, shredded (about 1 cup)

1. Prepare the dough through Step 2 of the dough recipe. If using a baking stone, place it in the oven. Preheat the oven to 500 degrees F for 30 minutes.

2. Heat the oil in a medium skillet. Add the onion and cook over medium heat, stirring occasionally, until golden, about 10 minutes. Do not let it brown. Remove from the heat. Stir in the olives and oregano.

3. Sprinkle a pizza peel or large rimless baking sheet with cornmeal and stretch the dough into a 12-inch circle as directed in the dough recipe. Evenly distribute the onion mixture over the dough, leaving a ½-inch border around the edge. Sprinkle the cheese over the top.

4. If using a stone, slide the pizza from the peel or baking sheet onto the preheated stone. Otherwise, place the baking sheet in the oven and bake until the crust starts to brown and the cheese turns golden brown in spots, 10 to 12 minutes.

5. Remove the pizza from the oven. Cut into wedges and serve immediately.

SERVING SUGGESTIONS

For a meal for four, serve the pizza with a soup, such as Chard and Spinach Soup with Lemon-Parsley Pesto (page 46), Lentil and Tomato Soup with Escarole (page 68) or Classic Minestrone with Pesto (page 60).

Pesto Pizza

MAKES ONE 12-INCH PIZZA

PESTO LIGHTENED WITH RICOTTA CHEESE makes a great pizza topping. I find that plain pesto is too strong to spread on pizza, but when mellowed with ricotta, the flavor is just right. Since the dough goes into the oven without any topping at first, it needs to be pricked all over to prevent large bubbles from forming. The pesto is spread over the dough for the last two minutes of baking.

- **½ recipe Basic Pizza Dough (page 440) or Whole Wheat Pizza Dough (page 442)**
- **1 cup packed fresh basil leaves**
- **1 medium garlic clove**
- **2 tablespoons pine nuts or walnuts**
- **3 tablespoons extra-virgin olive oil**
- **½ cup ricotta cheese, homestyle or supermarket**
- **¼ cup freshly grated Parmigiano-Reggiano cheese**
- **Salt and freshly ground black pepper**
- **Cornmeal for sprinkling**

1. Prepare the dough through Step 2 of the dough recipe. If using a baking stone, place it in the oven. Preheat the oven to 500 degrees F for 30 minutes.

2. Place the basil, garlic and pine nuts or walnuts in the work bowl of a food processor. Process, scraping down the sides of the bowl as needed, until finely chopped. With the motor running, slowly pour the oil through the feed tube and process until smooth. Scrape the pesto into a small bowl and stir in the ricotta and Parmigiano-Reggiano cheeses and salt and pepper to taste. Set aside.

3. Sprinkle a pizza peel or large rimless baking sheet with cornmeal and stretch the dough into a 12-inch circle as directed in the dough recipe. Prick the dough all over with a fork.

4. If using a stone, slide the pizza from the peel or baking sheet onto the preheated stone. Otherwise, place the baking sheet in the oven and bake until the crust starts to brown in spots, about 8 minutes.

5. Spread the pesto over the crust, leaving a ½-inch border around the edge. Continue baking the pizza until the pesto is heated through, about 2 minutes.

6. Remove the pizza from the oven. Cut into wedges and serve immediately.

Serving Suggestions

This pizza makes an appetizer for four or a main course for two. Serve it with a salad, such as Arugula, Tomato and Black Olive Salad (page 372), and a substantial vegetable side dish, such as Grilled Vegetables with Thyme and Garlic (page 365).

Potato, Arugula and Fontina Pizza

MAKES ONE 12-INCH PIZZA

THIS PIZZA REQUIRES A BIT OF PREPARATION, but the results are impressive. Slices of roasted potato are baked with the crust and then covered with chopped arugula and fontina just before the pizza is done. Sandwiched between the potatoes and the cheese, the greens do not dry out in the oven. Since the potatoes must brown as quickly as the crust, they need to be cut as thin as possible. Use a mandoline, the slicing blade of a food processor or a very sharp knife. Watercress or spinach may be substituted for the arugula. *See the photograph on page 204.*

- **½ recipe Basic Pizza Dough (page 440) or Whole Wheat Pizza Dough (page 442)**
- **1 large baking potato (about ¾ pound), scrubbed**
- **3 tablespoons extra-virgin olive oil**
- **Salt and freshly ground black pepper**
- **2 medium garlic cloves, minced**
- **2 cups stemmed arugula leaves (1 large bunch)**
- **Cornmeal for sprinkling**
- **3 ounces shredded Italian fontina cheese (about ¾ cup)**

1. Prepare the dough through Step 2 of the dough recipe.

2. Preheat the oven to 350 degrees F. Slice the potato crosswise into paper-thin slices. Toss the slices with 1 tablespoon of the oil on a large baking sheet and sprinkle generously with salt and pepper. Spread the slices in a single layer. Bake until just tender, about 10 minutes. Remove from the oven and set aside until cool enough to handle. If using a baking stone, place it in the oven. Raise the temperature to 500 degrees F.

3. Meanwhile, combine 4 teaspoons oil with the garlic and set aside. Wash, dry and coarsely chop the arugula. Toss the arugula with the remaining 2 teaspoons oil and set aside.

4. Sprinkle a pizza peel or large rimless baking sheet with cornmeal and stretch the dough into a 12-inch circle as directed in the dough recipe. Line the dough with concentric circles of slightly overlapping potato slices, leaving a ½-inch border around the edge. Brush the potatoes with the garlic oil.

5. If using a stone, slide the pizza from the peel or baking sheet onto the preheated stone. Otherwise, place the baking sheet in the oven and bake until the crust starts to brown and the potatoes are golden brown, about 10 minutes.

6. Sprinkle the arugula evenly over the pizza. Sprinkle the cheese over the arugula. Continue baking until the cheese melts, about 3 minutes.

7. Remove the pizza from the oven. Cut into wedges and serve immediately.

Serving Suggestions

Serve with a vegetable side dish with some sweetness, such as Slow-Browned Carrots with Butter (page 335), Roasted Fennel, Carrots and Red Onion (page 346) or Roasted Beets with Balsamic Vinegar and Parsley (page 333).

Pizza with Red Onions and Rosemary

MAKES ONE 12-INCH PIZZA

A TANGLE OF COOKED RED ONIONS makes a simple, yet satisfying pizza topping. A little grated cheese is sprinkled over during the last minute of baking for more flavor. This pizza can be served as a main course for two or as an appetizer or snack for four or six.

- ½ recipe Basic Pizza Dough (page 440) or Whole Wheat Pizza Dough (page 442)
- 3 tablespoons extra-virgin olive oil
- 4 medium red onions (about 1 pound), thinly sliced
- 1 teaspoon minced fresh rosemary leaves
- Salt and freshly ground black pepper
- Cornmeal for sprinkling
- ¼ cup freshly grated Parmigiano-Reggiano cheese

1. Prepare the dough through Step 2 of the dough recipe. If using a baking stone, place it in the oven. Preheat the oven to 500 degrees F for 30 minutes.

2. Heat the oil in a large skillet. Add the onions and cook over medium-low heat until lightly browned, about 15 minutes. Stir in the rosemary and salt and pepper to taste and remove from the heat.

3. Sprinkle a pizza peel or large rimless baking sheet with cornmeal and stretch the dough into a 12-inch circle as directed in the dough recipe. Evenly distribute the onion mixture over the dough, leaving a ½-inch border around the edge.

4. If using a stone, slide the pizza from the peel or baking sheet onto the preheated stone. Otherwise, place the baking sheet in the oven and bake until the crust starts to brown in spots, about 12 minutes. Sprinkle the cheese over the pizza. Continue baking just until the cheese melts, about 1 minute.

5. Remove the pizza from the oven. Cut into wedges and serve immediately.

SERVING SUGGESTIONS

If serving as a first course, follow it with a pasta dish, such as Orecchiette with Fava Beans, Plum Tomatoes and Ricotta Salata (page 94) or Fusilli with Spinach and Ricotta Puree (page 108).

Fresh Tomato Pizza with Oregano

MAKES ONE 12-INCH PIZZA

THIS SIMPLE NEAPOLITAN PIZZA is arguably the most famous in Italy. The tomatoes for the topping are often diced, but I like the look of thinly sliced circles. A tablespoon of minced fresh basil leaves can be used in place of the oregano if desired.

½ recipe Basic Pizza Dough (page 440) or Whole Wheat Pizza Dough (page 442)
2 large, ripe tomatoes (about 1 pound)
Cornmeal for sprinkling
2 tablespoons extra-virgin olive oil
2 medium garlic cloves, minced
1 teaspoon minced fresh oregano leaves
Salt and freshly ground black pepper

1. Prepare the dough through Step 2 of the dough recipe. If using a baking stone, place it in the oven. Preheat the oven to 500 degrees F for 30 minutes.

2. Core the tomatoes and slice them crosswise into very thin circles. Lay the slices on paper towels to absorb excess moisture.

3. Sprinkle a pizza peel or large rimless baking sheet with cornmeal and stretch the dough into a 12-inch circle as directed in the dough recipe.

4. Brush the dough with 1 tablespoon of the oil. Line the dough with concentric circles of slightly overlapping tomato slices, leaving a ½-inch border around the edge. Evenly distribute the garlic and oregano over the tomatoes and sprinkle with salt and pepper to taste. Drizzle the remaining 1 tablespoon oil over the tomatoes.

5. If using a stone, slide the pizza from the peel or baking sheet onto the preheated stone. Otherwise, place the baking sheet in the oven and bake until the crust starts to brown in spots, about 12 minutes.

6. Remove the pizza from the oven. Cut into wedges and serve immediately.

SERVING SUGGESTIONS

Serve with a green-vegetable side dish, such as Steamed Green Beans with Tarragon (page 347), Asparagus with Lemon-Shallot Vinaigrette (page 331) or Roasted Asparagus with Olive Oil (page 330).

Pizza with Tomatoes, Mozzarella and Basil

Makes one 12-inch pizza

Called Pizza Margherita in Italy, this pie takes its name from a nineteenth-century Italian queen. The colors of the topping—red tomatoes, green basil and white cheese—represent the colors of the country's flag.

- ½ recipe Basic Pizza Dough (page 440) or Whole Wheat Pizza Dough (page 442)
- Cornmeal for sprinkling
- 1 tablespoon extra-virgin olive oil
- 2 large, ripe tomatoes (about 1 pound), peeled, cored, seeded and diced
- ½ teaspoon salt
- ¼ cup chopped fresh basil leaves
- 5 ounces mozzarella cheese, shredded (about 1¼ cups)

1. Prepare the dough through Step 2 of the dough recipe. If using a baking stone, place it in the oven. Preheat the oven to 500 degrees F for 30 minutes.

2. Sprinkle a pizza peel or large rimless baking sheet with cornmeal and stretch the dough into a 12-inch circle as directed in the dough recipe.

3. Brush the dough with the oil. Evenly distribute the tomatoes over the dough, leaving a ½-inch border around the edge. Sprinkle the salt and basil over the tomatoes. Distribute the cheese evenly over the topping.

4. If using a stone, slide the pizza from the peel or baking sheet onto the preheated stone. Otherwise, place the baking sheet in the oven and bake until the crust starts to brown and the cheese turns golden brown in spots, about 15 minutes.

5. Remove the pizza from the oven. Cut into wedges and serve immediately.

Serving Suggestions

This classic pizza is a favorite with my family for weekend lunches. It also makes a light dinner, served with a tossed green salad, such as Red Leaf Lettuce, Arugula and Fennel Salad (page 374) or Tender Greens and Vegetables with Blood Orange Vinaigrette (page 376).

Three-Cheese Pizza

MAKES ONE 12-INCH PIZZA

THE THREE CHEESES IN THIS PIZZA—Gorgonzola, ricotta and Parmesan—complement each other very well. This combination is a favorite in Florentine pizzerias.

½ recipe Basic Pizza Dough (page 440) or Whole Wheat Pizza Dough (page 442)
1 cup ricotta cheese, homestyle or supermarket
2 ounces Gorgonzola cheese, crumbled (about ⅓ cup)
¼ cup freshly grated Parmigiano-Reggiano cheese
Freshly ground black pepper
Cornmeal for sprinkling
1 tablespoon extra-virgin olive oil

1. Prepare the dough through Step 2 of the dough recipe. If using a baking stone, place it in the oven. Preheat the oven to 500 degrees F for 30 minutes.

2. Combine the cheeses and the pepper to taste in a medium bowl.

3. Sprinkle a pizza peel or large rimless baking sheet with cornmeal and stretch the dough into a 12-inch circle as directed in the dough recipe. Evenly distribute the cheese mixture over the dough, leaving a ½-inch border around the edge. Drizzle the oil over the cheese.

4. If using a stone, slide the pizza from the peel or baking sheet onto the preheated stone. Otherwise, place the baking sheet in the oven and bake until the crust starts to brown and the cheese turns brown in spots, about 10 minutes.

5. Remove the pizza from the oven. Cool for 1 to 2 minutes, or until the topping stops bubbling and firms up. Cut into wedges and serve immediately.

SERVING SUGGESTIONS

Since this pizza is fairly rich, serve it with a tossed green salad, such as Radicchio, Arugula and Endive Salad with Balsamic Vinaigrette (page 373), Arugula, Tomato and Black Olive Salad (page 372) or Mixed Greens with Tomatoes, Yellow Pepper and Fennel (page 377).

Basic Pizza Dough

ENOUGH FOR TWO 12-INCH PIZZAS

THIS DOUGH CAN BE PREPARED IN A FOOD PROCESSOR or standing mixer or by hand with a wooden spoon. The food-processor method is the fastest and is my first choice. Shaping the dough is best done by hand. If the dough is too elastic and won't stretch as much as you would like, let it rest for five to ten minutes and try again. One 12-inch pizza is enough for a main course for two people or an appetizer or snack for four.

1¼ cups warm water (105-115 degrees F)
1 teaspoon active dry yeast (½ envelope)
2 tablespoons extra-virgin olive oil
3½ cups unbleached all-purpose flour
1½ teaspoons kosher salt
Cornmeal for sprinkling

1. **To make the dough in a food processor:** Pour the water into the work bowl of a food processor fitted with the metal blade. Add the yeast and oil and process for several seconds until smooth. Add the flour and salt and process until the dough comes together in a ball, about 30 seconds.

To make the dough by hand: Combine the water, yeast and oil in a large bowl, using a wooden spoon. Add the flour and salt and continue to stir until the dough comes together. Turn the dough out onto a floured surface and knead until smooth and elastic, about 6 minutes.

To make the dough in a standing mixer: Combine the water, yeast and oil in the large bowl of a mixer fitted with the paddle attachment. Stir in the flour and salt. When the dough comes together, replace the paddle attachment with the dough hook. Knead until the dough is smooth and elastic, about 4 minutes.

2. Turn the dough into a lightly oiled large bowl and cover with a damp cloth. Let rise until the dough is puffy and has almost doubled in bulk, about 1 hour. Divide the dough in half and place each half in a separate lightly oiled medium bowl. Let rise, covered, for 20 minutes. *(The dough can be refrigerated in separate airtight containers overnight or frozen for up to 1 month. Bring to room temperature before rolling out.)*

3. Lightly sprinkle a pizza peel or large rimless baking sheet with cornmeal. Flatten 1 dough ball into an 8-inch disk. Pat the disk several times to level out the dough. Slowly rotate the disk, stretching the dough to the side as you turn it. Thin the edge by flattening and stretching it with your fingertips. The circle of dough should have a diameter of about 12 inches.

4. Top and bake the pizza as desired. Repeat with the second dough ball, if using.

Whole Wheat Pizza Dough

ENOUGH FOR TWO 12-INCH PIZZAS

THIS DOUGH HAS A NUTTIER FLAVOR than the basic recipe. It contains a bit more oil to keep the dough supple and more yeast to promote a quicker rise. It can be used for any of the pizza recipes in this chapter.

- **1⅓ cups warm water (105-115 degrees F)**
- **2 teaspoons active dry yeast (1 envelope)**
- **3 tablespoons extra-virgin olive oil**
- **2 cups whole wheat flour**
- **1½ cups unbleached all-purpose flour**
- **1½ teaspoons kosher salt**
- **Cornmeal for sprinkling**

1. To make the dough in a food processor: Pour the water into the work bowl of a food processor fitted with the metal blade. Add the yeast and oil and process for several seconds until smooth. Add the whole wheat and all-purpose flours and salt and process until the dough comes together in a ball, about 30 seconds.

To make the dough by hand: Combine the water, yeast and oil in a large bowl, using a wooden spoon. Add the whole wheat and all-purpose flours and salt and continue to stir until the dough comes together. Turn the dough out onto a floured surface and knead until smooth and elastic, about 6 minutes.

To make the dough in a standing mixer: Combine the water, yeast and oil in the large bowl of a mixer fitted with the paddle attachment. Stir in the whole wheat and all-purpose flours and salt. When the dough comes together, replace the paddle attachment with the dough hook. Knead until the dough is smooth and elastic, about 4 minutes.

2. Turn the dough into a lightly oiled large bowl and cover with a damp cloth. Let rise until the dough is puffy and has increased in bulk by 1½ times, about 1 hour. Divide the dough in half and place each half in a separate lightly oiled medium bowl. Let rise, covered, for 20 minutes. *(The dough can be refrigerated in separate airtight containers overnight or frozen for up to 1 month. Bring to room temperature before rolling out.)*

3. Lightly sprinkle a pizza peel or large rimless baking sheet with cornmeal. Flatten 1 dough ball into an 8-inch disk. Pat the disk several times to level out the dough. Slowly rotate the disk, stretching the dough to the side as you turn it. Thin the edge by flattening and stretching it with your fingertips. The circle of dough should have a diameter of about 12 inches.

4. Top and bake the pizza as desired. Repeat with the second dough ball, if using.

Calzone with Mozzarella and Black Olives

SERVES 4

A CALZONE IS A SMALL PIECE OF PIZZA DOUGH rolled out into a circle, spread with topping, folded in half and sealed tight. Brushing the edges with a little cold water (rather than with an egg wash) ensures that the calzones will not open in the oven. The calzones in this recipe are good as is but are even better when served with Quick Tomato Sauce (page 522). Unlike pizza, calzone is delicious at room temperature and can be served at a picnic. The calzones can be made several hours in advance and reheated.

- ½ recipe Basic Pizza Dough (page 440) or Whole Wheat Pizza Dough (page 442)
- 8 ounces mozzarella cheese, shredded (about 2 cups)
- 10 large black olives, pitted and finely chopped
- 2 medium garlic cloves, minced
- 1 teaspoon minced fresh oregano leaves
- Salt and freshly ground black pepper
- Cornmeal for sprinkling

1. Prepare the dough through Step 2 of the dough recipe. If using a baking stone, place it in the oven. Preheat the oven to 450 degrees F for 30 minutes.

2. Combine the cheese, olives, garlic, oregano and salt and pepper to taste in a medium bowl.

3. Sprinkle a pizza peel or large rimless baking sheet with cornmeal. Divide the dough into 4 pieces. Use a rolling pin to roll out each piece into a 6-inch circle.

4. Divide the cheese mixture among the 4 pieces of dough, leaving a ½-inch border around the edge. Brush a little cold water around the edge of each. Fold the top of the dough over the filling so that it meets the bottom edge. Crimp the edges together with your fingers and turn them up.

5. If using a stone, slide the calzones from the peel or baking sheet onto the preheated stone. Otherwise, place the baking sheet in the oven. Bake until the calzones are puffy and golden brown in spots, about 20 minutes.

6. Remove the calzones from the oven and cool for several minutes to allow the filling to solidify. Serve immediately or at room temperature.

Serving Suggestions

Serve one calzone per person with a vegetable side dish or salad, such as Spinach Salad with Orange Juice Vinaigrette and Toasted Walnuts (page 380), Spicy Broccoli with Garlic (page 334) or Grilled Vegetables with Thyme and Garlic (page 365). If serving the calzones without tomato sauce, try a side dish with tomatoes, such as Grilled Zucchini and Eggplant Salad with Tomatoes and Balsamic Vinegar (page 398).

Calzone with Mozzarella, Tomatoes and Basil

SERVES 4

THESE CALZONES HAVE TOMATOES baked right into the filling along with cheese, basil and garlic.

- ½ recipe Basic Pizza Dough (page 440) or Whole Wheat Pizza Dough (page 442)
- 8 ounces mozzarella cheese, shredded (about 2 cups)
- 2 medium garlic cloves, minced
- 2 tablespoons minced fresh basil leaves
- Salt and freshly ground black pepper
- Cornmeal for sprinkling
- 1 cup canned crushed tomatoes

1. Prepare the dough through Step 2 of the dough recipe. If using a baking stone, place it in the oven. Preheat the oven to 450 degrees F for 30 minutes.

2. Combine the cheese, garlic, basil and salt and pepper to taste in a medium bowl.

3. Sprinkle a pizza peel or large rimless baking sheet with cornmeal. Divide the dough into 4 pieces. Use a rolling pin to roll out each piece into a 6-inch circle.

4. Divide the cheese mixture among the 4 pieces of dough, leaving a ½-inch border around the edge. Spread ¼ cup tomatoes over the cheese on 1 circle. Brush a little cold water around the edge of the circle. Fold the top of the dough over the filling so that it meets the bottom edge. Crimp the edges together with your fingers and turn them up. Repeat with the remaining 3 circles.

5. If using a stone, slide the calzones from the peel or baking sheet onto the preheated stone. Otherwise, place the baking sheet in the oven. Bake until the calzones are puffy and golden brown in spots, about 20 minutes.

6. Remove the calzones from the oven and cool for several minutes to allow the filling to solidify. Serve immediately or at room temperature.

SERVING SUGGESTIONS

These calzones make a good lunch with a leafy salad. For dinner, add a vegetable side dish, such as Wilted Escarole with Garlic and Lemon (page 343) or Swiss Chard with Raisins and Almonds (page 340).

Focaccia with Black Olives and Thyme

MAKES 1 LARGE RECTANGULAR FOCACCIA

FOCACCIA, AN ANCIENT FLATBREAD, is similar to pizza but rectangular in shape and thicker, usually about one inch thick. Toppings are simple, as for this focaccia with olives and thyme. Be sure to use large black olives that are not too salty. Oregano may be substituted for the thyme if desired.

- 1 recipe Basic Focaccia (page 456), Whole Wheat Focaccia (page 458) or High-Rise Focaccia (page 460), without topping
- 24 large black olives, drained
- 2 tablespoons extra-virgin olive oil
- ½-1 teaspoon kosher or coarse sea salt
- 1 teaspoon minced fresh thyme leaves

1. Follow the focaccia recipe of choice, dimpling the dough as directed.

2. Use the side of the blade of a heavy knife to crush the olives and loosen the pits. Remove the pits with your fingers and place 1 pitted olive in each dimple.

3. Drizzle the oil over the dough, sprinkle with salt and thyme and bake as directed in the master recipe.

SERVING SUGGESTIONS

This focaccia goes well with soups that have distinctive flavors, such as Chick-pea Soup with Fennel and Orange Zest (page 64), Chard and Spinach Soup with Lemon-Parsley Pesto (page 46) or Pureed Cauliflower Soup with Pesto (page 48).

Focaccia with Onions

MAKES 1 LARGE RECTANGULAR FOCACCIA

THINLY SLICED ONIONS caramelize in the hot oven heat while the focaccia bakes. Some people precook the onions (usually by sautéing them in oil), but I like the strong flavor that results from cooking them only once. Just before baking, sprinkle ½ teaspoon dried oregano or thyme over the focaccia if desired.

- 1 recipe Basic Focaccia (page 456), Whole Wheat Focaccia (page 458) or High-Rise Focaccia (page 460), without topping
- 2 medium onions, halved and very thinly sliced
- 3 tablespoons extra-virgin olive oil
- ½-1 teaspoon kosher or coarse sea salt

1. Follow the focaccia recipe of choice, dimpling the dough as directed.

2. Toss the sliced onions with 1 tablespoon of the oil and spread them evenly over the dimpled dough. Drizzle the remaining 2 tablespoons oil over the onions, sprinkle with salt and bake as directed in the master recipe.

SERVING SUGGESTIONS

Serve the focaccia with a vegetable main course, such as Zucchini Stuffed with Ricotta and Herbs (page 308), and a leafy salad.

Focaccia with Roasted Red Peppers

MAKES 1 LARGE RECTANGULAR FOCACCIA

YELLOW OR ORANGE BELL PEPPERS MAY BE USED in place of the red peppers if desired. Or use a mixture of colors.

- 1 recipe Basic Focaccia (page 456), Whole Wheat Focaccia (page 458) or High-Rise Focaccia (page 460), without topping
- 2 large red bell peppers (about 1 pound)
- 2 tablespoons extra-virgin olive oil
- ½-1 teaspoon kosher or coarse sea salt

1. Follow the focaccia recipe of choice, dimpling the dough as directed.

2. Roast and peel the peppers as directed on page 526. Core and seed them and cut them into thin strips. Spread the peppers evenly over the dough. Drizzle the oil over the peppers, sprinkle with salt and bake as directed in the master recipe.

SERVING SUGGESTIONS

Cut into small squares, the focaccia makes enough for eight people as a snack with drinks before dinner. It also makes a light meal for four when served with a substantial salad, such as Romaine Lettuce Salad with Gorgonzola and Walnuts (page 378), Fennel and Orange Salad (page 389), and/or a vegetable side dish, such as Gratinéed Asparagus with Parmesan (page 332).

Focaccia with Basil and Tomatoes

MAKES 1 LARGE RECTANGULAR FOCACCIA

THIS FOCACCIA IS SUBSTANTIAL and can be served as a lunch or light dinner for four or as a snack or an hors d'oeuvre for six to eight. The basil is sprinkled over the dough after it comes out of the oven, so it keeps its bright, green color.

- 1 recipe Basic Focaccia (page 456), Whole Wheat Focaccia (page 458) or High-Rise Focaccia (page 460), without topping
- 2 large, ripe tomatoes (about 1 pound), cored, seeded and cut into ½-inch cubes
- 2 tablespoons extra-virgin olive oil
- ½-1 teaspoon kosher or coarse sea salt
- ¼ cup minced fresh basil leaves

1. Follow the focaccia recipe of choice, pressing the dough into the pan as directed.

2. About 15 minutes before dimpling the dough, place the tomatoes in a strainer and allow some of the liquid to drain off.

3. Dimple the dough and then cover with the drained tomatoes. Drizzle the oil over the tomatoes, sprinkle with salt and bake as directed in the master recipe. As soon as the focaccia comes out of the oven, sprinkle it with the basil.

SERVING SUGGESTIONS

For a meal for four, serve the focaccia with a salad, such as Tender Greens and Vegetables with Blood Orange Vinaigrette (page 376). This focaccia is also a good accompaniment to many soups, especially Chickpea Soup with Fennel and Orange Zest (page 64).

Focaccia with Rosemary

MAKES 1 LARGE RECTANGULAR FOCACCIA

FRESH ROSEMARY IS ESSENTIAL for this focaccia. Also called *schiacciata,* it is a specialty of Florence that is offered in the afternoon to children as an after-school snack. It works well as an accompaniment to an Italian dinner.

- 1 recipe Basic Focaccia (page 456), Whole Wheat Focaccia (page 458) or High-Rise Focaccia page 460), without topping
- Several long sprigs fresh rosemary
- 2 tablespoons extra-virgin olive oil
- ½-1 teaspoon kosher or coarse sea salt

1. Follow the focaccia recipe of choice, dimpling the dough as directed.

2. Pull off 1-inch pieces of rosemary that contain several leaves each. You will need about 25 pieces. Press 1 piece fresh rosemary into each indentation.

3. Drizzle the oil over the dough, sprinkle with salt and bake as directed in the master recipe.

SERVING SUGGESTIONS

Serve squares of this bread with Pasta and White Bean Soup with Garlic and Rosemary (page 63) or Mixed Roasted Vegetables with Rosemary and Garlic (page 318).

Focaccia with Sage

MAKES 1 LARGE RECTANGULAR FOCACCIA

WHOLE SAGE LEAVES ARE PRESSED into the dough just before baking for a simple but attractive presentation.

1 recipe Basic Focaccia (page 456), Whole Wheat Focaccia (page 458) or High-Rise Focaccia (page 460), without topping
1 tablespoon chopped fresh sage leaves, plus about 25 whole fresh sage leaves
2 tablespoons extra-virgin olive oil
½-1 teaspoon kosher or coarse sea salt

1. Follow the focaccia recipe of choice, adding the chopped sage to the dough with the flour and salt.

2. After dimpling the dough, press 1 whole sage leaf into each indentation. Drizzle the oil over the dough, sprinkle with salt and bake as directed in the master recipe.

SERVING SUGGESTIONS
Serve this focaccia with Roasted Yellow Pepper Soup (page 53) or Grilled Portobello Mushrooms, Red Onions and Bell Peppers (page 320).

Parmesan Focaccia

MAKES 1 LARGE RECTANGULAR FOCACCIA

GRATED CHEESE SPRINKLED OVER THE DOUGH turns a rich golden brown when baked. This focaccia is especially nice with a hearty stew or soup. Pecorino Romano may be used in place of the Parmigiano-Reggiano if desired. Because of the generous topping of cheese, which has a salty taste, there is no need to sprinkle the risen dough with salt.

- 1 recipe Basic Focaccia (page 456), Whole Wheat Focaccia (page 458) or High-Rise Focaccia (page 460), without topping
- 2 tablespoons extra-virgin olive oil
- ⅔ cup freshly grated Parmigiano-Reggiano cheese

1. Follow the focaccia recipe of choice, dimpling the dough as directed. Drizzle the oil over the dough and sprinkle evenly with the cheese. (Do not sprinkle any salt over the dough.)

2. Bake as directed in the master recipe. When the cheese is a rich, golden brown color, the focaccia is done.

SERVING SUGGESTIONS

This focaccia is good with almost any meal. Serve it with Spring Vegetable Stew with Fennel, Carrots, Asparagus and Peas (page 322), Baked Tomatoes Stuffed with Pesto and Mozzarella (page 314) or Classic Minestrone with Pesto (page 60).

Focaccia with Sun-Dried Tomatoes and Garlic

MAKES 1 LARGE RECTANGULAR FOCACCIA

FOCACCIA DOUGH IS USUALLY NOT FLAVORED; or if it is, it is seasoned only with an herb. This recipe, however, calls for sun-dried tomatoes and garlic in the dough itself. A light topping of slivered sun-dried tomatoes is added just after baking. The best way to make this dough is in a standing mixer, which will tear the sun-dried tomatoes into small pieces, giving the dough a lovely rosy hue. If making the dough by hand, mince the sun-dried tomatoes before adding them with the flour.

DOUGH

- 6 sun-dried tomatoes packed in olive oil
- 3 medium garlic cloves, minced
- 2 teaspoons active dry yeast (1 envelope)
- 3½ cups unbleached all-purpose flour
- 1½ teaspoons kosher or coarse sea salt
- Nonstick vegetable oil spray

TOPPING

- 2 tablespoons extra-virgin olive oil
- ½-1 teaspoon kosher or coarse sea salt
- 6 sun-dried tomatoes packed in olive oil, drained and cut into long, thin slivers

1. Lift the sun-dried tomatoes from the oil and set aside. Drain off 2 tablespoons of the sun-dried tomato oil (add more extra-virgin olive oil if needed) and heat in a small skillet. Add the garlic and sauté over medium heat until golden, about 2 minutes. Remove from the heat and let cool to room temperature.

2. Combine 1⅓ cups warm water (105 to 115 degrees F), the yeast and cooled garlic and oil in the large bowl of a standing mixer fitted with the paddle attachment. Stir in the whole sun-dried tomatoes, flour and the 1½ teaspoons salt. When the dough comes together, replace the paddle attachment with the dough hook. Knead until the dough is smooth and elastic, about 4 minutes.

3. Turn the dough into a lightly oiled, large bowl and cover with a damp cloth. Let rise until puffy and doubled in bulk, 1½ to 2 hours.

4. Generously spray the bottom and sides of a 15½-by-10½-inch pan that measures at least 1 inch deep with vegetable oil. Flatten the dough and press it into the pan. Cover with a damp cloth and let rise until puffy and almost doubled, 1½ to 2 hours.

5. Preheat the oven to 425 degrees F. Just before baking, use your finger to dimple the dough at 2-inch intervals. Drizzle the 2 tablespoons oil over the dough, letting some collect in the indentations. Sprinkle the dough with the ½ to 1 teaspoon salt.

6. Bake until the bottom of the focaccia is richly colored and crisp and the top is golden brown, 20 to 25 minutes. As soon as the focaccia comes out of the oven, place 1 sun-dried tomato sliver in each dimple. Use a large spatula to remove the focaccia from the pan and slide it onto a wire rack to cool. Serve warm or at room temperature. *(Cool the focaccia, wrap it in plastic and then aluminum foil and freeze it for 1 month. Unwrap the frozen loaf and reheat it in a 375-degree oven for 10 to 15 minutes.)*

SERVING SUGGESTIONS

This focaccia takes on many guises in the kitchen. Cut into small pieces, it can be served as an antipasto for a crowd. Cut into squares and split, it can be filled to make sandwiches. Or serve the focaccia with soup, such as Roasted Yellow Pepper Soup (page 53) or Pureed Cauliflower Soup with Pesto (page 48). For a light dinner for four, serve it with a leafy salad and a vegetable side dish, such as Sautéed Zucchini with Lemon and Mint (page 363) or Grilled Vegetables with Thyme and Garlic (page 365).

Basic Focaccia

MAKES 1 LARGE RECTANGULAR FOCACCIA

THIS IS A MASTER RECIPE FOR FOCACCIA. The dough is topped with olive oil (use only the best quality) and coarse salt. This dough can be made in a standing mixer, in a food processor or by hand. A standing mixer delivers the best results because it does a more thorough job of kneading the dough.

DOUGH

- **1⅓ cups warm water (105-115 degrees F)**
- **2 teaspoons active dry yeast (1 envelope)**
- **3 tablespoons extra-virgin olive oil**
- **3½ cups unbleached all-purpose flour**
- **2 teaspoons kosher salt**
- **Nonstick vegetable oil spray**

TOPPING

- **2 tablespoons extra-virgin olive oil**
- **½-1 teaspoon kosher or coarse sea salt**

1. To make the dough in a standing mixer: Combine the water, yeast and oil in the large bowl of a mixer fitted with the paddle attachment. Stir in the flour and salt. When the dough comes together, replace the paddle attachment with the dough hook. Knead until the dough is smooth and elastic, about 4 minutes.

To make the dough by hand: Combine the water, yeast and oil in a large bowl, using a wooden spoon. Add the flour and salt and continue to stir until the dough comes together. Turn the dough out onto a floured surface and knead until smooth and elastic, about 6 minutes.

To make the dough in a food processor: Pour the water into the work bowl of a food processor fitted with the metal blade. Add the yeast and oil and process for several seconds until smooth. Add the flour and salt and process until the dough comes together in a ball, about 30 seconds.

2. Turn the dough into a lightly oiled large bowl and cover with a damp cloth. Let rise until the dough is puffy and has doubled in bulk, about 1½ hours.

3. Generously spray the bottom and sides of a 15½-by-10½-inch pan that measures at least 1 inch deep with vegetable oil. Flatten the dough and press it into the pan. Cover with a damp cloth and let rise until puffy and almost doubled, about 1½ hours.

4. Preheat the oven to 425 degrees F. Just before baking, use your finger to dimple the dough at 2-inch intervals. Drizzle the 2 tablespoons oil over the dough, letting some collect in the indentations. Sprinkle the dough with the ½ to 1 teaspoon salt.

5. Bake until the bottom of the focaccia is richly colored and crisp and the top is golden brown, 20 to 25 minutes. Use a large spatula to remove the focaccia from the pan and slide it onto a wire rack to cool. Serve warm or at room temperature. *(Cool the focaccia, wrap it in plastic and then aluminum foil and freeze it for 1 month. Unwrap the frozen loaf and reheat it in a 375-degree oven for 10 to 15 minutes.)*

Whole Wheat Focaccia

MAKES 1 LARGE RECTANGULAR FOCACCIA

IN ITALY, FOCACCIA IS TRADITIONALLY MADE WITH FLOUR similar to American all-purpose flour. A combination of whole wheat and all-purpose flour, however, gives the dough more flavor and a pleasant wheatiness without causing the bread to become dry or tough. Use this dough with any of the toppings in this chapter.

DOUGH

- 1⅓ cups warm water (105-115 degrees F)
- 2 teaspoons active dry yeast (1 envelope)
- 3 tablespoons extra-virgin olive oil
- 2 cups unbleached all-purpose flour
- 1⅓ cups whole wheat flour
- 2 teaspoons kosher salt
- Nonstick vegetable oil spray

TOPPING

- 2 tablespoons extra-virgin olive oil
- ½-1 teaspoon kosher or coarse sea salt

1. **To make the dough in a standing mixer:** Combine the water, yeast and oil in the large bowl of a mixer fitted with the paddle attachment. Stir in the all-purpose and whole wheat flours and salt. When the dough comes together, replace the paddle attachment with the dough hook. Knead until the dough is smooth and elastic, about 4 minutes.

To make the dough by hand: Combine the water, yeast and oil in a large bowl, using a wooden spoon. Add the all-purpose and whole wheat flours and salt and continue to stir until the dough comes together. Turn the dough out onto a floured surface and knead until smooth and elastic, about 6 minutes.

To make the dough in a food processor: Pour the water into the work bowl of a food processor fitted with the metal blade. Add the yeast and oil and process for several seconds until smooth. Add the all-purpose and whole wheat flours and salt and process until the dough comes together in a ball, about 30 seconds.

2. Turn the dough into a lightly oiled large bowl and cover with a damp cloth. Let rise until the dough is puffy and has doubled in bulk, 1½ to 2 hours.

3. Generously spray the bottom and sides of a 15½-by-10½-inch pan that measures at least 1 inch deep with vegetable oil. Flatten the dough and press it into the pan. Cover with a damp cloth and let rise until puffy and almost doubled, 1½ to 2 hours.

4. Preheat the oven to 425 degrees F. Just before baking, use your finger to dimple the dough at 2-inch intervals. Drizzle the 2 tablespoons oil over the dough, letting some collect in the indentations. Sprinkle the dough with the ½ to 1 teaspoon salt.

5. Bake until the bottom of the focaccia is richly colored and crisp and the top is golden brown, 20 to 25 minutes. Use a large spatula to remove the focaccia from the pan and slide it onto a wire rack to cool. Serve warm or at room temperature. *(Cool the focaccia, wrap it in plastic and then aluminum foil and freeze it for 1 month. Unwrap the frozen loaf and reheat it in a 375-degree oven for 10 to 15 minutes.)*

High-Rise Focaccia

MAKES 1 LARGE RECTANGULAR FOCACCIA

POTATO IS ADDED TO MANY FOCACCIA DOUGHS IN SOUTHERN ITALY, especially in Apulia. The result is a high-rising dough with a light, fluffy texture; the actual flavor of the potato is almost undetectable. Because this focaccia is so thick, it is especially well suited to sandwiches, since it is easy to slice in half. The dough can also be used with any of the toppings in this chapter, whenever a more cakelike texture is desired.

The potatoes make the dough a bit sticky, so moisten your hands when trying to stretch it into the pan. Knead this dough by hand or in a standing mixer. A food processor can make the potatoes gummy.

DOUGH

- **1 medium baking potato (8 ounces)**
- **1 cup warm water (105-115 degrees F)**
- **1½ teaspoons active dry yeast (¾ envelope)**
- **1 tablespoon extra-virgin olive oil**
- **3½ cups unbleached all-purpose flour**
- **2 teaspoons kosher salt**
- **Nonstick vegetable oil spray**

TOPPING

- **2 tablespoons extra-virgin olive oil**
- **½-1 teaspoon kosher or coarse sea salt**

1. Bring 1 quart water to a boil in a small saucepan. Peel and cut the potato into 2-inch chunks. Add the potato to the boiling water and simmer until tender, about 15 minutes. Drain and rice the potato. Set aside to cool to room temperature. There should be 1½ cups, lightly packed.

2. To make the dough in a standing mixer: Combine the water, yeast and oil in the large bowl of a mixer fitted with the paddle attachment. Stir in the riced potato, flour and salt. When the dough comes together, replace the paddle attachment with the dough hook. Knead until the dough is smooth and elastic, about 5 minutes.

To make the dough by hand: Combine the water, yeast and oil in a large bowl, using a wooden spoon. Add the riced potato, flour and salt and continue to stir until the dough comes together. Turn the dough out onto a floured surface and knead until smooth and elastic, about 8 minutes.

3. Turn the dough into a lightly oiled large bowl and cover with a damp cloth. Let rise until the dough is puffy and has doubled in bulk, about 1½ hours.

4. Generously spray the bottom and sides of a 15½-by-10½-inch pan that measures at least 1 inch deep with vegetable oil. Moisten your hands. Flatten the dough and press it into the pan. Cover with a damp cloth and let rise until puffy and almost doubled, about 1 hour.

5. Preheat the oven to 425 degrees F. Just before baking, use your finger to dimple the dough at 2-inch intervals. Drizzle the 2 tablespoons oil over the dough, letting some collect in the indentations. Sprinkle the dough with the ½ to 1 teaspoon salt.

6. Bake until the bottom of the focaccia is richly colored and crisp and the top is golden brown, 20 to 25 minutes. Use a large spatula to remove the focaccia from the pan and slide it onto a wire rack to cool. Serve warm or at room temperature. *(Cool the focaccia, wrap it in plastic and then aluminum foil and freeze it for 1 month. Unwrap the frozen loaf and reheat it in a 375-degree oven for 10 to 15 minutes.)*

PANINI AND BRUSCHETTA

FOR MANY YEARS, good bread was an afterthought for most Americans. This has never been the case in Italy. Every town or village, no matter how small, has a baker who turns out high-quality loaves. Regional specialties, such as the saltless bread of Tuscany, are commonplace. Like so much of Italian cooking, bread has not become nationalized or homogenized. This chapter includes two kinds of recipes that rely on good bread for their character.

Sandwiches are called *panini* in Italian, which literally translates as "little breads," or rolls. Panini are generally made with just a few well-chosen ingredients. At the tiny Italian places with a counter where they are sold, passersby stop to order and enjoy a glass of wine or sparkling water as they watch the panini being made, then eat standing up. Most panini are small enough to fit into the palm of one hand. (The "Italian" hero sandwich sold in many of our delicatessens is an American creation.)

Panini are intended to be made with items you are likely to have on hand: nothing exotic and no long lists of ingredients to shop for. If you keep cheese, tomatoes, olives, roasted peppers, marinated artichoke hearts, eggs, salad greens and fresh herbs in your kitchen, you have the makings for a dozen or more vegetarian panini.

Bruschetta, a large, thick slice of country bread that has been toasted, then rubbed with raw garlic cloves and brushed with the finest olive oil, is the original garlic bread. The word (pronounced brew-SKET-ta) comes from the Italian word *bruscare*, meaning "to roast over coals." Traditionally, the bread for bruschetta was toasted over an open fire. A broiler or toaster can stand in for a charcoal fire, although neither will add smoky flavor to the bread.

The bread should be toasted to a rich golden brown color for maximum crunch and flavor. This toasting also creates jagged edges that pull off tiny bits of the garlic. For a light garlic flavor, merely glide the clove across the hot toast. For a stronger flavor, scrape the garlic back and forth vigorously. Either way, a liberal brushing with extra-virgin olive oil comes next.

In its simplest form, bruschetta may be topped with coarse salt and nothing else. Add fresh herbs, tomatoes, grilled mushrooms or pureed beans for toasts of increasing heft. Lightly topped bruschetta can be served as an accompaniment to a meal or as an appetizer. More substantial toppings turn bruschetta into a light meal in itself, especially if served with a salad. For the following recipes, plan on one piece per person as an appetizer and two or three as a light meal.

Diminutive bruschetta, called crostini, are made with smaller pieces of toast and more delicate toppings. They are served as appetizers and are included in the antipasto chapter (see pages 17 to 41).

Cold Panini

Hot Panini

Bruschetta

Mozzarella Panini with Black Olive Paste

Makes 4 sandwiches

These sandwiches are simple yet full of flavor. I spread olive paste on a roll and then fill it with fresh mozzarella. Because it is packed in water, fresh mozzarella has to be patted dry before slicing. It is available in Italian groceries, gourmet shops and many supermarkets. When I lived in Florence, my local sandwich shop served a similar combination on individual rosemary focaccia. You can use store-bought focaccia or homemade (pages 456, 458 and 460) focaccia.

- **¾ pound fresh mozzarella cheese, packed in water**
- **½ cup Olivada (page 533)**
- **4 large sandwich rolls or squares of focaccia, split**

1. Lift the mozzarella from the water and pat it dry with paper towels. Thinly slice it.

2. Spread 2 tablespoons olive paste on the inside of each roll. Fill with slices of mozzarella cheese and serve immediately.

Serving Suggestions

Serve these sandwiches with a salad, such as Marinated Tomato and Red Onion Salad (page 395), Arugula Salad with Sliced Radishes and Carrots (page 371) or Red Leaf Lettuce, Arugula and Fennel Salad (page 374).

Bel Paese Sandwiches with Baby Spinach

MAKES 4 SANDWICHES

MILD, CREAMY BEL PAESE CHEESE is a good counterpoint to baby greens dressed with lemon juice and olive oil. Any cheese that is soft enough to spread can be used here, including goat cheese or mild *dolcelatte* Gorgonzola. Mesclun or arugula can be substituted for the baby spinach.

4 cups tightly packed baby spinach or other leafy greens
1 tablespoon lemon juice
Salt and freshly ground black pepper
2 tablespoons extra-virgin olive oil
8 ounces Bel Paese or other soft cheese, at room temperature
8 slices country white bread

1. Remove and discard the stems from the spinach or other greens. Wash the leaves in successive bowls of cold water until grit no longer appears in the bottom of the bowl. Shake the leaves to remove excess water and dry them thoroughly.

2. Place the spinach or other greens in a medium bowl. Drizzle with the lemon juice, sprinkle with salt and pepper to taste and toss gently. Drizzle the oil over the spinach and toss again.

3. Spread the cheese over 4 of the bread slices. Put some of the spinach on top of the cheese. Top with the remaining bread slices. Press down lightly on the sandwiches to bind the filling together. Cut the sandwiches in half and serve immediately.

SERVING SUGGESTIONS

Serve these sandwiches for lunch with a tomato salad, such as Marinated Tomato and Red Onion Salad (page 395) or Tomato Salad with Black Olives, Capers and Herbs (page 394).

Tomato Sandwiches with Basil Leaves and Garlic Mayonnaise

MAKES 4 SANDWICHES

THESE SANDWICHES COMBINE THE BEST OF SUMMER—ripe tomatoes and fresh basil—with garlicky mayonnaise. Top-notch tomatoes are a must. As for the bread, I like a dense, chewy country loaf.

- **½ cup Garlic Mayonnaise (page 534)**
- **8 slices country white bread**
- **4 medium, ripe tomatoes (about 1½ pounds), cored and cut crosswise into thin slices**
- **12 large fresh basil leaves**
- **Salt**

1. Thickly spread mayonnaise on 1 side of each slice of bread. Layer the tomatoes over 4 bread slices, adding a few basil leaves as you go. Sprinkle with salt.

2. Top with the remaining 4 bread slices. Cut the sandwiches in half and serve immediately.

SERVING SUGGESTIONS

Serve these sandwiches for lunch with a leafy salad, such as Red Leaf Lettuce, Arugula and Fennel Salad (page 374), and a bowl of Marinated Black Olives with Rosemary and Lemon Zest (page 20).

Tomato Panini with Basil Mayonnaise

MAKES 3 LARGE SANDWICHES

CRISP SLICES OF TOASTED BREAD, ripe summer tomatoes and a basil-flavored mayonnaise make an elegant but simple lunch. Other herbs, especially mint or tarragon, may be substituted for the basil. For this sandwich, I cut slices about seven or eight inches long from a large round loaf. One sandwich will satisfy a hearty appetite, while half a sandwich is enough for smaller appetites or when served with a salad.

If you are concerned about the health risks associated with eating raw eggs, choose another tomato sandwich.

- **1 large egg yolk**
- **2 teaspoons lemon juice**
- **Salt**
- **¼ cup extra-virgin olive oil**
- **¼ cup canola oil or other bland oil**
- **¼ cup minced fresh basil leaves**
- **6 large slices country white bread**
- **3 medium, ripe tomatoes (about 1 pound), cored and cut crosswise into ½-inch-thick slices**

1. Whisk the egg yolk, lemon juice and a pinch of salt together in a medium bowl. Combine the oils in a measuring cup. Very slowly whisk in the oil in a steady stream until it is fully incorporated. Stir in the basil and adjust the seasonings. *(The mayonnaise may be covered and refrigerated for 2 days.)*

2. Toast or grill the bread until the slices are golden brown. Thickly spread basil mayonnaise on 1 side of each slice of bread. Layer the tomatoes over 3 of the bread slices and top with the remaining bread slices. Cut the sandwiches in half and serve immediately.

SERVING SUGGESTIONS

For a more substantial meal, serve the panini with a vegetable salad, such as Spicy Broccoli Salad with Lemon (page 385) or Grilled Potato Salad with Red Pepper and Onion (page 392).

Mozzarella and Tomato Panini with Pesto

MAKES 4 SANDWICHES

PESTO HAS MANY USES IN MY KITCHEN, including as a sandwich spread. Because it is intensely flavored, you need only a little.

¾ pound fresh mozzarella cheese, packed in water
¼ cup Pesto, My Way (page 531)
4 crusty rolls, split
2 medium, ripe tomatoes (about ¾ pound), cored and cut crosswise into thin slices

1. Lift the mozzarella from the water and pat it dry with paper towels. Thinly slice it.

2. Spread 1 tablespoon pesto on the inside of each roll. Layer slices of mozzarella and tomato into each roll and serve immediately.

SERVING SUGGESTIONS

Serve the sandwiches alone or with a marinated vegetable salad, such as Spicy Broccoli Salad with Lemon (page 385), Marinated Cauliflower Salad with Olives (page 388) or Marinated Zucchini Salad with Lemon and Thyme (page 396).

Mozzarella and Arugula Panini with Roasted Red Pepper Spread

MAKES 4 SANDWICHES

BITTER ARUGULA LEAVES are balanced by thin slices of creamy fresh mozzarella and a slightly sweet sandwich spread made by pureeing a roasted red pepper with a little garlic and olive oil. I like to make these small sandwiches from a loaf of *ciabatta,* a Tuscan bread that is rectangular in shape and usually quite flat. Slice the loaf in half lengthwise, fill it and cut it into four pieces. The sandwiches may also be made on small crusty rolls.

1 medium red bell pepper
1 small garlic clove
1 tablespoon extra-virgin olive oil
1 ciabatta (about 12 inches long and 4 inches wide) or 4 small crusty rolls
8 ounces fresh mozzarella cheese, dried and thinly sliced
2 cups stemmed arugula leaves (1 bunch), washed, thoroughly dried and chopped

1. Roast and peel the pepper as directed on page 526. Core and seed the pepper.

2. Place the pepper and garlic in the work bowl of a food processor. Puree until smooth. With the motor running, slowly pour the oil through the feed tube and process until smooth. Scrape the sauce into a small bowl. *(The roasted pepper puree can be refrigerated for a few hours. The garlic flavor intensifies with time, so do not store for longer periods.)*

3. Cutting parallel to the work surface, slice the ciabatta or rolls in half. Spread the roasted pepper puree on both sides. Layer the cheese over the bottom half and cover with the arugula. Place the top half over the filling and cut the loaf into 4 sandwiches. Serve immediately.

SERVING SUGGESTIONS

These sandwiches make a nice light lunch. For a more substantial meal, add a vegetable salad, such as Marinated Cauliflower Salad with Olives (page 388) or Spicy Broccoli Salad with Lemon (page 385).

Grilled Eggplant and Red Pepper Sandwiches with Olivada

MAKES 4 SANDWICHES

SLICES OF GRILLED EGGPLANT AND RED BELL PEPPER on country bread make an excellent sandwich. The vegetables may be broiled, but they will lack the smokiness that comes from the coals.

- **2 large eggplants (about 1¾ pounds)**
- **2 large red bell peppers (about 1 pound), cored, seeded and cut into 2-inch wedges**
- **¼ cup extra-virgin olive oil**
- **Salt and freshly ground black pepper**
- **½ cup Olivada (page 533)**
- **8 slices country white bread**

1. Light the grill or make a charcoal fire. Trim and discard the ends from the eggplants and cut the eggplants lengthwise into ½-inch-thick pieces. Peel the outer slices. Lay the eggplant and peppers on a large baking sheet or platter. Brush them with the oil and sprinkle lightly with salt and pepper to taste.

2. Grill the vegetables over a medium-hot fire, turning once, until marked with dark stripes, about 10 minutes. Remove from the grill and cool until just warm or to room temperature. *(The vegetables can be covered and set aside at room temperature for several hours.)*

3. Spread 1 tablespoon olive paste over 1 side of each bread slice. Layer the eggplant and peppers over 4 of the slices, cutting them as needed to fit onto the bread. Top with the remaining bread slices. Serve immediately.

SERVING SUGGESTIONS

Serve these sandwiches with a leafy salad, such as Romaine Lettuce Salad with Gorgonzola and Walnuts (page 378) or Red Leaf Lettuce, Arugula and Fennel Salad (page 374).

Panini with Marinated Artichokes, Fontina and Basil

MAKES 4 SANDWICHES

FOR THESE SANDWICHES, marinated artichokes and basil are layered between slices of fontina cheese on toast and run under the broiler. Then they are covered with pieces of plain toast. Quartered marinated artichoke hearts are just the right size.

- **8 slices country white bread**
- **8 ounces Italian fontina cheese, very thinly sliced**
- **12 small pieces marinated artichoke hearts, drained on paper towels**
- **8 large fresh basil leaves**

1. Preheat the broiler. Place 4 bread slices on a large baking sheet and toast, turning once, until golden brown. Set aside.

2. Place the remaining 4 bread slices on the baking sheet. Cover each slice with a layer of cheese. Place 3 artichoke heart pieces and 2 basil leaves on each piece of bread and cover with another layer of cheese.

3. Broil until both layers of cheese melt and the edges of the bread turn golden brown. Top with the reserved toasted bread slices. Cut the sandwiches in half and serve immediately.

SERVING SUGGESTIONS

The sandwiches are fairly rich and can be served alone or with a vegetable accompaniment, such as Roasted Potato Salad with Herbs and Red Wine Vinegar (page 391).

Grilled Smoked Mozzarella and Arugula Panini

MAKES 2 SMALL SANDWICHES

SMOKED MOZZARELLA MAKES ESPECIALLY DELICIOUS grilled cheese sandwiches. These sandwiches are small but rich.

- **6 ounces smoked mozzarella cheese, thinly sliced**
- **2 long, thin slices country white bread, cut in half**
- **½ cup stemmed arugula leaves, washed and thoroughly dried**
- **2 tablespoons extra-virgin olive oil**

1. Lay several slices of the cheese over 2 of the bread slices. Top each with half of the arugula and then make a second layer of the cheese. Top with the remaining 2 bread slices.

2. Heat the oil in a large skillet set over medium heat. Add the sandwiches and cook, pressing down with a spatula to flatten them, until the bottoms turn golden brown, about 3 minutes. Turn and cook, occasionally pressing down on the sandwiches with the spatula, until golden brown on the second side, about 3 minutes. Serve immediately.

SERVING SUGGESTIONS

These little sandwiches are perfect for lunch or a light dinner with a bowl of soup, such as Roasted Yellow Pepper Soup (page 53) or Chilled Potato and Zucchini Soup with Fresh Tomato Garnish (page 55). The panini can also be served with a vegetable salad, such as Fennel and Orange Salad (page 389), to round out the meal.

Scrambled Egg Sandwiches with Red Peppers and Onions

MAKES 2 SANDWICHES

THESE SANDWICHES, on toasted (or grilled) country bread, make a quick lunch. Eggs are scrambled right in the pan with cooked onions and peppers.

- 1 large red bell pepper
- 2 tablespoons extra-virgin olive oil
- 1 medium onion, minced
- Salt and freshly ground black pepper
- 4 large slices country white bread
- 4 large eggs
- 1 tablespoon minced fresh parsley leaves

1. Core, seed and cut the pepper into very thin strips. Cut each strip in half and set aside.

2. Heat the oil in a large skillet. Add the onion and sauté over medium heat until slightly softened, about 2 minutes. Add the pepper strips and cook, stirring occasionally, until tender, about 10 minutes. Season with salt and pepper to taste.

3. While the onion and pepper are cooking, toast the bread. Set aside.

4. Beat the eggs, parsley and salt and pepper to taste in a small bowl. Add to the skillet and cook, stirring often, until set, about 2 minutes. Adjust the seasonings.

5. Divide the egg mixture between 2 slices of toast and top with the remaining slices. Cut the sandwiches in half and serve immediately.

SERVING SUGGESTIONS

For a more substantial lunch or light supper, add a salad, such as Arugula, Tomato and Black Olive Salad (page 372) or Spinach Salad with Orange Juice Vinaigrette and Toasted Walnuts (page 380).

Mozzarella Spiedini with Lemon-Caper Sauce

MAKES 4 SANDWICHES

MY WIFE CALLS THIS A "SIDEWAYS SANDWICH." Slices of Italian bread and mozzarella are threaded on skewers and baked on their sides just until the pieces of bread and cheese meld. Eat with a knife and fork. *See the photograph on page 201.*

¼ cup minced fresh parsley leaves
1 medium garlic clove, minced
1 tablespoon drained capers, rinsed and minced
1 tablespoon lemon juice
¼ cup extra-virgin olive oil
Salt
1 loaf Italian bread, cut into sixteen ½-inch-thick slices
¾ pound fresh mozzarella cheese, packed in water
Freshly ground black pepper

1. Preheat the oven to 450 degrees F. Combine the parsley, garlic, capers, lemon juice, 2 tablespoons of the oil and salt to taste in a small bowl. Set aside.

2. Lift the mozzarella from the water and pat it dry with paper towels. Cut into twelve ¼-inch-thick slices.

3. Starting and ending with a piece of bread, thread 4 slices of bread and 3 pieces of cheese onto each of 4 skewers.

4. Lightly brush a medium baking sheet with about ½ tablespoon oil. Place the skewers on the oiled sheet and brush the sandwiches with the remaining 1½ tablespoons oil. Lightly sprinkle the sandwiches with salt and pepper to taste.

5. Bake just until the edges of the bread turn golden brown and the cheese softens, 5 to 6 minutes. Do not overbake or the cheese may become runny.

6. Slide the sandwiches from the skewers onto individual plates. Drizzle the sauce over the sandwiches and serve immediately.

SERVING SUGGESTIONS

Serve with a tomato salad, such as Marinated Tomato and Red Onion Salad (page 395), or with Roasted Peppers Marinated in Garlic Oil (page 25).

Bruschetta with Tomatoes and Basil

MAKES 8 LARGE TOASTS

THIS IS THE CLASSIC BRUSCHETTA, simple, colorful and tasty. Grilled or toasted bread is rubbed with a raw garlic clove, brushed with top-quality olive oil and topped with tomatoes and fresh basil. Mint, oregano, thyme or marjoram, alone or in combination, may be substituted for the basil. Depending on the intensity of the herbs, you may want to reduce the amount.

- 4 medium, ripe tomatoes (about 1¾ pounds), cored and cut into ½-inch dice
- ⅓ cup shredded fresh basil leaves
- Salt and freshly ground black pepper
- 1 oblong loaf rustic country bread (about 12 inches long and 5 inches wide)
- 1 large garlic clove
- 3 tablespoons extra-virgin olive oil

1. Preheat the broiler or light the grill.

2. Place the tomatoes in a medium bowl. Add the basil and salt and pepper to taste and toss. Set aside.

3. Slice the bread crosswise into eight 1-inch-thick pieces. Save the ends for another use. Toast the bread until golden brown on both sides. Transfer to a large platter. Rub garlic to taste over the top of each slice. Brush the oil over the bread.

4. Using a slotted spoon, divide the tomato mixture among the toasts, leaving behind any juices in the bowl. Serve immediately.

SERVING SUGGESTIONS

Serve the bruschetta, one or two per person, as an antipasto before a zucchini dish, such as Fettuccine with Zucchini, Lemon and Mint (page 112) or Zucchini Frittata with Parmesan (page 259). Or serve with lightly dressed salad greens as a light lunch or dinner.

Bruschetta with Fresh Herbs

MAKES 8 LARGE TOASTS

THE FLAVORING HERE IS BASIC—olive oil with parsley, oregano and sage. Experiment and develop your own combination of fresh herbs.

- **5 tablespoons extra-virgin olive oil**
- **1½ tablespoons minced fresh parsley leaves**
- **1 tablespoon minced fresh oregano or thyme leaves**
- **1 tablespoon minced fresh sage leaves**
- **Salt and freshly ground black pepper**
- **1 oblong loaf rustic country bread (about 12 inches long and 5 inches wide)**
- **1 large garlic clove**

1. Preheat the broiler or light the grill.

2. Combine the oil, parsley, oregano or thyme, sage and salt and pepper to taste in a small bowl. Set aside.

3. Slice the bread crosswise into eight 1-inch-thick pieces. Save the ends for another use. Toast the bread until golden brown on both sides. Transfer to a large platter. Rub garlic to taste over the top of each slice. Brush the herb oil over the bread. Serve immediately.

SERVING SUGGESTIONS

Herb bruschetta fit in at any meal where bread would be served—as an appetizer, with any frittata or a bowl of soup or as a late-afternoon snack.

Bruschetta with Sliced Eggplant and Tomatoes

MAKES 8 LARGE TOASTS

THIS BRUSCHETTA IS LIKE AN OPEN-FACE SANDWICH. With broiled slices of eggplant and tomatoes, it is a substantial snack or light meal. You can grill the eggplant and bread slices and then broil the bruschetta to melt the cheese. If served with a salad, eight bruschetta are enough for three or four people. If serving as an antipasto, plan on one per person.

2 medium eggplants (about 1 pound)
¼ cup extra-virgin olive oil
Salt and freshly ground black pepper
1 oblong loaf rustic country bread (about 12 inches long and 5 inches wide)
1 large garlic clove
3 medium, ripe tomatoes (about 1¼ pounds), cored and cut crosswise into thin slices
½ cup freshly grated Pecorino Romano cheese

1. Preheat the broiler. Trim and discard the ends from the eggplants and cut the eggplants lengthwise into ½-inch-thick pieces. Peel the outer slices. Lay the slices on a large baking sheet. Brush both sides of each slice with 2 tablespoons of the oil and season generously with salt and pepper to taste. Broil, turning once, until golden brown on both sides, about 10 minutes. Transfer to a platter.

2. Slice the bread crosswise into eight 1-inch-thick pieces. Save the ends for another use. Place the bread on the baking sheet and slide it under the broiler. Toast the bread until golden brown on both sides. Rub garlic to taste over the top of each slice. Brush the remaining 2 tablespoons oil over the bread. Layer the eggplant and tomato slices on the bread and dust each slice with 1 tablespoon grated cheese.

3. Return the baking sheet to the broiler and cook just until the cheese melts, 1 to 2 minutes. Watch carefully to keep from burning. Transfer the bruschetta to a large platter and serve immediately.

SERVING SUGGESTIONS

To make a meal of this bruschetta, serve it with a leafy green salad, such as Red Leaf Lettuce, Arugula and Fennel Salad (page 374) or Tender Green Salad with Pine Nuts and Yellow Raisins (page 375).

Bruschetta with White Beans, Tomatoes and Herbs

MAKES 8 LARGE TOASTS

WHITE BEANS AND TOMATOES make a substantial topping for bruschetta. If you can find yellow tomatoes, use one yellow and one red in this recipe. Mint or parsley may replace the basil.

2 cups Basic Cannellini Beans (page 286)
2 large, ripe tomatoes (about 1 pound), cored, seeded and diced small
¼ cup extra-virgin olive oil
2 tablespoons minced fresh basil leaves
1 teaspoon minced fresh thyme or oregano leaves
Salt and freshly ground black pepper
1 oblong loaf rustic country bread (about 12 inches long and 5 inches wide)
1 large garlic clove

1. Preheat the broiler or light the grill.

2. Toss together the beans, tomatoes, 1½ tablespoons of the oil, the basil, thyme or oregano and salt and pepper to taste in a large bowl. Set aside.

3. Slice the bread crosswise into eight 1-inch-thick pieces. Save the ends for another use. Toast the bread until golden brown on both sides. Transfer to a large platter. Rub garlic to taste over the top of each slice. Brush the remaining 2½ tablespoons oil over the bread.

4. Spoon some of the bean mixture on each piece of toast and serve immediately.

SERVING SUGGESTIONS

These toasts are hearty enough to make a main course for two to four people, depending on how much other food is on the table. Serve with a vegetable side dish, such as Grilled Eggplant with Garlic and Herbs (page 341) or Sautéed Zucchini with Lemon and Mint (page 363). If you like, also serve a salad, such as Red Leaf Lettuce, Arugula and Fennel Salad (page 374).

Bruschetta with Mashed White Beans and Spinach

MAKES 8 LARGE TOASTS

A ROSEMARY-SCENTED BEAN PUREE slathered over toast prevents the bread from becoming soggy when wilted spinach is placed on top. Because the beans will be mashed, canned beans, rinsed well, can be used in this recipe.

- 6 tablespoons extra-virgin olive oil
- 1 tablespoon minced fresh rosemary leaves
- 2 cups Basic Cannellini Beans (page 286)
- Salt and freshly ground black pepper
- 1½ pounds flat-leaf spinach
- 3 medium garlic cloves, minced, plus 1 whole clove
- 1 oblong loaf rustic country bread (about 12 inches long and 5 inches wide)

1. Preheat the broiler or light the grill.

2. Heat 1½ tablespoons of the oil in a large skillet set over medium heat. Add the rosemary and cook until fragrant, about 30 seconds. Add the beans and cook, mashing with the back of a wooden spoon, until heated through. They need not be smooth; a few lumps are fine. Add salt and pepper to taste and keep warm.

3. Remove and discard the stems from the spinach. Wash the leaves in successive bowls of cold water until grit no longer appears in the bottom of the bowl. Shake the leaves to remove excess water but do not dry them.

4. Heat 2 tablespoons oil in a deep pot. Add the minced garlic and cook over medium heat until golden, about 2 minutes. Add the spinach and cook, stirring often, until wilted, about 4 minutes. Add salt and pepper to taste and keep warm.

5. Slice the bread crosswise into eight 1-inch-thick pieces. Save the ends for another use. Toast the bread until golden brown on both sides. Transfer to a large platter. Rub garlic to taste over the top of each slice. Brush the remaining 2½ tablespoons oil over the bread.

6. Spread some of the mashed beans over each piece of toast and top each with a portion of cooked spinach. Serve immediately.

Serving Suggestions

Two of these toasts per person are enough for lunch or a light meal. Serve them with a bowl of Roasted Yellow Pepper Soup (page 53). They can be served as a first course before any frittata that does not contain greens.

Bruschetta with Grilled Portobello Mushrooms

MAKES 8 LARGE TOASTS

LARGE PORTOBELLO MUSHROOM CAPS are grilled gills up to prevent the loss of juice and served over garlic-rubbed toasts. Since you are grilling the mushrooms, toast the bread on the grill as well. To serve, flip the mushrooms onto the bread and let their juices seep down into it.

- 4 medium portobello mushrooms (about 1¼ pounds)
- 6 tablespoons extra-virgin olive oil
- 1 tablespoon minced fresh rosemary leaves
- Salt and freshly ground black pepper
- 1 oblong loaf rustic country bread (about 12 inches long and 5 inches wide)
- 1 large garlic clove

1. Light the grill or make a charcoal fire.

2. Remove and discard the mushroom stems. Wipe the caps clean. Place the caps on a large baking sheet. Combine 3½ tablespoons of the oil, the rosemary and salt and pepper to taste in a small bowl. Brush the oil mixture on both sides of the mushrooms. Grill the mushrooms, gills up, until the caps are streaked with dark grill marks, 8 to 10 minutes.

3. Meanwhile, slice the bread crosswise into eight 1-inch-thick pieces. Save the ends for another use. Grill the bread until golden brown on both sides. Transfer to a large platter. Rub garlic to taste over the top of each slice. Brush the remaining 2½ tablespoons oil over the bread.

4. Cut the grilled mushrooms in half and place one half, gill side down, over each piece of toast. Serve immediately.

SERVING SUGGESTIONS

Serve these bruschetta as an antipasto, one per person. Follow with something else from the grill, such as Linguine with Grilled Plum Tomato Sauce (page 106), and a tossed green salad, such as Arugula, Pine Nut and Parmesan Salad (page 370).

Bruschetta with Red Onions, Herbs and Parmesan

MAKES 8 LARGE TOASTS

COOKING RED ONIONS almost to the point of caramelizing them makes them juicy and sweet.

- 5 tablespoons extra-virgin olive oil
- 4 medium red onions (about 1½ pounds), thinly sliced
- 2 tablespoons minced fresh chives
- 1½ tablespoons minced fresh mint leaves
- Salt and freshly ground black pepper
- Long piece of Parmigiano-Reggiano cheese, enough for 24 large shavings
- 1 oblong loaf rustic country bread (about 12 inches long and 5 inches wide)
- 1 large garlic clove

1. Heat 2½ tablespoons of the oil in a large skillet set over medium heat. Add the onions and cook, stirring often, until they soften completely, about 15 minutes. (Do not let them brown.) Stir in the chives, mint and salt and pepper to taste. Set aside.

2. Use a vegetable peeler to remove 24 long, thin curls from the piece of Parmigiano-Reggiano. Set aside.

3. Preheat the broiler. Slice the bread crosswise into eight 1-inch-thick pieces. Save the ends for another use. Place the bread on a large baking sheet and slide it under the broiler. Toast the bread until golden brown on both sides.

4. Rub garlic to taste over the top of each slice. Brush the remaining 2½ tablespoons oil over the bread. Divide the onion mixture among the toasts and place 3 cheese shavings on top of each toast.

5. Return the baking sheet to the broiler and cook just until the cheese melts, 1 to 2 minutes. Watch carefully to keep from burning. Transfer the bruschetta to a large platter and serve immediately.

SERVING SUGGESTIONS

Serve this bruschetta as an appetizer, with one per person. Or serve with soup, such as Chard and Spinach Soup with Lemon-Parsley Pesto (page 46), or with a leafy green salad.

Bruschetta with Roasted Red Peppers

MAKES 8 LARGE TOASTS

SILKY ROASTED RED PEPPERS make an excellent topping for bruschetta. Yellow or orange peppers (or a mixture) may also be used.

- **4 large red bell peppers (about 1¾ pounds)**
- **3½ tablespoons extra-virgin olive oil**
- **1½ tablespoons minced fresh mint or basil leaves**
- **Salt**
- **1 oblong loaf rustic country bread (about 12 inches long and 5 inches wide)**
- **1 large garlic clove**

1. Roast and peel the peppers as directed on page 526. Core and seed them and cut them into ½-inch-wide strips. Toss with 1 tablespoon of the oil, the mint or basil and salt to taste. Set aside.

2. Preheat the broiler or light the grill. Slice the bread crosswise into eight 1-inch-thick pieces. Save the ends for another use. Toast the bread until golden brown on both sides. Transfer to a large platter. Rub garlic to taste over the top of each slice. Brush the remaining 2½ tablespoons oil over the bread. Divide the peppers among the toasts and serve immediately.

SERVING SUGGESTIONS

Serve the bruschetta as a first course before egg, pasta and rice dishes, such as Asparagus Frittata with Basil, Shallots and Parmesan (page 245), Orecchiette with Fava Beans, Plum Tomatoes and Ricotta Salata (page 94) or Lemon Risotto (page 162).

Bruschetta with Garlicky Zucchini

Makes 8 large toasts

In this bruschetta, the garlic is cooked into the topping. If you want raw garlic flavor, rub a whole clove over the toasts as well.

- **5 tablespoons extra-virgin olive oil**
- **1 medium onion, minced**
- **4 medium garlic cloves, minced**
- **4 medium zucchini (about 1½ pounds), scrubbed, ends trimmed and cut into ½-inch dice**
- **8 large fresh basil leaves, shredded**
- **Salt and freshly ground black pepper**
- **1 oblong loaf rustic country bread (about 12 inches long and 5 inches wide)**

1. Heat 3 tablespoons of the oil in a large skillet. Add the onion and sauté over medium heat until translucent, about 4 minutes. Add the garlic and cook until lightly colored, about 1 minute. Add the zucchini and cook, stirring often, until quite soft, 15 to 20 minutes. Stir in the basil and season with salt and pepper to taste. Set aside.

2. Preheat the broiler or light the grill. Slice the bread crosswise into eight 1-inch-thick pieces. Save the ends for another use. Toast the bread until golden brown on both sides. Transfer to a large platter. Brush the remaining 2 tablespoons oil over the bread.

3. Divide the zucchini mixture among the toasts and serve immediately.

Serving Suggestions

Serve the bruschetta as a first course. Follow with Summer Rice Salad with Tomatoes, Cucumber and Yellow Pepper (page 175) and a leafy green salad, such as Arugula, Pine Nut and Parmesan Salad (page 370).

DESSERTS

IN ITALY, the conclusion of a meal is generally signaled by the appearance of a bowl of fruit on the table, accompanied, perhaps, by a few cookies. The rich, sweet confections sold in Italian-American bakeries are not part of everyday eating but are reserved for holidays and other special occasions. The desserts in this chapter represent that simple approach, although most would be appropriate to serve as the finale when entertaining.

The chapter begins with a number of fruit preparations: poached and baked fruit as well as fruit dressed with honey or balsamic vinegar.

Several recipes for cookies follow, along with bread pudding and rice cake. Included here are Pine Nut Macaroons, my family's favorite cookie. I make them every Christmas, along with an extra tin for my mother and grandmother. These cookies are not overly sweet and are delicious with coffee, fresh fruit and gelato or sorbet.

Also meant for dunking are the crisp Italian cookies called *biscotti*. The name means "twice cooked" and comes from the fact that the dough is first shaped into a log and baked, then cut into individual cookies and baked again. The almond and cappuccino versions in this chapter, perfect for dipping into coffee or dessert wine, are examples of the hard, crisp style. The cornmeal biscotti, which are traditional in northern Italy, contain butter and are much softer and more crumbly.

The second half of the chapter is devoted to Italian frozen desserts: gelato, sorbet and granita. Both gelato and sorbet are churn-frozen and require an ice-cream maker. An electric model, either with a built-in freezer or a separate canister that goes into the freezer overnight, will produce the best results.

Gelato is similar to American ice cream but has a more intense taste. It has less butterfat and fewer eggs and is also served softer, so its flavors are more apparent.

SORBET, CALLED *sorbetto* IN ITALIAN, is a perfectly smooth dairy-free ice. Traditional recipes call for a sugar syrup—water and sugar simmered until the sugar dissolves and then cooled. Sugar syrups make sense for chefs who create a dozen different flavors a day, but for the home cook, carefully stirring the sugar and fruit juice or puree together saves time and works just as well. A whisk is a good tool for this job, which should take no more than five minutes.

Once the sorbet mixture has been combined, it must be chilled to at least 40 degrees F. This can be done in the refrigerator over the course of several hours. If you are pressed for time, combine the ingredients in a metal bowl set over a larger bowl filled with ice water. As you whisk to dissolve the sugar, the sorbet mixture will cool down rapidly. Like other churned frozen desserts, sorbets are soft when they come out of most ice-cream makers. They need a few hours in the freezer to become firm.

Unlike sorbet, the coarsely textured granita does not require an ice-cream maker. The word comes from the Italian word meaning "grain," referring to the tiny crystals of flavored ice in a well-made granita. Since it contains little sugar and usually no dairy products, granita should taste of fruit (or espresso) and not much else.

The classic technique calls for pouring a flavorful base (fruit juice, fruit puree or espresso, mixed with sugar and lemon juice or liqueur) into a shallow pan and occasionally scraping the mixture with a spoon as it hardens in the freezer. This scraping/freezing process continues for several hours or until small, distinct ice crystals have formed. The consistency is similar to that of a snow cone.

The traditional method calls for on-and-off attention over several hours. As soon as the granita has properly solidified, it should be served. If you wait too long, the individual crystals will freeze into a solid mass. If you start the granita several hours before dinner, the timing should work. For greater flexibility and less hands-on work, you can freeze the granita without stirring it and whir it in a food processor just before bringing it to the table.

Fruit Desserts

Cookies, Puddings and Cakes

Gelato, Sorbet and Granita

Apricots and Raspberries with Mint

SERVES 4

APRICOTS ARE A SURE SIGN OF SUMMER. Since the fruit is not particularly juicy, a little freshly squeezed orange juice is added to moisten the dish. The raspberries give the juice a bright pink color.

- **1 pound apricots, halved, pitted and thinly sliced**
- **1 cup raspberries**
- **½ cup freshly squeezed orange juice**
- **8 large fresh mint leaves, cut into thin strips**

1. Toss the apricots, raspberries and orange juice in a medium serving bowl. Let the fruit stand at room temperature for 15 minutes. *(The fruit can be refrigerated for up to 2 hours. Bring it to room temperature before serving.)*

2. Sprinkle the mint over the fruit and toss again. Serve immediately.

SERVING SUGGESTIONS

Pine Nut Macaroons (page 502) go well with this dessert as does Prosecco Sorbet (page 514).

Macerated Strawberries with Balsamic Vinegar

SERVES 4

THIS IS A CLASSIC RECIPE FROM EMILIA-ROMAGNA, the region famous for balsamic vinegar. Fresh berries are tossed with sugar and set aside to macerate until the sugar forms a rich syrup. A touch of balsamic vinegar balances the sweetness and gives the syrup more body. Although any balsamic vinegar can be used, an aged vinegar is best because of its low acidity and complex woody bouquet. This preparation is ideal for early-season berries that are not as sweet as you might like.

2 pints fresh strawberries
3-4 tablespoons sugar
1 tablespoon aged balsamic vinegar

1. Wash the strawberries, hull them and trim any unripe portions. Slice small berries lengthwise in half; cut larger berries into 3 or 4 thick slices.

2. Place the berries in a large glass or ceramic bowl and toss gently with 3 tablespoons of the sugar. If the berries are particularly tart, add 1 more tablespoon sugar, or to taste.

3. Let the berries stand at room temperature, tossing occasionally to dissolve the sugar. After about 30 minutes, the sugar will form a thick, red syrup.

4. Add the vinegar and toss. Divide the berries and syrup among individual bowls or goblets. Serve immediately.

SERVING SUGGESTIONS

Serve the berries alone or with a plate of cookies, such as Pine Nut Macaroons (page 502). You could also serve them with a scoop of Rich Vanilla Gelato (page 505).

Pears and Parmesan Drizzled with Honey

SERVES 4

THIS DESSERT REQUIRES REALLY RIPE FRUIT and the finest Parmigiano-Reggiano. I particularly like red Anjou pears in this dish. They have a lovely russet-colored skin and are very fragrant. The honey should be warmed to make it easier to pour. This may be done in the microwave (20 seconds on high is enough time) or in a small pan set over medium heat.

3 large, ripe pears, cored and thinly sliced
Small piece of Parmigiano-Reggiano cheese (at least 2 ounces)
2 tablespoons honey, warmed

1. Arrange the pear slices on 4 dessert plates. With a vegetable peeler, remove long, paper-thin curls from the cheese, letting the curls fall onto the pears. Make at least 8 or 10 curls for each plate.

2. Use a small spoon to drizzle warmed honey over each plate. Serve immediately.

SERVING SUGGESTIONS

This dish is a good way to end a fall or winter meal, especially one that does not contain much cheese.

Oranges Poached in Syrup

SERVES 6

THIS IS A DRAMATIC FRUIT DESSERT with glazed oranges served with a garnish of soft orange zest.

6 medium navel oranges
1 cup sugar
2 tablespoons orange liqueur, such as Grand Marnier

1. Use a vegetable peeler to remove the colored zest from the oranges, leaving behind the bitter white pith. Use a small, sharp knife to cut the zest into very thin, long strips. Place the zest in a small saucepan and cover with cold water. Bring to a boil and simmer for 1 minute. Drain the zest and refresh it in a bowl of cold water. Set aside in the cold water.

2. Use a knife and your fingers to remove all the pith from the oranges. They should be as clean as possible.

3. Place the sugar and ½ cup cold water in a 2-quart saucepan. Bring to a boil, stirring often to dissolve the sugar. Simmer the syrup for 1 to 2 minutes, or until completely clear. Add 3 of the oranges and cook, turning often, until nicely glazed, about 4 minutes. Lift the oranges from the syrup with a slotted spoon and transfer them to a medium bowl. Add the remaining 3 oranges to the boiling syrup and cook for 4 minutes. Transfer to the bowl.

4. Drain the orange zest and add it to the simmering syrup. Add the liqueur and cook for 2 minutes, or until the zest softens slightly. Pour over the oranges.

5. Cover the bowl with the oranges and chill for several hours. *(The oranges can be refrigerated in the syrup for 2 days.)* When ready to serve, spoon 1 orange into each individual dessert bowl. Garnish with strips of zest and pour a spoonful of syrup over each orange.

SERVING SUGGESTIONS

Serve the oranges alone or with a few cookies, such as Pine Nut Macaroons (page 502) or Cornmeal Biscotti with Dried Cherries (page 501). They also can be served with a small scoop of Rich Vanilla Gelato (page 505) or on top of a slice of pound cake.

Peaches Poached in Chianti with Lemon and Fennel

SERVES 4

THIS POACHING TECHNIQUE can be used with any stone fruit—peaches, nectarines, plums, even apricots. Select a combination or one kind of fruit that is firm but ripe. A fruity red wine, like a young Chianti, is the best choice for poaching fruit. *See the photograph on page 207.*

- **2 cups Chianti or other fruity red wine**
- **½ cup honey**
- **1 medium lemon**
- **1 teaspoon fennel seeds**
- **2 pounds ripe peaches, nectarines or plums, peeled, halved and pitted**
- **Fresh mint sprigs and/or very thin slices of lemon for garnish (optional)**

1. Mix the wine, 1 cup water and honey in a large nonreactive saucepan. Use a vegetable peeler to remove a long strip of the zest from around the equator of the lemon. Add the lemon zest and fennel seeds to the pan. Bring to a boil and boil for 10 minutes.

2. Add the fruit halves to the poaching liquid. Reduce the heat and cook at the barest simmer until the fruit can be easily pierced with a metal skewer, 5 to 10 minutes, depending on the fruit's ripeness. Use a slotted spoon to transfer the fruit to a large bowl, leaving behind the lemon zest and as many of the fennel seeds as possible.

3. Raise the heat to high and boil the poaching liquid until it is reduced to 1½ cups, about 10 minutes. Pour through a fine-mesh strainer into the bowl with the fruit; discard the fennel seeds and lemon zest. Cool the fruit and syrup to room temperature, cover and refrigerate for several hours until well chilled. *(The fruit can be refrigerated in the syrup for several days.)*

4. To serve, divide the fruit among individual dessert bowls. Cover with as much poaching syrup as desired. Garnish with sprigs of fresh mint and/or lemon slices, if using.

SERVING SUGGESTIONS

Serve the peaches with a small plate of cookies, such as Pine Nut Macaroons (page 502).

Baked Peaches Stuffed with Almond Macaroons

SERVES 4 TO 6

BAKED PEACH HALVES FILLED with crushed almond macaroons are a traditional summer dessert in many regions of Italy. The cookies, known in Italian as *amaretti*, are not too sweet and complement the natural sugars in the fruit. Crushing the cookies in a plastic bag with a mallet produces fine crumbs with a minimum of mess and work. The crumb mixture can be stuffed into nectarines as well. Choose fruit that is ripe but not overly soft. Look for amaretti in Italian markets and gourmet stores.

- 4 large, ripe peaches
- 15 medium amaretti cookies (about 3 ounces)
- 3 tablespoons sugar
- 1 large egg yolk
- 1 teaspoon vanilla extract
- 2 tablespoons unsalted butter

1. Preheat the oven to 375 degrees F. Working over a large bowl to catch any juice, cut each peach lengthwise in half. Remove the pits. Use a small spoon to scoop out some pulp from the center of each peach half to enlarge the cavity. Add the pulp to the bowl with the peach juice.

2. Place the cookies in a small plastic bag and seal. Crush with a mallet or rolling pin into small crumbs. There should be about ¾ cup crumbs.

3. Add the amaretti crumbs, sugar, egg yolk and vanilla to the bowl with the peach pulp. Mix well to form a wet paste. Spoon some of the filling into each peach half. Mound the filling over the peach and press firmly with your fingers to compact the filling.

4. Use 1 tablespoon of the butter to grease a baking dish just large enough to hold the peach halves in a single layer. Cut the remaining 1 tablespoon butter into 8 small pieces. Place the filled peaches in the dish and dot each with a piece of butter.

5. Bake until the peaches are soft and the filling begins to brown, about 40 minutes. Cool slightly and serve warm. *(The peaches may be covered and kept at room temperature for several hours. If desired, warm the peaches just before serving.)*

SERVING SUGGESTIONS

Serve the peaches as is or with a scoop of Rich Vanilla Gelato (page 505).

Peaches with Ricotta-Walnut Filling

SERVES 6

RIPE SUMMER PEACHES are transformed into a special summer dessert when filled with sweetened ricotta enriched with toasted walnuts. Look for homestyle ricotta. It is more flavorful than supermarket ricotta. You can find it in Italian markets, gourmet shops and some large supermarkets.

1 cup ricotta cheese, preferably homestyle
½ cup walnut halves
2 tablespoons sugar
Pinch of freshly grated nutmeg
6 large, ripe peaches

1. If using supermarket ricotta, line a small colander or mesh sieve with several layers of paper towels. Spread the cheese over the towels and let drain until thickened and creamy, about 1 hour. Remove the cheese from the colander and discard the paper towels; they should be quite moist. (Homestyle ricotta does not need to be drained.)

2. Place the walnuts in a medium skillet set over medium heat. Toast, shaking the pan occasionally to turn the nuts, until fragrant, about 5 minutes. Transfer to a plate. Set aside 12 attractive walnut halves. Finely chop the remaining walnuts. Stir the chopped walnuts, ricotta, sugar and nutmeg in a small bowl until smooth. *(The cheese mixture may be covered and refrigerated for several hours.)*

3. Cut each peach lengthwise in half. Remove the pits. Use a small spoon to scoop out some pulp from the center of each peach half to enlarge the cavity.

4. Mound some of the ricotta mixture into each peach half. Place a reserved walnut half on top. Place 2 peach halves on each plate and serve immediately.

SERVING SUGGESTIONS

This dish makes a light ending to any summer meal where cheese has not already been featured.

Classic Almond Biscotti

MAKES ABOUT 24 BISCOTTI

THIS IS THE CLASSIC TUSCAN RECIPE, loaded with toasted almonds and rich with eggs. Biscotti, which means "twice cooked" in Italian, bake much longer than most cookies, but there's no need to portion the dough into individual cookies or stand by the oven and make batch after batch. Just shape the dough into long logs and slice them after the first baking. The cookies are then crisped in the oven.

1 cup whole almonds with skins
2 cups unbleached all-purpose flour
1 cup sugar
½ teaspoon baking powder
Pinch of salt
3 large eggs
2 large egg yolks
1 teaspoon vanilla extract

1. Preheat the oven to 350 degrees F. Spread the almonds on a large baking sheet in a single layer. Toast until fragrant, about 8 minutes. Set aside to cool. Do not turn off the oven. Grease and flour another large baking sheet.

2. Use a whisk to combine the flour, sugar, baking powder and salt in a large bowl.

3. Beat 2 of the eggs, the egg yolks and vanilla in a small bowl with a fork. Pour over the dry ingredients and use the fork to combine them. When the liquid ingredients have been incorporated, knead the dough with your hands until smooth.

4. Coarsely chop the cooled almonds (each nut need only be broken into 2 or 3 pieces) and knead them into the dough. Turn the dough out onto a lightly floured surface and divide it in half. With your hands, shape each half into a flat log about 12 inches long and 3 inches across. Place the logs on the baking sheet, about 4 inches apart.

5. Beat the remaining 1 egg with a fork. Lightly brush the beaten egg over the 2 logs. Bake until the logs are firm to the touch and lightly browned on top, about 35 minutes. Remove from the oven and reduce the heat to 325 degrees. Wearing oven mitts, cut the logs on the diagonal into 1-inch-wide slices.

6. Lay the slices flat on the baking sheet and return them to the oven. Bake until crisp, about 10 minutes. Remove from the oven and cool on wire racks. *(The biscotti can be kept in an airtight container for at least 1 week.)*

SERVING SUGGESTIONS

Dunk these cookies in coffee or sweet Italian wine or serve them with fruit or with a sorbet or granita.

Cappuccino Biscotti with Almonds and Chocolate

MAKES ABOUT 24 BISCOTTI

THESE ESPRESSO-FLAVORED BISCOTTI are full of chopped almonds and chocolate chips. You can use small chunks of high-quality bittersweet or semisweet chocolate in place of chocolate chips if you like. *See the photograph on page 208.*

- 2 cups unbleached all-purpose flour
- 1 cup sugar
- ½ teaspoon ground cinnamon
- ½ teaspoon baking powder
- ½ teaspoon baking soda
- ½ teaspoon salt
- ¼ cup espresso or strong coffee, cooled slightly
- 2 tablespoons milk
- 1 large egg yolk
- 1 teaspoon vanilla extract
- ⅔ cup whole almonds with skins, coarsely chopped
- ½ cup semisweet chocolate chips

1. Preheat the oven to 375 degrees F. Grease and flour a large baking sheet.

2. Use a whisk to combine the flour, sugar, cinnamon, baking powder, baking soda and salt in a large bowl.

3. Combine the espresso or coffee, milk, egg yolk and vanilla in a small bowl. Mix well and add to the dry ingredients. Mix with an electric mixer until the dough is smooth, about 1 minute. Stir in the almonds and chocolate.

4. Turn the dough out onto a lightly floured surface and divide it in half. With your hands, shape each half into a flat log about 12 inches long and 3 inches across. Place the logs on the baking sheet, about 4 inches apart.

5. Bake until the logs are firm to the touch, about 30 minutes. Remove from the oven and reduce the heat to 325 degrees. Wearing oven mitts, cut the logs on the diagonal into 1-inch-wide slices.

6. Lay the slices flat on the baking sheet and return them to the oven. Bake until crisp, about 10 minutes. Remove from the oven and cool on wire racks. *(The biscotti can be kept in an airtight container for at least 1 week.)*

SERVING SUGGESTIONS

Serve these biscotti with coffee or a frozen dessert, such as Hazelnut Gelato (page 506).

Cornmeal Biscotti with Dried Cherries

MAKES ABOUT 24 BISCOTTI

CORNMEAL COOKIES ARE POPULAR throughout northern Italy. I like to add dried cherries, which are available in gourmet stores, natural-food stores and many supermarkets. Although these cookies look like classic crisp biscotti, they are much softer and a little smaller and have an almost crumbly texture. Butter, which is not used for the other biscotti, makes the difference. They are best served within a day of baking.

- **1 cup unbleached all-purpose flour**
- **½ cup yellow cornmeal**
- **¼ cup sugar**
- **½ teaspoon baking powder**
- **⅛ teaspoon salt**
- **12 tablespoons (1½ sticks) unsalted butter, softened and cut into small pieces**
- **1 large egg**
- **1 teaspoon vanilla extract**
- **½ teaspoon grated lemon zest**
- **¾ cup dried cherries, chopped**

1. Preheat the oven to 350 degrees F. Line a large baking sheet with parchment paper.

2. Use a whisk to combine the flour, cornmeal, sugar, baking powder and salt in a large bowl. Add the butter. Beat with an electric mixer until the mixture resembles coarse crumbs.

3. Whisk the egg, vanilla and lemon zest in a small bowl. Pour over the dry ingredients and lightly beat until the dough comes together. Do not overmix. Gently stir in the dried cherries.

4. Turn the dough out onto a lightly floured surface and divide it in half. With your hands, shape each half into a log about 12 inches long and 1 inch across. Place the logs on the baking sheet, about 4 inches apart.

5. Bake until the logs are firm to the touch, about 20 minutes. Remove from the oven and let cool until firm, about 10 minutes. Using a chef's knife, cut the logs on the diagonal into 1-inch-wide slices.

6. Lay the slices flat on the baking sheet and return them to the oven. Bake until crisp, about 8 minutes. Remove from the oven and cool on wire racks. *(The biscotti can be stored in an airtight container for only 1 day.)*

SERVING SUGGESTIONS

These soft cookies are not meant for dunking. They can be eaten alone or with Raspberry Sorbet (page 513) or Blood Orange Sorbet (page 512).

Pine Nut Macaroons

MAKES 18 LARGE COOKIES

HOMEMADE ALMOND PASTE—blanched almonds, sugar and egg whites—is the basis for these pine-nut-covered clusters. The dough can be messy to handle, but the results are impressive. For a more elegant look, sift confectioners' sugar over the cookies just after they come out of the oven.

- **1⅔ cups blanched slivered almonds**
- **1⅓ cups sugar**
- **2 large egg whites**
- **1 cup pine nuts**

1. Preheat the oven to 375 degrees F. Grease 2 large baking sheets.

2. Place the almonds and sugar in the work bowl of a large food processor and grind until quite fine. Add the egg whites and process until smooth. (The dough will be wet.) Scrape the dough into a large bowl. Pour the pine nuts into a shallow bowl.

3. Take a rounded tablespoon of the dough and shape it into a rough ball about the size of a walnut. Roll the ball in the pine nuts just until the outside is covered. Place the balls on the baking sheets, leaving 2 inches between each one.

4. Bake until the cookies turn light golden brown, 13 to 15 minutes. Do not let the nuts turn dark brown or burn. Cool the cookies on a wire rack. *(The cookies can be stored in an airtight container for 1 or 2 days.)*

SERVING SUGGESTIONS

Serve these elegant cookies with a glass of chilled dessert wine or a cup of espresso.

Bread Pudding with Grappa-Soaked Raisins

SERVES 8

DAY-OLD BREAD GETS NEW LIFE when baked with custard into a rich bread pudding. Grappa, which is used to soak the raisins in this dish, is a clear brandy made from the skins that remain after grapes are pressed to make wine.

½ cup dark or yellow raisins
¼ cup grappa or brandy
6 large eggs
¾ cup sugar
3 cups whole milk
2 teaspoons vanilla extract
4 cups day-old country white bread, cut into ½-inch cubes

1. Place the raisins and grappa or brandy in a small bowl. Soak for at least 1 hour or overnight if desired.

2. Preheat the oven to 375 degrees F. Butter a shallow 2-quart glass or ceramic baking dish. Place the baking dish in a roasting pan large enough to hold it comfortably. Put a filled kettle on to boil.

3. Whisk together the eggs and sugar in a large bowl until smooth. Whisk in the milk and vanilla. Stir in the bread cubes and the raisins with the soaking liquid.

4. Pour the bread mixture into the baking dish. Place the roasting pan and baking dish in the oven. Add enough boiling water to come halfway up the sides of the baking dish.

5. Bake until the pudding is set and a knife inserted in the center comes out clean, about 1 hour. Remove the baking dish from the roasting pan and cool on a wire rack. The bread pudding may be served warm or chilled. *(The pudding can be refrigerated for 1 day.)*

SERVING SUGGESTIONS

Rich Vanilla Gelato (page 505) or Hazelnut Gelato (page 506) would be a welcome addition.

Creamy Rice Pudding Cake

SERVES 8 TO 10

THIS HUMBLE CAKE, KNOWN AS *TORTA DI RISO*, is made in many parts of Italy, especially in the north. Think of rice pudding baked into a moist cake that resembles a cheesecake, and you have it. My version has a little lemon zest and juice to balance the richness of the eggs. The cake needs no adornments and may be served warm or chilled.

- **1 cup Arborio rice**
- **4 cups whole milk**
- **1⅓ cups sugar**
- **1 tablespoon unsalted butter**
- **2 tablespoons semolina or plain bread crumbs**
- **6 large eggs**
- **1 teaspoon grated zest and 1 tablespoon juice from 1 large lemon**

1. Place the rice and milk in a large saucepan. Bring to a boil over medium-high heat, stirring frequently. Reduce the heat to low and simmer, stirring often, until the rice is al dente, about 20 minutes. Near the end of the cooking time, you should be stirring almost constantly to prevent the rice from sticking and burning. Scrape the rice into a large bowl, stir in the sugar and cool to room temperature.

2. Preheat the oven to 350 degrees F. Use the 1 tablespoon butter to grease a 9-inch springform pan. Sprinkle the bread crumbs into the pan. Working over the sink, turn the pan to coat the bottom and sides with crumbs. Shake out the excess.

3. Beat the eggs and lemon zest and juice with a whisk until light and foamy. Fold into the cooled rice and mix well.

4. Scrape the rice mixture into the pan. Bake until a toothpick inserted in the center comes out clean and the edges start to turn golden brown, 60 to 70 minutes. Cool and unmold. The cake may be served slightly warm, at room temperature or cold. *(The cake may be tightly wrapped and refrigerated for 2 days.)*

SERVING SUGGESTIONS

Serve this cake with citrus fruit, such as clementines or mandarin oranges.

Rich Vanilla Gelato

SERVES 6

THIS GELATO CONTAINS FOUR EGG YOLKS for extra smoothness and creaminess. Two teaspoons of vanilla extract can be substituted for the vanilla bean, although the flavor will not be quite as intense. Stir the extract into the chilled custard just before churning.

- **2 cups whole milk**
- **¾ cup sugar**
- **5-inch piece of vanilla bean**
- **4 large egg yolks**
- **1 cup heavy cream**

1. Place the milk and ¼ cup of the sugar in a large saucepan. Slit the vanilla bean lengthwise and scrape the seeds into the milk mixture. Add the bean to the pan. Heat, stirring occasionally to dissolve the sugar and break up the vanilla seeds, until the milk reaches 175 degrees F on an instant-read or candy thermometer. Do not heat the milk above this point.

2. While the milk is heating, beat the remaining ½ cup sugar and the egg yolks in a medium bowl until pale yellow, about 2 minutes with an electric mixer or 4 minutes with a whisk. Gradually whisk ½ cup of the hot-milk mixture into the yolk mixture. Whisk the yolk mixture back into the saucepan and, stirring constantly, slowly heat the custard to 180 degrees.

3. Pour the custard through a fine-mesh strainer into a bowl. Discard the vanilla bean. Stir in the cream. Refrigerate until chilled to at least 40 degrees.

4. Churn-freeze in an ice-cream machine. Transfer the gelato to an airtight container and freeze until firm. *(The gelato can be stored in the freezer for up to 2 days.)*

SERVING SUGGESTIONS

Like vanilla ice cream or whipped cream, this gelato is a welcome accompaniment to many desserts, including Macerated Strawberries with Balsamic Vinegar (page 492) and Oranges Poached in Syrup (page 494). Or top it with sliced seasonal fruits, such as berries, mango or melon, or serve it with cookies.

Hazelnut Gelato

SERVES 6

ITALIAN ICE CREAM, called gelato, is generally lower in butterfat than American versions. But don't think of this as a compromise. Any gelato is powerfully flavored. In this one, for example, the reduced amount of butterfat keeps the focus on the nuts, with intense results. Hazelnut skins are bitter, so remove as much as possible.

2 cups hazelnuts
3 cups whole milk
¾ cup heavy cream
¾ cup sugar
3 large egg yolks
1 tablespoon hazelnut liqueur, such as Frangelico (optional)
Few drops of vanilla extract

1. Preheat the oven to 350 degrees F. Spread the nuts on a baking sheet in a single layer. Toast in the oven until fragrant, about 8 minutes. Wrap the hot nuts in a kitchen towel and rub vigorously to remove as much of the skin as possible. Place the nuts in the work bowl of a food processor and grind until quite fine.

2. Combine the milk, ½ cup of the cream and the ground nuts in a large saucepan. Bring almost to a boil. Remove from the heat and steep for 30 minutes. Pour the mixture through a fine-mesh strainer, pressing down on the nuts with a large spoon to extract as much liquid as possible. Discard the nuts and return the liquid to a clean saucepan.

3. Add ½ cup of the sugar to the milk mixture. Heat, stirring occasionally to dissolve the sugar, until the milk reaches 175 degrees on an instant-read or candy thermometer. Do not heat the milk above this point.

4. While the milk is heating, beat the remaining ¼ cup sugar and the egg yolks in a medium bowl until pale yellow, about 2 minutes with an electric mixer or 4 minutes with a whisk. Gradually whisk ½ cup of the hot-milk mixture into the yolk mixture. Whisk the yolk mixture back into the saucepan and, stirring constantly, slowly heat the custard to 180 degrees.

5. Pour the custard through a fine-mesh strainer into a bowl. Stir in the remaining ¼ cup cream and liqueur, if using. Refrigerate until chilled to at least 40 degrees.

6. Stir in the vanilla and churn-freeze in an ice-cream machine. Transfer the gelato to an airtight container and freeze until firm. *(The gelato can be stored in the freezer for up to 2 days.)*

SERVING SUGGESTIONS

Serve the gelato as is, with Cappuccino Biscotti with Almonds and Chocolate (page 500) or with a sprinkling of toasted, skinned and chopped hazelnuts.

Gianduia Gelato

SERVES 6

THE COMBINATION OF HAZELNUTS AND CHOCOLATE called gianduia is popular in candy, cake and gelato, especially in the northern Italian city of Turin. Dutch-process cocoa is less harsh than natural cocoa and is preferred in this recipe.

- **2 cups hazelnuts**
- **3 cups whole milk**
- **¾ cup heavy cream**
- **¾ cup sugar**
- **3 large egg yolks**
- **2 ounces bittersweet chocolate, melted**
- **¼ cup unsweetened cocoa powder, preferably Dutch process**
- **Few drops of vanilla extract**

1. Preheat the oven to 350 degrees F. Spread the nuts on a baking sheet in a single layer. Toast in the oven until fragrant, about 8 minutes. Wrap the hot nuts in a kitchen towel and rub vigorously to remove as much of the skin as possible. Place the nuts in the work bowl of a food processor and grind until quite fine.

2. Combine the milk, ½ cup of the cream and the ground nuts in a large saucepan. Bring almost to a boil. Remove from the heat and steep for 30 minutes. Pour the mixture through a fine-mesh strainer, pressing down on the nuts with a large spoon to extract as much liquid as possible. Discard the nuts and return the liquid to a clean saucepan.

3. Add ½ cup of the sugar to the milk mixture. Heat, stirring occasionally to dissolve the sugar, until the milk reaches 175 degrees on an instant-read or candy thermometer. Do not heat the milk above this point.

4. While the milk is heating, beat the remaining ¼ cup sugar and the egg yolks in a medium bowl until pale yellow, about 2 minutes with an electric mixer or 4 minutes with a whisk. Beat in the melted chocolate and cocoa until smooth. Gradually whisk ½ cup of the hot-milk mixture into the yolk mixture. Whisk the yolk mixture back into the saucepan and, stirring constantly, slowly heat the custard to 180 degrees.

5. Pour the custard through a fine-mesh strainer into a bowl. Stir in the remaining ¼ cup cream. Refrigerate until chilled to at least 40 degrees.

6. Stir in the vanilla and churn-freeze in an ice-cream machine. Transfer the gelato to an airtight container and freeze until firm. *(The gelato can be stored in the freezer for up to 2 days.)*

SERVING SUGGESTIONS

Serve this gelato as is. If you want to embellish it, sprinkle each serving with a few chocolate-covered espresso beans.

Strawberry Gelato

Serves 6 to 8

Ripe fruit that is red through to the center should be selected for this recipe. The strawberry puree contains chunks of berries.

- **2 cups whole milk**
- **¾ cup sugar, plus 2 tablespoons for the strawberries**
- **4 large egg yolks**
- **1 cup heavy cream**
- **1 pint strawberries, washed, hulled and sliced**
- **1 teaspoon vanilla extract**

1. Place the milk and ¼ cup of the sugar in a large saucepan. Heat, stirring occasionally to dissolve the sugar, until the milk reaches 175 degrees F on an instant-read or candy thermometer. Do not heat the milk above this point.

2. While the milk is heating, beat the remaining ½ cup sugar and the egg yolks in a medium bowl until pale yellow, about 2 minutes with an electric mixer or 4 minutes with a whisk. Gradually whisk ½ cup of the hot-milk mixture into the yolk mixture. Whisk the yolk mixture back into the saucepan and, stirring constantly, slowly heat the custard to 180 degrees.

3. Pour the custard through a fine-mesh strainer into a nonreactive bowl. Stir in the cream. Refrigerate until chilled to at least 40 degrees.

4. While the custard is chilling, place the strawberries in a medium bowl. Sprinkle with the 2 tablespoons sugar and the vanilla. Crush the fruit lightly with a potato masher and let stand for 1 hour. Stir the berry mixture into the custard and chill again if necessary until the temperature falls below 40 degrees.

5. Churn-freeze in an ice-cream machine. Transfer the gelato to an airtight container and freeze until firm. *(The gelato can be stored in the freezer for up to 2 days.)*

Serving Suggestions

Serve with a scoop of Rich Vanilla Gelato (page 505).

Pink Grapefruit Sorbet

SERVES 4

PINK GRAPEFRUITS ARE SWEETER than white grapefruits, so they require less sugar to make a smooth sorbet. Their bright pink color is another reason to choose them. Tiny flecks of grated yellow peel and lime juice give the sorbet extra citric kick.

3 medium pink grapefruits
1 cup plus 2 tablespoons sugar
1 tablespoon lime juice

1. Grate the zest from the grapefruits until you have 2 teaspoons. Halve and juice the grapefruits. There should be 2 cups. Discard the seeds. Combine the zest and juice in a medium bowl. Add the sugar and lime juice and stir on and off for several minutes until the sugar has dissolved. (Rub your finger along the bottom of the bowl to make sure it has dissolved.)

2. Refrigerate the mixture and chill to at least 40 degrees F. Churn-freeze in an ice-cream machine. Transfer the sorbet to an airtight container and freeze until firm. *(The sorbet can be stored in the freezer for up to 2 days.)*

SERVING SUGGESTIONS

Serve this sorbet with a drizzling of Campari over each serving.

Blood Orange Sorbet

SERVES 4

CRIMSON-FLESHED BLOOD ORANGES were once a rarity in the United States, but in recent years, California has been supplying these special oranges to the rest of the country. While this recipe will work with regular oranges, the shocking pink-purple color and the flavor of the blood oranges are unique. *See the photograph on page 208.*

- **6 medium blood oranges**
- **1 cup sugar**
- **1 tablespoon lemon juice**

1. Grate the zest from the oranges until you have 2 teaspoons. Halve and juice the oranges. There should be 2 cups. Discard the seeds. Combine the zest and juice in a medium bowl. Add the sugar and lemon juice and stir on and off for several minutes until the sugar has dissolved. (Rub your finger along the bottom of the bowl to make sure it has dissolved.)

2. Refrigerate the mixture and chill to at least 40 degrees F. Churn-freeze in an ice-cream machine. Transfer the sorbet to an airtight container and freeze until firm. *(The sorbet can be stored in the freezer for up to 2 days.)*

SERVING SUGGESTIONS

Serve with Cappuccino Biscotti with Almonds and Chocolate (page 500) or crumble a few leftover Classic Almond Biscotti (page 498) over this sorbet if you like.

Raspberry Sorbet

SERVES 4

THIS IS ONE OF THE EASIEST SORBETS IMAGINABLE but also one of the most delicious. You have to strain out the seeds, though. A fine-mesh strainer will do the job easily.

- **3 cups raspberries**
- **1 cup sugar**
- **1 tablespoon lemon juice**

1. Place the raspberries and ½ cup cold water in the work bowl of a food processor and puree until smooth. Pour the raspberry mixture through a fine-mesh sieve, pressing on the solids to extract as much liquid as possible. There should be 2 cups. Discard the seeds.

2. Combine the raspberry liquid, sugar and lemon juice in a medium bowl. Stir on and off for several minutes until the sugar has dissolved. (Rub your finger along the bottom of the bowl to make sure it has dissolved.)

3. Refrigerate the mixture and chill to at least 40 degrees F. Churn-freeze in an ice-cream machine. Transfer the sorbet to an airtight container and freeze until firm. *(The sorbet can be stored in the freezer for up to 2 days.)*

SERVING SUGGESTIONS
Serve this sorbet garnished with fresh raspberries and mint leaves and with Pine Nut Macaroons (page 402).

Prosecco Sorbet

SERVES 6

PROSECCO, A SLIGHTLY SWEET ITALIAN SPARKLING WINE from the Veneto, makes an interesting sorbet. Offer it as a palate cleanser between courses at an elaborate meal. Given its high alcohol content, it should be served in small portions. In addition, because of the alcohol, it requires several hours in the freezer after churning to become firm enough to scoop.

1 medium lime
1½ cups prosecco (Italian sparkling wine)
¾ cup sugar

1. Grate the zest from the lime until you have ½ teaspoon. Halve and juice the lime. There should be 1 tablespoon. Discard the seeds. Combine the zest and juice, prosecco, ¾ cup cold water and sugar in a medium bowl. Stir on and off for several minutes until the sugar has dissolved. (Rub your finger along the bottom of the bowl to make sure it has dissolved.)

2. Refrigerate the mixture and chill to at least 40 degrees F. Churn-freeze in an ice-cream machine. Transfer the sorbet to an airtight container and freeze until firm. *(The sorbet can be stored in the freezer for up to 2 days.)*

SERVING SUGGESTIONS

Turn the sorbet into dessert by garnishing it with berries or pieces of melon. Or serve the sorbet with cookies, such as Cornmeal Biscotti with Dried Cherries (page 501).

Rosemary Sorbet

SERVES 4 TO 6

THIS AROMATIC SORBET has an inviting, fresh flavor. Serve small portions between courses or as a light dessert. Since fresh herbs vary greatly in intensity, taste often as the rosemary steeps in the sugar syrup, keeping in mind that freezing will mellow the flavor. When the mixture is fairly strong, strain it and discard the rosemary.

- ½ cup sugar
- ½ cup chopped fresh rosemary sprigs

1. Bring 2¼ cups water and the sugar to a boil in a small saucepan, stirring occasionally until the sugar dissolves. Stir in the rosemary and remove from the heat. Steep until the rosemary flavor is fairly strong, 20 to 40 minutes.

2. Strain the mixture and discard the rosemary. Refrigerate and chill to at least 40 degrees F. Churn-freeze in an ice-cream machine. Transfer the sorbet to an airtight container and freeze until firm. *(The sorbet can be stored in the freezer for up to 2 days.)*

SERVING SUGGESTIONS

Serve this sorbet with sliced strawberries and chunks of fresh pineapple for an elegant dessert. This sorbet is also delicious over a slice of warm apple tart.

Caffè Latte Granita

SERVES 4

MILK MELLOWS THE COFFEE FLAVOR of this granita and colors it a warm beige. Very strong-brewed coffee may be used in place of the espresso. When you serve this granita after dinner, make it with decaffeinated coffee. If you would like to make the granita in advance, see page 517.

- 1 cup brewed espresso
- 1 cup whole milk
- ¼ cup sugar

1. Combine the espresso, milk and sugar in a medium bowl. Stir on and off for several minutes until the sugar has dissolved. (Rub your finger along the bottom of the bowl to make sure it has dissolved.)

2. Pour the mixture into a 13-by-9-by-2-inch glass or ceramic baking dish. Place in the freezer for 30 minutes. Using a large metal spoon, stir the frozen crystals from around the edges of the pan back into the liquid. As the mixture continues to freeze, scrape the spoon against the sides and bottom to loosen and break up any frozen crystals. Repeat this scraping process every 30 minutes or so, until the mixture is frozen and a bit creamy, about 3 hours total. Scoop the crystals into individual bowls or goblets and serve immediately.

SERVING SUGGESTIONS

Serve this granita on hot summer nights in place of coffee.

Food Processor Shortcut for Making Granita

INSTEAD OF POURING THE GRANITA MIXTURE into a large pan, freezing it and stirring every 30 minutes, you can freeze the mixture in ice-cube trays and break the cubes into tiny crystals at serving time using a food processor. This method allows for more flexibility, especially when entertaining.

1. Pour the granita mixture into 2 ice-cube trays and freeze until very firm, at least 3 hours. *(The cubes can be transferred to a zipper-lock plastic bag and frozen for up to 1 week.)*

2. When ready to serve, place a single layer of cubes in the work bowl of a food processor fitted with the metal blade. Pulse 10 to 12 times (each time for 2 to 3 seconds), or until no large chunks of ice remain and the granita has been evenly ground. Scoop into individual bowls or goblets. Repeat with the remaining cubes and serve immediately.

Blackberry Granita

SERVES 4

LIGHTLY SWEETENED BLACKBERRIES can be transformed into a deep purple ice that is perfect for a hot summer day. This recipe has a conservative amount of sugar, which keeps the fruit flavor at the forefront; adjust the amount according to the sweetness of the berries and your own taste. This recipe may also be prepared with raspberries. If you would like to make the granita in advance, see page 517.

3 cups fresh blackberries
⅓ cup sugar

1. Place the blackberries and 1½ cups cold water in the work bowl of a food processor and puree until smooth. Pour the blackberry mixture through a fine-mesh sieve, pressing on the solids to extract as much liquid as possible. There should be 2 cups. Discard the seeds.

2. Combine the blackberry liquid and sugar in a medium bowl. Stir on and off for several minutes until the sugar has dissolved. (Rub your finger along the bottom of the bowl to make sure it has dissolved.)

3. Pour the mixture into a 13-by-9-by-2-inch glass or ceramic baking dish. Place in the freezer for 30 minutes. Using a large metal spoon, stir the frozen crystals from around the edges of the pan back into the liquid. As the mixture continues to freeze, scrape the spoon against the sides and bottom to loosen and break up any frozen crystals. Repeat this scraping process every 30 minutes or so, until the mixture is frozen and a bit creamy, about 3 hours total. Scoop the crystals into individual bowls or goblets and serve immediately.

SERVING SUGGESTIONS

Serve the granita as is or with Pine Nut Macaroons (page 502).

Lemon Granita

SERVES 4

TINY PIECES OF YELLOW LEMON ZEST add flavor and color to this ice. Any lemon variety can be used, but this granita is especially good when made with the small, sweet Meyer lemons that grow in California. If you would like to make the granita in advance, see page 517.

3 large lemons
½ cup sugar

1. Grate the zest from the lemons until you have 2 teaspoons. Halve and juice the lemons. There should be ½ cup. Discard the seeds. Combine the zest and juice in a medium bowl. Add 1½ cups cold water and sugar and stir on and off for several minutes until the sugar has dissolved. (Rub your finger along the bottom of the bowl to make sure it has dissolved.)

2. Pour the mixture into a 13-by-9-by-2-inch glass or ceramic baking dish. Place in the freezer for 30 minutes. Using a large metal spoon, stir the frozen crystals from around the edges of the pan back into the liquid. As the mixture continues to freeze, scrape the spoon against the sides and bottom to loosen and break up any frozen crystals. Repeat this scraping process every 30 minutes or so, until the mixture is frozen and a bit creamy, about 3 hours total. Scoop the crystals into individual bowls or goblets and serve immediately.

SERVING SUGGESTIONS

Serve the granita as is, garnished with sliced strawberries or whole raspberries, or with Classic Almond Biscotti (page 498).

Watermelon-Campari Granita

SERVES 4

CAMPARI IS A RUBY-RED ITALIAN APERITIF made with herbs and oranges. Lemon juice may be substituted for the Campari, but you will lose some color and the mysterious aftertaste. If you would like to make the granita in advance, see page 517.

2½ pounds watermelon
¼ cup sugar
2 tablespoons Campari

1. Remove the rind from the watermelon. Pick out and discard the seeds. Cut the flesh into large chunks and place them in the work bowl of a food processor. Puree until smooth. Pour the watermelon puree through a fine-mesh strainer, pressing on the pulp to extract as much liquid as possible. There should be about 2 cups. Discard the pulp.

2. Combine the watermelon juice, sugar and Campari in a medium bowl. Stir on and off for several minutes until the sugar has dissolved. (Rub your finger along the bottom of the bowl to make sure it has dissolved.)

3. Pour the mixture into a 13-by-9-by-2-inch glass or ceramic baking pan. Place in the freezer for 30 minutes. Using a large metal spoon, stir the frozen crystals from around the edges of the pan back into the liquid. As the mixture continues to freeze, scrape the spoon against the sides and bottom to loosen and break up any frozen crystals. Repeat this scraping process every 30 minutes or so, until the mixture is frozen and a bit creamy, about 3 hours total. Scoop the crystals into individual bowls or goblets and serve immediately.

SERVING SUGGESTIONS
Serve this granita as is or layered with Lemon Granita (page 519) in tall goblets.

Sauces and Other Basics

Quick Tomato Sauce

MAKES ABOUT 3 CUPS

THIS IS MY MOST BASIC TOMATO SAUCE. Using canned crushed tomatoes reduces the cooking time to just 10 minutes.

3 tablespoons extra-virgin olive oil
2 medium garlic cloves, minced
1 28-ounce can crushed tomatoes
2 tablespoons minced fresh basil or parsley leaves
Salt and freshly ground black pepper

1. Heat the oil in a medium saucepan. Add the garlic and sauté over medium heat until golden, about 2 minutes.

2. Add the tomatoes, basil or parsley and salt and pepper to taste. Bring to a simmer, lower the heat and simmer until the sauce thickens, about 10 minutes. Adjust the seasonings. Use immediately or store in an airtight container. *(The sauce can be refrigerated for 2 days or frozen for several months.)*

Nana's Slow-Cooked Tomato Sauce

MAKES ABOUT 4 CUPS

THIS IS A TOTALLY SMOOTH, VERY RICH TOMATO SAUCE made by my grandmother Katherine Pizzarello. She serves it over ziti or spaghetti. It's also good in baked pasta dishes like lasagne.

½ cup extra-virgin olive oil
3 large garlic cloves
2 29-ounce cans tomato puree
2 tablespoons minced fresh parsley leaves
Several sprigs of fresh basil
1 teaspoon dried oregano leaves
Salt and freshly ground black pepper

1. Heat the oil in a large, heavy saucepan. Add the whole garlic cloves and cook, turning often, over medium heat until golden brown, about 5 minutes. Remove and discard the garlic.

2. Add the tomato puree, parsley, basil and oregano, taking care not to spatter any oil onto your hands. Partially cover to prevent excessive spattering and simmer slowly over very low heat until the sauce has become quite thick, about 1½ hours. Add salt and pepper to taste. Use immediately or store in an airtight container. *(The sauce can be refrigerated for 2 days or frozen for several months.)*

Mom's Favorite Pink Tomato Sauce

MAKES ABOUT 2 CUPS

A LITTLE HEAVY CREAM turns a basic tomato sauce a bright orange-pink color. It also adds sweetness (which is reinforced by the sautéed carrot and onion) as well as richness. My mother loves this sauce, especially with gnocchi. It is good over fresh fettuccine with freshly grated Parmesan or Pecorino Romano cheese and can be served as an accompaniment to soufflés and frittatas.

3 tablespoons unsalted butter
1 small onion, minced
1 medium carrot, peeled and minced
1 28-ounce can crushed tomatoes
Salt
½ cup heavy cream

1. Melt the butter in a medium saucepan. Add the onion and carrot and sauté over medium heat until they soften, 8 to 10 minutes. (Do not let them brown.)

2. Add the tomatoes and salt to taste. Bring to a boil, reduce the heat to medium-low and simmer until the sauce thickens considerably, 25 to 30 minutes.

3. Scrape the sauce into a food processor or blender and puree until smooth. Scrape the sauce back into the saucepan and stir in the cream. Simmer, stirring constantly, just until the sauce thickens again, about 2 minutes. Adjust the seasonings. Use immediately or store in an airtight container *(The sauce may be refrigerated for 2 days or frozen for several months.)*

Oven-Dried Tomatoes

MAKES 1½ CUPS

OVEN-DRIED TOMATOES are quite different from sun-dried ones. Sun-dried tomatoes, even those packed in olive oil, tend to be a bit leathery and have a strong, sometimes harsh flavor. Oven-drying removes much but not all of the moisture, so the tomato halves become very wrinkled but still have some juice in them. The tomatoes can be marinated in olive oil, herbs and/or hot red pepper flakes. If packed in olive oil and refrigerated, they will last about a week.

10 medium plum tomatoes (about 2 pounds)
½ teaspoon salt

1. Preheat the oven to 200 degrees F. Set a large cross-woven wire rack over a large baking sheet. Trim a thin slice from the stem end of each tomato to remove the core. Slice the tomatoes in half lengthwise. Place them cut side up on the rack and sprinkle with the salt.

2. Place the baking sheet in the oven. Oven-dry the tomatoes until they are wrinkled and greatly reduced in size, 6 to 7 hours. Do not dry them completely; some moisture should remain.

3. Remove the baking sheet from the oven and cool the tomatoes completely. Transfer to an airtight container and refrigerate. *(Dried tomatoes can be refrigerated for several days. Bring the tomatoes to room temperature before using.)*

Roasted Bell Peppers

ROASTING PEPPERS UNTIL THEY ARE BLACKENED, then removing their skins, gives them a mellow, rich, slightly smoky flavor.

Red, yellow or orange bell peppers

1. To roast the peppers under the broiler in a gas or electric oven: Preheat the broiler. Place the peppers on a rack set over a baking pan so that they are 1 to 2 inches from the heating element. Broil, turning carefully several times with tongs and taking care not to puncture the peppers, until the skins are lightly charred but not ashen on all sides, about 15 minutes.

To roast the peppers over a gas flame: Hold 1 pepper at a time with a pair of tongs (a fork will puncture the skin and permit the loss of flavorful juices) over a gas flame on top of the stove, turning often, until lightly charred on all sides, no more than 2 to 3 minutes.

2. Place the charred peppers in a large bowl, cover with plastic wrap and set aside to steam for about 10 minutes, or until the skins pucker. When cool enough to handle, peel the peppers, working over a bowl to catch the juice. Use your fingers to remove the skin, then core and seed them. Cut them as directed in the recipes. *(Roasted peppers can be stored in their juices in the refrigerator for 1 to 2 days. For longer storage, cover them with a film of extra-virgin olive oil. They should stay fresh for about 1 week.)*

Classic Béchamel

Makes about 3 cups

This is the Italian version of the classic French white sauce. Although the sauce is traditionally stirred with a spoon, a whisk greatly reduces the risk of lumps.

- **3 cups whole milk**
- **6 tablespoons (¾ stick) unsalted butter**
- **4½ tablespoons unbleached all-purpose flour**
- **½ teaspoon salt, or to taste**

1. Heat the milk in a small pan until hot but not scalded or boiling. While the milk is heating, melt the butter in a medium saucepan. When it is foamy, whisk in the flour until smooth. Stir-cook for 2 minutes over medium heat. Do not let the flour brown.

2. Add several tablespoons of the hot milk and whisk vigorously. Continue adding milk in small increments, whisking until it is incorporated. Eventually, you will be able to add it in greater amounts until it has all been incorporated into the sauce.

3. Add the salt and cook over medium-low heat, stirring often, until the sauce thickens to the consistency of heavy cream, 3 to 5 minutes.

4. Remove the pan from the heat to prevent further thickening. Use immediately or cool to room temperature and whisk until smooth before using. *(The sauce can be refrigerated for up to 2 days. Before using, bring to room temperature and whisk until smooth.)*

Low-Fat Béchamel

MAKES ABOUT 3 CUPS

DESPITE ITS THICK, CREAMY TEXTURE, regular béchamel is not especially high in fat. You can reduce the fat by using low-fat milk instead of whole and switching from butter to olive oil. The color will be more yellowish than traditional béchamel. Note that the technique for making this sauce is not the same as for the classic sauce.

3 cups low-fat milk
3½ tablespoons extra-virgin olive oil
3½ tablespoons unbleached all-purpose flour
½ teaspoon salt, or to taste

1. Heat the milk in a small pan until hot but not scalded or boiling. While the milk is heating, heat the oil in a medium nonstick saucepan. Whisk in the flour until smooth. Stir-cook for 2 minutes over medium heat. Do not let the flour brown.

2. Whisk in the hot milk all at once and continue whisking to break up any lumps. Bring to a boil and reduce the heat to a simmer. Stir often as the sauce thickens, making sure that it does not stick to the bottom of the pan.

3. After 10 minutes or so, the sauce should have the consistency of light cream. Remove the pan from the heat and stir in the salt. Pour the sauce through a fine-mesh strainer or briefly whip it in a blender if any lumps remain. Use immediately or cool to room temperature and whisk until smooth before using. *(The sauce can be refrigerated for up to 2 days. Before using, bring it to room temperature and whisk until smooth.)*

Vegetable Stock

MAKES ABOUT 8 CUPS

THIS ALL-PURPOSE STOCK IS LIGHT AND DELICATE. It can serve as a base for soups, pasta sauces, rice dishes and stews. The secret of a good vegetable stock is to sauté the vegetables in olive oil to bring out their flavor. This step requires a few extra minutes but is well worth the effort.

2 medium leeks
2 tablespoons extra-virgin olive oil
6 celery ribs with leaves, chopped
4 small carrots, chopped
2 medium onions, chopped
Peelings from 2 large potatoes
4 medium garlic cloves, unpeeled
16 sprigs fresh flat-leaf parsley
4 sprigs fresh thyme
4 bay leaves
2 teaspoons whole black peppercorns

1. Trim and discard the dark green tops and tough outer leaves from the leeks. Remove the roots along with a very thin slice of the nearby white part. Halve the leeks lengthwise and wash them under cold running water. Gently spread apart but do not separate the inner layers to remove all traces of soil. If the leeks are particularly sandy, soak them in several changes of clean water. Chop the leeks.

2. Heat the oil in a large soup kettle or stockpot. Add the leeks, celery, carrots and onions and sauté over medium heat until the vegetables soften and are just beginning to color, about 15 minutes.

3. Add 12 cups cold water and the remaining ingredients. Bring to a boil, lower the heat and simmer for 1 hour.

4. Pour the stock through a fine-mesh strainer set over a large container. Press on the solids to extract as much liquid as possible. Discard the solids and cool the stock to room temperature.

5. Use a spoon to skim off the oil that rises to the surface. Use immediately or store in an airtight container. *(The stock may be refrigerated for 2 days or frozen for 2 months.)*

Light Tomato Stock

MAKES ABOUT 8 CUPS

WITH PLENTY OF GARLIC AND FRESH BASIL, this stock has more character than my standard vegetable stock. Tomatoes give it a light rosy color. It is appropriate in any soup, pasta sauce, rice dish or stew that contains tomatoes.

- 2 medium leeks
- 2 tablespoons extra-virgin olive oil
- 6 celery ribs with leaves, chopped
- 4 small carrots, chopped
- 2 medium onions, chopped
- Peelings from 2 large potatoes
- 3 medium plum tomatoes (about 8 ounces), chopped
- 8 medium garlic cloves, unpeeled
- 16 sprigs fresh flat-leaf parsley
- 16 large fresh basil leaves, cut into thin strips
- 4 sprigs fresh thyme
- 4 bay leaves
- 2 teaspoons whole black peppercorns

1. Trim and discard the dark green tops and tough outer leaves from the leeks. Remove the roots along with a very thin slice of the nearby white part. Halve the leeks lengthwise and wash them under cold running water. Gently spread apart but do not separate the inner layers to remove all traces of soil. If the leeks are particularly sandy, soak them in several changes of clean water. Chop the leeks.

2. Heat the oil in a large soup kettle or stockpot. Add the leeks, celery, carrots and onions and sauté over medium heat until the vegetables soften and are just beginning to color, about 15 minutes.

3. Add 12 cups cold water and the remaining ingredients. Bring to a boil, lower the heat and simmer for 1 hour.

4. Pour the stock through a fine-mesh strainer set over a large container. Press on the solids to extract as much liquid as possible. Discard the solids and cool the stock to room temperature.

5. Use a spoon to skim off the oil that rises to the surface. Use immediately or store in an airtight container. *(The stock may be refrigerated for 2 days or frozen for 2 months.)*

Pesto, My Way

MAKES ¾ TO 1 CUP

HERE'S MY VERSION OF THE CLASSIC BASIL SAUCE. Many recipes call for a combination of Parmesan and Pecorino cheese, but I use only Parmesan because the scant amount of Pecorino doesn't merit a special trip to the market. To heighten the flavor of the nuts, toast them in a dry skillet until golden. Walnuts may be used in place of pine nuts. I find the food processor to be the easiest tool for making pesto. A blender will work, although you may need to add a little extra oil. A mortar and pestle produces a coarse texture that is more authentic. If using the pesto to sauce gnocchi, add only ¼ cup cheese so that the pesto stays a bit runny.

- **2 tablespoons pine nuts**
- **2 cups tightly packed fresh basil leaves**
- **2 medium garlic cloves**
- **½ cup extra-virgin olive oil**
- **¼-⅓ cup freshly grated Parmigiano-Reggiano cheese**
- **Salt**

1. Place the pine nuts, basil and garlic in the work bowl of a food processor. Process, scraping down the sides of the bowl as needed, until the ingredients are finely chopped. With the motor running, slowly pour the oil through the feed tube and process until smooth.

2. Scrape the sauce into a small bowl and stir in the cheese and salt to taste. Use immediately or refrigerate in an airtight container. *(The pesto may be refrigerated for several days. For longer storage in the refrigerator, pour a thin film of olive oil over the pesto.)*

Salsa Verde

MAKES ABOUT ¾ CUP

THIS PIQUANT GREEN SAUCE has countless variations. Some cooks add anchovies, others lemon juice and still others red wine vinegar. Some like parsley alone, others a combination of fresh herbs. Some prefer capers in it, others olives. My version calls for garlic, parsley as well as basil, capers *and* olives and plenty of lemon juice and extra-virgin olive oil. The sauce should be a little chunky, so mince the ingredients by hand.

Traditionally, this sauce is served with boiled meats and fish. I like it with eggs (it's a great way to perk up scrambled eggs), drizzled over steamed or boiled vegetables, spread on slices of toast, tossed with pasta or mixed into rice. Remember that a little goes a long way.

¼ cup minced fresh parsley leaves
10 large green olives, pitted and minced
2 tablespoons minced fresh basil leaves
1 tablespoon drained capers, rinsed and minced
2 medium garlic cloves, minced
2 tablespoons lemon juice
⅓ cup extra-virgin olive oil, or more as needed
Salt

1. Place the parsley, olives, basil, capers, garlic and lemon juice in a medium bowl. Slowly beat in the ⅓ cup oil with a fork. Add more oil as needed until the sauce is smooth and just a little runny.

2. Taste and add salt if necessary. Use immediately or refrigerate in an airtight container. *(The sauce may be refrigerated for several days. For longer storage in the refrigerator, pour a thin film of olive oil over the sauce.)*

Olivada

MAKES ABOUT 1 CUP

OLIVADA IS A SILKY, PUNGENT SPREAD made with olives, thyme, garlic and olive oil. Gaeta olives are particularly good. I add basil and lemon juice; other versions contain capers and/or anchovies. Olivada has many uses in my kitchen: spread on crostini for a quick antipasto; spread on sandwiches to moisten the bread; or served over linguine or spaghetti after being thinned with a little cooking liquid from the pasta.

2 medium garlic cloves
8 large fresh basil leaves
1 tablespoon fresh thyme leaves
1½ cups drained black olives (about 7 ounces), pitted
2 tablespoons lemon juice
3 tablespoons extra-virgin olive oil

1. Place the garlic, basil and thyme in the work bowl of a food processor. Process, scraping down the sides of the bowl as needed, until the ingredients are finely chopped. Add the olives and lemon juice and pulse, scraping down the sides of the bowl several times, to form a coarse paste.

2. For a coarse paste, add the oil all at once and pulse until it is just incorporated. For a smooth paste, add the oil in a steady stream through the feed tube with the motor running. Scrape the olive paste into an airtight container and adjust the seasonings. *(The olive paste may be refrigerated for several days. For longer storage in the refrigerator, pour a thin film of olive oil over the paste.)*

Garlic Mayonnaise

MAKES ¾ TO 1 CUP

HOMEMADE MAYONNAISE bears little resemblance to what you buy in a jar. This mayonnaise is thick and eggy, but the garlic helps cut the richness. Making mayonnaise in a blender minces the garlic into extremely fine pieces; it is a foolproof method. I find that using all olive oil can be overpowering. A blend of canola or another mild oil and extra-virgin olive oil tastes better to me.

Note that this recipe contains a raw egg: Use a very fresh egg. If you are concerned about health risks of raw eggs, you may want to add minced garlic to store-bought mayonnaise, though the flavor will not be comparable.

- **1 large egg**
- **1 tablespoon lemon juice**
- **3 medium garlic cloves**
- **½ teaspoon salt, plus more to taste**
- **6 tablespoons canola or other bland oil**
- **6 tablespoons extra-virgin olive oil**

1. Place the egg, lemon juice, garlic and ½ teaspoon salt in a blender. Process until smooth.

2. Combine the oils in a measuring cup. With the blender running, slowly add the oil until the mayonnaise thickens. (It should take 1 to 2 minutes to add all the oil.) Taste and adjust the seasonings.

3. Scrape the mayonnaise into an airtight container. *(The mayonnaise may be refrigerated for 2 days.)*

APPENDIX

Key Ingredients

THE FOLLOWING VEGETABLES, cheeses and pantry items have a regular place in any Italian kitchen. I have included basic information on purchasing, storing and preparing each item.

ARTICHOKES

Artichokes are the flower bud of a Mediterranean thistle plant. Like flower buds, the leaves on an artichoke should be tightly closed. Size is not a function of age ("baby" artichokes come from a different place on the plant), but it does matter. I prefer medium artichokes, about eight ounces each. Large specimens are often woody and should be avoided. If possible, buy artichokes with the stems attached; they keep the artichokes fresh and are edible when peeled.

Since cut artichokes turn gray almost immediately, rub them with a lemon half as you clean them. Once one artichoke has been cleaned, drop it into a bowl of cold lemon water while you work on the next. Remove all dark green portions of the artichoke, since they are tough and will not soften, even with prolonged cooking. In addition, remove several layers of outer leaves, the tips of the inner leaves, the outer skin on the stem and the base of the torn leaves that surrounds the bottom of the artichoke once the leaves have been snapped off. Finally, remove the fuzzy part in the center, called the choke.

The alternatives to fresh artichokes are not very appealing. Frozen artichokes are mushy and bland. Marinated quartered artichoke hearts are fine for sandwiches and salads but are so highly seasoned that they cannot be used for much else.

ARUGULA

This leafy green grows wild throughout southern Italy. When shopping, buy fresh-looking arugula with dark green leaves. Arugula can range in flavor from spicy to fairly mild. Taste the leaves and consider blending the arugula with mild leaf lettuces for salads. Arugula wilts and bruises very quickly. To prolong freshness, do not detach the stems or wash the leaves until the last possible moment. Arugula is often quite sandy. Wash stemmed leaves in successive bowls of cold water until they are free of grit.

Asparagus

Asparagus comes in sizes ranging from pencil-thin to as fat as two fingers. Large spears are often woody and stringy; I prefer those about the same thickness as the pinkie on an average adult hand. Buy asparagus of similar thickness so that the spears cook evenly. Tightly closed top buds indicate freshness. When you are ready to cook asparagus, snap off the tough ends of the spears, one at a time. The tough portion should break off at just the right spot.

Beans (dried)

Keep an assortment of dried beans on hand, especially **cannellini beans**, also known as white kidney beans, and **chickpeas**. Both require soaking before cooking. You can use an eight-hour or overnight soak (see page 286) or the quick-soak method (see page 286), which produces the same results as longer soaking.

Cranberry or **borlotti beans**, both of which need soaking, can be used in any cannellini bean recipe. Two other legumes, **lentils** and **dried split fava beans**, are good for faster meals, since they do not need to be soaked.

Simmering (as opposed to boiling) helps keep the bean skins intact. Do not add salt until the beans are almost done, or you may toughen them. The freshness of dried beans varies greatly; taste often to determine when they are done. Cool them right in the pot and store in their cooking liquid to keep them moist. The liquid can be added to soups and sauces—another good reason not to drain beans after cooking.

Beans (fresh)

Buy fresh green and yellow beans that are not too thick or swollen with immature bean pods. Younger, thinner beans have a better flavor (they are generally sweeter) and texture. Green beans do not need to be stringed; but the ends should be snapped off.

Beets

Beets present a challenge to the uninitiated. They can be a mess, staining everything in their path. Although recipes often call for boiling them, this method of cooking dilutes their sweet flavor and causes them to "bleed."

Roasting is a better method because it concentrates their flavor, and leaving the skins on during cooking keeps the bleeding to a minimum. Wash the beets and wrap them in foil before roasting. Allow about an hour for smaller beets, longer for larger ones. When the beets are done, let them cool slightly. With a paper towel, slip off the skins.

Choose beets of similar size so they will all be done at the same time. Try to get bundles with the greens attached. Cut off the greens one to two inches above the beets (they must be used almost immediately) and cook them as you would spinach or swiss chard.

Bread

Good bread is an essential part of any Italian meal. If you do not have a ready supply, stock up when you can get good bread; it freezes remarkably well. To freeze, wrap a loaf tightly in foil and place it in a large zipper-lock plastic bag. Bread will keep for months in the freezer. Defrost the bread (still wrapped in foil) at room temperature for several hours, place it in a 325-degree-F oven to heat through, then remove the foil and let it crisp in the oven for about five minutes. If you forget to take the bread out of the freezer, defrost it in a hot oven for about 20 minutes. Keep the loaf wrapped in foil to prevent burning. When the bread is defrosted (slide a skewer into the center to see if it is still hard), unwrap it and let it crisp in the oven for several minutes.

Bread Crumbs

Toasted bread crumbs sometimes replace grated cheese as a topping for pasta dishes or vegetables or can be used to coat buttered baking dishes for soufflés and tortas. Make your own bread crumbs from stale bread. Grind cubed stale bread (either white or whole wheat) in the food processor until fairly fine. Homemade crumbs will be coarser than the commercial kind but should not be too large. Store the crumbs in the freezer and toast them as needed in a dry skillet on top of the stove or on a baking sheet in a 350-degree-F oven.

Broccoli

Choose bunches with tightly closed florets that are dark green or even purple in color (darker florets indicate a higher concentration of vitamin C). If you plan to use the whole spears, do not pick bunches with extremely wide stalks, which are often woody.

Broccoli Rabe

Broccoli rabe, also called rapini or *broccoletti di rape*, is a nonheading variety of broccoli that is especially popular in southern Italy. It has more in common with bitter leafy greens like collards than with broccoli. Look for broccoli rabe with thin stalks and tightly closed buds that show no signs of yellow flowers. Like other leafy greens, broccoli rabe can be briefly boiled, drained and then sautéed. Or it can be wilted in a covered pan with some oil and the moisture that clings to the leaves after washing. Choose the first method if you prefer more tender greens, the second method if you want more of the natural bitterness in the greens.

Butter

Most of the recipes in this book call for olive oil as the fat, but some take butter. I prefer unsalted (sweet) butter for cooking. It has a fresher flavor than salted butter and allows you to control how much salt goes into your food. Keep butter in the freezer, moving a stick to the refrigerator as needed.

CABBAGE AND KALE

Cabbage and kale find many uses in vegetarian cooking, in soups, rice and polenta dishes and the like. Savoy cabbage, with its crinkly green leaves, is my favorite. The flavor is milder and nuttier than other green cabbages. Standard green cabbage can be used in its place. Pick firm heads that are heavy for their size.

A member of the cabbage family, kale has thick, ruffled leaves that are dark green. Cut off and discard the tough stems and tear off the leafy part on either side of the thick central vein running through each leaf; discard the veins.

CAPERS

Capers are the flower buds of a bush that grows all around the Mediterranean. They add a salty note to many dishes. I prefer small capers packed in balsamic vinegar as opposed to white vinegar (look for them in markets and supermarkets with a good selection of foods imported from Italy); the flavor is not quite as sharp. Larger capers are fine but will require chopping. Keep opened jars of capers in the refrigerator. Do not drain the brine; it will keep the capers moist for months.

CARROTS

Choose firm, medium carrots (six to eight to a pound). Healthy-looking greens are a sign of freshness, but the greens should be discarded before the carrots are refrigerated, since the leaves can rob the roots of flavor over time. For all the recipes in this book, the carrots are peeled.

CAULIFLOWER

Cauliflower has many of the nutritional benefits of broccoli without the sulfur flavor. For that reason, cauliflower takes to a number of preparations, such as Salsa Verde (page 532), that would clash with stronger-tasting broccoli. Look for cauliflower heads with no discoloration or black spots. The florets should be firm to the touch.

CHEESES

Italian cheeses are wonderful, but most supermarkets have a poor selection. You need to find a reliable source for authentic Italian cheese, such as a gourmet shop or an Italian market. Real Italian cheeses have much more flavor than imitations produced in other European countries or in this country.

Italian fontina from the Valle d'Aosta is rich and creamy, with a nutty, buttery flavor. (Danish, Swedish or American fontina has a rubbery texture and little flavor.)

Dolcelatte, or "sweet milk," Italian **Gorgonzola** is creamy and mild. If I cannot find it, I avoid crumbly, dry Gorgonzola and choose instead creamy **Saga Blue** cheese.

Mascarpone is an Italian cream cheese. Look for imported mascarpone in plastic tubs. Processed American cream cheese cannot be substituted; mascarpone has a much more buttery flavor and a creamier texture.

Mozzarella and **ricotta** are the two exceptions to the rule about buying imported Italian cheeses. Both are fresh cheeses and are well made by local artisans in most major American cities. Fresh mozzarella comes packed in water, which should be changed every day or two. It is available at specialty shops and many large supermarkets. It is a better option than Italian buffalo-milk mozzarella *(mozzarella di bufala)*, which rarely tastes good by the time it reaches American markets. Commercial mozzarella that is shrink-wrapped in plastic and sold in the supermarket should never be used in a dish where the cheese is not cooked. Since commercial mozzarella contains less moisture than fresh, however, it is easier to work with as a topping for pizzas or tarts and in baked pasta. If you use fresh mozzarella in these dishes, slice or shred it and press the pieces between layers of paper towels to remove as much liquid as possible.

Many gourmet stores and Italian markets sell **homestyle ricotta**, which is similar to the ricotta sold in Italy and far superior to the supermarket kind. (Italian ricotta is not imported into the United States; it is strictly a local product.) Because it is pasteurized at a lower temperature than supermarket versions, homestyle ricotta is dry and firm, more akin to goat cheese in texture than cottage cheese. Good homestyle ricotta should be a little sweet, with a strong milk flavor. It stays fresh for about one week in the refrigerator. Supermarket ricotta is too watery to be used as is in many recipes. Draining it in a small colander or sieve lined with paper towels improves its texture but not its flavor.

In Italy, fresh ricotta is salted and pressed to make **ricotta salata**, a crumbly cheese with a texture reminiscent of feta but with a milder and much less salty flavor. Ricotta salata is not nearly as perishable as fresh ricotta and is increasingly available in supermarkets as well as specialty shops. It has some of the sharpness of Pecorino but is creamy and soft. Ricotta salata can be used in savory tarts to give fresh ricotta a boost or mixed with a spicy tomato sauce to make a creamy pasta sauce.

Parmigiano-Reggiano is the king of Italian cheeses. There is no substitute, so look for the real thing. The beige rind should have the words Parmigiano-Reggiano stenciled on it. This cheese is expensive, but a little adds a lot of flavor. Other Parmesan cheeses are not worth the bother. Buy a small piece and grate it as needed.

Pecorino Romano is a sheep's milk cheese, generally more salty and pungent than Parmigiano-Reggiano. It is especially important in the cooking of southern Italy. Some American-made Pecorinos taste of salt and little else. Authentic imported Pecorino has a more balanced flavor.

Eggplant

Whenever possible, buy small eggplants (8 ounces or less), which are usually sold at farmers' markets. They have fewer seeds and little bitterness, in contrast to two-pound eggplants, which need to be salted to draw off the bitter juices. Eggplants should be firm and unblemished.

Eggplants are spongelike and will soak up as much oil as you give them; therefore, use low-fat cooking methods, such as grilling, broiling, roasting and stewing.

Eggs

Really fresh eggs make a tremendous difference in dishes like the frittata, where they command attention. Local organic eggs generally have bright orange yolks and have a superior flavor compared with supermarket eggs. All recipes in this book call for large eggs. You may use five extra-large eggs in place of six large.

Endive

Belgian endive, a member of the chicory family, can range from somewhat bitter to mild with some sweetness. Use it in salads, slicing the leaves crosswise into thin strips. Cooking endive mellows its flavor. Look for tight heads with crisp outer leaves that show no signs of limpness or browning around the edges.

Fava Beans

Fava beans are a springtime delicacy in Italy. The very first ones are so tender they can be eaten raw. Many Italian families gather around the table and slip the beans out of their pods and dip the beans into olive oil as an antipasto. You rarely find fava beans that fresh in this country. Instead, you have to remove the thin outer coating from the shelled beans. To do this, drop the shelled beans into boiling water for a few minutes. Drain and refresh the beans in cold water. Use your fingernails to scrape away part of the skin, then squeeze out the dark green bean. (It's fine if it splits in two.) Use the shelled and skinned fava beans in pasta sauces, rice dishes or salads. Fresh fava beans are available in produce stores and many supermarkets.

Fennel

Bulb fennel, called *finocchio* in Italian, is remarkably versatile. Its crisp texture and licorice flavor make it refreshing in salads, but when it is cooked, the licorice flavor fades, leaving a smooth sweetness behind. Look for creamy white bulbs with light green stems and feathery dark green fronds. The stems are generally discarded, but the fronds can be minced and used like an herb to add color and flavor to a dish just before serving. Fennel can be used in rice dishes and pasta sauces or served as a vegetable side dish.

Directions for preparing fennel appear in each recipe, but in general, start by removing the tough or blemished outer layers and a slice from the root end. (For wedges for grilling or braising, cut only a very thin slice from the base.) At this point, the fennel can be cut into fan-shaped wedges or halved, cored and cut into thin strips.

FLOUR

Recipes in this book were tested with unbleached all-purpose flour.

GARLIC

Along with onions and herbs, garlic is the predominant seasoning in Italian food. When cooking without meat, I find it helpful to use a fair amount of garlic. As long as the garlic is sautéed until golden, it will lose any harshness and give vegetable, grain and bean dishes a rich, full flavor that is hard to duplicate by other methods.

Look for large, firm bulbs with no signs of sprouting. Keep garlic at room temperature to prolong freshness. To remove the papery skins from the cloves, crush them with the side of a chef's knife. This loosens the skins quickly and without much fuss. (This technique is appropriate only when the garlic is going to be crushed or minced.)

HERBS

Fresh herbs are my first and only choice for the recipes in this book. Dried herbs usually have little flavor. If you do any gardening at all, plant herbs. Otherwise, pick them up whenever you go to market. Most supermarkets now stock the basics—flat-leaf parsley, basil, mint, thyme, oregano, rosemary, tarragon and chives.

Store all herbs, with the exception of basil, in the refrigerator in unsealed dry plastic bags. Thyme and rosemary will keep for several weeks there; more delicate herbs like parsley and mint will last for a few days. Because basil blackens at cold temperatures, keep it at room temperature, with the stems (or roots) in water. If you change the water daily, the basil should stay fresh for several days.

I'm a firm believer in substituting one fresh herb for another, as opposed to using the dried form. The only trick is to match the intensity of the herb you are replacing. Taste and use your judgment. Parsley and basil are the mildest herbs, followed by mint, chives and tarragon, and then thyme, oregano, marjoram and rosemary.

KALE

See Cabbage.

LEEKS

Leeks are part of the allium family, which also includes garlic, onions, shallots and chives. Leeks have a milder flavor than the others and can be used as a seasoning for soups and sauces or as a vegetable in their own right. Choose crisp and firm leeks, about one inch thick.

Since leeks can be very sandy, they must be thoroughly cleaned before slicing or chopping. Directions appear in recipes where leeks are used.

Lemons

Lemons are plentiful in Italy, and the juice and the zest are used in every kind of dish from pasta and risotto to salads and vegetable dishes, as well as for garnish. For zesting a lemon, a flat fine-tooth grater does the best job. Rub the lemon over the teeth on the grater, turning the lemon to avoid grating the bitter white pith. Room-temperature lemons give up their juices more easily than cold ones. Roll them on the counter and press them before juicing. This technique works with oranges also.

Lettuce

In recent years, American supermarkets have begun to carry an assortment of salad greens almost as extensive as that of produce markets in Italy. For escarole, romaine and leaf lettuces, choose heads that look fresh and crisp and use them as soon as possible; they are highly perishable. Wash lettuce shortly before using. Soak leaves in successive bowls of cold water until clean, spin them dry in a salad spinner and then pat off any remaining water with paper towels. You may place the greens in a salad bowl, cover with plastic and refrigerate for a few hours.

Mushrooms

For this book, several kinds of mushrooms were used, including **white button** mushrooms and **creminis**, which I generally prefer. Similar to button mushrooms in size and shape but light brown in color, they have a much stronger flavor. They are also firmer and give off less water when cooked. With either kind, trim a thin slice from the stem end and wipe the mushroom clean with a paper towel before slicing or chopping. Do not rinse mushrooms; exposure to water makes them soggy.

Portobellos are actually giant cremini mushrooms. Everything about them is big, including their meaty flavor. The stems are tough and should be discarded. Portobellos take well to grilling and roasting. To keep their juices from oozing out during cooking, place them gill side up on the grill or in the oven.

Italians can buy fresh **porcini** mushrooms, but we Americans have to make do with dried porcini, which re-create the flavor but not the texture of the fresh. Dried porcini should be tan or light brown in color, not black. Avoid packages with lots of dust or crumbled bits. Directions for rehydrating dried porcini are given in the recipes in which they are called for.

The soaking liquid is highly flavorful. Pour it through a strainer lined with a paper towel to trap the sediment. The liquid can be used in sauces, soups or stocks.

NUTS

There are two key points to remember with nuts. First, due to their high oil content, they can become rancid. Store them in the freezer, and this will not be a problem. Second, they need to be toasted to bring out their flavor. Toast them either in a dry skillet on top of the stove or on a baking sheet in a 350-degree-F oven. Watch carefully so that they don't burn.

OLIVE OIL

It's impossible to imagine Italian cooking without olive oil. Unlike most other oils, it adds flavor to everything. For most uses, I prefer the greater nuances of extra-virgin olive oil. Use one of the supermarket brands of extra-virgin oil imported from Italy (whatever is on sale) for sautéing. For deep-frying, I use ordinary olive oil, as do most Italians. I also keep a special artisanal extra-virgin olive oil from Italy or Spain on hand for vinaigrettes and for drizzling over vegetables. It may cost as much as $15 or $20 a bottle, but it lasts for months.

OLIVES

Good olives are so much better than bad ones that it's hard to imagine what went wrong with the inferior samples. Do not buy canned olives, which are tasteless and watery. If you like, buy imported olives in jars. Better yet, go to a good gourmet store or an Italian market and choose olives in brine. (The "gourmet mix" available from many stores usually has a good selection in various colors and sizes.) Try to get olives that are not too salty. You should be able to taste the olive itself and not just the salt.

ONIONS

Yellow onions are standard in the Italian kitchen. Red onions are a bit sweeter and not as sharp as yellow onions. Because of their appealing color, I use red onions in dishes where the onions are not cooked or the cooking time is minimal. Like garlic, onions keep better at room temperature.

To peel an onion, make a shallow incision from one end to the other and gently lift off the outer layer of skin. Cut the onion in half through the ends and lay the halves down on a work surface. To chop or mince, slice the onion in half again, cutting parallel to the work surface. Next, make several cuts down the length of the onion. Finally, cut across it to turn out pieces of the desired size.

Pasta

Keep dried pasta in several different shapes and sizes in your cupboard. I prefer Italian brands (DeCecco is my personal favorite) because they make so many unusual shapes. American brands cook up just fine.

If you plan to make fresh pasta, invest in a hand-cranked pasta machine from Italy, such as the Atlas (see page 554).

Peas

When peas are fresh, they are marvelous, but when they are old, they are a lot more work than the frozen and not as good. Open a few fresh pods in the market and taste the peas. If they are mealy and bland, walk over to the freezer section. As a rule of thumb, one pound of fresh pods yields a little more than one cup shelled peas.

Peppers

Bell peppers are relatively new to Europe (they came back with Columbus from the Americas), but they are now an integral part of the Italian vegetable larder. I prefer red, yellow and orange varieties. Green peppers are unripe (other peppers all pass through a green stage) and often bitter. Purple peppers are really green peppers with a thin purple skin that changes to a muddy green color when cooked. Red, yellow and orange peppers may be used interchangeably in the recipes in this book.

For roasting directions, either over a gas flame on a stovetop burner or under the broiler, see page 526.

Polenta

Polenta, a dish of cooked cornmeal, is a staple in northern Italy. **Stone-ground cornmeal**, which can be found in the baking aisle of most supermarkets, is your cheapest and best option. Because it contains both the germ and the bran, it has light and dark specks. Fine cornmeal, like Quaker or Goya brands, produces gummier polenta. Imported cornmeal, labeled "polenta," is often quite good, although generally more expensive than domestic cornmeal. Look for the words ***polenta integra***, which means whole grain. I have noticed, however, that Italian polenta sometimes contains bugs, so when buying it, look for clear bags that you can inspect. One imported product worth buying is **quick-cooking** or **instant polenta**. The preparation is the same as for regular cornmeal, but the cooking time is just five minutes. Keep cornmeal in the refrigerator to prolong its freshness.

Potatoes

Americans tend not to associate potatoes with Italian cooking, and yet they are quite widely used, most notably for gnocchi. Buy baking or russet potatoes for both gnocchi and mashed potatoes, since they have little moisture. For mashing, choose Yukon Gold potatoes, which have a low moisture content and pale yellow flesh. Do not use this variety for gnocchi, where their color would be out of place. Buy red new potatoes (or other varieties of new potatoes with white or yellow flesh and brown skin) for roasting. Freshly dug potatoes have more moisture and do not dry out as much when exposed to oven heat. Do not use them for mashing, as they become gummy.

Radicchio

Radicchio, a red chicory with a bracing bitterness, originated in Italy. By now, it has worked its way into almost every supermarket in America. Use it in salads or cook it in rice dishes or on its own as a side dish. Look for heads with crisp outer leaves and no discoloration.

Rice

Arborio rice, which is grown in northern Italy, is a medium-grain rice with a unique balance of starches. The grains cook up tender, retaining some firmness in the center and releasing starches slowly to form a creamy sauce. No American or Asian rice can achieve a similar effect. Other Italian rices, like Carnaroli and Vialone Nano, are similar to Arborio but are less widely available.

Salt

Since every palate reacts differently to salt, I have suggested that you add "salt to taste" in most recipes. Only where tasting is impractical, as in pizza dough and cookies, have I specified an amount. I use kosher salt in my kitchen for everything but desserts and recommend that you do too. (For cookies and other sweet baked goods, the fine granules of table salt dissolve more easily.) Kosher salt has a cleaner flavor than table salt, which is processed with chemicals to keep the crystals from clumping together.

Because kosher salt is less salty than regular salt (the granules are larger and hence fewer fit in a teaspoon), the two cannot be used interchangeably without some adjustments.

Many cooks prefer sea salt, but it is more expensive and less widely available than kosher salt. Depending on how fine the grind is, it can be slightly saltier. Coarse sea salt is ideal for sprinkling on focaccia.

Shallots

Shallots have a slightly sweet flavor, which makes them preferable to onions in some recipes. Buy full, firm bulbs that have not sprouted green shoots and store them at room temperature with onions and garlic.

Spinach

The curly-leaved spinach sold in plastic bags is often dried out, tough and tasteless. A better option is flat-leaf spinach, which is sold in bundles in most supermarkets. Its spade-shaped leaves tend to have thin, less fibrous stems that do not need to be discarded, and its leaves are not as stringy as those of curly spinach, with a flavor far superior and sweeter. In addition to flat-leaf spinach, many supermarkets sell baby spinach in bulk. It is excellent in salads.

Buy spinach shortly before you intend to use it, because it is quite perishable, and clean it thoroughly as described in each recipe. The spinach may be cleaned up to several hours in advance and refrigerated.

SQUASH

Winter squash is commonly used in pasta fillings, especially for "pumpkin" ravioli. Squash also works well as an ingredient in risotto or can be roasted and served as a vegetable side dish.

Among American squashes (varieties in Italy are somewhat different), butternut is the best choice. This sweet, creamy variety is not as watery as other hard squashes and has the best flavor; use it for pasta fillings. Choose butternut squash that is firm and heavy for its size. The skin should be smooth and a deep tan color.

When you are ready to use the squash, split it lengthwise in half and scoop out and discard the stringy fibers and seeds. If the squash needs to be peeled, use a knife or heavy-duty vegetable peeler to remove the skin and greenish layer of flesh just below it.

SWISS CHARD

Chard is similar to spinach, though somewhat more bitter in taste. It can be used almost anywhere spinach is called for. Swiss chard must be deribbed as well as stemmed. Pull off the leafy portion from either side of the central stalk and discard the stalks or save them to be braised or gratinéed under a blanket of béchamel and Parmigiano-Reggiano. There are two varieties of chard: white and red; they taste much the same.

TOMATOES (FRESH)

The tomato was unknown to Italians until after the discovery of the New World. Although not immediately embraced, it eventually became an integral part of Italian cuisine. Buy round tomatoes only in season from nearby farms. At other times of the year, buy plum tomatoes; although rarely good enough to eat raw, they are fine for cooked sauces. Look for plum tomatoes that are a rich red color and not rock-hard.

For some sauces, I prefer tomato flesh without skin or seeds. Unless the tomato is very soft, the skin can be removed with a heavy-duty vegetable peeler (see page 552): Remove the core of the tomato and pull down pieces of skin. To remove the skin the old-fashioned way (or if the tomato is very soft), drop the tomato into a pot of simmering water for 20 seconds, turning it so that all parts of the skin come into contact with the hot water. Lift the tomato from the water, cool it slightly and scrape off the skin with your fingernails. To seed a tomato, cut it crosswise in half. Gently squeeze the tomato over a bowl to remove the seeds and some of the juice.

Store tomatoes at room temperature, never in the refrigerator; they lose all flavor when chilled and never recapture it.

Tomatoes (canned)

Tomatoes are one of the few vegetables that can well, and canned tomatoes are the cook's salvation. Keep several kinds of canned tomatoes in your pantry. Crushed tomatoes are good for smooth sauces that need to be ready in a flash. Canned whole tomatoes add texture to a dish. For a meatier texture, roughly seed the tomatoes over a bowl, opening them with your fingers and pushing out the seeds. When moisture is needed in a dish, dice the whole tomatoes and consider adding some of the packing liquid. For this reason, choose tomatoes packed in juice, not puree. As to brands, I have found that Italian tomatoes often have a metallic taste, probably picked up in their long journey across the Atlantic. California tomatoes have a sweeter, more consistent flavor. Canned organic tomatoes, now widely available, are a good option.

Tomatoes (dried)

Sun-dried tomatoes have been used by generations of Italians to preserve a taste of summer for winter and to add intense flavor to pasta sauces, eggs or tarts. A few sun-dried tomatoes go a long way. Buy sun-dried tomatoes packed in high-quality oil and drain them well before using. Store open jars of sun-dried tomatoes in the refrigerator. If the oil congeals, place the jar in hot water to liquefy it.

You can also oven-dry your own plum tomatoes, which allows you to get that just-picked summer taste any time of the year. The flavor is fresher and not nearly as salty as that of many commercial sun-dried tomatoes. See page 525 for details.

Vegetable Stock

I make vegetable stock (see page 529) myself and keep it in the freezer in small containers. In a pinch, you can substitute vegetable bouillon cubes, but get them at a natural-foods store that carries brands without MSG. Canned vegetable stock is not an acceptable option. Brands I've tasted seem to be either oddly bitter or overly sweet. It's better to use plain water or a cube.

VINEGARS

Always keep an assortment of high-quality imported vinegars on hand. **Aged red wine vinegar** is my first choice for most dressings. **White wine vinegar** has a slightly less sharp flavor and is best when a colorless vinegar is required.

Aged balsamic vinegar has only a hint of sharpness. It should be thick and mellow. I particularly like Cavalli or Masserie de Sant'Eramo, two brands widely available in gourmet stores or by mail (see page 554). Expect to spend $10 to $15 for a small bottle. If the vinegar in your cabinet cost $3, it's probably not the real thing and is just cheap red wine vinegar with caramel coloring.

Even the best balsamic vinegar has limited uses, however. Its distinctive sweet-sharp flavor is too overpowering in many instances. Add a little to a salad dressing, preferably one that contains red wine vinegar as well, or drizzle some over roasted vegetables or even sliced strawberries.

ZUCCHINI

As with so many other vegetables, small zucchini have the sweetest and most delicate flavor. Look for zucchini no larger than six to eight ounces each, with smooth, firm skin. (Larger zucchini can be full of seeds and watery.) Scrub the skin but do not peel it. If a quick wash does not remove the grit, soak the zucchini in a bowl of cold water for 10 minutes to loosen it.

Key Specialty Equipment

YOU PROBABLY ALREADY OWN the equipment needed to make most of the recipes in this book. Occasionally, however, you'll need specialty items. See page 554 for information on how to buy equipment by mail.

Baking Stone

A large ceramic baking stone conducts heat much better than a metal baking sheet, making pizza crusts and breads crisper. There are few kitchen tools that deliver such dramatic results for so little money (about $20). Choose the largest size that can fit in your oven. Rectangular stones are more versatile than round ones. Preheat the stone at 500 degrees F for at least 30 minutes before baking.

Ice-Cream Machine

Making ice cream at home changed about 20 years ago with the invention of the Donvier, which rendered messy rock salt and wooden buckets obsolete. This type of ice-cream machine comes with an aluminum canister filled with supercoolant. The canister is put in the freezer overnight, then slipped into a plastic housing. A chilled mixture is added and is churned by hand.

Newer models made by other companies have electric churning mechanisms that beat in more air and yield a better product. (Krups makes one with an electric churning paddle for $60 that I particularly like.) If money is no object, get an Italian model with a built-in freezer. (I use a Simac machine.) This Rolls Royce of ice-cream makers costs around $500 but is worth every penny if you make ice cream a lot. Fashioned after commercial machines, the unit weighs 30 pounds and does not require prefreezing the canister or any other parts. Simply pour the mixture into the ice-cream maker and turn on the churning and freezing mechanisms. About 30 minutes later, you have perfect gelato or sorbet.

Nonstick Skillet

A nonstick skillet makes preparing eggs much easier and healthier. A frittata doesn't stick in a nonstick skillet, so the amount of oil can be reduced to a minimum. Choose a nonstick skillet with a heatproof handle (made from metal, not wood or plastic) so that you can put the frittata under the broiler without worrying about the handle burning or melting. Smooth nonstick surfaces are preferable; textured surfaces are more difficult to clean and don't release food as well.

Pasta Machine

A manual pasta machine that clamps onto a counter or worktable is essential for making homemade pasta. Rolling pins require a lot of effort and never get the pasta thin enough. Electric pasta machines that knead and extrude the dough are expensive and do not work well. Buy an Atlas manual pasta machine from Italy: It costs about $40 and delivers excellent results.

The rollers can be successively narrowed to turn disks of pasta dough into thin, translucent sheets. Most models come with two cutting blades. The wider fettuccine cutters are better than the thin linguine cutters, which often do a poor job of separating individual strands of pasta. Most manual machines can be fitted with attachments to produce ravioli and other filled pastas, but these delicate shapes are better made by hand with long, wide sheets of pasta and a knife or pastry wheel.

Pizza Peel

Thin aluminum or wooden peels are helpful for sliding pizza dough or bread onto a baking stone in a hot oven. The peel should have a diameter of at least 14 inches so that you can roll out a 12-inch circle of dough and have plenty of space around the edges. Aluminum peels with heat-resistant wooden handles are preferable to all-wood ones because they can be washed and cleaned easily. Just wipe wooden peels clean. A rimless baking sheet can serve in a pinch, but a peel will quickly become indispensable if you bake often.

Tart Pan

Fluted metal tart pans with removable bottoms come in a variety of sizes for individual and large tarts. Once cool, the outside ring can be lifted off and the tart on the bottom plate slid onto a serving dish. A 10-inch pan is the most useful size. Any store that carries cookware or bakeware will stock tart pans. Use either the shiny metal ones or the dark black ones; it makes no difference.

Vegetable Grid

If the grates on your grill are widely spaced, small vegetables like onions or mushrooms may fall between the spaces and down onto the coals. A metal vegetable grid that rests directly on the grates prevents this. The cross-weaves on the rack allow heat to get through but keep the food in place. Most hardware stores or other shops with a good selection of grilling equipment stock this inexpensive item, which generally costs about $15.

Vegetable Peeler

My favorite peeler is the heavy-duty swivel peeler from Oxo Good Grips. It looks like a regular swivel peeler except that the blade is made of stainless steel and is much sharper than that of most flimsy peelers. The molded plastic handle is especially large and comfortable, so it's easy to grip, even when your hands are wet. For $7, it's an excellent investment.

Mail-Order Sources

IF YOU LIVE NEAR A GOOD SUPERMARKET, Italian market or gourmet store, you should be able to buy all the ingredients in this book. Here's a list for when you can't get what you need locally.

A Cook's Wares
211 37th Street
Beaver Falls, PA 15010
(412) 846-9490
This mail-order business has an excellent selection of kitchenware, including Atlas manual pasta machines from Italy, pizza peels, baking stones and Oxo Good Grips utensils, such as the swivel peeler with a molded plastic handle. The store also carries an assortment of vinegars, oils, rices and dried mushrooms.

Chef's Catalog
3215 Commercial Avenue
Northbrook, IL 60062
(800) 338-3232
The catalog carries a good selection of equipment, including the Simac ice-cream machine, Oxo Good Grips utensils and vegetable grids for grilling.

Dean & DeLuca
560 Broadway
New York, NY 10012
(800) 221-7714
This famous New York gourmet store has an excellent selection of Italian ingredients, including a wide assortment of fine olive oils, vinegars, Arborio rice, beans (including borlotti and dried split favas), olives and dried porcini mushrooms.

Gray's Grist Mills
Box 422
Adamsville, RI 02081
(508) 636-6075
This mill is known for its selection of high-quality cornmeals.

Williams-Sonoma
P.O. Box 7456
San Francisco, CA 94120
(800) 541-2233
The chain of upscale kitchenware stores has a good mail-order catalog featuring oils, vinegars, Arborio rice and the Krups ice-cream maker.

Zingerman's Delicatessen
422 Detroit Street
Ann Arbor, MI 48104
(313) 769-1625
This top-notch gourmet store has an excellent selection of Italian ingredients, especially olive oils.

Index

(Numbers in boldface indicate photographs.)